Environmental Planning and Management

Environmental Planning and Management

John H. Baldwin

Westview Press / Boulder and London

All rights reserved. No part of this publication may be reproduced or transmitted in any form or by any means, electronic or mechanical, including photocopy, recording, or any information storage and retrieval system, without permission in writing from the publisher.

Copyright © 1985 by Oregon State Board of Higher Education

Published in 1985 in the United States of America by Westview Press, Inc., 5500 Central Avenue, Boulder, Colorado 80301; Frederick A. Praeger, Publisher

Library of Congress Cataloging in Publication Data
Baldwin, John H.
  Environmental planning and management.
  Bibliography: p.
  1. Environmental policy—United States. 2. Environmental protection—United States. I. Title.
HC110.E5B36 1985   363.7′056′0973   84-2281
ISBN 0-86531-723-2
ISBN 0-8133-0063-0 (pbk.)

Printed and bound in the United States of America

10   9   8   7   6   5   4   3   2

*To Erin Elizabeth Baldwin
for a safe, healthy, and happy future*

Contents

List of Tables and Figures   xi
Acknowledgments   xv

1 / Introduction   1

Environmental Planning and Management   4
Natural Laws and Social Systems   6
Natural Laws and the Evolution of Social Systems   14
Natural Laws and the Industrial Order   18
The Goals of Environmental Planning and Management   21

2 / Land Use Planning and Controls   25

Land Use in Ancient Civilizations   25
Land Use Issues in the United States   28
The Debate over Land Use Planning   45
Federal and State Land Use Programs   47

3 / Methods of Land Use Planning and Analysis   57

An Ecological Approach to Land Analysis   58
Geology and Topography   60
Soils   63
Hydrology   66
Biota   73
Human Activities   74
Techniques of Analysis   75
Land Management Tools   84
Recommendations   88

4 / Natural Resource Management   90

RESOURCE MANAGEMENT: ISSUES AND OPTIONS   91

Cornucopians Versus Neo-Malthusians   92

viii / Contents

    Conventional Approaches to Resource Management   94
    Alternative Approaches to Resource Management   98

  WATER RESOURCE MANAGEMENT   101

    Local Water Resource Management Problems   101
    Local Water Resource Management   107
    Federal and State Programs   112

  COMMUNITY ENERGY PLANNING AND MANAGEMENT   114

    Conventional Input Approaches   115
    Throughput Management   118
    Rationale for Community Planning and Management   119
    Community Energy Planning and Management   121

5 / Residuals Management   126

    The Materials Balance Model and Pollution Control   126
    The Market System and Pollution   127
    U.S. Pollution Control Policy   130
    Alternative Approaches to Residuals Management   132
    Local Roles in Residuals Planning and Management   136

6 / Air and Water Quality Management   141

  AIR QUALITY MANAGEMENT   141

    U.S. Air Pollution Control Policy   141
    The Clean Air Act Under Fire   151
    Air Quality in the United States   153
    Air Pollution Control   158

  WATER QUALITY MANAGEMENT   162

    Types and Sources of Water Pollution   163
    Water Quality in the United States   165
    U.S. Water Pollution Control Policy   168
    Water Quality Planning and Management   174
    Water Pollution Control   175

7 / Hazardous and Solid Waste Management   184

  HAZARDOUS WASTE MANAGEMENT   184

Federal and State Responses to Hazardous Waste
   Problems   187
Methods of Hazardous Waste Management   193
Hazardous Waste Planning and Management   197

SOLID WASTE MANAGEMENT   199

Federal and State Responses to Solid Waste Problems   201
Solid Waste Planning and Management   203

8 / Economic Impacts of Environmental Controls   216

The Costs and Benefits of Environmental Controls   217
The Distributive Effects of Environmental Controls   230
Techniques of Analysis   237
Cost Subsidies and Adjustment Assistance   239
Economic Development and the Environment   240

9 / Environmental Impact Assessment   243

The NEPA   244
The CEQ Regulations for EIS Preparation   246
Local Roles in EIS Development   262
EIS Review   263
The NEPA and the Courts   266
State Environmental Policy Acts   267
The Evolution of the EIS   275

10 / Local Environmental Planning and Management   277

Local Planning and Management   278
Citizen Participation   289
The Role of Government   290
Case Study: Village Homes, Davis, California   293
Conclusions   295

Appendix: The National Environmental Policy Act of 1969, as Amended   297
Acronyms   303
Bibliography   305
Other Titles of Interest from Westview Press   318
About the Book and Author   319
Index   321

Tables and Figures

Tables

1-1	The Characteristics of "Pioneer" and "Climax" Ecosystems	3
2-1	State Protection of Significant Natural Resources Under CZMA	33
2-2	Floodplain Development in Selected U.S. Cities	35
2-3	Growth in Preservation and Recreation Lands, 1969–1979	42
2-4	Federal Laws Affecting Private Land Use Practices	50
2-5	Summary of State Laws Protecting Critical Natural Resources	54
3-1	Damage Under Various Grading Codes in Los Angeles, California, from 1969 Storms	62
3-2	Soil Limitation Criteria for Lane County, Oregon	67
3-3	Annual Sediment Yields from Colma Creek Basin, California, in 1967 and 1970	73
4-1	Seventy-Year Lifetime Resource Use and Pollution by the Average American	91
4-2	Estimated 1976 World Reserves of Selected Minerals and Life Expectancies at Two Different Rates of Demand	93
4-3	U.S. Import Dependence for Twelve Key Raw Materials	97
4-4	Municipal Water Consumption in the United States	104
4-5	National Interim Primary Drinking Water Standards	106
4-6	Water Conservation Measures	110
4-7	Potential Fuel Conservation by Sector and Activity	119
5-1	Waste Discharges and Control Costs of Eight Hypothetical Firms	132
6-1	Characteristics, Sources, and Health Impacts of Major Pollutants	142
6-2	The National Ambient Air Quality Standards	144
6-3	Compliance Status of Major Air Pollution Sources for Industry, 1980	151
6-4	Frequency of Violations of the National Ambient Air Quality Standards for Federal Air Quality Regions by County, 1978	152

xii / *Tables and Figures*

6-5   Comparison of PSI Values, Pollutant Levels, and General Health Effects   154
6-6   Ranking of 40 Standard Metropolitan Statistical Areas Using the PSI, 1976–1978   156
6-7   Types, Sources, and Impacts of Water Pollution   164
6-8   Thresholds Used in the CEQ Analysis of National Surface Water Quality   165
6-9   Costs of Water Pollution Controls, 1970–1975   173
6-10 Sewage Treatment Processes and Their Impacts   179
6-11 Alternative Wastewater and Sludge Technology   183
7-1   Summary of Major Federal Hazardous Substances Control Legislation   188
7-2   Evaluation of State Hazardous Substances Management Programs   194
7-3   Costs of Several Methods of Hazardous Waste Disposal   197
7-4   Estimated Solid Waste Production of the United States in 1975   201
7-5   Projected Costs and Revenues for Energy Recovery Systems in the Kansas City Area in 1978   211
7-6   Comparison of Source Separation and Centralized Waste Processing for Municipal Waste Disposal   212
8-1   Estimated Incremental Pollution Abatement Expenditures, 1979–1988   218
8-2   Estimated Incremental Pollution Control Expenditures, 1976–1983   220
8-3   Estimated Impacts on Individual Industries   221
8-4   Jobs Affected: Actual and Threatened Closings Where Pollution Control Costs Were Alleged to Be a Factor, January 1971 to December 1976   223
8-5   Areas with Highest and Lowest Per Family Gross Benefits Under the 1970 Clean Air Amendments   233
8-6   Areas with Highest and Lowest Per Family Costs Under the 1970 Clean Air Amendments   234
8-7   Areas with Highest and Lowest Per Family Net Benefits Under the 1970 Clean Air Amendments   235
8-8   Annual U.S. Per Family Air Pollution Control Costs and Benefits by Income, Class, and Race   236
9-1   CEQ Prescribed EIS Format   252
9-2   A Sample Attribute Package   258
9-3   A Simplified Matrix Analysis   261
9-4   Checklist Analysis for a Proposed Activity and Alternatives   262
9-5   EPA Draft and Final EIS Review Classification   265
9-6   State Environmental Impact Statement Requirements, June 1, 1979   268

Tables and Figures / xiii

Figures

1-1 The Kaibab Plateau Deer Population Eruption and Crash Resulting from a Predator Control Program 11
1-2 The Materials Balance Model 19
2-1 Prime Farmland Diverted to Other Uses, 1967–1977 28
2-2 Desertification in North America 30
2-3 Flood Frequency Curve for the Eel River, California, 1932 to 1959 36
3-1 The Standard Textural Triangle of the Soil Conservation Service 64
3-2 A Stream Hydrograph Depicting the Change in Flow Response to a Given Amount of Rainfall Before and After Urbanization 69
3-3 Increase in Flood Frequency (Ratio of Overbank Flows After and Before Urbanization) for Varying Degrees of Urbanization 70
3-4 Increase in Flood Magnitude (Ratio of Peak Discharge After and Before Urbanization) for Varying Degrees of Urbanization 70
3-5 The Relative Threshold Velocities for Runoff Erosion of Different-Sized Particles 72
3-6 Composite Mapping Technique 77
3-7 Computer Printout Indicating View Prominence in the South Hills of Eugene, Oregon 79
3-8 Computer Analysis of the Suitability of the South Hills of Eugene, Oregon, for Residential Development 80
3-9 The Land Use Guidance System Planning Process 81
4-1 Territorial Claims in Antarctica 95
4-2 Water Supply and Consumption in the United States, 1900 to 2020 103
4-3 Water Supply Deficiencies in the United States by Watershed Region 104
4-4 Energy Demand and Fuel Supply in the United States, 1900 to 1979 114
4-5 Entropy and Energy 117
4-6 Hudson-Jorgenson Total Primary Energy Consumption Forecasts, 1980–2000 120
5-1 The Optimum Level of Pollution Control Model 128
6-1 National Trends in Urban PSI Levels, 1974–1978 155
6-2 Estimated National Exposures to Pollutants Above the Short-Term Ambient Health Related (Primary) Standards, 1978 157
6-3 Techniques of Particulate Removal from Exhaust Gases of Industrial and Power Plants 160

6-4 Violations of EPA Water Quality Criteria in 1978   166
6-5 Water Quality Management System   176
6-6 Design of a "Typical" Primary, Secondary, and Tertiary Sewage Treatment Plant   178
6-7 The Design of a "Typical" Septic System   181
7-1 Generation of Residential and Commercial Solid Waste in the United States, 1960 to 1977   200
7-2 A "Typical" Sanitary Landfill   205
7-3 Flow Diagram of a Typical Resource Recovery System   210
8-1 The Estimated Amount of Spending for Environmental Protection, 1979 to 1988   219
8-2 Unemployment Rate With and Without Environmental Controls   225
8-3 Percent Annual Increase in Consumer Price Index With and Without Environmental Controls   226
8-4 Real Gross National Product With and Without Environmental Controls   229
8-5 Estimated Losses, Savings, and Costs for Managing Geologic Hazards in California from 1970 to 2000   231
9-1 EIS Development Steps   249
9-2 Procedure for Developing an Environmental Impact Analysis   256
9-3 Value Function Graphs   260
10-1 The Cycle and Relationships of Land Use, Resources, and Residuals   281
10-2 Interrelationships Among Components of an Environmental Guidance System   288
10-3 The Layout of the Village Homes Subdivision in Davis, California   294

Acknowledgments

During the preparation of this book, several people made valuable contributions. I thank Iris Gould and Diane Baldwin, who typed the original manuscript, and Mary Gilland and Carol Cogswell, who assisted with the photographs and graphics. I also thank my parents, Reverdy and Helen Baldwin, for editorial assistance.

John H. Baldwin

It must be remembered that there is nothing more difficult to plan, more uncertain of success, nor more dangerous to manage than the creation of a new order to things. For the initiator has the enmity of all who would profit by the preservation of the old institutions, and merely lukewarm defenders in those who would gain by the new ones.

Machiavelli, *The Prince*

1 / Introduction

According to the U.S. government's *The Global 2000 Report to the President*, world resource supplies by the year 2000 will be insufficient to meet the demands of an estimated global population of 6.35 billion people (Council on Environmental Quality and U.S. Department of State, 1980). According to the report, serious regional water and food shortages will occur by the year 2000. Although global food production will increase by more than 15 percent, the global population will have grown by more than twice that percentage, with billions of people in the developing countries facing famine. By the year 2000, soil erosion will annually result in deserts equal in total size to Maine, and an area half the size of California will be deforested each year. In addition, mineral and energy resources will become increasingly scarce and more inequitably distributed between the developed and developing nations of the world. Thus, the scale of need and the interdependencies of nations created by resource trade and improved communications will more closely intertwine the problems of rich and poor nations. This may foster a climate of increased international cooperation or confrontation.

U.S. citizens have contributed more than their share to these problems. Since the American revolution, the United States has developed an industrial economy in which resources are acquired, processed, and discarded at a rate unprecedented in human history. Today, the United States, with less than 6 percent of the global population, annually accounts for nearly 33 percent of global consumption and generates nearly 50 percent of all global solid wastes and pollution (Miller, 1982).

However, as we Americans enjoy the fruits of our labors, we are becoming painfully aware of growing global environmental problems. We sense that profound changes are in the making. Ames (1981) has stated, "Like a plains thunderstorm, we feel it coming long before it hits. Economists, politicians and other observers of the American system do not openly savor the rumblings on the horizon of the new decade. Privately many of them express doubt and cynicism. The public itself is not far behind in its perception that uninvited changes are in the works." These changes reflect the transition of U.S. socioeconomic systems from a "pioneer" to a "mature" state. Rapid economic growth, high birth rates, and even harmful technologies can be tolerated in natural ecosystems having plentiful resources and high assimilative capacities. However, as our resource base shrinks, as the human population swells, and as we use increasingly harmful technologies for war and commerce, the ability of our maturing system to tolerate these insults is diminishing. The result is increasing socioeconomic problems, resource shortages, environmental contamination, and damage to human and ecological systems.

If we survive the transition, terms such as power, prestige, economic growth, and exploration will be replaced with terms such as efficiency, conservation, diversity, stability, cooperation, and recycling. These latter terms are created in the image of natural ecological processes. In biological terms we are engaged in a transition from a primary succession stage to that of a climax community or a steady state. Howard Odum (1978) stated, "Whenever an ecosystem reaches its steady state after periods of succession, the rapid net growth specialists are replaced by a new team of higher diversity, higher quality, longer living, better controlled and stable components. Collectively through division of labor and specialization, the climax team gets more energy out of the steady flow of available source energy than those specialized in fast growth could."

Table 1-1 contrasts the characteristics of pioneer and climax ecosystems, drawing the analogy to industrial and ecological communities. The socioeconomic goal of the new ecological community is both compatible with and complementary to the limits of the local ecology. Such harmony between socioeconomic and ecological systems must include recognition of the opportunities and constraints embodied in each. Some developmental activities severely damage ecological systems—some environmental constraints (e.g., flooding, topography, earthquakes, hurricanes) severely limit human activities. Conversely, the environment offers considerable opportunity for economic activity with minimal environmental impact, and socioeconomic systems can be used to protect the health, safety, and welfare of ecological as well as human systems. The key is to preserve and develop by taking advantage of the opportunities afforded by both systems, yet remain within their economic, ecological, and resource constraints. Perhaps the most important step in accomplishing this is to change our linear system of acquiring, processing, "consuming," and discarding resources to one of a more circular pattern based on efficiency, recycling, and maximum use of renewable resources (discussed in Chapter 4). The end result would be the use of a more "appropriate technology" to develop a more "appropriate community."

Public support in the United States for preserving and protecting our natural environment is growing. In the summer of 1980, the president's Council on Environmental Quality (CEQ) released the results of a national public opinion poll on environmental issues (Resources for the Future, 1980). The survey of 1,576 adults found that:

- 62 percent of the respondents said that their views were in sympathy with the environmental movement

Table 1-1. The Characteristics of "Pioneer" and "Climax" Ecosystems (from Coates, 1981).

Pioneer State (Industrial Cities)	Climax State (Ecological Cities)
Few species with one or few dominant species (simplicity)	Many species with relative equality among species (diversity)
Quantitative growth	Qualitative growth
Competition among species, with few symbioses	Cooperation among species, with many symbioses
Short, simple life cycles	Long, complex life cycles
Mineral and nutrient cycles relatively open, rapid and linear	Mineral and nutrient cycles circular and slow
Detritus relatively unimportant in nutrient regeneration	Detritus relatively important in nutrient regeneration
Rapid growth	Growth controlled and limited by complex feedback circuits
Relatively inefficient use of energy	Efficient use of energy
Energy flows linear (in large increments through simple channels)	Energy flows circular (in small increments through multiple channels)
Low degree of structure and order (high entropy)	High degree of structure and order (low entropy)
Low stability to external perturbation	High stability to external perturbation

- 82 percent said that the government should screen new chemicals for safety before they are placed on the market
- 61 percent stated that solar energy should be the energy source that the nation should "concentrate on most"
- 73 percent stated that "an endangered species must be protected, even at the expense of commercial activity"
- support for the environmental movement cuts across nearly all demographic groups, including the elderly, poor, and persons of different educational levels

In spite of the recent recession, a Lou Harris poll published in May 1982 found that public support for retaining or strengthening the Clean Air Act was expressed by an astounding 93 percent of the respondents (Harris, 1982). In addition, not a single segment of the public polled wanted a relaxation of environmental laws. The percentages for (and against) retaining or strengthening clean air regulations were: big city residents, 83 to 14 percent; people under 30, 90 to 10 percent; women, 82 to 13 percent; union members, 82 to 16 percent; Democrats, 84 to 13 percent; Republicans, 76 to 22 percent; conservatives, 76 to 21 percent; and people who voted for Ronald Reagan in 1980, 76 to 22 percent (Harris, 1982).

The message is clear that people want a clean environment . . . but will they vote that way in upcoming elections? As Harris (1982) expressed it:

> Fully 45 percent of the voters nationwide say that the vote of a candidate for Congress on clean air would probably or certainly affect their vote for that candidate this fall, even if they agreed with him or her on most issues. . . . A big 39 percent say that a candidate who votes for a bill that weakens the clean air act will lose their vote. Only a small six percent say they would vote against a candidate who votes to keep the Act as strict as it is or votes to make it stricter. This means that an incredible net of 33 percent of the voters this fall are prepared to defeat candidates for Congress who yield on clean air.

Thus, people of all ages, from all segments of the U.S. population, want to protect their air, land, water, and natural heritage from environmental destruction. This is a lasting and solid foundation upon which local environmental planning and management programs can be developed.

Environmental Planning and Management

Environmental planning and management can be defined as the initiation and operation of activities to direct and control the acquisition, transformation, distribution, and disposal of resources in a manner capable of sustaining human activities, with a minimum disruption of physical, ecological, and social processes (Rowe et al., 1978; *The Random House Dictionary*, college ed., Random House, New York, 1968).

For several important reasons, the emphasis of this text is on local environmental planning and management: (1) the majority of environmental monitoring, analyzing, and enforcing activities are accomplished by local agencies, (2) local planning and management tends to focus on long-term development (e.g., land use plans) and higher levels of government vary considerably in environmental policy with changes in administration, (3) the demand for environmental quality is strongest at home, (4) the combined effects of the decentralist approach of Reagan's "New Federalism" and the growing "home rule" movement will result in increasing emphasis on local planning and management, and (5) local decision-making processes are more readily influenced because they are relatively open and accessible to the public.

The response of state and federal governments to growing environmental problems has been poorly planned and implemented. The reasons for this inadequate response are many, including lack of accurate information, expediency, political compromise, bureaucratic ineptness, administrative turnovers, and incompatible socioeconomic theories. Nowhere is this more apparent than in the difference in environmental policies and programs between the Carter and Reagan administrations (see Friends of the Earth, 1982). For example, under the Carter administration, the energy policy focus was on conservation, renewable sources of energy, and synfuels. Under the Reagan administration, the emphasis is on nuclear power and "free" markets. The abrupt changes in policy have significantly fragmented and inhibited federal management programs. Because most state and local energy and environmental management programs rely on the federal government for leadership, guidance, and funding, federal policy changes significantly disrupt state and local programs, resulting in failure to protect the public health, safety, and welfare.

In many cases, criticisms of state and federal environmental management programs by industry, environmental organizations, and citizens are valid. Excessive reliance on absolute prohibitions, zero-discharge legislation, and inflexible requirements for large capital-intensive construction projects can often not be justified on scientific and economic grounds. However, to be fair, it should be noted that environmental management is particularly difficult because of the following:

- the complexity and interrelatedness of environmental problems and solutions
- the infancy of the environmental planning and management field
- the frequent omission or discounting of environmental goods and services during conventional value analysis
- lifestyle changes, which are often required to resolve environmental conflicts, are difficult to accomplish
- environmental goals often appear to conflict with other community development goals
- the difficulty in establishing environmental priorities and defining tradeoffs
- the lack of commitment of resources to environmental quality control programs (making management efficiency a compelling issue)
- a general lack of sufficient and accurate information for proper decision making

It is apparent that changes are needed in the orientation and management of environmental quality programs. The decision making processes of these programs need to be more flexible, open, and equitable; the enforcement procedures should be more direct; and program investments of time and labor need to be more efficient. Clearly, a new approach to environmental planning and management is warranted.

This new approach will probably involve a multitude of diverse local actions, each accomplished with an awareness of its larger context. In the words of René Dubos, "we must think globally and act locally." Former Oregon Governor Tom McCall stated (RAIN, 1981):

> The new decade has brought with it a tough set of issues which will only broaden the challenges of the last ten years. We must now grapple with the impacts of increasingly scarce resources, energy and capital, inflated costs of goods and services, and the decline of big government's willingness and even ability to meet social needs. The old growth and quality of life questions have not gone away—they've just gotten more complex. Nowhere is this more apparent than on the local level. The 1980's will require that the grass roots level performs as it has never performed before.

In the United States, the goal of decentralization of control and activity is often hidden in political rhetoric, with either big business or big government the perceived enemy. However, the dark-horse trend toward increased localization is beginning to seriously challenge the past trends toward centralization. Many futurists are predicting that decentralist, participatory movements will become one of the primary driving forces for the next two decades (Ames, 1981).

Environmentalists are in the forefront of this decentralist, participatory trend, for nowhere else are the global problems more obvious, the need to solve them more compelling, and the tangible benefits of proper management more immediate. The most obvious example of a decentralist, participatory movement in the United States is the drive toward energy conservation. In recent years, the actions of millions of citizens have significantly diminished the growth rate in U.S. energy consumption. This has resulted in a reduction in both energy expenditures and the detrimental impacts of energy production and consumption. Similar actions by people of all nations can significantly improve the global balance of resources and population. By handling resources and residuals more conservatively and responsibly, local governments could take complementary actions that contribute to community development, stability, and quality of life and promote self-determination.

Natural Laws and Social Systems

In scientific terms, a "system" can be defined as a group of interacting components with a defined boundary working toward a common goal. Under this definition, a system can be one amoeba, human, community, nation, or world. Systems scientists tell us that all systems are structured and function through the interaction of mass, energy, and information. For example, a single-celled plant comprises a multitude of organic and inorganic molecules. Its energy is obtained from the capture of solar energy and the manufacture of organic molecules whose bond energy can be used to do the work of the cell. The "information" of the cell (how to produce food, obtain energy, reproduce, etc.) is obtained from the nucleic acids (DNA and RNA) of the cell.

It is important to note that the information system of "higher forms" of life contains, in addition, an important learned component. Unlike the single-celled plant, we can use our knowledge to consciously manipulate our environment to make it more suitable for human needs. Thus, the quality of information we pass on from generation to generation is critical for human development (a good argument for maintaining the best information, education, and communication systems possible).

Similar relationships of mass, energy, and information can be found in all living, physical, and social systems. The manner in which mass, energy, and information is handled by a system can have a profound impact on the structure and function and, therefore, the perpetuation of that system. Although the permutations of the interactions of mass, energy, and information are almost limitless, the interactions are governed by what are called "universal natural laws." Knowledge of these laws is essential for the comprehension of the causes and consequences of environmental problems and provides a biophysical foundation for the development of socioeconomic systems. The basic assumption is that the more a socioeconomic system is developed to comply with natural laws, the more stable and compatible that system will be with its surrounding environment.

Physical Laws

The principles that govern the interaction of mass and energy are the *law of conservation of mass* and the *first* and *second law(s) of thermodynamics*. (See Miller, 1979, for a discussion of these laws.) The law of conservation of mass simply states that mass can be neither created nor destroyed. That is, materials are never really "produced" or "consumed." They change in form from raw materials to products to wastes and residuals without a change in quantity. Thus, over time, in any stable system, the amount of matter moving into the system must equal the amount of matter stored plus the amount moving out. The only exception to this rule is expressed in Einstein's Theory of Relativity. Under the special conditions of a thermonuclear reaction, the energy produced (E) is equal to the amount of equivalent mass destroyed (m) times the square of the speed of light (c, or 3×10^8 m/s) or $E = mc^2$. However, the special thermonuclear conditions for this conversion occur naturally only in our sun and other stars or are created artificially by the detonation of nuclear weapons or controlled reactions in nuclear power plants.

Energy relationships are governed by the first and second laws of thermodynamics. The first law, the law of conservation of energy, states that energy can be neither created nor destroyed (outside a thermonuclear reaction). Although energy can be changed in form and distribution, the quantity remains the same. Thus, the terms "energy production" and "energy consumption" are misnomers. Energy is neither produced nor consumed; it is only converted from one form to another. For example, when energy in the form of fossil fuels is "consumed," creating mechanical, electrical, or thermal energy, only the form of energy has changed.

The second law of thermodynamics or "entropy law" governs the change of form or "quality" of energy. The second law states that in any closed system the amount of energy in forms available to do useful work diminishes over time. This loss of available energy represents a diminished capacity to maintain "order" through time. Thus, in any closed system, over time, disorder (or entropy) increases.

It is extremely important to understand the relationship of the second law of thermodynamics to social and natural systems. The law holds that to sustain or enlarge any system (e.g., organism or community) requires the "expenditure" of energy. Expenditure is defined as the conversion of a "useful" or "available" (to do work) form of energy to a less useful, unavailable or "bound" form. The law applies to all human activities from cleaning your room to building a nation.

Entropy (or disorder) in strictly physical terms is defined as an increased requirement to expend available energy to maintain the health, safety, and welfare (or perpetuation) of a system. This definition applies in any number of physical, ecological, and social problems. Classic examples include the diminishing returns on investment and the frequent shortages resulting from high levels of production and consumption of nonrenewable resources. The expenditure of increasing amounts of available energy is required to sustain production, manage shortages, or find alternatives. Similarly, available energy must be spent to protect public health, safety, and welfare from the detrimental effects of pollution, ecological disruption, or social problems such as crime, antisocial behavior, and poor mental health.

Thus, the resource and residuals control problems addressed by planners and managers can be attributed to entropy changes, which inevitably result from human activities. When these impacts occur in a state and/or at a rate with which natural processes cannot deal, socioeconomic and environmental problems result. When the natural capacity to assimilate entropic changes is exceeded, resources and energy must be expended to deal with resulting problems.

One final important lesson of the second law of thermodynamics is that, all things being equal, the larger the ordering process or the faster the rate of resource and energy "consumption," the greater the disorder created. Further, the entropy resulting from ordering processes need not occur at the location of the process. The evolution of life forms on earth from simple to complex depended on the use of available sunlight. The entropy has occurred in the sun in the conversion of available hydrogen fuel to a less available form—helium. Solar energy thus represents a "free" form of energy to the biosphere because the detrimental effects of this energy source are isolated by space and distance from the natural systems of the earth. In contrast, the socioeconomic ordering of recent times, based on the conversion of nonrenewable fossil fuels, cannot escape problems associated with increasing entropy. The result has been a constant increase through time of problems such as pollution, resource shortages, economic disruption, social stress, increased morbidity and mortality, and the loss of amenities and our natural heritage.

In summary, the challenge of the next decades involves the recognition of entropy and its origins and the management of entropy to channel these inevitable detrimental impacts into forms less damaging to human and natural systems.

Evolutionary and Ecological Principles

The evolutionary and ecological principles that govern the interaction of organisms and their environments also have direct application to environmental planning and management. For instance, living systems in the biosphere possess the capacity to transmit and to inherit genetic information—a capacity that is not found in nonliving, or "abiotic," systems. This genetic capacity makes possible *evolution by natural selection*, a principle that was formally announced in a joint paper read to a scholarly audience in London in 1858 by Charles Darwin and Alfred Russel Wallace. Darwin's book *On the Origin of Species . . .* (1859) became famous for its articulation of the principle. In a nutshell, the principle ensures the selection of the most adapted organism for a given environment—the "survival of the fittest." This is accomplished by the production of a genetically variable set of offspring, not all of which will survive. The resulting competition for limited indigenous resources results in the survival of those individuals with the most useful genetic qualities for their particular environment. Over time, as local environments change, natural selection results in changes in the kinds, numbers, and interrelationships of the surviving genetic types.

One aspect of the principle of evolution by natural selection that is very important to understand is that a species has a genetically fixed rate of potential adaptation to environmental change. However, organisms with a relatively short life span and large number of offspring (such as insects) have a faster rate of evolution than organisms with long life spans and few offspring (such as humans). Thus, in times of environmental change, some species can readily adapt, whereas others experience difficulty. Fortunately, certain "higher" animals (including humans) have learned to manipulate changing or hostile environments to reduce the negative selection pressures. However, if the environmental changes exceed the genetic and/or learned capacity to evolve or to manipulate the environment, the result may be extinction.

Another ecological principle important to environmental planning and management is "Ashby's Law of the Requisite Variety in Cybernetic Systems" (see Margalef, 1970). This is more commonly articulated as the law of *diversity and stability*, more recently refined by ecologists to hold that "stability leads to diversity." The principle states that stable environments tend to develop diverse ecological communities over geologic time. Conversely, less diverse communities in unstable environments (e.g., desert, tundra, alpine habitats) or less diverse communities in general (e.g., monocultural crops) tend to be more vulnerable to environmental disruption. The simplest way of expressing this principle is "don't put all your eggs in one basket." For example, a food system that relies primarily on one crop is vulnerable to crop failure and famine, as was the case in the 1848 potato blight in Ireland. A similar situation is found in the monocultural second-growth spruce forests in the Northeast, which are very vulnerable to diseases and insect infestations (e.g., spruce budworm outbreaks). Corbett (1981) has stated, "It appears that a similar principle applies to human communities. Those communities with the greatest diversity in energy sources, in forms of economic enterprise, and in food sources will tend to be more stable and to adapt most successfully and painlessly to severe changes, be they environmental, political, economic, or social."

A third important ecological principle, the *Brontosaurus principle*, states that "up to a point, the bigger the better; beyond that point, the bigger the worse" (Miller, 1979). The Brontosaurus dinosaur was selected as the example of this principle because it was the largest land animal ever known (up to 65 feet long and weighing between 35 and 40 tons) and it became extinct at the end of the Cretaceous period (approximately 75 million years ago). No one is certain why the Brontosaurus, or for that matter, the other species of dinosaurs that dominated the Mesozoic era (the "age of the reptiles") became extinct. Most likely the cause was an inability of these creatures to adapt to changing physical conditions (e.g., the elimination of lowland habitat due to mountain building, climatic change, radiation caused by changing landforms or cosmic events) or ecological conditions (e.g., epidemics, the eating of dinosaur eggs by early mammals) (Swinton, 1954). Whatever the cause, the ponderous Brontosaurus failed to adapt to a changing environment and paid the price of extinction.

The Brontosaurus principle applies not only to the size of living organisms, but also to the size of socioeconomic units such as communities, unions, corporations, and governments. For example, in a

Figure 1-1. The Kaibab Plateau Deer Population Eruption and Crash Resulting from a Predator Control Program.

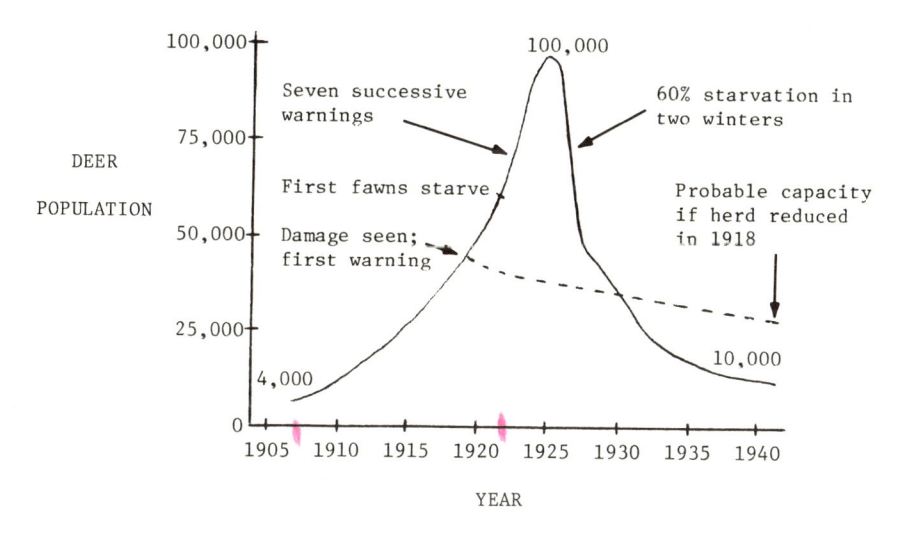

```
DEER
POPULATION

100,000 ┤
                    Seven successive        100,000
                    warnings                              60% starvation in
 75,000 ┤                                                 two winters
                    First fawns starve
 50,000 ┤                                                 Probable capacity
                    Damage seen;                          if herd reduced
                    first warning                         in 1918

 25,000 ┤
                                                                  10,000
          4,000
      0 ┴────┼────┼────┼────┼────┼────┼────┼────
         1905  1910  1915  1920  1925  1930  1935  1940
                              YEAR
```

Source: Adapted from C. S. Southwick, *Ecology and the Quality of Our Environment,* 2nd ed. Copyright 1976 by PWS Publishers.

community—from its early small size to a population of hundreds of thousands—the benefits of continued growth in the provision of public services and cultural amenities may clearly outweigh (to some people) the costs in loss of personal space, increased density, and so on. However, a point is reached where the marginal benefits of growth diminish as the intrusion on personal space and freedom increases significantly, reversing the benefit/cost ratio. Thus, bigger is better; however, a point is reached beyond which continued growth becomes a liability rather than an asset. This principle, in reality, is closely related to the economist's "law of diminishing returns" or the physician's "continued growth of cells in maturity is cancer." Relationships like those in the community example are seen in the growth and development of industry, unions, and government.

A fourth ecological principle important to environmental planning and management is the concept of *carrying capacity*. Carrying capacity is formally defined as the maximum population that can be sustained by an ecosystem over time (Miller, 1979). As noted by Kormondy (1969) in the classic study of the population dynamics of the deer herd on the Kaibab Plateau on the northern side of the Grand Canyon in Arizona, the carrying capacity of an ecosystem for a population can change significantly over time (see Figure 1-1).

In 1907 the deer population on the isolated, 727,000-acre plateau was estimated to be 4,000. Between 1907 and 1923, predator control programs removed 816 cougars, 30 wolves, and 7,388 coyotes from the plateau, allowing the population of deer to expand unchecked by depredation. By 1918 the deer population had expanded by more than ten times, and by 1924 the population reached an estimated 100,000. The overbrowsing and trampling of plateau vegetation resulting from this population explosion caused a famine and population crash. Between 1924 and 1926 more than 60,000 deer starved to death. The population continued to decline through the 1930s to a number about half that which could have theoretically been sustained had the population not exploded beyond the level of 1918. The lessons of this example are apparent. Overpopulation can diminish the carrying capacity of an ecosystem for a species through ecosystem destruction.

What is the carrying capacity of the earth for humans? The debate rages over what level of human population can be achieved (at all cost) versus sustained (in a manner that will not permanently disrupt life-sustaining ecosystems). Many ecologists believe that the carrying capacity of the earth for humans has already been exceeded (Ehrlich and Ehrlich, 1974; Hardin, 1974). These scientists are concerned for the existing quality of life for billions of people in developing nations and for the integrity of natural ecosystems that sustain human and nonhuman life. Others, such as Clark (1963) and an expert panel of the National Academy of Sciences (1969), believed that the population can achieve more than 30 billion *at a minimum subsistence level*. The issue is one of quality and sustainability of life. Eugene Odum (1971) stated, "The optimum for quality is always less than the maximum quantity that can be sustained. . . . The earth can support more "warm bodies" sustained as so many domestic animals in a polluted feedlot than it can support quality human beings who exercise the right of a pollution-free environment, a reasonable chance for personal liberty, and a variety of options for the pursuit of happiness."

Thus, we can theoretically achieve a level of population at orders of magnitude above existing levels if we are willing to sacrifice basic human rights and freedoms (already not achieved in many areas of the world today) and jeopardize the integrity of our life-sustaining natural ecosystems. Finally, as our population grows exponentially the pace of change in the everyday lives of human beings must accelerate. To accommodate the resource and energy demands of a burgeoning population will require "a breakthrough a day to keep the crisis away." This accelerated pace of change, if it can be achieved through time, becomes a source of stress in itself.

The concept of environmental carrying capacity has several applications important to environmental planning and management above and beyond the calculation of the global carrying capacity for humans. If the limitation of a human activity can be supported by scientific data on carrying capacity, the resulting decisions and actions could more easily win public support and be defended in the courts (Godschalk and Parker, 1975).

The three primary uses of the concept of environmental carrying capacity for environmental planning and management are in impact studies of the effects of human actions on natural ecosystems, in standard setting for pollution control, and in developing sustained-yield renewable resource management. The concept of carrying capacity is embodied in studies that determine the threshold of human activities that will cause ecological damage to a natural environment. The best example is studies of the impact of hikers and campers on vegetation in wilderness areas. How many hikers and campers can be allowed in an area before the natural vegetation is damaged? How can the hikers and campers be managed to reduce the vegetative impacts to allow greater human access to the area?

The second use of the concept of carrying capacity is in the development of impact thresholds (such as air and water quality standards) that, if exceeded, will damage certain aspects of the environment (e.g., human health and property). The threshold can be used to calculate the pollution reduction necessary to meet the standard or it can be used to calculate the amount of additional pollution allowed before significant damage will occur.

A final common use of the carrying capacity concept in environmental planning and management is to calculate the sustained yields of renewable resources that are possible without damaging the resource base for the future. In essence, the calculation is used to prevent exceeding the environmental carrying capacity (overgrazing, forest destruction, groundwater depletion) so that over time the commercial yield of resources can be sustained in a manner that does not diminish the overall environmental quality of the area.

In summary, the concept of carrying capacity can be very important in delimiting the ultimate growth of human populations on the earth, can be used for ecological studies of human activities in natural environments, can be used to set pollution standards based on environmental thresholds, and can be used in resource management to establish sustained-yield limits to renewable resource development. Thus, the concept of carrying capacity is one of the most important in environmental planning and management (Godschalk and Parker, 1975).

The final ecological principle of relevance to environmental planning and management can be called the *connection principle*, which states that "everything is connected to everything else—the question is 'how?'" Corbett (1981) stated:

> Every living thing survives by numerous and subtle relationships with all living things and the inanimate environment. When all living things are considered together, these relationships appear as

complex, interdependent, and self-regulating structures or ecosystems, in which any one form of life depends on the rest of the system to provide the conditions necessary for its existence. Human beings are as much a part of this ecosystem as any other form of life, and depend on the rest of the ecosystem for food, a breathable atmosphere, drinkable water, and a survivable climate. The earth has not always provided a suitable environment for humans, but was made hospitable over the millennia by functioning ecosystems.

The connection principle can also be applied to socioeconomic structures and interactions. For example, high interest rates for mortgages have, in part, contributed to a collapse of the homebuilding industry which, in turn, has led to the near demise of the forest products industry in the Pacific Northwest. With a reduction of revenues from commercial, industrial, and income taxes, county and state budgets have been cut. The result has been the layoff of thousands of public employees in addition to the tens of thousands out of work in the timber and homebuilding industries. This has subsequently led to an increase in the incidence of crime and other social problems related to poverty and uncertainty.

Thus, all things great and small are intertwined in a complex web of hidden and subtle relationships that are often beyond the capacity of human comprehension (see, for example, Forrester, 1971). The message is clear that when our economic, social, and physical lives depend on that web for nourishment and sustenance, we had better be careful and deliberate in our actions that could upset the delicate balances of nature.

In conclusion, these physical laws and evolutionary and ecological principles provide an essential foundation for the relationships of human and natural systems. It is important to note that during the Renaissance, when the redevelopment of the natural and social sciences was occurring, several of these natural laws were embodied in the developing socioeconomic theories of economics, law, and government. Considerable insight can be gained into the opportunities and constraints of our existing socioeconomic system through the study of the parallel evolution of the natural and social sciences.

Natural Laws and the Evolution of Social Systems

The Renaissance or "age of intellectual rebirth," which began in the fourteenth century in Florence, could be characterized as a period during which many of the old myths of science, philosophy, medicine, and theology were debunked. Questioning, reasoning, and rationalization replaced tradition and faith for the natural and social sciences.

Scientists such as Francis Bacon, Galileo, and Johannes Kepler rejected the theological and contemplative philosophies of the day. In his *Novum Organum* of 1620, Francis Bacon openly criticized the contemplative sciences of the day that were founded in ancient Greek philosophy. According to Rifkin (1980), Bacon stated that the Greeks "assuredly have that which is characteristic of boys, they are prompt to prattle but cannot generate; for their wisdom abounds in words but is barren of works." In essence, Bacon was calling for a more rational science oriented toward the control and utilization of nature for the welfare of mankind. As the sciences developed and flourished, the contemplative aspects of science (or "why") were replaced by a more productivist and mechanistic (or "how") orientation.

This new "mechanical world paradigm" is manifested in many of the great works of Renaissance scientists. The mathematician and philosopher René Descartes believed that mathematics could be used to explain all physical things (Randall, 1940): "Give me extension and motion . . . and I will construct the universe."

Later, Sir Isaac Newton's writings about the laws of gravity and motion, along with the works of the astronomers Galileo, Kepler, and Copernicus, provided the tools for scientific analysis and insights into the nature of humans and the universe. The mechanical world paradigm held that there was a natural order for things that could be observed and quantified simply, predictably, and accurately through scientific investigation for the utilization and benefit of mankind (Rifkin, 1980). Hazel Henderson, in her book *The Politics of the Solar Age* (1981), wrote:

> This philosophical approach, which was a rejection of religious dogma and developed from the investigations of Descartes's older contemporaries Francis Bacon, Galileo, and Johannes Kepler, led to the greatest flowering of scientific and technological achievement since the earliest civilizations of China, as well as toward the materialistic goals of production of worldly goods and luxuries, the increasing domination of nature, and the rise of the manipulative rationality of the industrial age. This, in turn, gave rise to specific rationales for such goals and value shifts and the new institutions they created in law, custom, and political life. The new academic pursuits it engendered gave rise to a proliferation of theorizing about a new set of specific phenomena that suddenly stood out in sharp relief; economic activities, production, exchange, distribution, moneylending, trade, and merchant "venturing"—all of which not only required description and explanation but also rationalization.

Thus, the process of rationalization was not limited to the works of the natural scientists. Social scientists began to question the faiths and philosophies underlying the often chaotic and repressive economic, legal, and political systems of the day. For instance, in his political theories, John Locke (1632–1704) attempted to establish a "natural" basis for politics and government. This influential British physician and philosopher took "God" out of politics by challenging the notion of the "divine right of kings." Like the natural scientists, he discounted the traditional and spiritual in favor of the measurable and quantifiable. Locke held that people possess a natural right to life and property and that the purpose of the individual is to accumulate and protect property. He believed that the proper function of government is to allow people to exercise their rights and power over nature to produce wealth and that government should only be given sufficient power to protect the "natural rights" of the individual without infringing upon them (Strauss, 1953). Many of these principles became embodied in the U.S. Constitution. For instance, the U.S. government cannot infringe upon the rights of citizens unless the activities are allowed by the U.S. Constitution (e.g., taxing, spending, waging war, or regulating commerce).

Sir William Blackstone (1723–1770), a distinguished English judge, teacher, and writer, was most influential in developing the legal concepts of private property rights embodied in the U.S. Constitution. Blackstone believed in the absolute sanctity of private property. He held that a private property owner had no obligation to the "public good" in making land use decisions. In 1765 Blackstone published his *Commentaries on the Laws of England* (derived from a series of Oxford lectures) which, as it turned out, was one of the few major published works on English law for nearly a century. In his commentaries, Blackstone expressed opinions that countered, to a certain extent, British legal principles that the nation had a vested interest in the use of its lands. Blackstone's theories about absolute private property rights were widely read in the American colonies and later embodied in constitutional law.

Adam Smith in *The Wealth of Nations* in 1776 applied a similar mechanical world view to economics. In a free market with competition and self-interest, Smith believed, resources would naturally be allocated to their highest and best use. Intrusion into a free market by government or monopoly inhibited free trade and was, thus, unnatural. Like Locke, Smith held that the purpose of government was to protect and promote natural processes of competition and trade. It should be noted that the process of allocating resources through competition and free trade is not significantly different from the process of allocating resources to living organisms in nature through natural selection and survival of the fittest. Adam Smith's "invisible hand" is nothing more than the concept of survival of the fittest that was articulated formally for the biological sciences by Darwin and Wallace eighty-three years later. Henderson (1981) wrote:

> [This] concept liberated the merchants of the day from the moral law of "just" prices. [It] became another cornerstone of economics and was elevated to the status of the laws of mechanics, and persists

today as the bedrock model used in neoclassical economic analysis: supply and demand equilibrated by price. It also fitted perfectly with the new mathematics developed in 1666 respectively by Isaac Newton as "fluxions" and by Gottfried von Leibniz as differential calculus. If enough a priori assumptions were made, economists could now assign "objective" scientific status to the determination of wages (by designating workers as a "supply of commodities" in relatively greater or lesser demand), to subjective desires (today's revealed preference functions, marginal "utilities"), etc.

Thus, through the combined efforts of natural and social scientists during the Renaissance, the mechanical world view was both popularized and institutionalized. Science and technology were viewed as a means to subjugate the natural world, accumulate wealth, and create a more ordered world (Rifkin, 1980). Hazel Henderson (1981) stated:

> The sixteenth- and seventeenth-century mercantilism, feudalism, and the divine right of monarchs gave way to the liberalism and social revolution of the Enlightenment, which ushered in the period of classical and "laissez-faire" economic individualism, representative government, and property rights. This Enlightenment period was midwifed by a crescendo of critical reasoning against feudalism and aristocracy. "Natural law," always invoked as a higher court in periods of social criticism, was invoked again as a more comprehensive frame of reference from which to argue and engulf the old values, and as a way of displaying their limited relativity to the newly proclaimed absolute.

We can say, then, that our legal, political, and economic systems in the United States were founded in the "natural law" of the sixteenth and seventeenth centuries. This natural law, based upon freedom, individualism, competition, and survival of the fittest, laid out the ground rules and provided the framework for unlimited opportunities. However, at the time, this natural law did not include the second law of thermodynamics. The second law was not discovered until 1827 (by a French army officer) and was not articulated until 1868 by German physicist Rudolf Claussius (Rifkin, 1980). The first and second laws of thermodynamics, the premier laws of all sciences, describe the constraints placed upon all physical activities of the universe. In the words of chemistry Nobel Prize winner Frederick Soddy, the laws of thermodynamics (Rifkin, 1980) "control, in the last resort, the rise and fall of political systems, the freedom or bondage of nations, the movements of commerce and industry, the origins of wealth and poverty, and the general welfare of the race." Further, our leading scientists have stated that there are no exceptions to the second law of thermodynamics. According to Miller (1971), Albert Einstein once said, "A theory is more impressive the greater is the simplicity of its premises, the more different are the kinds of things it relates and the more extended its range of applicability. Therefore, the deep impression which classical thermodynamics made on me. It is the only physical theory of universal content which I am convinced, that within the framework of applicability of its basic concepts, will never be overthrown."

The ramifications of the second law to the currently held mechanical world paradigm are significant. For every ordering process (for an organism or a civilization), disordering of greater magnitude occurs, perhaps elsewhere. In the past, the entropy caused by rapid development was either within the assimilative capacity of the natural environment or occurred at the "elsewhere" where the negative effects were not readily apparent.

Our limited perception of time, space, and matter may prevent a true reading of cause and effect for the detrimental impacts of human development activities. However, as the world's economic systems continue to grow, the stresses on physical systems will inevitably increase and the capability to incur negative effects elsewhere will be constantly diminishing. The laws of thermodynamics tell us that continued conventional economic development on a finite planet is impossible. Even if unlimited energy resources were available, the continued process of conversion of resources to products will result in increasingly difficult entropic problems of thermal pollution (resulting in changes in climate), contamination, and resource shortages. The harder and faster we work to "conquer the earth," the more extensive and rapid the rate of deterioration (Rifkin, 1980).

To summarize, the economic, legal, and political systems of the United States were founded on theories of individual rights, competition, and unlimited opportunities, and the theories were based on the scientific thought of the sixteenth and seventeenth centuries. However, that scientific thought was seriously flawed by not incorporating the second law of thermodynamics. Thus, the emerging socioeconomic systems had rules for gaining wealth and opportunity that did not allow for the inevitable entropic constraints expressed in the second law.

Natural Laws and the Industrial Order

Conventional economic theory depicts the flow of resources (land, labor, and capital) in an industrial economy through the use of a production and consumption model (Figure 1-2) (Freeman et al., 1973). The "production" sector (which includes mining, transportation, and processing) provides goods and services to consumers in exchange for purchases. In addition, the "consumption" sector supplies labor to the production sector in exchange for wages. Thus, the economic system is portrayed as a circular flow of money (wages and purchases) accompanied by an opposite flow of productive factors (goods, services, and labor) between producers and consumers. This conventional model

Figure 1-2. The Materials Balance Model. Dotted lines indicate the circular flow of money. Solid lines indicate energy and materials flows.

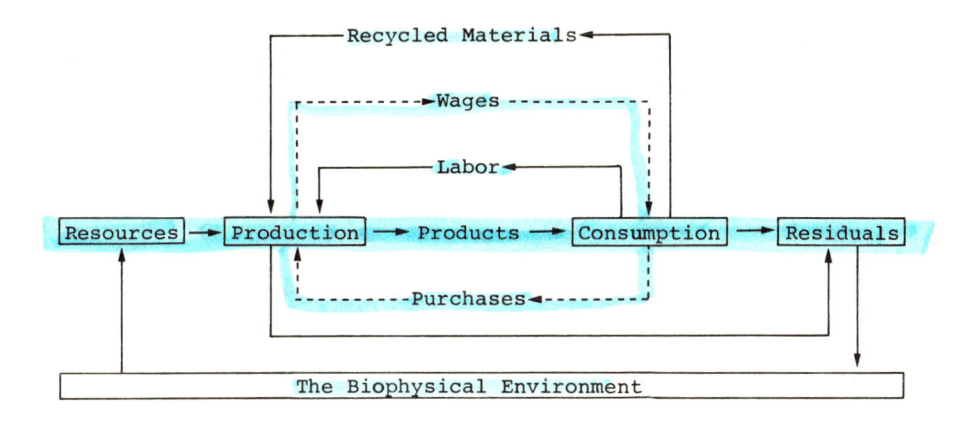

```
                    ┌──── Recycled Materials ◄────┐
                    │                             │
                    │    ┌─────── Wages ──────┐   │
                    │    │                    ▼   │
                    │    │    ┌── Labor ◄──┐  │   │
                    ▼    │    ▼            │  │   ▼
[Resources]──►[Production]──► Products ──►[Consumption]──►[Residuals]
    ▲              ▲                            │             │
    │              └──────── Purchases ◄────────┘             │
    │                                                         ▼
    │                                                         │
    └──────────── The Biophysical Environment ────────────────┘
```

According to the Law of Conservation of Mass
and the First Law of Thermodynamics:

Resources	=	Products & Services	+	Residuals
Mass In	=	Mass Stored	+	Mass Out
Energy In	=	Energy Stored	+	Energy out

of production and consumption is particularly deficient, however, both in its failure to consider the biophysical foundations of the economic system and in its failure to incorporate important nonmonetary considerations in its calculations.

The circular flow model of production and consumption ignores the biophysical foundation of the economy as well as the importance of energy and material resources to the economy. The economy functions within the natural environment, which serves as the platform for all activities and as a source for resources and sink for residuals (Figure 1-2). Applying the physical laws of conservation of mass and of thermodynamics, we see that material and energy resources are transformed from raw material to product to waste in a one-way flow through the economy called "throughput." In a physical sense, our present system is based on moving a constantly increasing volume of resources in a one-way flow and then trying to fight the resulting entropy through resource recovery, concentration, containment, storage, and treatment. The materials balance model provides a broader, more accurate picture of the existing situation.

For example, in 1972 the U.S. economy used 4.4 billion tons of raw materials and 72 quadrillion BTUs of energy to produce a gross national product of $1.15 trillion. Approximately 50 percent of this material (2.1 billion tons) ended as solid waste. The remaining material was deposited in the environment as pollution or was circulated in the economy for a time before becoming solid waste or pollution. It is important to note that in 1972 the U.S. economy recycled only 6.2 percent of all discarded resources (Miller, 1979).

As previously mentioned, the conventional model of production and consumption omits important nonmonetary considerations. This omission—standard for most schools of economics from Marxism to capitalism—results in emphasizing and managing only those sectors of production and consumption that are monetized. Most real production and consumption of goods and services in the world, especially in developing countries, occurs outside the formal monetized economy. The majority of people in the world sustain themselves (provide their own food, clothing, energy, and shelter) in an informal nonmonetary economy a peasant agriculture, cooperative settlements, and barter. Hazel Henderson (1981) has stated:

> One of the aspects of the crises of industrial development is that it begins to suck all such informal, use-value production and consumption into the monetized economies, drawing populations into the cities, denuding rural agricultural areas, dissolving the cultural glue of village life and reciprocal community systems of food-sharing, care of the young and elderly, and folk medicine, and destroying inherited cultural wisdom learned in coping with diverse ecological conditions. Thus, industrialism and the economic logic underpinning it tacitly view the industrialization process as also one of monetization of all production and consumption and the accumulation of investment "capital" or "surplus" (viewed as money whether denominated as dollars, rubles, pounds, or yen). As industrialization and monetization spread and colonize more and more of the informal, use-value production, consumption, accumulation, and exchange systems that are non-monetized, limits to this process are reached. Symptoms of these limits show up as anomalies in trying to "monetize" environmental resources and place cash value on air, water, open space, and even human life and the loving, caring relationships that allow humans in all societies to provide services to each other free of charge.

Finally, the materials balance model provides a useful framework for analyzing alternative methods of resource and residuals management. The model indicates that the entropic production-consumption-waste flow of resources can be managed through the control of throughput. Thus, although entropy cannot be avoided, it can be minimized through proper management. One important goal of environmental management should be, therefore, to reduce the rate of flow of matter and energy in society in order to diminish the negative effects of entropy. To do so requires a fundamental realignment of our productive and consumptive sectors that acknowledges their biophysical foundations. In the words of Hazel Henderson (1981), "We are going to repeal the divine right of capital, because it is just as arbitrary as the divine right of kings."

The Goals of Environmental Planning and Management

As we proceed into the final decades of the twentieth century, the opportunities to develop and inhabit new frontiers of our planet are diminishing. Our search is now taking us into areas that have serious climatic and/or physical limitations (e.g., Antarctica and the sea bed) that increase the environmental risks and diminish the returns on investments. The age of abundance of relatively cheap natural resources is waning. In addition, growing interdependencies and mass communications are diminishing our capability to leave entropic costs to other nations; it is becoming increasingly difficult for developed nations to maintain themselves as islands of wealth in a sea of poverty. Thus, the negative entropic or external effects of our industrial economy are going to be increasingly internalized.

The result will be a growing need to manage the entropic effects of economic activities. To date, the approach of all levels of government has been to attack each problem as if it were unrelated to other problems. Social programs have been developed to treat poverty and protect the family; environmental laws have been passed to protect human health and safety; economic development plans and deficit spending have been used in an attempt to bolster faltering economies; and emergency plans have been developed (and quickly forgotten) as a result of preliminary bouts with resource shortages. This piecemeal approach is only partially treating problems and is masking them rather than addressing and curing the root cause—entropy. Many of these related problems can be alleviated by reorganizing our industrial economy to minimize its impacts. This involves a conscious effort to accomplish three goals: (1) to minimize the entropic effects of economic activities, (2) to do so at minimum costs and (3) to do so in as just and equitable a manner as possible.

The first goal, to minimize entropic effects, can be further broken down into three objectives: (1) reduction of throughput in our economic system, (2) protection of public health and safety and natural ecosystems from the detrimental effects of the improper handling of land, resources, and residuals, and (3) stabilization and perpetuation of our socioeconomic system. The third goal, to be as just and equitable as possible in distributing benefits and costs, is an essential consideration in environmental planning and management. Planning and management based solely on controlling entropy and economic efficiency will continue to create difficulties in being fair and equitable. Below is a summary of the goals and objectives; it contains a series of suggested actions derived from physical laws and ecological principles that can assist in achieving these goals and objectives.

Goal 1. Decrease the entropic effects of economic activities
  Objective 1. Decrease throughput in our economic system
   Actions:
   1. Limiting resource inputs into production by:
      a. increasing worker productivity
      b. developing more efficient industrial processes and machinery
      c. improving maintenance and repair
      d. replacing raw materials with recycled materials as resource inputs
   2. Decreasing the amount of resources in products
   3. Decreasing per capita consumption of resources
   4. Lowering the overall level of economic activity
   5. Increasing the longevity of resource use by:
      a. improving the durability of products
      b. improving the capability to repair products
  Objective 2. Protect public health and safety and natural ecosystems from improper handling of resources and residuals
   Actions:
   1. Improving knowledge of the impacts of human activities
   2. Protecting sensitive, unique, and ecologically significant lands
   3. Avoiding human development on hazardous lands
   4. Choosing the optimal time and place to release residuals
   5. Augmenting the capacity of the environment to assimilate residuals
   6. Treating residuals through various combinations of collection, concentration, containment, detoxification, recycling, and isolation from human and ecological systems
   7. Internalizing costs to give a competitive advantage to less polluting goods and services
  Objective 3. Stabilize and perpetuate the socioeconomic system
   Actions:
   1. Diversifying the economy
   2. Limiting the size and power of corporations, unions, and government, thereby promoting competition and preventing excessive dependency and control
   3. Promoting the sustained-yield use of renewable resources (often termed the earth's "free income" because the entropy

resulting from the production of renewable resources occurs outside the biosphere)
4. Promoting the maximum use of indigenous resources to prevent unnecessary dependencies
5. Conserving and stockpiling essential nonrenewable resources
6. Developing emergency plans for resource shortages and residuals spills

Goal 2. Provide this protection at minimum economic cost (so that management resources are not wasted)

Goal 3. Provide these services in as just and equitable a manner as possible

To allocate resources in the most economically efficient manner, planners are constantly involved in calculating the net costs and/or benefits of human activities. For instance, using conventional economic models, a resource planner may attempt to minimize costs and maximize the value of water use, perhaps seeking to reduce water pollution in a stream to an economically optimal level. However, communities in general are less capable of organizing, assessing, and assembling a collective bid for clean drinking water than an industry is for using water for the dispersal of residuals. The benefits to a community in safe drinking water, recreation, and so on, are more difficult to quantify than the benefits to industry in forgone costs of pollution control. Thus, it is highly unlikely that a citizen group or community could collectively organize and outbid an industry for water rights. The result is a misallocation of water.

In addition, the question must be asked: Is it fair to require communities to bid on and pay for clean air, land, water, and a pleasant living environment? Is it fair to require citizens to pay for services that have been free for generations? By allocating a commons to the highest bidder, we lose the concepts of fairness and natural rights to the commons. In that situation the assumption is made that a dirty environment is all we are entitled to, with a clean one only for those willing and able to pay. Therefore, it is important that the rights to clean air, land, water, and a decent, healthy living environment be vested with the citizenry. Intrusions into the environmental quality of any citizen should result in compensation to that citizen for infringement upon his or her natural rights. By combining the social and physical rationales for environmental planning and management, a conserving, efficient, fair, and equitable foundation for residual and resource management is established (Beatley, 1981).

In conclusion, environmental planning and management involve the control of the inevitable entropic effects of developing socioeconomic systems. But perhaps even more important at this stage of human endeavor is changing the existing mechanical world paradigm to incorporate the concept of limits—limits that occur in all systems of the universe. As Hazel Henderson (1981) put it: "Today, as liberal, 'laissez-faire,' and free-market values and institutions lose their organizing power, a new wave of critical reasoning has emerged. This reasoning also invokes new concepts of "natural law" as a higher court for indictment of the old values. . . ."

2 / Land Use Planning and Controls

Land use planning provides a means for managing human developments to ensure maximum use of a limited resource base and to retain for future generations a maximum number of available alternatives (Griggs and Gilchrist, 1983). The way in which land is used significantly influences many social characteristics, including spatial relationships, resource use, energy consumption, pollution accumulation and resultant ecosystem damage, availability of recreation, allocation of public services, and degree of integrity of the natural environment. In essence, the land use plan is the centerpiece for comprehensive environmental management. Land use controls can be, and have been, used for a variety of purposes, including (1) conservation of energy, material, and natural resources, (2) reduction of air, water, and noise pollution, (3) proper siting of public service, waste disposal, and recycling facilities, (4) promotion of quality development, and (5) enhancement of the visual quality of human environments.

On the other hand, the abuse and misuse of land can detrimentally affect a community and the lives of citizens in a number of ways, including (1) causing floods, landslides, and so on, (2) destroying important natural resources like waterways, beaches, and wetlands, (3) wasting economically productive soils, forests, aquifers, and renewable energy resources, and (4) creating major public health hazards like toxic waste and radiation contamination.

Land Use in Ancient Civilizations

History is rich with examples of the impacts of the misuse and exploitation of land. Many lands that once nourished great civilizations are today arid and uninhabitable. Centuries of intensive use and abuse of the land through deforestation, overgrazing, and inappropriate practices in agriculture have created expanding areas of desert in Africa, Asia, Australia, and the Americas. These man-made deserts today cover approximately 6.7 percent of the earth's surface (Eckholm and Brown, 1977).

Because of the growing awareness of desertification, scientists and historians have recently come to recognize that land use problems played an important historic role in the rise and fall of empires. A study of the cultural antecedents of modern technological societies provides valuable insights into past and present causes and effects of land abuse.

Before the advent of civilization, the Middle Eastern and Mediterranean basins had lush, diverse ecological communities. As late as 7000 B.C. the headwaters of the Tigris and Euphrates rivers were covered with forests and grasslands (Southwick, 1976). Greece, with a land area approximately half that of the British Isles, originally had more than three times the number of flowering plants in existence in the British Isles today. The Mediterranean Basin was covered with diverse wetland, forest, chaparral, and alpine ecological communities, many of which were destroyed by cultivation and settlement (Hughes, 1975). Southwick (1976) stated:

> The span of history from 5,000 B.C. to 200 A.D., which we know primarily as the period of great civilizations—Sumeria, Babylonia, Assyria, Phoenicia, Egypt, Greece, and Rome—was also a period of unprecedented environmental disturbance. We tend to concentrate our attention on the superb achievements of these civilizations in literature, art, government, and science, while we virtually forget their incompetence in land management. These golden civilizations prospered at the expense of their environments. They left a landscape which has never recovered, and a legacy to future civilizations which ushered in a period of dark ages lasting for more than a thousand years.

In the Fertile Crescent, deforestation and agricultural activities carried on by the Assyrians, Sumerians, and Phoenicians (who destroyed the cedars of Lebanon) denuded the countryside, causing enormous erosion and siltation problems. By approximately 3000 B.C., increased siltation from the Tigris and Euphrates rivers had extended the delta more than 180 miles farther into the Gulf (Southwick, 1976). Today the once Fertile Crescent supports only a fraction of the people it did in ancient times, and lost cities of former grandeur are found in areas too arid to support life.

In contrast, the ancient Egyptian civilization along the Nile endured for more than 6,000 years. This was due, in part, to the sparsely populated headwaters of the Nile, the annual flooding that replenished the soil and removed salts, and the Egyptian reverence for the natural world. Unlike the Mesopotamian cultures, which saw nature as a monstrous chaos to be battled, the Egyptians viewed nature as cyclical, replenishing, and friendly. In Egypt, nature was protected and worshipped (Hughes, 1975).

The ancient Greek culture had a similar benign attitude toward nature. The Greek gods were nature deities (Zeus, weather; Poseidon, seas; Demeter, plants; and Artemis, animals and wilderness). In the contemplative sciences of the Greeks, nature was studied and protected.

Hippocrates believed that sicknesses resulted from a mistreated environment—for instance, that improper handling of sewage and wetlands disruption resulted in malaria. But even given the benign attitudes of the Greeks, centuries of deforestation, mining, overgrazing, and intensive agriculture resulted in denudation and destruction of the land. This destruction was one cause of the development of sea-based trading systems (primarily by Athens) and war (e.g., Sparta conquering Messenia to obtain slave labor for agriculture). In the Hellenistic period, laws were passed to prevent the development of agricultural lands and protect wetlands, but too late. Today, approximately one-tenth of Greece is forested; in the past more than half the country was covered by forests (Hughes, 1975). Plato in *Critias* commented on the deforestation of Attica in two careless generations: "What now remains compared to what then existed is like the skeleton of a sick man, all the fat and soft earth having washed away, and only the bare framework being left."

As the Greek city-states deteriorated, Rome flourished on the fertile Italian peninsula. The Roman culture was much more utilitarian than that of the Greeks. Roman gods were gods of utility (Ceres, grain; Insiter, sowing; and Liber, wine). The Romans conquered much of the known world, but their achievements were shadowed by the destruction of their homeland. Deforestation, intensive cultivation, overgrazing, and war devastated the Roman countryside. Flooding, erosion, and siltation resulted in food shortages by the second century A.D. and forced the closing of seaports (i.e., Ravenna, Ostia, and Poestrum) (Hughes, 1975).

The city of Rome became a decidedly unpleasant place to live. Noise, crowding, air pollution, water pollution, flooding, food shortages, and disease became chronic problems. Diocletian's "Edicts on Prices and Occupations" (wage and price controls) were passed to deal with chronic food shortages. Building codes and transportation laws (limiting vehicular travel during daylight hours) were passed to reduce hazards. Air, water, and noise pollution laws were strictly enforced. Cries of anger echoed throughout Rome whenever Nero ostentatiously bathed at the intake of the Aqua Marcia (a major drinking water aqueduct) (Hughes, 1975).

As living conditions deteriorated, the wealthy developed posh suburbs and country estates. This concentration of land ownership by the noble class resulted in calls for agrarian reform by the first and second centuries A.D. This movement was dealt with harshly by the state, resulting in the exercise of police power and even assassination, as in the case of the Gracchi brothers. By the third century A.D., burning, pillaging, and the leveling of cities, a common practice by armies of rival political factions, destroyed what little remained of the Roman countryside (Hughes, 1975).

Strangely, the achievements of Rome that are so often admired— their armies, aqueducts, roads, etc.—hastened the destruction of their

28 / *Land Use Planning and Controls*

Figure 2-1. Prime Farmland Diverted to Other Uses, 1967–1977 (Sheets, 1981). © *U.S. News and World Report.* Reprinted with permission.

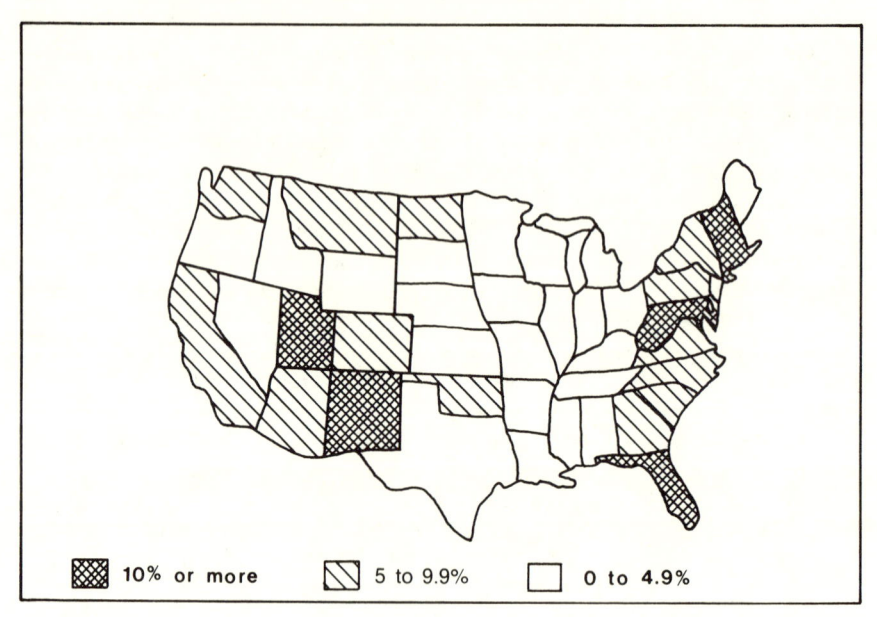

resource base, which contributed to the fall of Rome. Roman engineering, technology, and military prowess sowed the seeds of destruction through exploitation and war. Today, the technologies, attitudes, and problems of many Western cultures parallel those of ancient Rome. Dasmann (1966) has written, "Until industrial man, armed with powers greater than his ancestors ever imagined, makes use of the wisdom his ancestors so painfully acquired, he remains in peril. Like the gods of old, he can make the earth into a paradise if he so chooses, or he can destroy it."

Land Use Issues in the United States

Loss of Agricultural Lands

Precious U.S. farmland is disappearing at an alarming rate. Of the 368 million acres of potential cropland in the United States, an estimated 3 million acres are being lost each year to subdivisions, highways, parking lots, factories, shopping centers, and other nonagricultural uses. This amounts to a loss of twelve square miles of potential farmland each day (CEQ, 1980; Sheets, 1981).

Farmland losses are particularly heavy in the industrial states of the east coast (see Figure 2-1). Approximately 50 percent of the available farmland in New England has been lost, and the Mid-Atlantic states have lost an estimated 22 percent. If present trends continue to the year 2000, Florida could lose virtually all its prime farmland and California nearly 15 percent (Sheets, 1981).

In addition, an estimated 4 million acres are lost to wind and water erosion each year. The General Accounting Office has claimed that topsoil losses to erosion today are worse than those in the dust bowl years of the 1930s. Approximately two-thirds of the agricultural lands in the United States are eroding faster than they are being replenished. Fifteen tons of topsoil roll out of the mouth of the Mississippi each second. In Illinois, two bushels of topsoil are lost for each bushel of corn produced. In the last century, the average depth of the topsoil in Iowa has decreased from sixteen to eight inches (Sheets, 1981).

The cumulative effects of these losses could lead to higher agricultural prices and food shortages. The U.S. Department of Agriculture has estimated that the physical limits of agricultural productive capacity may be reached by the year 2030, if not earlier. However, long before these physical limits are reached, economic, social, and environmental constraints could diminish production capacity (CEQ, 1980).

A recent study by the U.S. Department of Agriculture and the Council on Environmental Quality (1981) estimated that U.S. farmers will need to plant an additional 84 million to 143 million acres of land by the year 2000 to meet anticipated domestic and foreign demands for food. The study also called for additional, stronger initiatives to protect agricultural land from development.

In forty-three states, farmland property tax assessments are based on the agricultural value rather than on the potential development value of the land. In some areas, zoning is also used to protect farmland. For example, special agricultural districts have been established in New York State to provide tax breaks to farmers who agree not to sell their land for development. Farmers who do sell their land must pay five years of back taxes on the land's market value (Sheets, 1981).

Some areas, such as Suffolk County, Long Island, have established programs to purchase outright the development rights of land from farmers. In Wisconsin and Michigan, farmers are offered property tax credits if their taxes exceed a specified percentage of family income when they keep their land in agriculture uses. Finally, Vermont, Connecticut, and Montana levy capital gains taxes on profits made from land speculation (Sheets, 1981). Despite these many and varied efforts, experts remain worried about the continuing loss of one of the most precious of U.S. resources.

Desertification

The long-term productivity and habitability of many lands in North America are being diminished by desertification. Groundwater and

30 / *Land Use Planning and Controls*

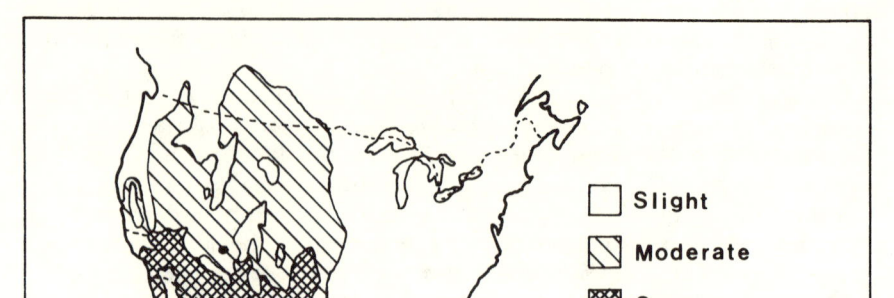

Figure 2-2. Desertification in North America (Dregne, 1977).

surface water supplies are being depleted and contaminated by overgrazing, intensive irrigation and cultivation, large water-diversion projects, industrialization, and urbanization. This is resulting in the destruction of soils and biological communities, especially in the West (CEQ, 1980).

A substantial land area in North America is affected by desertification (see Figure 2-2). An estimated 37 percent of the arid lands in North America (1.1 million square miles) have undergone severe desertification, characterized by devegetation, invasion of undesirable brush, or reduction of more than 50 percent in crop yields resulting from soil salinization. An estimated 10,500 square miles of North America have undergone very severe desertification, characterized by the presence of large sand dunes, gullies, salt crusts, and/or nearly impermeable soils (Dregne, 1977). Nearly 10 percent of the lands in the continental United States have undergone severe desertification, and nearly twice that amount of land is threatened (CEQ, 1980).

One principal cause of desertification in western North America is chronic overgrazing. A prime example is in the 511,916-acre Rio Puerco Basin just west of Albuquerque, New Mexico. More than a century ago, the area was known as the "bread basket of New Mexico." Livestock grazing began in the late 1700s, and by the 1870s the basin supported 240,000 sheep and 9,000 cattle (U.S. Bureau of Land Management, 1978). However, by the late 1880s water tables were dropping, the arroyo was cut, and erosion accelerated. Grazing in the basin peaked in 1910 and steadily diminished afterward. Between 1885 and 1962 an estimated 1.1 billion to 1.5 billion tons of soil were lost from the basin. By the late 1950s many formerly productive agricultural communities were ghost towns (CEQ, 1980).

In 1975 the U.S. Bureau of Land Management, which manages 170 million acres of rangeland in the West, estimated that 50 percent of this range was in fair condition, 28 percent in poor condition, and 5 percent in bad condition. Only 17 percent of the rangeland was classified as being in good or excellent condition, and of that, 16 percent was found to be deteriorating. Approximately one-third of all federal lands in the West are used to support an estimated four million cattle and nine million sheep—yet these lands provide only 3 percent of the forage consumed by livestock nationwide (Washington State University, 1976).

The ten-million-acre San Joaquin Basin, in the southern Central Valley of California, is another area that has suffered problems related to desertification. Irrigation, intensive agriculture, and overgrazing have extensively altered the landscape. The original lakes, wetlands, vegetation, and wildlife have all but vanished from the basin. More than 400,000 acres of the basin have crop and vegetative damage from excessive irrigation and salinization. By the year 2000, an additional 300,000 acres could be affected, causing an estimated $321 million in crop damage annually. Agricultural irrigation is depleting the natural aquifers of the basin at a rate of 1.5 million acre-feet per year. As a result, some lands in the western basin have subsided nearly thirty feet (CEQ, 1980).

The problem of soil salinization has plagued agricultural civilizations for centuries. In arid or semiarid climates, the trace amounts of salts present in irrigation water remain in the soil as the water evaporates from the soil surface. Over time the salts accumulate to levels toxic to most agricultural plants. Without periodic removal, by flooding for example, the salts destroy the vegetative cover of the land, thereby adding to the problem of desertification. This has been a problem in the Mediterranean Basin, the Middle East, the Indus Valley (where nearly thirty-six thousand square miles of agricultural lands suffer from salinization), and the San Joaquin and Imperial valleys of California (where nearly one million acres are expected to be adversely affected) In light of this problem, building the Aswan Dam to control the annual spring flooding in Egypt may have been a massive mistake. The spring flooding annually rejuvenated the soils, nourishing the Egyptian civilization for tens of thousands of years while many other ancient civilizations perished (Griggs and Gilchrist, 1983).

Nearly 80 percent of the four million acres of private rangeland in the San Joaquin Basin have been damaged by overgrazing (U.S. Department of Agriculture, 1977). These grazing practices and intensive agriculture have left the land vulnerable to water and wind erosion. An estimated 2.2 million acres of land have been damaged by serious water erosion (U.S. Department of Agriculture, 1977). In December 1977, a single windstorm in the southern San Joaquin Basin removed more than 25 million tons of topsoil from 373 square miles. In some areas nearly 24 inches of topsoil were lost (U.S. Geological Survey, 1978).

Wetlands and Coastal Zones

The protection of wetlands and sensitive coastal environments from dredging, draining, and filling is an important national concern. These areas are extremely important for wildlife, fisheries, and the integrity of land and water resources. Pressures are increasing to develop these sensitive areas for urban housing, industry, new energy facilities, deep-water ports, and offshore oil and gas drilling. To date, approximately one-third of all wetlands and coastal estuaries of the contiguous forty-eight states have been converted to homes, recreational developments, airports, industrial parks, highways, parking lots, and other uses. Regionally, these losses can be significant. For example, California has lost two-thirds of its original estuaries to development, and two-thirds of the remaining estuaries are polluted (Miller, 1979; CEQ, 1979a; Interagency Task Force, 1979).

Since 1900, more than 13,000 people in the United States have been killed by hurricanes. Yet, an estimated 80 percent of the 40 million people living on the Gulf and Atlantic coasts (where most of the storm damage has occurred) have never experienced a major storm (Griggs and Gilchrist, 1983). Despite the thousands of deaths and billions of dollars of property damage from hurricanes, barrier islands, spits, and beaches are being developed at twice the rate of other U.S. lands. Of all environments, these are among the least stable for development and most important in their natural state, yet federal subsidies are used to promote coastal zone and barrier island development. The federal money is used to prevent erosion and to provide disaster relief, flood insurance, and the public roads, bridges, sewers, and water systems necessary to make these areas livable (CEQ, 1980).

Under section 404 of the Clean Water Act, the Army Corps of Engineers was given authority to use a permit system to regulate the dredging and filling of wetlands. In addition, as of 1979, fifteen states had adopted separate legislation regulating the development and use of wetlands (Interagency Task Force, 1979).

In 1972 the Coastal Zone Management Act (CZMA) was passed to assist states and territories in establishing voluntary programs for the protection and management of coastal environments. Between 1974 and 1979 the federal government spent more than $70 million in matching funds for state programs. As of 1979 approximately twenty states had received federal approval for their programs (CEQ, 1979). However, the Reagan administration has cut CZMA funding, and several of these programs have been diminished or eliminated.

Table 2-1. State Protection of Significant Natural Resources under CZMA (NOAA, 1979).

State	Wetlands	Floral & Faunal Habitats	Beaches & Dunes	Barrier Islands	Reefs
Alabama	X	P	P		
Alaska	X	X		X	
California	X	X	X		
Connecticut	X				
Delaware	X	X	X		
Florida	X	X	X		X
Georgia	X	X	X		
Guam	X	X	X		X
Hawaii		X	X		X
Illinois	X		X		X
Indiana	X				
Louisiana	X		P	P	
Maine	X	X		X	
Maryland	X	X	X		
Massachusetts	X	X	X		
Michigan	X	X	X		X
Minnesota	X				X
Mississippi	X		X	X	
New Hampshire		P	P	P	
New Jersey	X	X	P		
New York	X	X			
North Carolina	X	X	X	X	
N. Marianas					
Ohio	X	P	P		X
Oregon	X	X	X		X
Pennsylvania	X	P			
Puerto Rico	X	X	X		P
Rhode Island	X	X	X	X	
(Am.) Samoa					
South Carolina	X	X	X	X	
Texas	X		X		
Virgin Islands	X	X	X	X	X
Virginia	X		X		
Washington	X	X	X		X
Wisconsin	X	X	X		X

X = Pre-existing law or program incorporated in Coastal Management Program or new or expanded law or program directly attributable to CZM participation.
P = Proposed law or program to be part of CMP.

To date, thirty-one of thirty-five eligible states and territories have either adopted new statutes or regulations or improved the implementation of existing laws to protect wetlands, native flora and fauna, beaches, dunes, barrier islands, and reefs. A summary of these programs is given in Table 2-1. As federal programs are cut by the Reagan administration, more and more of the burden for wetland and coastal zone management is falling upon state and local governments.

Floodplain Development

Unwise development in floodplains has resulted in increasing losses of life and private property and in the reduction of uses compatible with periodic inundation, such as wildlife habitat, recreation, forestry, and agriculture. Floodplains, including barrier islands, account for 6 to 8 percent of the land area of the United States. An estimated 6.4 million dwelling units plus a substantial number of industrial and commercial facilities have already been built in these zones. The recent acceleration in floodplain development, caused in part by federal assistance programs, has resulted in increased property losses from flooding.

The U.S. Geological Survey recently studied the extent of development of twenty-six moderate to large U.S. cities. The study found that an average of 52.8 percent of the total floodplain area of the cities was urbanized (see Table 2-2). The highest values were for Great Falls, Montana (97 percent); Phoenix, Arizona (89.2 percent); and Tallahassee, Florida (83.9 percent) (Griggs and Gilchrist, 1983).

The Water Resource Council (WRC) has estimated that annual flood losses doubled from 1967 to 1977. If present settlement and property investments continue, the WRC predicted, annual losses from flooding will reach $5 billion (in 1979 dollars by 1985) (CEQ, 1980; Platt, 1979).

The flooding problem provides an excellent example of the two basic approaches available for the management of geological hazards. The difference in the approaches is clearly illustrated by the contrast between massive public works projects and floodplain land use restrictions. The former "engineering approach" attempts to eliminate the problem, whereas the latter approach involves an adjustment in the development pattern to live within the natural constraints of the hazard (Griggs and Gilchrist, 1983).

The engineering approach to solving floodplain problems has been used almost exclusively. Yet despite the expenditure of hundreds of billions of dollars, the problems are getting worse. In many areas it is prohibitively expensive to protect poorly sited urban and rural developments. To begin with, it is economically and technically impossible to provide complete control through the engineering approach. When a rare geological phenomenon that exceeds control capacity occurs, the damage is extensive and in many cases exacerbated by the attempted control. For example, many watersheds are managed to control the 100-year flood (i.e., the probability is one in one hundred of so severe a flood occurring in a given year). Because the engineering works are in place, accelerated development of the floodplain is allowed. Thus, when the dams and diversions fail because of poor design, sedimentation, accelerated urban and rural runoff, or the rare 100-year flood, enormous damage results.

When the costs are low and the control of hazards easy to accomplish, the engineering approach may be best. However, we have arrived at a point where, in many cases, it is much safer, easier, and cheaper to change the development pattern rather than try to control the hazard.

Table 2-2. Floodplain Development in Selected U.S. Cities (Griggs and Gilchrist, 1983).

Urbanized area	Floodplain Area (sq.mi.)	Percent of urbanized area	Developed Area (sq.mi.)	Percent of floodplain total
Asheville, NC	1.6	4.4	1.0	65.0
Boise, ID	2.5	8.5	2.1	84.0
Boston, MA	62.4	9.4	11.9	19.1
Charleston, SC	39.8	40.1	21.2	53.3
Chicago, IL	131.8	10.3	75.1	57.0
Dallas, TX	146.1	21.7	28.0	19.2
Denver, CO	30.6	10.5	19.1	62.2
Fargo—Moorhead, ND–MN	9.4	40.0	5.1	54.3
Great Falls, MT	2.0	9.2	1.9	97.0
Harrisburg, PA	9.7	12.4	8.1	83.5
Lansing, MI	4.8	6.5	.9	18.8
Lincoln, NB	13.8	26.5	6.9	49.6
Lorain—Elyria, OH	5.3	5.0	.6	11.3
Monroe, LA	32.5	81.0	26.8	82.4
Norfolk—Portsmouth, VA	59.2	19.8	15.5	26.2
Omaha—Council Bluffs, NB–IA	50.6	33.5	23.1	45.5
Phoenix, AZ	71.2	18.4	63.5	89.2
Portland, OR	14.5	5.4	8.5	58.7
Reno, NV	2.0	5.3	.9	45.0
Richmond, VA	12.9	8.9	1.7	13.2
St. Louis, MO–IL	136.1	29.6	91.7	67.4
Salt Lake City, UT	12.9	7.0	10.1	78.3
San Jose, CA	80.0	28.8	67.9	84.7
Spokane, WA	1.9	2.4	.9	47.4
Tallahassee, FL	3.1	10.4	2.6	83.9
Texarkana, TX–AR	4.7	13.8	2.1	44.2
Total	941.4		497.2	
Weighted average		16.2		52.8

Source: Griggs, Gary B., and John A. Gilchrist. *Geologic Hazards, Resources, and Environmental Planning*, 2nd ed. © 1983 by Wadsworth Inc. Reprinted by permission of Wadsworth Publishing Co., Belmont CA 94002.

This applies not just to flood hazards but also to those associated with other climatological and geological hazards, such as tornados, hurricanes, volcanos, earthquakes, and shifting coastal dunes. In these examples, an ounce of prevention may be worth a ton of cure.

Over the years more than 8,000 flood control dams have been built in the United States. A recent survey of about half of these dams by the Army Corps of Engineers revealed that approximately one-third were unsafe. U.S. history is rich with examples of flooding and disasters created by the failures of unsafe dams (from the famous Johnstown

36 / Land Use Planning and Controls

Figure 2-3. Flood Frequency Curve for the Eel River, California, 1932 to 1959. The graph indicates how often a given level of discharge will occur (Griggs and Gilchrist, 1983).

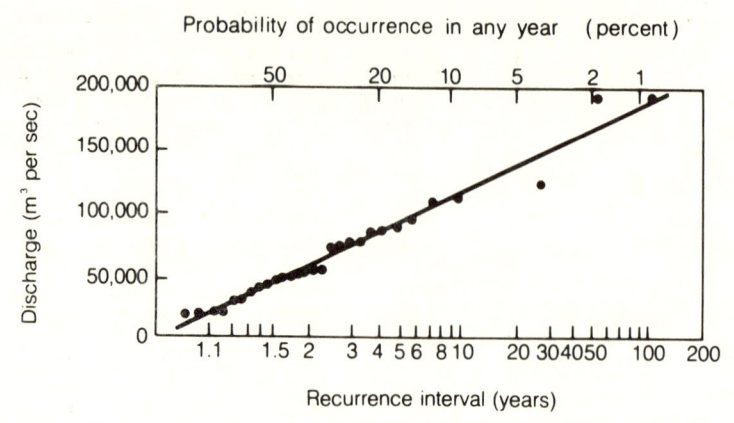

Source: Griggs, Gary B., and John A. Gilchrist. *Geologic Hazards, Resources, and Environmental Planning*, 2nd ed. © 1983 by Wadsworth Inc. Reprinted by permission of Wadsworth Publishing Co., Belmont CA 94002.

flood in the early part of the century to the more recent failure of the Teton Dam in Idaho) (Griggs and Gilchrist, 1983).

Similar problems have been experienced in the development of diversion, dike, and levee projects. One of the most destructive dike failures in history occurred in Vanport City, Oregon, in the late 1940s when a railroad dike was breached by a flood of the Columbia River. The town was totally destroyed, leaving 19,000 residents homeless (Griggs and Gilchrist, 1983). If the engineering approach to watershed management is so costly and potentially hazardous, why then has it been so favored? Several of the principal reasons are tradition, attitudes of supremacy over nature, simplicity of administration, and politics. In the last category, politicians and legislators find it very much to their political benefit to develop structural water projects, whereas the alternative—floodplain development controls—is often regarded as a potential political liability (e.g., if it were to be seen as government intrusion into private property rights). In addition, nonstructural floodplain development controls are viewed by many as a constraint on community development because the availability of developable land is reduced and land is withdrawn from the tax base.

The first step in floodplain management is the identification of the location, extent, and frequency of flooding in the watershed. This information is readily available for most major watersheds and urban areas from the U.S. Geological Survey. Figure 2-3 provides a representative flood frequency curve, where the stream discharge is plotted against a log scale of the recurrence interval (see Dunne and Leopold, 1978).

For planning purposes, the 100-year flood is the most important flood frequency statistic. Most floodplain controls are based on directing development activities in the "floodway" (area of active downstream water flow) and "floodplain fringe" (area of standing water) during a typical 100-year flood. The most frequently used controls include zoning of the floodway for open space, recreation, agricultural, and other nonstructural uses that would not be seriously damaged by flooding or inhibit the flow of floodwaters. Building codes and subdivision regulations are commonly used to "floodproof" structures allowed in the floodplain fringe (e.g., by anchoring or elevating structures) (Griggs and Gilchrist, 1983).

In order to curtail the development of floodplains, Congress enacted the National Flood Insurance Program through the 1968 Federal Flood Insurance Act. The program offered federally subsidized flood insurance to communities that implemented floodplain development controls. Unfortunately, few communities chose to participate voluntarily in the program because they feared and/or resented federally mandated land use controls. There was also little incentive to join the program because of the continued availability of federal money for floodplain development, disaster relief, and other floodplain development problems (Dingham and Platt, 1977).

In 1973 the act was amended to provide more affordable federally subsidized insurance for homeowners against flooding, mudslides, and shore erosion. Communities that are entirely or partly within a 100-year flood zone are first notified by the U.S. Department of Housing and Urban Development (HUD) that they are flood prone. The community must enter the program within a specified period or lose eligibility for loans from the Veterans Administration, Federal Housing Administration, Small Business Administration, and federal lending institutions. An estimated 14,800 flood-prone communities have joined the federal program (Griggs and Gilchrist, 1983).

Under the program a community must adopt stringent land use controls that prohibit development, construction, grading, and filling on the floodway and require either floodproofing or elevating structures in the floodplain fringe. In addition, communities are encouraged to develop comprehensive floodplain management plans for the flood-prone areas. These include such measures as open space tax incentives, acquisition of development rights, emergency planning, flood warning systems, and floodproofing criteria (Griggs and Gilchrist, 1983).

Unfortunately, in 1977 Congress passed another amendment to the act removing the federally subsidized loan sanctions from the program. Lending institutions must merely warn builders that they will not be entitled to disaster relief funds if they develop in floodplains. However, it is the buyer of a structure, not the builder, who bears the burden for flood damage, so the development continues (Myers and Rubin, 1978).

In May 1977, President Carter, by executive order, directed federal agencies to issue or amend existing regulations and procedures on floodplain management and wetlands protection. The Water Resource Council issued formal guidelines for compliance in February 1978, but agency compliance with the guidelines has been slow and incomplete (CEQ, 1979a).

Surface Mining

Approximately 6.5 million acres of land in the United States have been mined at the surface and not reclaimed. In the next two decades, an estimated 15 million acres of land will be mined. If not reclaimed, the resulting 21.5 million acres of wasteland would equal the combined land areas of Connecticut, Delaware, New Jersey, Rhode Island, Vermont, New Hampshire, and Washington, D.C. (Miller, 1979; CEQ, 1976).

Surface mining is undergoing a geographic shift from the middle Appalachian states to the arid, coal- and mineral-rich Great Plains states of New Mexico, Colorado, Montana, Wyoming, North Dakota, and South Dakota. These areas contain approximately 75 percent of the U.S. coal reserves that can be recovered by surface mining at reasonable cost.

The serious impacts associated with surface mining or reclamation vary with geographic region. In the Midwest, surface mining is destroying prime agricultural lands. In the West, some areas targeted for mining are so arid that they could not be reclaimed (National Academy of Sciences, 1974), and others could be reclaimed only through an intensive, long-term effort. The key issue is water. Even without surface mining, groundwater reserves in many areas of the West are dropping. Large surface mines could seriously deplete and contaminate what little remains and disrupt the current patterns of water resource allocation (Atwood, 1975).

To control the environmental impacts of the strip mining of coal, Congress passed and the president signed the Surface Mining Control and Reclamation Act (1977). Major features of this act include:

1. The requirement that mine operators post a reclamation bond before a mining permit is issued
2. The requirement that land be restored to its former use
3. The prohibition of surface mines from certain sensitive lands and the granting of veto rights to farmers and ranchers (even if they do not own the mineral rights to their land) over mining of their lands
4. The requirement that mine operators use the best available technologies to prevent surface water and groundwater contamination

5. The establishment of a $4.1 billion fund from a tax on coal for restoring previously unreclaimed lands

If adequately funded and enforced, this law should substantially decrease the environmental impacts of the strip mining of coal at a minimal cost. Similar legislation is needed to govern the surface mining of all other materials.

In its effort to accelerate coal leasing and production, the Reagan administration has stated its intention to turn the Office of Surface Mining (OSM) (which enforces the Surface Mining Control and Reclamation Act) into a technical service bureau for the strip mining companies. The administration has cut the enforcement staff of the OSM by 57 percent, has cut the inspection staff by 70 percent, and threatened to close the Denver office of the OSM (Friends of the Earth, 1982; *Newsweek,* 1981). Because of the weakening of the enforcement of the surface mining act, state, regional, and local governments may need to strengthen their regulatory efforts and be very cautious in developing commercial strip-mining operations.

One increasingly important aspect of land use planning is the proper management of mining activities and sites. At the onset, a zoning district for mineral extraction may be used to prevent unwanted, premature, or unwise development of a site. This is particularly important, for example, in protecting cheap, local sources of gravel (one of the most important basic resources for our urban development) from urban encroachment. The zoning ordinance should specify the conditions and types of activities permitted in the mineral extraction zone as well as general operational standards for setbacks, landscaping, access, and air, water, and noise pollution.

Another approach is the conditional use permit. A conventional governmental review procedure is employed to determine whether a permit will be granted and under what conditions. In addition to the standards discussed in the previous paragraph, permit reviewers should consider devegetation, soil conservation and strata compatibility with adjacent soils and hydrology, soil compaction and the creation of impervious soil layers, runoff, erosion, sedimentation, disposal of overburden, disposal of chemical by-products, and site rehabilitation (Griggs and Gilchrist, 1983).

Mining operators should also be required to berm sites to create noise and visual barriers and to provide siltation basins to reduce erosion, flooding, and siltation. Further, the mining operation should be planned in phases so that part of the mining profits are constantly being used for site restoration. When mining and restoration are planned and implemented together, the costs of restoration and the likelihood of the local community being left with an abandoned mine are significantly reduced. Reclaimed mines can be and have been restored as agricultural and grazing lands, parks, gardens, and storage areas.

Finally, to assure that the restoration effort is completed after the mining operation shuts down, a performance bond should be posted (Young, 1968).

Forest Lands

Forests are renewable resources if they are managed wisely and not overharvested for lumber, firewood, paper, recreation, agriculture, and mining. In addition to these uses, forests serve extremely important ecological functions by influencing wind, temperature, humidity, and rainfall; by recycling water, oxygen, carbon, and nitrogen; by controlling flooding; by providing habitat for wildlife; by absorbing air pollution and reducing noise; and by providing solitude and beauty.

To date, human activities on the earth have reduced its forests by one-third to one-half. Nearly one-third of the original forest lands of the United States have been lost (Eckholm, 1976); the loss has resulted in stripped hillsides, extensive erosion, siltation of streams, and increasing problems due to flooding.

Today, the National Forest System of the United States consists of 155 national forests and 19 national grasslands, totaling 191 million acres or nearly one-eighth of the land area of the United States (Frome, 1984). These lands are managed by the Forest Service under the Multiple-Use–Sustained-Yield Act of 1960, the 1974 Forest and Rangeland Renewable Resources Planning Act, and the 1976 National Forest Management Act. In theory, forests should be managed according to the principles of sustained yield (balancing cutting and planting to prevent depletion) and multiple use (for timbering, mining, recreation, grazing, wildlife, and soil and water conservation). In practice, however, the majority of our forest lands are open for timber cutting, to the detriment of the other forest uses.

To balance the economic, environmental quality, and social value factors of forest land management, the Forest and Rangeland Renewable Resources Planning Act (RPA) was passed in 1974. This act requires the U.S. Department of Agriculture to inventory and assess the nation's forests and rangelands every ten years and to recommend a management program to the president every five years. The National Forest Management Act of 1976 amended the RPA and required the secretary of agriculture to issue land and resource management planning regulations (*Federal Register,* 1979) specifying how the Forest Service should prepare management plans for forests and regions. These plans must be completed by the end of 1985 for all administrative units and each of the nine regions (CEQ, 1980).

The land and resource management planning regulations deal with a number of controversial issues, including:

1. Limitations on the maximum allowable size of a clearcut by geographic region

Land Use Planning and Controls / 41

2. Protection of riparian areas
3. Determination of suitability of lands for timber production based on physical, biological, and economic criteria
4. Specified procedures for departures from the requirements

During its first three years in office, the Reagan administration's policy has been to abandon the multiple use, sustained-yield policies established by Congress and to promote commercial cutting of our national forests to the detriment of wildlife, recreation, and soil and water conservation. This change of policy is reflected, for instance, in the Forest Service request in 1982 for an increase in timber sales from 8.3 billion to 12.3 billion board feet, despite a depressed economy and a backlog of more than 36 billion board feet of timber. In addition, the proposed 1983 budget for the Forest Service included reductions in fish and wildlife management allocations of 64 percent, in soil and water protection of 99 percent, and in trail construction of 90 percent (Friends of the Earth, 1982). These reductions may cause considerable damage to wildlife, soil, water, and recreation resources in the national forests.

Preservation and Recreation Lands

The three major public lands recreation and preservation systems are the National Park System, the National Wildlife Refuge System, and the National Wilderness Preservation System. As of 1979 more than 125 million acres were protected by these three systems. In the 1970s more than 57 million acres were added to these systems (81.5 percent of the present system), a reflection of strong public support and continued demand for recreation and resource preservation (CEQ, 1980) (see Table 2-3).

In November 1978 Secretary of the Interior Cecil D. Andrus temporarily withdrew 110 million acres of Alaskan lands from development using section 204(c) of the Federal Land Policy and Management Act of 1976. The action was taken to protect the areas until Congress provided a legislative solution. A month later President Carter, invoking the Antiquities Act of 1906, designated seventeen national monuments totaling 56 million acres in Alaska, thereby prohibiting mining, logging, and other commercial developments unless authorized by Congress. Most of these lands were those previously withdrawn by Secretary Andrus.

Finally, in November 1980 Congress passed and the president signed the Alaska Lands Bill. The bill provided protection for 103 million acres of federal lands in Alaska, nearly 28 percent of the land area of the state. The bill supersedes and generally incorporates prior executive actions taken by the Carter administration. Although the bill fell short of the hopes and expectations of the Alaska Coalition (a coalition of

Table 2-3. Growth in Preservation and Recreation Lands, 1969-1979 (CEQ, 1980).

System	Acres (thousands) 1969	Acres (thousands) 1979	Miles (thousands) 1969	Miles (thousands) 1979
Preservation systems				
National Park System	29,496	76,721 [a]		
National Wildlife Refuge System	30,540	34,974 [b]		
National Wilderness Preservation System [c]	9,925	15,301		
Other systems				
Wild and Scenic Rivers System			789	2,318
National Trails System				
Scenic Trails			4,450	7,550
Historic Trails			0	9,037
Recreation Trails			0	4,403
Total Trails			4,450	20,990

[a] Includes 42 million acres designated in Alaska in 1979 as National Park Service Monuments by Executive action.

[b] Does not include the 40 million acres withdrawn by Secretarial action or the 11.8 million acres designated as National Monuments by Executive action in 1978 because the areas were not officially added to the Refuge System until 1980.

[c] Includes only Forest Service and Bureau of Land Management lands, which comprise 80 percent of the Wilderness System.

the principal national conservation organizations) and congressional advocates, the significance of the achievement should not be overlooked. The bill more than doubled the acreage of the National Park and Wildlife Refuge systems and trebled the size of the National Wilderness Preservation System (Duscha, 1981).

Between 1950 and 1970 the annual number of visitors to state parks increased from 100 million to 600 million. During the same period, the annual number of visitors to the thirty-seven national parks increased from about 40 million to an estimated 280 million. As the number of people visiting parks dramatically increased, park budgets were reduced, exacerbating problems of park management. Currently, overcrowding, congestion, noise, litter, pollution, vandalism, crime, and drug abuse occur in many parks (Allen, 1976; Kephart, 1977).

Three recent management decisions in our national parks reflect the stresses placed upon them by overuse. In early 1980 the National Park Service Management Plan for the Grand Canyon established limited use levels, redistributed launching times, established environmental protection regulations, and called for a phasing out of all motorized river craft over a five-year period. In a similar decision the Park Service issued regulations limiting the number of tour boats in Glacier Bay in an effort to protect endangered bowhead whales. Finally, a recent management plan for Yosemite calls for the relocation of facilities and housing for 1,900 park and concession employees outside park boundaries and calls for the elimination of automobile traffic from Yosemite Valley (CEQ, 1980).

Urbanization

In 1800 only five percent of the U.S. population lived in urban areas. Today, 75 percent, and by the year 2000, an estimated 80 to 90 percent will live and work in urban environments. This rapid growth in urbanization has created a myriad of problems, including crowding, ugliness, pollution, hazards, stress, sprawl, excessive resource consumption, and loss of valuable resource lands.

In the past, urbanization has progressed in three major shifts. Between 1800 and 1950, 70 percent of the U.S. population moved from rural areas to cities. This rural-to-urban shift created rapid development of central city areas and urban neighborhoods. Between 1950 and 1970, large numbers of middle- and upper-income citizens moved into the suburbs. They did so largely because of deteriorating central city conditions, a desire to live in a more rural environment, improving economic conditions, tax and loan subsidies for single-family dwellings, and expanding automobile transportation systems that made the central city more readily accessible from the suburbs. These new metropolitan areas inundated large areas of land, especially on the East and West coasts and in the Great Lakes region of the United States. In the 1970s a third population shift began: away from the largest metropolitan areas, toward the South and West, and back into rural environments. This was primarily due to disenchantment with urban life, improved communications and transportation, and improved rural employment (Morrison and Wheeler, 1976).

This third shift may have the greatest land use impacts in the decades to come. Small communities and rural counties, especially in the South and West, will be faced with the pressures of rapid development. Pressure will increase to develop agricultural, forest, and floodplain lands. Local governments will be hard pressed to provide housing, schools, sewage disposal, and other public services. Without proper land use planning and controls, urban sprawl could exacerbate problems of rural land conservation and destroy the rural character of small communities.

A 1974 study prepared by the Real Estate Research Corporation compared the costs of low-density urban sprawl with those of high-density planned developments. The study concluded that the high-density planned development would (1) reduce total capital costs by 56 percent, (2) reduce operation and maintenance costs by 11 percent, (3) save 43 percent in development land costs, 40 percent in land costs for streets, and 63 percent in land costs for utilities, (4) reduce local government costs by 50 percent (5) reduce automobile air pollution by 50 percent, reduce air pollution from space heating and other natural gas uses by 40 percent, reduce water sedimentation by 30 percent, and reduce storm water runoff by 20 percent, and (6) reduce energy consumption by 44 percent and water consumption by 35 percent. Thus, good land use planning can save money, improve environmental quality, and promote the efficient use of resources in a developing community.

Land use planning can also be useful in providing and maintaining urban open spaces. Many people recognize the aesthetic and recreational functions of urban open space, but few understand that open spaces also provide physical and ecological buffers between and within urban areas; can be used to block harmful patterns of development; can reduce flooding and air and water pollution; can be used to maintain biological diversity; and can be useful in moderating climatic extremes.

The most overlooked and perhaps the most important urban open spaces are the small strips and patches of unused lands found throughout urban areas. For example, utility and transportation rights-of-way and dry stream beds can be used for walkways and bike paths. Abandoned lots can be developed as small parks or playgrounds.

Parks and cluster developments are frequently used by land use planners to provide urban open spaces. Central Park in New York City and Golden Gate Park in San Francisco are excellent examples of heavily used urban parks. Cities must anticipate and plan for the provision of such parks and be prepared to defend them against the inevitable onslaught of pressures for development or use as transportation corridors. In recent years many communities have been using cluster developments and planned unit developments to preserve urban open spaces. Such developments must be carefully planned, constructed, and maintained to prevent problems from overcrowding, congestion, and noise (Whyte, 1968).

Attempts have been made to provide large areas of urban open space and contain sprawl through the use of greenbelts. A classic example is the six- to ten-mile-wide greenbelt surrounding the city of London. Such greenbelts are successful in providing open space and preserving land use choices, but they are often underutilized and inaccessible to the urban poor (Whyte, 1968). Greenbelts have also been relatively unsuccessful in controlling urban growth and sprawl. Suburbs simply "leap frog" over the belts, exacerbating transportation, energy consumption, air pollution, and land development problems.

Land Ownership

One issue that is seldom addressed but very important for land planning and management is land ownership. The land management philosophy of land owners to a large extent determines the degree of abuse of the land. Knowledge of land ownership patterns is important in formulating and implementing land use plans. The more a regulator knows about the people and lands being regulated, the greater the likelihood of a more sensitive, effective regulatory program. Land resources, ownership patterns, and land use regulations in combination ultimately determine patterns of development (Popper, 1979).

Approximately one-third of the land in the United States is owned and managed by the U.S. government. Approximately 5 percent of the citizens of the United States own two-thirds of the remaining private lands (Barnes and Gasalino, 1972). Most of us "own" (mortgage) small urban lots and homes that are really owned by lending institutions. Throughout the last century, as rural landowners sold their lands and moved into the cities, more and more land came under the control of wealthy individuals, corporations, and institutions (Barnes, 1971). Thus, the real wealth of the nation—forests, minerals, fields, and streams—is currently owned and increasingly being managed for maximum short-term economic gain. The ecological and intrinsic values of land, along with the long-term impacts of the current development patterns, are often ignored.

The Debate over Land Use Planning

One fundamental cause of the land use problems discussed in the previous section is that landowners view land as a private commodity to be bought and sold freely in open markets with little or no government intervention. These potential opponents of land use planning adhere strongly to the theories of John Locke and Adam Smith and to the mechanical world paradigm. They tend to believe that a private landowner has no obligation to consider the public good when making a land use decision and that free markets are the ideal mechanism for allocating land resources.

This commodity concept ignores the intrinsic and ecological values of land and the external impacts of abusive development. Because land is treated as a commodity, its greatest value is realized in its most intensive development: Developers receive greater profits and governments receive higher tax revenues. Forest, farm, park, and preserve lands reduce profits and revenues and are, therefore, often overlooked.

Opponents of land use planning often cite the Fifth Amendment of the U.S. Constitution as support for their views. The Fifth Amendment states "private property shall not be taken for public use without just compensation" and "no person shall be deprived of property without due process of law." These property rights of owners came to apply at the state level when the Fourteenth Amendment to the U.S. Constitution was ratified. Many people interpret the Fifth and Fourteenth amendments to mean that a landowner may own and use property in any way he or she chooses as long as it does not infringe on a neighbor's similarly held property rights. However, a long history of legal and regulatory precedents dating back to colonial building codes clearly indicates that government is empowered to use its "police power" to regulate land use for the benefit of the community. In recent history, beginning with the landmark case *Village of Euclid* v. *Amber Realty Company* of 1926 (see Haar, 1959, for text), the courts have clearly established the rights of communities to regulate land use through zoning, building codes, subdivision regulations, and so on, when there is a clear public benefit.

In summary, no governmental agency may interfere with or take away private property rights without compensation to the owner. However, compensation is unnecessary if the "taking" of private property rights (e.g., development restrictions) is clearly in the public interest. Courts have allowed local governments to restrict property rights to the point of allowing only open space uses where clear hazards or very valuable resources exist. Courts have rejected restrictions, however, when a reasonable basis for the restriction does not exist. Because many of the "takings" are based on environmental constraints (e.g., the local groundwater's capacity to assimilate organic pollutants from septic tanks), care must be taken to fully document the local environmental conditions before a restriction is proposed (Griggs and Gilchrist, 1983).

In addition, Margerum (1979) concluded that local governments may actually be held liable for failing to prohibit or properly site new developments in areas of known or suspected hazards. If this liability, which applies for both public and private structures, is upheld in the courts, it would provide major impetus for proper land use planning (Griggs and Gilchrist, 1983).

In general, federal, state, and local governments and the courts have been fairly conservative in protecting private property rights. Regulatory efforts have been relatively successful in eliminating clearly obtrusive, damaging, and incompatible land uses. However, these management tools and philosophies have clearly failed when it comes to the more subtle, long-term problems of protecting unique, sensitive, or productive environments. In fact, Bergin (1978) concluded that a new theory for land use planning is needed—one that can encompass the concepts of beauty, harmony, permanence, and perpetuity.

Land is not a commodity, or even a resource; it is a priceless irreplaceable, finite resource *base* from which we draw many of the goods and services necessary for life (Andrews, 1979). It provides the sustenance and the foundation for all human activities. Unlike most commodities, land is immovable, finite, and physically variable from one location to another. In addition, land can have historic, cultural, religious, and symbolic values to many. In American Indian cultures, for example, the land is viewed and treated with reverence. In the mid-1800s Chief Seattle said:

> We know that the white man does not understand our ways. One portion of the land is the same to him as the next, for he is a

stranger who comes in the night and takes from the land whatever he needs. The earth is not his brother, but his enemy, and when he has conquered it, he moves on. He leaves his fathers' graves behind, and he does not care. He kidnaps the earth from his children. He does not care. His fathers' graves and his children's birthright are forgotten. He treats his mother, the earth, and his brother, the sky, as things to be bought, plundered, sold like sheep or bright beads. His appetite will devour the earth and leave behind only desert.

Those who argue for conventional market allocation of land resources to the "highest and best use" ignore the fact that the market fails to value many of the finite, essential, and irreplaceable goods and services provided by the land. Further, the allocation of land to the highest and best use does not incorporate the concepts of fairness and equity, nor does it provide a time frame for evaluation. Thus, the poor and/or powerless can be deprived of an essential, life-sustaining resource, and the long-term degradation of lands is not brought into the process of market valuation.

Our system has overemphasized the commodity value of land and underemphasized its value as a natural resource base. The key to any efforts to improve our management of the land is the development of a new land ethic. In the words of Aldo Leopold in *A Sand County Almanac* (1966), "We abuse land because we regard it as a commodity belonging to us. When we see land as a community to which we belong, we may begin to use it with love and respect."

Finally, land use planning can be justified on four bases (Erwin et al., 1977):

1. Land is a resource base, providing irreplaceable sustenance for social as well as natural systems. It should, therefore, be carefully and consciously allocated.
2. Many of the negative externalities resulting from poor land use practices do not pass through markets. The conventional control system of zoning is inadequate in dealing with these externalities because it is an indirect approach using spatial separation and is without sufficient incentives or accounting of costs of regulation.
3. Good planning can provide an optimal level of public goods such as parks, open spaces, vistas, and so on.
4. Land use planning can assist in providing public services such as sewers, transportation, and fire and police protection in an efficient and equitable manner.

Federal and State Land Use Programs

Several attempts were made in the early and middle 1970s to pass a comprehensive federal land use policy bill. In January 1970 the late

Senator Henry Jackson submitted the first federal land use bill to the Senate, stating:

> For nearly three centuries the American people moved ever westward seeking land and opportunity, seeking a better place to live, to work and to play. Rapid urbanization along the Pacific coast testifies to the end of this era of abundant and open land. No longer will there always be more land over the next rise. Yet the "pioneer land ethic" remains with its commonly accepted principle that the ownership of the land carries with it the right to do with the land as one pleases—to buy and sell, to use and deplete.
>
> Although the notion of unlimited land may have lost acceptance, the tendency to view land in monetary and ownership terms continues. Will Rogers succinctly, albeit unwittingly, described our present perception of land when he admonished us to "Buy land; they ain't making any more of it."
>
> We must modify further our concept of land. We must treat land not as a commodity to be consumed or expended but as a valuable finite resource to be husbanded.
>
> It is . . . essential that we develop a framework within which the myriad proposals to use or consume natural resources can be balanced against one another and measured against the demands they collectively impose upon the environment. Put simply, we need a focal point upon which we can compare alternative proposals to achieve our goals. That focal point, I submit, should be the use of the land. (Committee on Interior and Insular Affairs, 1972, pp. 3 and 6.)

The bill provided funding for the development of state land use programs, established a framework for developing management structures to inventory and protect significant land resources, and designated the Water Resources Planning Council as the federal administrative agency. The bill was passed by the Senate Committee on Interior and Insular Affairs, but was never voted on by the Senate.

Senator Jackson's bill was reintroduced in the Senate in January 1971. In February 1971 President Nixon, calling for better management of the nation's land resources, introduced his own, similar national land use bill. The president's version, however, recommended state regulation only for those land use activities of greater than local significance, thereby leaving land use decisions of local concern in the hands of local government (see American Law Institute, 1974; Carter, 1973).

In 1972 compromise bills regulating only areas and uses of greater than local concern were introduced in the Senate (S 632) and the House of Representatives (HR 7211). Under the terms of these bills, state land use programs could serve either to direct state land use planning or to review and approve local land use plans. Further, if state programs failed to comply with federal guidelines, federal airport, highway, and land and water conservation funding would be reduced and eventually withdrawn. In September 1972 the Senate bill passed, but the House version never made it to the floor (Environmental Policy Division, 1973).

Congressional activities concerning land use in 1973 were a mirror image of those in 1972, with the Senate passing a bill (S 268) and the House version never reaching the floor. Because the Senate passed a land use bill in the first session of the Ninety-third Congress in 1973, there was no need for Senate activities concerning land use in the second session in 1974. The 1974 House version, sponsored by Representative Morris Udall, passed the House Committee on Interior and Insular Affairs by a vote of 26 to 11. Although President Nixon once called this legislation a "high priority" environmental measure, he reversed his decision on the Udall bill after a meeting with conservative Representative Samuel Steiger (the bill's leading opponent) on February 6, 1974. On June 11, 1974, the Udall bill was tabled indefinitely *without debate* in a House vote of 211 to 204. The lack of support by the administration was decisive. The *New Republic* (1974) concluded:

> In Washington this summer nothing is untainted by impeachment politics, and land use is no exception. Representative Udall has thought since February that the White House was playing games on a number of issues, the chips being the vote of representatives on impeachment. After the defeat of Udall's bill, he charged the President with "grandstanding for the right wing." "Absolute nonsense," said Representative Steiger, a blunt-speaking cattle rancher, at a press conference: "The President never reversed his position; he just was never aware of what was in the committee bill when he endorsed land use legislation." Steiger maintains that the impeachment issue did not come up during his session with the President. He says he convinced Mr. Nixon that under the Udall approach, the federal government would get excessively entangled in what should be local land use decisions.

If the Nixon administration really did want some kind of land use law, such as a more limited measure than the Udall bill, it could have blocked the effort to table the issue indefinitely (four votes were needed) and pushed for the weaker Steiger substitute or for amendments to the Udall bill (*New Republic*, 1974).

Land use bills were introduced in both the Senate and the House in 1975. However, the Ford administration was on record as opposing any new spending program unless related to energy or the economy. Thus, a bill incorporating a national land use policy, originally slated as the centerpiece for federal environmental programs was never passed.

Although a comprehensive federal land use plan was never achieved, many laws that affect land use decisions were passed in the 1970s. These laws are summarized in Table 2-4. Although the majority of

Table 2-4. Federal Laws Affecting Private Land Use Practices (CEQ, 1979a).

Name (citation)	Administering Agency	Primary Purpose	Land Use Effect
Natural Resource Laws			
National Environmental Policy Act (42 USC §4321 et seq.)	Council on Environmental Quality	Reduce the degradation of the human environment and achieve a balance between development and resource use.	Requires federal agencies and licensees to analyze impacts of actions on land and water resources and to choose the environmentally preferable alternative or to explain why that alternative was not chosen.
Land and Water Conservation Fund (16 USC §4601-5)	Heritage Conservation and Recreation Service	Provide financial incentives for state and local governments to provide recreation areas and opportunities.	Requires adoption of 5-year State Comprehensive Outdoor Recreation Plans to guide recreation land acquisition and development activities.
Coastal Zone Management Act (16 USC §1451 et seq.)	Office of Coastal Zone Management	Assist coastal and Great Lake states in preparing and implementing state coastal plans.	Requires states to adopt acceptable coastal plans as condition for continued federal assistance; plans generally designate permissible uses of coastal lands.
Floodplain Management Executive Order (E.O. 11988)	Council on Environmental Quality, Water-Resources Council and Federal Emergency Management Administration	Reduce the risk of flood loss and restore or preserve natural floodplains.	Prohibits federal agencies and licensees from building in the 100-year floodplain unless there is no practicable alternative.
Protection of Wetlands Executive Order (E.O. 11990)	Council on Environmental Quality	Minimize the destruction of wetlands.	Requires federal agencies to avoid construction in wetlands unless there is no practicable alternative.
Fish and Wildlife Coordination Act (16 USC § 661 et seq.)	Fish and Wildlife Service	Ensure wildlife conservation needs receive agency consideration when water-related impacts will result from federal projects.	Fish and Wildlife Service and state wildlife agencies can recommend modifications of projects to reduce impacts on wildlife habitat.

Act	Agency	Purpose	Description
Water Resources Planning Act (42 USC § 1962 et seq.)	Water Resources Council	Encourage the conservation, development, and utilization of water on a coordinated basis.	Establishes River Basin commissions to coordinate water and related land development; statewide water resource planning must be consistent with these planning policies.
Agricultural Marketing Agreement Act of 1973; Agricultural Adjustment Act of 1938 (7 USC § 601 et seq.) (7 USC § 1231 et seq.)	Agricultural Stabilization and Conservation Service	Stabilizes prices, markets, and farm incomes and conserves resources.	Affects land use and crop management practices through set-aside programs, acreage allotments, and marketing limitations and subsidies.
Consolidated Farm and Rural Development Act of 1961 (7 USC § 1921 et seq.)	Farmers Home Administration	Finance real estate, operating, and emergency loans for soil and water conservation and rural industrialization.	Provides money for watershed and erosion protection, flood prevention, and soil and water projects.
Surface Mining Control and Reclamation Act of 1977 (30 USC § 1201 et seq.)	Office of Surface Mining	Protect society and environment from adverse effects of surface coal mining.	Regulates surface mining on both private and public lands and prohibits mining on critical lands.
Marine Protection, Research, and Sanctuaries Act of 1972 (16 USC 1431–1434)	Office of Coastal Zone Management	Designate marine areas as sanctuaries for conservation, recreation, or ecological purposes.	Allows only activities compatible with marine sanctuaries protection to be conducted within sanctuary boundaries.
Endangered Species Act of 1973 (16 USC § 1531 et seq.)	Fish and Wildlife Service	Conserve ecosystems for the use of endangered or threatened species.	Requires that federal agency actions anticipate threats to and be consistent with survival of endangered and threatened species and their critical habitats, whether or not the area is designated as critical habitat.
Watershed Protection and Flood Prevention (16 USC § 1001 et seq.)	Soil Conservation Service	Prevent floods, conserve and utilize water and land resources.	Helps local organizations plan for community development and forecast demands for residential, commercial, industrial and recreational facilities in a comprehensive manner.

Table 2-4 (Continued)

Name (citation)	Administering Agency	Primary Purpose	Land Use Effect
Community Development Laws			
Housing and Community Development Act of 1974 (42 USC § 5301)	Department of Housing and Urban Development	Encourage comprehensive planning for the development of human and natural resources by state, region.	Provides grants for the planning and development of community facilities and services such as housing projects and recreation.
National Flood Insurance Act of 1968 (42 USC § 4001)	Federal Emergency Management Administration	Reduce the risk of loss due to flooding.	Requires designated flood-prone communities to develop flood mitigation measures including land use, elevation and building requirements as a condition for flood insurance coverage.
Disaster Relief Act (42 USC § 5121)	Federal Emergency Management Administration	Mitigate losses from disasters and provide emergency assistance for major natural disasters.	Requires state and local governments to adopt measures which may discourage building on hazard-prone lands.
National Historic Preservation Act (16 USC § 470 et seq.)	Advisory Council on Historic Preservation	Protect districts, buildings, sites and objects significant to American history.	Requires that federal agency actions consider impacts of their actions on property registered in or eligible for the National Historic Register.
Federal-Aid Highway Act (23 USC § 101 et seq.)	Federal Highway Administration	Develop state and interstate highway system.	Provides grants to states for the construction of highway systems.
Urban Mass Transit Act of 1964 (49 USC § 1601 et seq.)	Urban Mass Transit Administration	Encourage the reconstruction and expansion of urban transit systems.	Provides grants to urban areas for public transportation.
Public Works and Economic Development (42 USC § 3121 et seq.)	Economic Development Administration	Stimulate community development through a wide range of subsidized community projects.	Provides grants to communities to develop facilities such as public works and roads.
Water Resources Development Act of 1974 (33 USC § 701 et seq.)	Army Corps of Engineers	Reduce the loss of life and property due to floods through dam and reservoir projects.	Provides for the construction of dams and reservoirs to reduce uncontrolled flooding and provide recreational benefits.

Pollution Control Laws

Law	Agency	Purpose	Description
Clean Water Act (33 USC § 1251 et seq.)	Environmental Protection Agency; U.S. Army Corps of Engineers	Reduce water pollution and the discharge of toxic and waste materials into all waters.	Makes grants for sewage treatment plants, which may encourage or permit growth; requires state to regulate land use practices to control pollution from indirect (nonpoint) sources such as urban areas; requires wetland concerns to be considered in U.S. Army Corps of Engineers dredge and fill permits. Permits Environmental Protection Agency to veto federal agency and licensee projects that could contaminate the watershed of a municipality's only source of drinking water.
Safe Drinking Water Act (42 USC - 300 (F))	Environmental Protection Agency	Assure public is provided safe drinking water.	Limits development in pristine areas, and affects siting of new industrial facilities in all areas.
Clean Air Act (42 USC § 1857 et seq.)	Environmental Protection Agency	Reduce air pollution dangerous to public health, crops, livestock, and property.	
Resource Conservation and Recovery Act of 1976 (42 USC § 6901 et seq.)	Environmental Protection Agency	Control of waste disposal and hazardous wastes.	Requires that all solid wastes, other than hazardous wastes be disposed of in sanitary landfill or utilized for resource recovery.
Rivers and Harbors Act of 1899 (33 USC § 401 et seq.)	Army Corps of Engineers	Protect navigation, water quality, fish and wildlife, ecology, and aesthetics of navigable waters.	Requires that effects on wildlife habitat, wetlands, historic resources, and coastal zones be considered before granting a permit for activities in navigable waters.
Deepwater Port Act of 1974 (33 USC § 150- et seq.)	United States Coast Guard	Regulate the construction and operation of deepwater ports on the seas to transfer oil from tankers to shore.	Requires land-based development effects to be considered in any port license and be consistent with state environmental laws or coastal zone programs.

Table 2-5. Summary of State Laws Protecting Critical Natural Resources (CEQ, 1979a).

States	Tidal Wetlands	Nontidal Wetlands	Floodplains	Coastal areas (including Great Lakes)	Agricultural Lands	Endangered Species
Alabama (C)	P a			P	T	
Alaska (C)	P b			CMP	T,O	
Arizona			P o		T	
Arkansas			P c		T	
California (C)	CMP		P o	CMP	T,O	P
Colorado			P		T	P
Connecticut (C)	P c	P o	P o	P	T,O	P
Delaware (C)	P d			P e	T	P
Florida (C)	P f			P g	T	P
Georgia (C)	P			P		P
Hawaii (C)	P b		P i	CMP	T	P
Idaho					T	
Illinois (C)			P		T	P
Indiana (C)			P	P j	T	P
Iowa			P o		T,O	P
Kansas			P c		T	P
Kentucky			P		T	P
Louisiana (C)			P		T	
Maine (C)	P	P	P	CMP	T,O	P
Maryland (C)	P	P	P	CMP	T,O	P
Massachusetts (C)	P	P	P	CMP	T,O	
Michigan (C)			P	CMP	T	P
Minnesota (C)		P k	P o	P o	T	P
Mississippi (C)						
Missouri					T	P
Montana					T	P
Nebraska			P c		T	P
Nevada					T	P
New Hampshire (C)	P	P			T,O	
New Jersey (C)	P		P o	CMP	T,O	P
New Mexico					T	P
New York (C)	P	P o	P	P	T,O	P
North Carolina (C)	P		P	CMP	T	
North Dakota					T	
Ohio (C)				P j	T,O	P
Oklahoma					T	P
Oregon (C)	CMP			CMP	T,O	P
Pennsylvania (C)			P		T,O	P
Rhode Island (C)	P	P		CMP	T	P
South Carolina (C)	P m			P	T	P
South Dakota					T	P
Tennessee					T,O	P
Texas (C)	P a			P o	T	P
Utah					T	
Vermont	P p	P p	P o		T	P
Virginia (C)	P o				T,O	P
Washington (C)	CMP	CMP	P	CMP	T,O	P
West Virginia					T	
Wisconsin (C)	CMP	CMP	P o	CMP	T,O	P
Wyoming					T	

P   =permits required for activities affecting the resource. *Note:* numbers indicate conditions or limitations on permit requirements.
CMP=regulated under a federally approved coastal management plan
T   =preferential taxation scheme used
O   =other farmland protection scheme used
(C) =denotes coastal state as defined by the Coastal Zone Management Act of 1972

ᵃ **Activities on coastal wetlands require permits under the state's coastal regulation.**
ᵇ Applies to state-owned wetlands and intertidal zones only.
ᶜ State law authorized local units to adopt regulations pursuant to state standards. In the absence of local control the state regulates.
ᵈ State's coastal act requires permits for industrial development in wetlands.
ᵉ State coastal act prohibits the siting of new heavy industry, permits required for the siting of light industry.
ᶠ Dredge, fill, and construction activities in certain tidal areas regulated.
ᵍ Activities seaward of established coastal setback lines regulated.
ʰ State land use act requires permits for activities on wetlands.
ⁱ State land use act requires permits for activities on floodplains.
ʲ Permits required for activities in lakes and their shorelands.
ᵏ Permits required under shorelands zoning regulation.
ˡ A beach protection regulation applies to Lake Erie.
ᵐ Permits required for activities in wetlands within defined critical coastal areas
ⁿ Permits required for activities affecting public wetlands.
ᵒ **Regulation applies only to public coastal lands.**
ᵖ Vermont site plan review act establishes standards and requires approval for most resource disturbing activities.

---

these laws were not specifically intended to promote wise land use, they are important in protecting critical, unique, and fragile ecological and cultural resources. Collectively, these laws are very important in discouraging improper uses of wetlands, aquifers, floodplains, agricultural lands, shoreline habitats, other habitats, wilderness, and culturally significant lands (CEQ, 1979a).

State land use planning programs vary significantly according to the nature and degree of the land use problems of the state and the willingness of state government to engage in statewide land use planning. State land use planning activities generally fall into four categories (Patterson, 1979; Healy, 1979) as follows:

1. *State land use planning.* Hawaii, Florida, and Vermont have passed legislation requiring a state land use plan as a guide for local and regional planning. California's state planning office issues guidelines for the preparation of environmental impact statements for specified developments. Oregon's state planning office prepares both goals and guidelines for use in judging the adequacy of local plans and controls.
2. *Statewide zoning.* Hawaii is the only state with statewide zoning (passed in 1961). The state is zoned into four categories: urban,

rural, agricultural, and conservation. In the areas designated as urban, more detailed local zoning is allowed.

3. *Planning and controls for critical substate areas.* This approach parallels the recommendations of the American Law Institute's 1974 model land-development code. In Oregon, protection is afforded to "areas of statewide significance." Florida has passed legislation directed toward "developments of regional impact." In either case, the state can adopt plans and controls if local governments fail to do so. Vermont has passed legislation dealing with the planning and control of developments involving more than ten dwelling units or developments at altitudes exceeding 2,500 feet. As previously discussed, several states have coastal-zone management programs.

4. *Statewide mandatory local planning.* Florida and Oregon both have legislation requiring local planning. In Oregon, the state is required to prepare and adopt plans for localities that fail to do so themselves.

Several states have also passed legislation that directly and indirectly affects private land use decisions. In many cases, state laws are stronger than federal laws in protecting critical resources and influencing land use decisions (CEQ, 1979a). A summary of state laws is given in Table 2-5.

3 / Methods of Land Use Planning and Analysis

Local jurisdictions vary considerably in their approaches to land use and urban planning. The most widely used and least effective planning technique is simple extrapolation of existing trends into the future. This approach can be successful in the short term, but for the longer term it can be disastrous. A second widely used and ineffective technique is simple reaction to crisis, wherein agencies are established to deal with short-term problems rather than long-term planning. Such approaches fail to capture the efficiencies and economies of "an ounce of prevention."

A third, more sophisticated technique involves the modeling and simulations of urban and land systems. In building models, testing alternatives and assumptions, and projecting future trends, systems analysis can be very useful in developing optimal plans under specified assumptions. However, models are no better than the data and assumptions upon which they are based. Too often, models are developed using a narrow economic or engineering approach that fails to incorporate a wide range of unquantifiable, intangible, long-term variables. For example, a survey by Walsh et al. (1982) found that 2.6 million acres of wilderness in Colorado were worth an estimated $1.9 billion (or approximately $730 per acre) in tangible recreation and preservation benefits alone. Walsh et al. concluded that this value would increase rapidly as recreational demand for wilderness increases in the next half century and found that access of future generations to wilderness areas would be one of the most important components of value. These calculations of the tangible economic value of wilderness are significant. However, the authors cautioned: "There may be long-run ecological values that are not included here. It is difficult for biologists to predict what these might be, let alone measure and incorporate them into an economic benefit estimate. The inability of economic analysis to place a dollar value on unknown ecological effects should be recognized in making decisions about future wilderness designations."

The final technique of land use planning involves the ecological approach. This approach seeks to protect sensitive, unique, and productive natural environments from human disturbance and to protect human settlements from environmental hazards. The ecological approach usually involves the creation of overlay maps of critical resources and environmental hazards, which are used to determine land suitability for various types of development (McHarg, 1971). Growth guidance programs are then used to promote development in the most suitable areas.

An Ecological Approach to Land Analysis

Extensive knowledge of a site is essential for proper land use planning and management. At the outset, it is extremely important to carefully define both the target area and its relationship to the wider region (e.g., to the regional watershed and airshed) and to inventory and analyze important environmental factors. The analysis should emphasize the integration of these factors into a whole to make possible the identification of important (to man and nature) ecosystem components and interrelationships. For ease of analysis the following progression of study is suggested:

PHYSICAL FACTORS
- Surface and subsurface geology
- Hazards
  earthquakes
  hurricanes
  volcanos
  landslides
  subsidence
  coastal erosion
- Topography
  slopes
  special features: vistas and unusual landforms
- Soils
  types and properties
  hazards
  suitable uses (agriculture, forestry, etc.)
- Hydrology
  watershed drainage patterns
  surface water bodies—recreation sites
  groundwater systems
  water supply: quantity and quality
  floodplains
- Climate: regional and local (micro)

BIOLOGICAL FACTORS
- Community characteristics
- Ecological functions
- Biological resources
- Endangered species
- Fire hazards

Methods of Land Use Planning and Analysis / 59

HUMAN FACTORS
- Land use patterns and conflicts
- Land ownership patterns
- Existing laws and regulations (e.g., zoning ordinances and plans)

Careful assessment of the physical and ecological factors in a land area can indicate the subareas that are most and least suitable for human development. This type of analysis can be used to (1) increase the efficiency of human investments, (2) minimize hazards to life and property, (3) protect water quality by minimizing soil erosion and identifying important aquifers and recharge areas, (4) preserve open space and sensitive and unique natural lands, and (5) identify potential development conflicts in the area (Kellogg, 1966).

Many of these factors will be discussed in this and subsequent chapters of this book. However, it is beyond the scope of this work to discuss all in detail. The information necessary for a complete analysis is readily available from the following sources:

1. *U.S. Geological Survey:* topographic maps—often used as base maps; quadrangle maps of surface and subsurface geology; geological investigations; interpretive reports; water resource investigations; circulars; open-file reports; professional papers and bulletins; water supply papers.

2. *U.S. Soil Conservation Service:* soil surveys and suitability maps.

3. *U.S. Army Corps of Engineers:* geological and hydrological studies; harbor, beach, and coastal maps and studies; floodplain maps and studies.

4. *All U.S. government agencies:* engineering reports; environmental impact statements.

5. *State geological surveys:* geology; minerals; hydrology.

6. *State environmental quality and resource agencies:* resource maps—forest, agricultural areas, water resources, etc.; pollution problems; waste management.

7. *City and county departments of planning, public works, and building inspection:* maps of local geology; development projects; hazard maps; land use maps, plans, guidelines; floodplains.

8. *Universities and colleges—geology, geography, and planning departments:* planning maps; environmental impact statements; geology; geologic hazards; hydrology; minerals.

9. *Professional organizations to consult:* Association of Engineering Geologists; Geological Society of America; American Planning Association.

An important new source of geological and biological data has developed from remote-sensing programs. Aerial photographs, for instance, can provide valuable information on fault traces, landslides, slope stability, hydrology, coastal pollution, and biological communities.

60 / *Methods of Land Use Planning and Analysis*

Data gathering has also been done using conventional color cameras, multiband cameras, multispectral scanners, gamma ray spectrometers, radiometers, and side-looking radar. For instance, infrared sensors have provided information on volcanic eruptions, hydrology, coastal resources, and the thermal plumes of power plants. Ultraviolet and color photography have been used to detect oil spills. Radar imagery from high altitude is also useful in identifying geologic features, such as domes, faults, or potentially oil-bearing anticlines. Considerable information is available from the LANDSAT 1, 2, and 3 satellites launched in 1972, 1975, and 1978, respectively, for the purpose of resource and environmental monitoring. Given the availability of these tools, Griggs and Gilchrist (1983) considered the opportunities for the use of remote-sensing data in environmental planning to be increasingly promising.

Finally, if all else fails, there is nothing that can compare to a field survey conducted by a professional scientist or engineer to provide needed information where existing data are nonexistent, inaccurate, or unclear.

Geology and Topography

Knowledge of local geology provides a foundation for understanding the natural processes of an area. For example, the type of rock largely determines topography, hydrology, and soils. These, in turn, influence the nature and distribution of flora and fauna. Thus, to assess the environmental impacts of human actions, one must "know the rocks."

Knowledge of local geology provides valuable information on (1) unstable areas in the subsurface (e.g., earthquakes) and surface (e.g., landslides and shifting dunes); (2) soil characteristics; (3) hydrology and water quality (e.g., erosion and sedimentation); (4) possible flora and fauna; and (5) sensitive ecological environments (e.g., primary dunes and wetlands) (McHarg, 1971).

One of the most important topographic features for land use planning is the slope of the land. The slope is calculated using the equation:

$$S = (V/H) \times 100$$

where S = the slope (in percent)
V = vertical rise
H = horizontal distance represented by that rise

It should be noted that a slope of 100 percent is equivalent to a 45-degree slope.

The slope of the land affects virtually every land use. With all other variables held equal, steeper slopes have faster runoff and greater soil erosion. Steeper slopes are not well suited for urban development and septic drainfields. Ideally, septic tank drainfields should be constructed with slopes of less than 3 percent to promote a slow, gradual flow of effluent with sufficient time for proper degradation of the wastes. The use of a slope greater than 8 percent may result in surface seepage near the lower end of the drainfield (Marsh, 1978).

The suitability of an area for development varies widely with uses, soil structure and texture, and climate. The Soil Conservation Service (SCS) (1981b) stated that (1) slopes greater than 25 percent are unsuitable for development, (2) slopes greater than 15 percent have severe development limitations, (3) slopes between 8 and 15 percent have moderate limitations, and (4) slopes less than 8 percent have only slight limitations (e.g., wetness problems). The severe limitations of steeper slopes can be overcome, but the costs commonly are prohibitive and the potential ecological damage is more severe (McHarg, 1971).

In hilly areas with unstable soils and heavy development, landslides are a frequent problem. For instance, a single storm in 1982 caused landslides that damaged or destroyed more than 6,500 homes and killed 19 people in the greater San Francisco Bay area (Griggs and Gilchrist, 1983). The fact of the matter is that the vast majority of landslides are caused by improper development by humans and are therefore easily controlled through proper siting, design, and construction. More than 80 percent of all landslides in Contra Costa County, California, and more than 90 percent of the landslides in Allegheny County, Pennsylvania, can be attributed to land development by humans (Nilson and Turner, 1975; Briggs et al., 1975).

The single most important step in controlling landslides is to require a detailed geotechnical investigation prior to construction in suspected landslide-prone areas. For example, landslide repair costs in New York State were reduced by more than 90 percent between 1969 and 1976 by improved geotechnical techniques (Chassie and Goughnour, 1976). In areas that are unsuitable for development, a community should clearly specify the location and nature of the hazard and should zone the area for open space or a similar compatible use.

Areas with minor construction hazards also should be carefully identified and defined, and fair, accurate, and enforceable construction standards and engineering specifications (e.g., land use, grading, engineering, construction, clearing, runoff and drainage controls) should be developed.

The evolution of grading ordinances in southern California provides an excellent example of successful regulation of construction practice (see Table 3-1). Prior to 1952, Los Angeles had no grading code and no requirements for soil engineering or engineering geology studies before construction. A heavy storm during the winter of 1951–1952 prompted the city to enact its first grading code and requirements for soil engineering studies and basic geological studies. Finally, beginning

Table 3-1. Damage under Various Grading Codes in Los Angeles, California, from 1969 Storms (modified from Slosson, 1969).

Pre-1952	1952–1962	1963–1969
No grading code, no soil engineering, no engineering geology	Semiadequate grading code. Soil engineering required. Very limited engineering geology but status and responsibility not qualified	New modern grading codes, soil engineering and engineering geology required during design and construction. Design Engineer, Soil Engineer, and Engineering Geologist all hold legal responsibility
Approx. 10,000 sites constructed	Approx. 27,000 sites constructed	Approx. 11,000 sites constructed
Approx. $3,300,000 damage	Approx. $2,767,000 damage	Approx. $182,400 damage
Approx. 1,040 sites damaged	Approx. 350 sites damaged	Approx. 17 sites damaged
An average of $330 per site for the total produced	An average of $100 per site for the total produced	An average of $7 per site for the total produced
Predictable failure percentage: 10.4%	Predictable failure percentage: 1.3%	Predictable failure percentage: 0.15%

in 1963 the codes were strengthened to require design, soils, and engineering studies, and the professional geologists and engineers undertaking the studies are to be held legally responsible. Table 3-1 graphically presents the success of the new codes by contrasting the damage done by storms in 1969 to those sites constructed before 1952, between 1952 and 1963, and from 1963 until 1969. More than 10 percent of all the sites constructed before 1952 sustained damage. Only 1.3 percent of the sites constructed between 1952 and 1962 and only 0.15 percent of those constructed after 1963 sustained damage. In addition, the strengthening of the grading code reduced damage per site from $330 to $7 (Slosson, 1969). Similar modern grading codes have been widely implemented in southern California and have served as the basis for the adoption of the grading and excavation section of the Uniform Building Code. Finally, it is extremely important to rigorously enforce construction codes. The severe storms of 1978 caused 0.7 percent slope failure for recent development in the city of Los Angeles, whereas the county of Los Angeles, with a similar code but apparently less quality control and enforcement, experienced slope failures in 20.5 percent of recent development sites (Griggs and Gilchrist, 1983).

If a landowner insists on developing a hazardous site, a community can protect itself from excessive service costs and poor business practices by insisting that the owner assume liability for any repairs and damages. This can be done through formal recording procedures and can include the liability for damages to adjacent properties. In addition, a community can require that hazards and liability clauses be clearly recorded in the property deed. These measures can discourage further development of property in all but the most desirable and densely populated areas (Griggs and Gilchrist, 1983).

Soils

Soils constitute the top layer of the earth's surface and are formed by the weathering of rocks. They contain air, water, and organic materials and are capable of supporting plant growth. Each type of soil has characteristic physical and chemical properties that are important for development or resource use. For instance, in undeveloped or unincorporated areas, sewage must be disposed of through the use of septic tanks and drainfields, which require thick, well-drained soils in relatively flat or gently sloping terrain. Soils that are compressible (e.g., organic soils) or that shrink and swell due to changes in moisture content (e.g., clays) are poorly suited for structural foundations, bridges, and highways. The physical and chemical characteristics of soils also determine their erodability and stability, corrosiveness (to human structures), and resource value (e.g., potential use for forestry or agriculture or as construction materials). The soil survey (available from the SCS) has become one of the most important tools in land use planning.

A very important characteristic of soil, from the standpoint of land use planning, is texture, which determines to a large extent its ecological and economic properties. The SCS soil classification scheme is based on three texture or particle size categories: sand (0.0625 to 2 millimeters in diameter), silt (0.004 to 0.0625 millimeters), and clay (less than 0.0004 millimeters) (see Figure 3-1, bottom). Because soils are not discrete units of particle sizes, but rather a continuum of mixtures of the various particle sizes, the SCS has developed a textural triangle for the classification of soils (see Figure 3-1). Each side of the textured triangle is scaled from 0 to 100 percent for either sand, silt, or clay, and labeled areas within the triangle represent soil types that comprise all three categories. Soils containing all three particle sizes plus a small amount of organic matter are placed in a fourth textural category—loam. In the system of nomenclature, the last constituent listed in the name of the soil is that making up the greatest percentage of the soil. For instance, a silty clay loam by percentage weight is mostly loam, followed by clay and silt, respectively. Soils are separated for textural classification through the use of wire-meshed sieves.

As previously indicated, knowledge of soil texture is extremely important in successful land use planning. Coarse soils that are well drained and have a high bearing capacity are well suited for urban

64 / *Methods of Land Use Planning and Analysis*

Figure 3-1. The Standard Textural Triangle of the Soil Conservation Service.

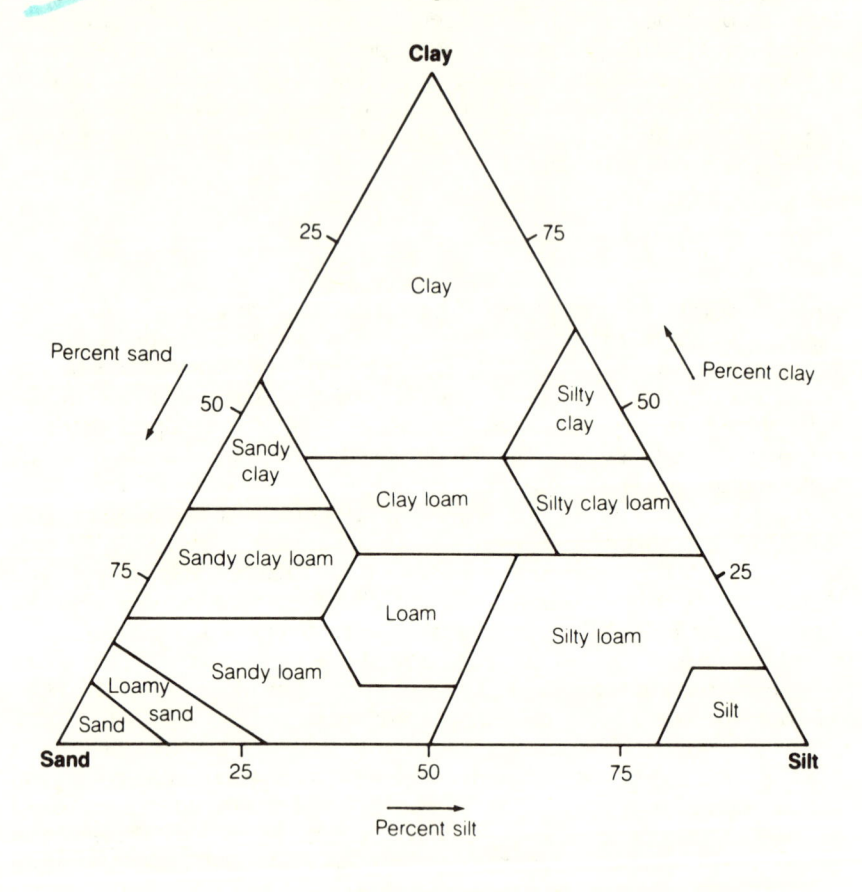

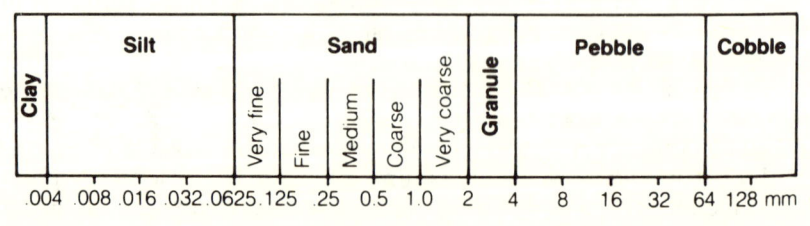

development. Clayey soils, which have a high "shrink-swell" potential (propensity to change in volume with changes in soil moisture content) and "plasticity" (tendency to change from a solid to a liquid or "plastic" state when water is added) pose serious problems for structural foundations, roads, and bridges because of their instability. Fine, organic soils (e.g., muck or peat) often form in poorly drained areas and have a low bearing capacity. These soils are relatively unsuitable for urban development or for septic tanks and drainfields in rural environments (Marsh, 1978).

There are many other soil properties that can indicate opportunities or constraints for urban or resource uses. For example, some soils are corrosive to steel and concrete. The corrosiveness of a soil varies significantly with soil acidity, texture, drainage, electrical conductivity, and the presence of sodium or magnesium sulfate (which corrodes concrete). Corrosive soils may damage foundations and steel piping (frequently used for drinking water systems).

Another important property of soil is its "depth to bedrock." "Shallow bedrock" may necessitate costly excavations for homes, roads, utility lines, septic drainfields, and so on, and may pose significant drainage, erosion, and slippage problems during rainy seasons because of the restricted downward flow of water (SCS, 1981a).

Perhaps the most important and frequently neglected soil property is its shrink-swell capacity. Soils that readily expand and contract with changes in water content have a high shrink-swell capacity. These soils annually cause more than $7 billion in damage in the United States—more than hurricanes, earthquakes, tornadoes, and floods combined. The most common problems are structural damage and cracking of walls, foundations, highways, airfields, and utility lines (Griggs and Gilchrist, 1983).

The shrink-swell capacity of a soil is dependent on the amount of clay it contains. For example, soils with large amounts of bentonitic clays tend to be very expansive, cracking foundations and creating landslides. These soils underlie approximately 20 to 25 percent of U.S. lands, but the problems are most acute for areas that have pronounced wet and dry seasons (e.g., the Southwest and southern California) (Griggs and Gilchrist, 1983). According to Jones and Holtz (1973), more than 250,000 new homes per year are built on expansive soils, and approximately 10 percent of these will experience significant damage (a change in as little as 3 percent volume can do considerable damage).

In hot climates, another particularly difficult problem involves the tendency of water to migrate from warmer to cooler soils. Because building foundations and roads shade the soil and prevent water from evaporating, they tend to accumulate water beneath them. If the soils are expansive, this can lead to cracking, warping, and structural failure. To prevent such damage, structures need to be (1) heavily reinforced, (2) anchored in pilings in bedrock and/or nonexpansive soils, or (3) the site must be excavated (Griggs and Gilchrist, 1983).

The most useful and readily available source of soil information for the land use planner is the SCS county soil survey. The heart of the soil survey is the classification of soils into soil series. Soils of the same series have very similar profiles (or vertical cross sections of topsoil, subsoil, and bedrock). Each soil series is named (1) for the town or geographical feature near where the series was first identified and (2) for the texture of the soil (e.g., Waldport fine sand series). A series can be further subdivided on the basis of slope, surface texture, stoniness, and so on, into phases. For example, the Waldport fine sand series is divided into three slope phases of 0 to 12 percent, 12 to 30 percent, and 30 to 70 percent. Each phase is assigned a number, which appears on the soil map (SCS, 1981a).

The series and phases are frequently mapped on aerial photographs at a scale of 4 inches per mile (3.168 inches per mile when published). Because of the scale, it is nearly impossible to accurately represent all soils in all locations, and the planner should be aware that the mapping process simplifies the existing soil conditions (see SCS, 1981a).

Despite its extensive mapping effort, the SCS cannot possibly map the soils at each individual building site. Add to this the fact that soil properties can vary considerably over short distances, and the necessity for a soil study prior to construction is obvious. This is especially true for larger projects or uses dependent on subsurface conditions, like foundations and septic tanks. The study should be done by a competent soil scientist or engineer.

In most regions of the country, soil characteristics have been analyzed by local, county, regional, state, or federal agencies for soil suitability or limitations for development. For example, the *Soil Survey for Land County, Oregon* (SCS, 1981b) contains information on (1) the origins of soils, (2) textural classifications and the depth of topsoil and subsoils, (3) key soil properties, and (4) the suitability of each soil for broad categories of development (see Table 3-2). The soils were rated for suitability (good, fair, poor) or limitations (slight, moderate, severe) for various uses of the land. Such information, if locally available to a land use planner, can be extremely valuable.

Hydrology

Hydrology concerns the manner in which water flows into, is stored in, and eventually flows out of an area, and it involves the local climate (e.g., precipitation patterns) and surface water and groundwater movements. Hydrologic data can be very valuable in determining the suitability of an area for development and in pinpointing erosion, slippage, and flooding hazards and land unsuitable for septic tank and foundation construction. Hydrologic information can also be useful in identifying and conserving groundwater aquifers and recharge zones. Finally, hydrologic data can be used in evaluating the suitability of rural lands for commercial agriculture and forestry dependent on the seasonal availability of water or intensive irrigation.

Table 3-2. Soil Limitation Criteria for Lane County, Oregon (modified from SCS, 1981b).

A. Local Roads and Streets

Property	Slight	Limitations Moderate	Severe
1. USDA texture	--	--	permafrost
2. Depth to bedrock (inches)			
Hard	>40	20 - 40	<20
Soft	>20	<20	--
3. Depth to cemented pan (inches)			
Thick	>40	20 - 40	<20
Thin	>20	20	--
4. Depth to high water table (ponding and wetness) (ft.)	>2.5	1.0-2.5	0 - 1.0
5. Slope (%)	0 - 8	8 - 15	>15
6. Flooding	none	rare	common
7. Potential frost action	low	moderate	high
8. Shrink-swell	low	moderate	high
9. Large stones (>3 inches)(%)	<25	25 - 50	>50

B. Dwellings Without Basements

1. USDA texture	--	--	permafrost
2. Flooding		--	rare, common
3. Depth to high water table (ponding and wetness) (ft.)	>2.5	1.5-2.5	0 - 1.5
4. Shrink-swell	low	moderate	high
5. Slope (%)	0 - 8	8 - 15	>15
6. Depth to bedrock (inches)			
Hard	>40	20 - 40	<20
Soft	>20	<20	--
7. Depth to cemented pan (inches)			
Thick	>40	20 - 40	<20
Thin	>20	<20	--
8. Large stones (>3 inches)(%)	<25	25 - 50	>50

C. Septic Tank Absorption Fields

1. USDA texture	--	--	permafrost
2. Flooding	none	rare	common
3. Depth to bedrock (inches)	>72	40 - 72	<40
4. Depth to cemented pan (inches)	>72	40 - 72	<40
5. Depth to high water table (ponding and wetness) (ft.)	>6	4 - 6	0 - 4
6. Permeability (inches/hour) (24 - 60 inches depth)	2.0 - 6.0	0.6 - 2.0	<0.6
7. Slope (%)	0 - 8	8 - 15	>15
8. Large stones (>3 inches)(%)	<25	25 - 50	>50

Drainage Characteristics

The drainage characteristics of soil, specifically permeability and degree of runoff and infiltration, are extremely important in determining the suitability of an area for urban or commercial uses. Permeability is defined as the ability of the soils to transmit water. Infiltration is defined as the permeability of the soil surface to water. Runoff is water that never infiltrates past the soil surface but rather flows over the surface.

Permeability and infiltration are greatly affected by soil texture and water content. For example, soils with high clay content do not transmit water readily because the tightly packed pore spaces around the clay allow little room for water. In addition, strong cohesive bonds between clay particles restrict water flow. Thus, clay soils commonly have drainage problems. Clayey soils or any soil with a high water content (that does not transmit water rapidly) are also poorly suited for the use of septic tanks and drainfields. Because the waste water does not readily pass from the drainfield into the soil, surface seepage problems, which are expensive to remedy and pose a potential health hazard, may occur (Marsh, 1978).

At the other end of the soil spectrum are sandy soils, which have plenty of pore space, little cohesion, and high permeability (SCS, 1981a). Because fluids (including sewage and water pollutants) pass rapidly through these soils, groundwater contamination is a potential hazard in sandy soil areas.

Permeability is expressed as the rate of water transmission through a given quantity of soil in a given time period.

$$\text{Permeability} = \frac{\text{Amount of water through soil (inches)}}{\text{Time (minutes)}}$$

The SCS (1981a) classifies soil permeability from "rapid" (two to six inches of water pass through a soil sample in one hour) to "very slow" (requiring years for detectable migration).

As permeability decreases, water that does not infiltrate the surface moves over the surface at a rate and in a direction dictated by the slope and shape of the land and the nature of the vegetative cover. Vegetation tends to reduce the volume and intensity of runoff by (1) capturing some precipitation so that it never strikes the ground, (2) extending the period of time for precipitation to strike the ground (reducing the intensity of rainfall), and (3) reducing the velocity of water on the ground by friction (Marsh, 1978).

The combination of bare ground, low permeability (e.g., clay soils, impermeable rooftops and pavement), and steep slopes results in the highest runoff rates. Thus, urban developments in clayey soils may require expensive drainage systems (ditches, large storm sewers, tiled

Figure 3-2. A Stream Hydrograph Depicting the Change in Flow Response to a Given Amount of Rainfall Before and After Urbanization (Leopold, 1968).

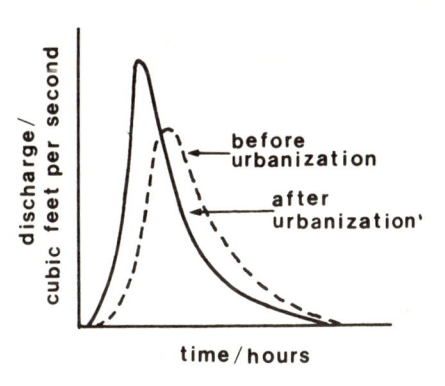

yards, etc.) to prevent flooding and drainage problems. In addition, as the development pattern progresses from rural to high-density urban, storm discharge increases in both magnitude and frequency; then flooding (see Figure 3-2), soil erosion, and water quality problems are exacerbated. Graphic depictions of flood frequency (Figure 3-3) and magnitude (Figure 3-4) are presented.

Dunne and Leopold (1978) provided a simple method for calculating the amount of increased runoff expected from any change in the permeability of the soil surface during peak runoff events:

$$Q_{PEAK} = CIA$$

where Q_{PEAK} = peak runoff rate (ft³/sec)
C = rational runoff coefficient
I = rainfall intensity (in./hr)
A = drainage area (acres)

In the equation, C represents the percentage of rainfall that runs off and is therefore a function of the infiltration rate, slope, vegetative cover, and so on, of the soil surface. For example, C values for urban streets and parking lots can be 0.70 to 0.95; for residential areas, 0.25 to 0.70; and for pasture, 0.15 to 0.45 (Dunne and Leopold, 1978).

If the surface conditions before and after development are known, the expected change in runoff can be calculated. The equation can also be used to calculate the effects of mitigation measures (recharge zones, catch basins, etc.) on downstream flooding.

If summaries of the water discharge rate (in ft³/sec) can be obtained, they can be extremely useful in understanding local hydrology and for water and floodplain management. Plots of water discharge rate can indicate (Kazmann, 1972):

Figure 3-3. Increase in Flood Frequency (Ratio of Overbank Flows After and Before Urbanization) for Varying Degrees of Urbanization (Leopold, 1968).

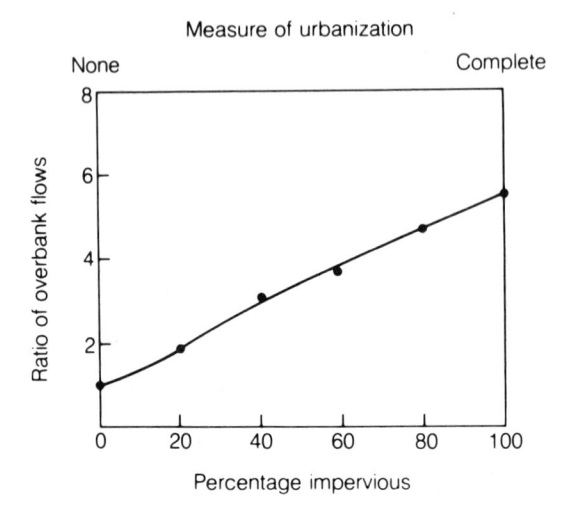

Figure 3-4. Increase in Flood Magnitude (Ratio of Peak Discharge After and Before Urbanization) for Varying Degrees of Urbanization (Leopold, 1968).

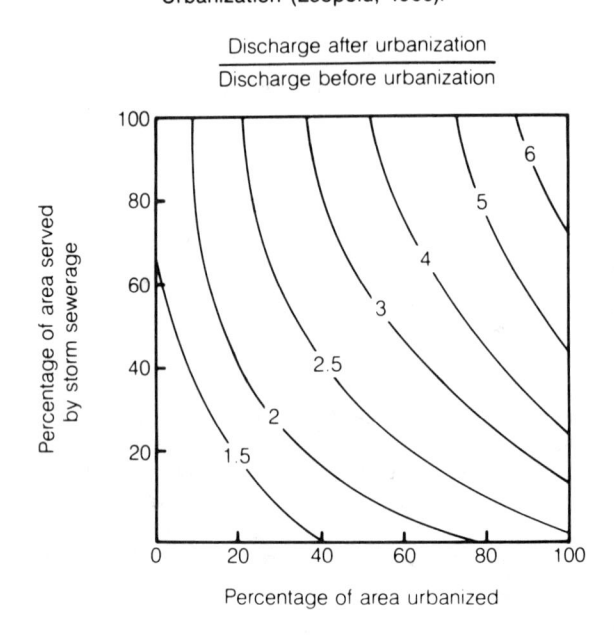

- water availability throughout the year
- dilution (of pollution) capacity of local streams throughout the year
- the amount of water available for cooling, municipal use, or irrigation throughout the year
- the minimum stream flow necessary to sustain fish and wildlife populations and to recharge aquifers

As was previously mentioned, urban runoff can contain a variety of pollutants, including petroleum, nitrates, phosphates, organic materials, heavy metals, pesticides, and bacteria. Urban runoff, especially in the first hour of a moderately heavy storm, can contribute more pollutants to waterways than would the city's raw sewage during the same period of time (Santor et al., 1974). This problem can be reduced considerably by the installation of off-channel facilities such as check dams, ponds, treatment lagoons, infiltration basins, and roadside swales. Many of these can serve the multiple purposes of reducing flooding, reducing contamination, and recharging groundwater reservoirs (the level of organic, particulate, nitrate, phosphate, and bacterial pollution can be reduced considerably over time through natural ecological processes).

Considerable progress has recently been made in the development of a porous asphaltic pavement that allows the percolation of storm water into the underlying soils. In the future, the use of such pavement could substantially reduce storm water runoff, and, because the asphalt also acts as a filter to remove many physical and biological contaminants, it could improve groundwater recharge (Griggs and Gilchrist, 1983).

Permeability, infiltration, and runoff are so closely related that soil scientists have developed a comprehensive summary of drainage features in which soils are divided into four hydrologic groups. The soils in hydro group A have low runoff potential and high permeability and infiltration rates (e.g., well-drained sandy soils). Hydro group B soils have moderate permeability and infiltration and moderately low runoff potential (e.g., sandy silts and silty loams). Hydro group C soils have a moderately high runoff potential and low permeability and infiltration rates (e.g., soils with moderately fine to fine texture or a restrictive hardpan layer, which often experience seasonally high water tables). Finally, hydro group D soils have a very low permeability and infiltration and a very high runoff potential. These are the clay soils, soils with a permanent high water table, soils with a restrictive clay layer or hardpan, or shallow soils over impervious bedrock (SCS, 1981a).

These hydro groups can be extremely valuable in managing land and water resources. The hydro groups can help pinpoint, for example, areas that have high potential erosion, severe wetness or drainage problems, drought problems, or high potential groundwater contamination.

Figure 3-5. The Relative Threshold Velocities for Runoff Erosion of Different-Sized Particles (modified from Marsh, 1978).

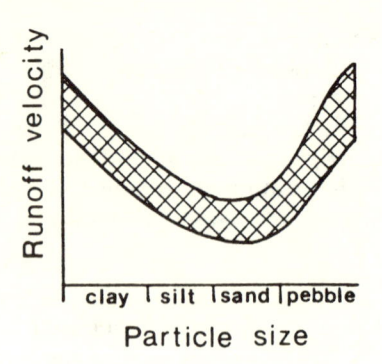

Erosion Potential

The erosion potential or erodibility of soils is generally a function of soil texture and cohesiveness, vegetation, slope, and the frequency and intensity of precipitation and wind. Many studies have indicated that vegetation is the most influential factor in reducing soil erosion. In addition to reducing the magnitude and increasing the duration of precipitation, plants tend to bind soil aggregates with their roots and thereby increase soil resistance to erosion.

A vegetative cover also ensures that the frictional interface of the wind with the land occurs in the foliage rather than on the soil surface, significantly diminishing the wind speed at the soil surface and thereby reducing soil erosion. Wind erosion is of particular concern in the case of bare, cultivated fields, arid environments, and coastal dunes.

If vegetation is removed, what types of soil are most prone to erosion? Figure 3-5 indicates the threshold velocities for erosion by runoff of clay, silt, sand, and pebble soils. The figure shows that sandy soils erode at the lowest runoff velocity. Pebble and clay soils exhibit a higher threshold runoff velocity because of weight and cohesiveness, respectively (Marsh, 1978).

The manner in which land is developed and used can have a striking impact on soil erosion and the attendant problems of water sedimentation. Those development activities that remove vegetative cover (e.g., agricultural or construction activities) maximize the potential for erosion in nearly any given environment. Table 3-3 presents the results of a two-year study of the sedimentation of a small drainage basin in the San Francisco Bay area. As indicated in the table, the sediment loads of soil erosion from agricultural and construction activities are orders of magnitude higher than those from activities on open space or urban lands.

Table 3-3. Annual Sediment Yields from Colma Creek Basin, California, in 1967 and 1970 (Knott, 1973).

Land use	Average tons per square mile per year
Open space	382
Agricultural	25,400
Construction	32,750
Urban	938

Depth to Water Table

Water tables that are within six feet of the land surface pose many potential problems, including destabilization of building foundations, soil erosion, and septic tank failure and the resultant leaching of untreated sewage into the water table or to the land surface. Great care should therefore be taken to monitor the level of the water table after storms or for seasonal variation. Further, fluctuations in the water table may be caused by human activities such as excessive withdrawal or "overdraft" of groundwater, creation of cuts or extensive fills, or the creation of new surface bodies of water. The excessive withdrawal of groundwater (exceeding the rate of recharge) may result in secondary problems of subsidence and, in coastal environments, salt water intrusion.

The amount of fresh water stored as groundwater is 150 times as large as the amount of surface water and 50 times larger than the average annual runoff in the United States. These groundwater aquifers are particularly valuable resources: they are cheap and easy to tap, relatively free of pollutants (in their natural state), and do not take up any valuable surface area. Although groundwater systems are only 20 percent of the total water supply in the United States, they can provide most of an area's available water, especially in relatively arid regions of the Midwest and Southwest. Great care should, therefore, be taken to protect these resources from overdraft and contamination (Griggs and Gilchrist, 1983).

Biota

With knowledge of the geology, hydrology, and soils, one can begin to analyze and comprehend the interrelationships of the physical and biological processes of an area. It is important to understand existing biological conditions as well as the dynamics of population changes to find communities that are unique or very sensitive to human developments. These include the vegetation in areas where vegetative cover helps to prevent soil erosion (e.g., old-growth Douglas fir forests of the Cascades) or to prevent movement or erosion of dunes in coastal environments. In addition, careful analysis of the physical conditions of an area can allow the accurate assessment of sustained-yield timbering of forest lands. The local vegetative community also provides a valuable service in sustaining wildlife populations and providing amenities to humans. In the process of assessing wildlife populations and their distribution, one must be careful to consider the migration patterns of key species that may reside part of the year or move only periodically through an area. To the trained biologist, the distribution of plants and animals can also be a diagnostic tool that indicates soil conditions and the possible contamination of soil and/or water. Finally, data from a biological survey or aerial photographs can provide valuable information on unique ecological environments (e.g., bogs, wetlands, old-growth forests, etc.) that are sensitive to human intrusion and that warrant protection.

Riparian habitats are especially important, both to ecological stability and the local economy. Riparian lands are the banks and adjacent terrestrial environments of bodies of fresh water and surface-emergent aquifers. These habitats have a much more diverse biological community than do adjacent terrestrial habitats and serve many valuable functions which include (1) providing a source of forage and refuge for wildlife adjacent to water bodies, (2) acting as a sediment trap, (3) helping to regulate water temperature, (4) reducing shoreline and riverbank erosion, (5) reducing the severity of flooding, and (6) providing valuable recreational sites and other amenities.

In an effort to protect these habitats, the State of Oregon in 1981 adopted an innovative tax incentive program. This program, which went into effect in January 1983, provides an *ad valorem* property tax exemption for riparian lands that are protected and enhanced and grants a 25-percent personal or corporate income-tax credit for costs incurred in fish-habitat improvement projects. Innovative approaches such as this may become quite popular in the future as governments begin to stress incentive rather than regulatory programs to control land use.

Human Activities

After the best and worst sites for human activities have been established, additional information on existing land uses, use conflicts, land ownership patterns, and existing laws, regulations, and plans can be very useful in defining the tradeoffs involved in designating certain lands for specific uses. Local, regional, state, and federal agencies should be consulted about laws and regulations restricting the uses of certain lands (e.g., historic and archaeological sites, parklands, public lands, endangered species habitats). In addition, state agencies often restrict development on poorly drained or erodable soils and areas that are considered unique (e.g., wetlands) or sensitive (e.g., coastal dunes). The latter are commonly termed "areas of critical concern," "conservation zones," "critical areas," or "resource lands." These areas may be already designated and mapped, or it may fall to the analyst to assure that no incompatible development occurs in these areas (Marsh, 1978).

In addition, important social obstacles, such as land ownership and public opinion, should be assessed to determine if a development or preservation action is politically and administratively feasible. For example, there may be considerable opposition to a utility right-of-way through prime agricultural lands, an interstate highway through an urban neighborhood, the siting of a solid waste or sewage treatment facility, or the prevention of land development for most profitable use. Careful attention to these factors can help to assess the level and nature of socioeconomic "feedback" just as the natural systems' inventory can help to assess the environmental "feedback" (disruption and destruction) from development by humans in the natural environment.

Techniques of Analysis

Suitability Mapping

The three primary applications of environmental information are to (1) identify environmental constraints on human activities, (2) discover environmental opportunities for resource and urban development, and (3) assess the changes in environmental conditions resulting from proposed actions (discussed in Chapter 9). The most frequently used technique for organizing and displaying information on land areas best and least suited for development activities is the comprehensive suitability map. Pertinent environmental information can be organized, analyzed, and displayed in a manner easily understood by the lay person, especially those coincidental relationships in the distribution of a number of factors. It is also easy to display alternative sets of factors.

The first step in developing a suitability map is to obtain an adequate base map (commonly a U.S. Geological Survey topographic map or an SCS county soil map). Individual "categories" (e.g., degree of slope, type of vegetation) of relevant environmental "factors" (e.g., slope, soils, vegetation, drainage) are mapped according to the degree of opportunity or constraint judged to be represented by the category (see Table 3-2). Because of the potential for litigation in land use matters, it is extremely important to base the suitability ratings on the most reliable and accurate data possible. An individual suitability overlay map is developed for each relevant environmental factor. When superimposed over the base map, the resulting composite reveals areas with a variety of development suitability (see Figure 3-6).

There are many methods of representation of overall suitability. For example, each overlay can be differentially shaded in proportion to the degree of suitability, the darkest areas being least suitable. This method is fairly inexpensive and easy to accomplish, but the relative influence of the individual factors is not represented and can be very important in land use planning. For instance, sandy soils and steep slopes may individually represent only a modest constraint for a given form of development, but the enormous combined potential for erosion could significantly limit the development potential. Figure 3-6 presents the most popular method used to indicate the relative constraints of the factors, both visually and quantitatively. In addition, a combined numerical and color scheme (usually overlaying the primary colors) is commonly used (see McHarg [1971] for examples of each method).

A more quantitative and advanced method, the "factor combination" method, combines related factors and categories prior to suitability rating and mapping. The factor combination method thus accounts for interaction among the factors and categories. However, great difficulty is experienced when a large number of factors and categories are analyzed. For example, although two factors with three categories each produces only nine categories (3^2) for suitability ratings, four factors with four categories each results in 128 categories (4^4). The number of subjective judgments for suitability ratings can thus become prohibitively large (Chapin and Kaiser, 1979).

The process of analyzing environmental opportunities involves the assessment of natural potentials of an area for various land uses. The technique of analysis is quite similar to that of determining environmental constraints. However, instead of determining constraints for a specific action, the analysis is intended to determine the optimal use of the land for a variety of actions. Thus, opportunity suitability analysis is often more comprehensive than constraint suitability analysis, which focuses on only one potential land use (Marsh, 1978).

Opportunity mapping may involve the search for the best site for a specific land use (e.g., recreation facility or ski area), the identification of the best use of a specific site, resource mapping, or the location of the best sites for public functions (utility rights-of-way, energy facilities siting, or highways). Usually, however, opportunity mapping involves the identification of environmental constraints that are to be considered before opportunities are assessed. What represents a constraint to one type of development may be an opportunity for another. For instance, floodplains are poorly suited for residential development, but well suited for recreation and open space preservation. Opportunities and constraints can be simultaneously represented on suitability maps by differential shading, coloring, or numerical rating schemes.

Although suitability mapping is widely used in land use planning, one should be aware of its major drawbacks: (1) the subjective ranking

Figure 3-6. Composite Mapping Technique. A composite map is assembled from four overlays ranked for residential development suitability with a five-category classification system (modified from Marsh, 1978).

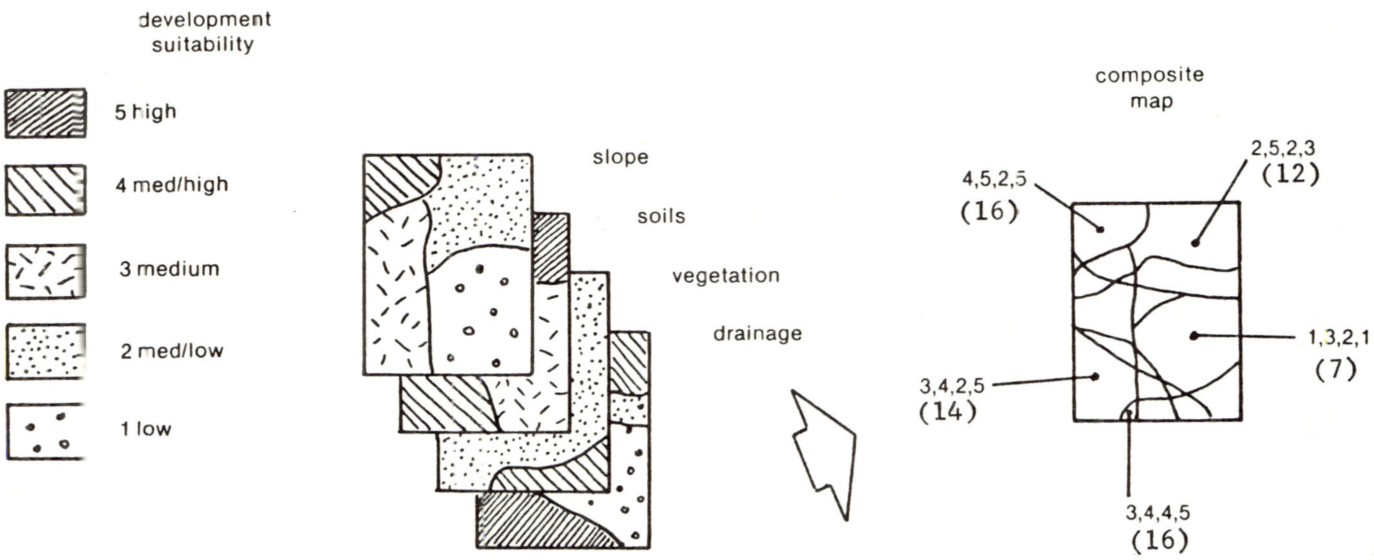

78 / *Methods of Land Use Planning and Analysis*

of suitability (based on the best information available), (2) the large number of combinations possible from only a few categories and factors mapped, (3) the difficulty of manipulating and updating a large number of acetate overlays, and (4) the difficulty in evaluating and translating the large volume of data from base maps to acetate sheets.

Computer Applications of Analysis

Many of the problems just discussed can be alleviated through the use of computer mapping systems. Data programmed into a computer can be stored, manipulated, evaluated, and updated easily and efficiently. Further, the computer can print out information for different geographic scales and alternative schemes of scaling and weighting in digital or graphic form or both (see Figures 3-7 and 3-8).

Like any automated system, computers have limitations. Computer output is only as accurate as input and the assumptions embodied in the evaluations. Impressive computer outputs may mask poor assumptions, subjective decisions, and/or incomplete or inaccurate data bases. In addition, information input, access, and retrieval may become centralized and remote from the planning staff if not properly managed. The dependence on computers and technicians and the need to digitize all data may create bottlenecks and prevent effective use of the information. Despite these drawbacks, there is an extremely bright future for the use of computers in land use and environmental planning.

Guidance System Planning Approach

In the past few decades, concern has been increasing among citizens, professional planners, and government officials for systematically improving the effectiveness of implementing land use plans and policies. This concern has resulted in the development of innovative legislation and programs, reorganizations of government, and proposals for the development of growth guidance systems to control the timing, location, and quality of urban development. The land use guidance system is the most frequently used systematic method for formulating, implementing, and monitoring the performance of a land use plan. Figure 3-9 outlines the six principal steps of the guidance system approach to land use planning (EPA, 1974a; Patterson, 1979).

Step 1. Problem Identification and Analysis. The first step in developing a land use guidance system is the establishment of an information base to assist in defining problems, formulating goals and objectives, analyzing alternatives, and establishing a baseline for monitoring the performance of the program. Information should be obtained on past, present, and predicted land uses. In addition, the inventory should include detailed physical, ecological, and socioeconomic features of the land. Once this

Figure 3-7. Computer Printout Indicating View Prominence in the South Hills of Eugene, Oregon. The study assumes that steep slopes and high elevations are more visually prominent than low, flat areas. Differential shading according to elevation and slope reveals the areas with high visual prominence (darker areas) (courtesy of Prof. Eugene Bressler, University of Oregon).

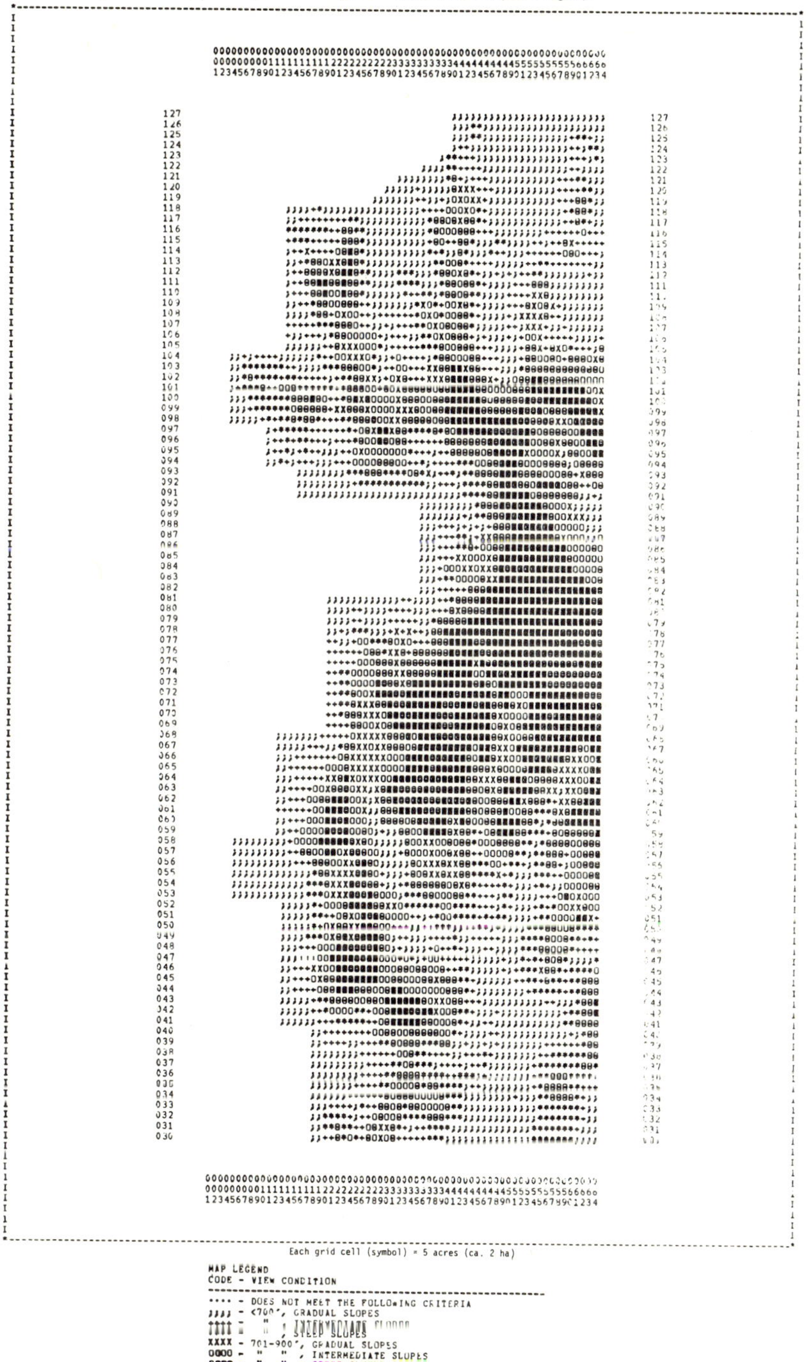

Each grid cell (symbol) = 5 acres (ca. 2 ha)

MAP LEGEND
CODE - VIEW CONDITION

- .... - DOES NOT MEET THE FOLLOWING CRITERIA
- ;;;; - <700', GRADUAL SLOPES
- ++++ - " , INTERMEDIATE SLOPES
- **** - " , STEEP SLOPES
- XXXX - 701-900', GRADUAL SLOPES
- 0000 - " " , INTERMEDIATE SLOPES
- 8888 - " " , STEEP SLOPES
- @@@@ - >901', GRADUAL SLOPES
- ■■■■ - " , INTERMEDIATE SLOPES
- ████ - " , STEEP SLOPES

THIS MODEL EVALUATES EVERY CELL IN THE STUDY AREA FOR ITS VIEW PROMINENCE. IT IS BASED ON ELEVATION AND SLOPE. THE LOGIC IS BASED ON THE ASSUMPTION THAT THE HIGHER THE ELEVATION OF THE CELL, THE MORE VISUALLY PROMINENT IT IS. IN ADDITION, IF A CELL HAS A FLAT SLOPE, IT IS LESS VISUALLY PROMINENT THAT IF IT HAS A STEEP ONE.

BASED ON THESE ASSUMPTIONS, A CELL WITH A HIGH ELEVATION AND A STEEP SLOPE WILL BE MORE VISUALLY PROMINENT THAT A CELL WITH A LOW ELEVATION AND A FLAT SLOPE. IF A CELL HAS A HIGH VISUAL PROMINENCE (HIGH ELEVATION AND STEEP SLOPE), THEN IT CAN BE ASSUMED THAT IT ALSO HAS A GOOD VIEW OUT OVER THE LANDSCAPE.

Figure 3-8. Computer Analysis of the Suitability of the South Hills of Eugene, Oregon, for Residential Development. The output is based on view prominence, biosupport (agricultural or forest lands), and potential for mass movements (landslides). In general, the lighter areas are best suited for residential development (courtesy of Prof. Eugene Bressler, University of Oregon).

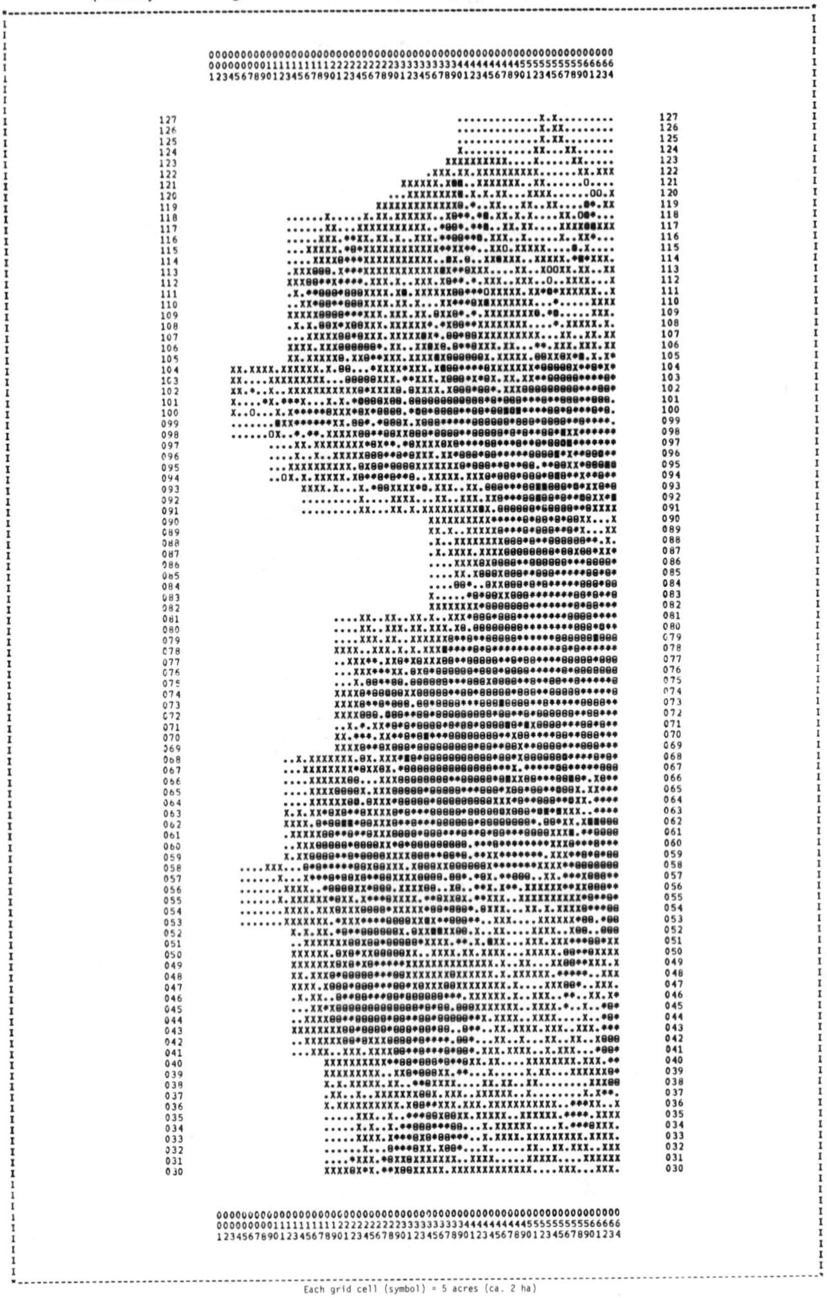

Each grid cell (symbol) = 5 acres (ca. 2 ha)

MAP LEGEND

CCEE – COMPOSITE CONDITION

- •••• – NOT IN THE SOUTH HILLS STUDY AREA
- ♦♦♦♦ – NONE OF THE FOLLOWING CONDITIONS
- ●●●● – MEETS THE VIEW CRITERIA
- XXXX – HAS THE POTENTIAL FOR BIO-SUPPORT
- OOOO – HAS A MASS MOVEMENT POTENTIAL
- ⊕⊕⊕⊕ – HAS THE POTENTIAL FOR BIO-SUPPORT, AND MEETS THE VIEW CRITERIA
- ⊛⊛⊛⊛ – MEETS THE VIEW CRITERIA, AND HAS A MASS MOVEMENT POTENTIAL
- ▓▓▓▓ – HAS THE POTENTIAL FOR BIO-SUPPORT, AND HAS A MASS MOVEMENT POTENTIAL
- ████ – HAS POTENTIAL FOR MASS MOVEMENT AND BIO-SUPPORT, AND MEETS THE VIEW CRITERIA

THE PURPOSE OF THIS MAP IS TO CORRELATE THOSE AREAS COMPILED FROM THE MASS MOVEMENT MODEL, BIO-SUPPORT MODEL, AND THE VIEW MODEL.

Figure 3-9. The Land Use Guidance System Planning Process (EPA, 1974).

	STAGE 1	STAGE 2	STAGE 3	STAGE 4	STAGE 5	STAGE 6
THEORETICAL RATIONAL PLANNING PROCESS	Problem identification and analysis	Goals, objectives and choice criteria	Formulation of alternatives	Evaluation of alternatives	Action decisions	Feedback
LAND USE PLANNING ACTIVITIES	Inventorying, monitoring, prediction interpretation	Formulating general goal oriented decision guides	Formulating specific decision guides and action instruments	Testing alternative plans and predictions	Selecting and implementing action instruments	Monitoring the urban environmental system and performance action instruments
OUTPUTS OF PLANNING ACTIVITIES	Background studies, status reports, suitability maps	Goal plans, choice criteria, policies, strategies	Specific Budgets, policies plans, programs, projects, model regulations incentives	Effectiveness and environmental impact analyses	Indirect actions: Regulations Incentives Public investments Direct actions: Public investments	Monitoring environmental quality indicators Public surveys Political activities
CONSEQUENCES	Local Government's Course of Action for Promoting Environmental Quality					
	The Urbanization Process and Urban Environmental Quality					

81

information base is complete, potential land use problems can be identified and analyzed.

Step 2. Formulation of Goals and Objectives. The process of developing goals and objectives is one of the most important in the land use planning process. In setting goals and objectives, considerable attention should be given to the interface between land conservation and development in an attempt to resolve potential conflicts. It is, therefore, essential that representatives from a wide variety of community groups become involved in this process.

The goals and objectives should address the desired plan orientation and the level and breadth of control activities. Because a land use plan is often the centerpiece for environmental management and an important element in other community planning activities, it is important that the land use goals and objectives be consistent with those of other community activities. It may be desirable to set separate goals and objectives for different urban and rural environments such as critical resource protection lands, rural lands under development pressures, and urban environments.

Step 3. Formulation of Specific Alternative Decision Guides and Strategies. To develop an appropriate land use control program, one must convert goals and policies into action proposals. The planning staff, in conjunction with public administrators, experts, and citizens, should analyze the implementation tools and strategies (or "action instruments") available to accomplish the local land use goals. If there are large volumes of data, computers could be used to process information, to test alternative combinations of control activities, and to facilitate periodic updating of information. The integration of control activities into community processes should also be studied to avoid conflicting or noncomplementary programs

Step 4. Evaluation of Alternative Plans. Once the available alternative action instruments have been clearly defined, their effectiveness in achieving the objectives should be assessed in conjunction with their physical, ecological, and socioeconomic impacts. Probable combinations of alternatives should also be tested. The planning agency should be very explicit about the techniques, instruments, criteria, priorities, and weighting factors used.

Step 5. Selection of Action Instruments. After local land-use problems, goals, objectives, and the effectiveness and impacts of action instruments have been evaluated, a land use management program can be developed. Planning agencies frequently use various combinations of geological, ecological, and land use overlay maps to delineate sensitive, unique, productive, or hazardous environments in which development should be carefully managed, limited, or prohibited (Twiss and Heyman, 1976). Management plans are then developed for each sensitive land use, using direct controls (public investments, intervention, etc.) and indirect controls (regulations, incentives, tax policies, etc.). The tools used in a guidance system should be capable of achieving the following objectives (Patterson, 1979):

1. The control of the location and timing of the development
2. Provision of the necessary infrastructure for development in accordance with land use and financial plans and policies
3. The control over incompatible land uses
4. The control of aesthetic and historic structures, sites, and neighborhoods
5. Encouragement of quality, harmonious, aesthetically pleasing development
6. Provisions for compensation where the use of police power could be reasonably construed as a "taking"

The most common approach to implementing the land use plan is the establishment of a governmental review process. For a proposed private development, the process generally involves a review by a city or county planning staff for compliance with the established procedures and goals (policies, ordinances, requirements of environmental impact statements, etc.). After review, the proposal is acted upon by a planning commission of community residents who are usually appointed to the job. The commission can review the proposal and staff recommendations and take public testimony about the proposal. If a legislative action is involved (e.g., ordinance amendment, rezoning, etc.), the final decision is usually deferred to a city council or county board of supervisors. Citizens should be very careful in monitoring these procedures because of the enormous vested interests involved and the political nature of the proceedings (Griggs and Gilchrist, 1983).

The political compromise often involved in decision making can be very frustrating to the land use planner and scientist. Although their recommendations may be well based on scientific principles, scientists seldom become involved in the actual decision-making process. Thus, the decision maker may not have been made familiar with the scientific reasoning behind a staff recommendation, and in the process of political compromise, extremely important physical considerations may be ignored or glossed over.

A good example of this has been recorded by Flawn (1970). In 1959 a U.S. Geological Survey bulletin (Miller and Dobrovolny, 1959) warned that the Bootlegger Cove clay, which underlies most of Anchorage, was unstable to vibrations when wet and that great care should be exercised in developing certain areas. According to Flawn (1970):

84 / *Methods of Land Use Planning and Analysis*

They published the engineering properties of the clay. They said that shocks such as those associated with earthquakes set into motion material that is stable under most conditions. They pointed out that Anchorage is an earthquake region. They documented a number of previous slumps and slides within the Bootlegger Clay. Nowhere in this report, however, did the authors condemn the Bootlegger Clay as material that provided an unsafe foundation for structures. This report apparently passed unnoticed and unappreciated by city authorities.

After the earthquake of 1964, the Geological Survey personnel reviewed the extent of the damage to Anchorage (Hansen, 1965). The report concluded that most of the damage to nearly thirty city blocks of residential and commercial development resulted from the failure within the Bootlegger clay.

Step 6. Feedback and Monitoring. The final step in the land use guidance process involves the development of a system to evaluate the performance of the program in accomplishing its goals and objectives. The feedback and monitoring system provides the information necessary for ongoing program revision as development pressures, problems, and public values and attitudes change. The planning agency should develop appropriate indicators, sampling techniques, instruments, and sites and an administrative forum to accommodate these changes.

The land use guidance process should adhere to the requirements and coordinate the plans, policies, programs, and implementation activities of federal, state, regional, and local government entities to take maximum advantage of their programs and to avoid duplication and conflicts. To be politically acceptable, the guidance system must encourage the full participation of elected officials, civic and professional groups, planning professionals, and citizens in planning, policy making, and preparation of implementation programs.

Land Management Tools

Most tools used for carrying out land use planning were adapted rather than designed for planning processes. For instance, zoning and subdivision regulations were designed to solve specific land development problems independent of the planning process and have often been used in the absence of land use planning. The fact that many of these tools were not designed for land use planning has created difficulty in developing and coordinating land use control programs that effectively accomplish their goals and objectives (Patterson, 1979).

Most legal tools for land management, such as codes and ordinances, are under the jurisdiction of county and municipal governments through grants of authority from the state. The legal tools consist of the exercise of eminent domain, police, taxing, and spending powers. Land use planning tools, based on the police powers of government, are generally designed to protect and enhance the public health, safety, and welfare. These include comprehensive or general plans; zoning; subdivision regulations; building, health, and fire codes; official maps; and aesthetic and historic preservation ordinances (Patterson, 1979).

A *comprehensive or general plan* is a local government's officially adopted development guide. The plan commonly consists of a set of development goals and guidelines, a present and future land use map (ten and twenty years into the future), and a summary of the means of implementation (e.g., zoning ordinances, subdivision regulations, etc.). In general, the maps designate the future location of residential, commercial, industrial, and open space land uses. In the open space category, considerable opportunity exists for the preservation of unique or sensitive habitats and areas poorly suited for development (e.g., steep slopes and floodplains). General plans that are more than ten years old seldom acknowledge environmental quality as a community goal. By updating and revising these plans, communities can avoid serious land use problems as well as capture many new opportunities. If properly developed and used, a general plan can significantly influence the pattern of community development.

Zoning is the most common method of land use control in the United States. Zoning involves the prohibition of certain types of developments or activities in specified areas. Zoning processes, however, are highly vulnerable to development pressures if not administered properly. In addition, the legal costs of defending and enforcing zoning decisions can be significant. Often, so many local jurisdictions are involved in zoning that regional planning for agricultural, forest, or open space lands preservation is all but impossible (Moss, 1976; CEQ, 1974). In spite of disadvantages, conventional zoning can be effective in spatially separating incompatible land uses if it is properly designed, enforced, and supported by the public.

If a community has properly inventoried its natural environment, a zoning ordinance can be a very powerful tool for protecting valuable resource lands and for avoiding the development of hazardous areas. Unfortunately, in many cases the ordinance is based more on ownership patterns than on natural opportunities and constraints.

In the past few decades, several zoning innovations have been proposed that hold considerable promise in improving land use management. The first, *planned unit development* zoning, allows relief from conventional development standards (i.e., structure types, density, and location) for certain parcels of land in exchange for certain concessions (i.e., housing type, open space, and protection of unique and sensitive environments) from the developers. This flexibility is achieved through a prescribed site-design review process that gives vested rights to both the community and the developer (HUD, 1977).

Incentive zoning offers a prestated financial bonus or incentive to developers in return for some desired amenity (e.g., open space, bike paths, solar access). Without the bonus, the desired public amenity presumably would not be economically feasible (HUD, 1977).

Impact zoning relates land use demands to land use capacities by including an assessment of the consequences of proposed land use changes in view of performance standards. Developers are required to state and prove the impacts of proposed land use changes, which are then compared to performance standards in an ongoing process of negotiation between the developers and a community (HUD, 1977).

The *transfer of development rights* system is a relatively new tool for the management of private land uses without the expenditure of public funds for land acquisition. The system separates the right to develop a parcel of land from the land itself. The right to develop parcel A can be sold by the owner of A to another landowner in another area, who is then allowed to develop his/her parcel B to a greater density (e.g., more dwelling units per acre) than normally would be allowed. Parcel A is then kept as open space or in a low density use. The system automatically compensates the owner of parcel A (with a lowering of property taxes and the revenue from the sale of the development right) and captures some of the windfall profits of the owner of parcel B (in higher taxes and the outlay for the purchase of the development rights). In addition, the level of development can be carefully regulated by the number of assigned development rights. Thus, development on hazardous, unique, sensitive, or productive lands can be controlled at no cost to the public and without a reduction of the tax base. To be effective, however, the management agency must have a sound master plan, properly assign development rights, and be capable of resisting the pressures for unsound development (CEQ, 1974; Griggs and Gilchrist, 1983).

Zoning can be even more effective in controlling harmful forms of development when it is coupled with *taxation policies*. For example, developers in Vermont must meet certain specifications before a development permit is issued. In addition, the higher the development profits and the shorter the period the property is held by the developer, the higher the property taxes (Healy, 1979).

In the past, state property taxes were based on the highest value of potential land use (usually high density development) rather than the value of actual use. Thus, lands on the periphery of urban areas were taxed as potential development lands. Faced with higher tax levies, rural landowners were forced to sell or develop their lands. To relieve these development pressures, approximately half the states now base property taxes on the value of actual land uses (Foin, 1976).

Preferential tax assessments in the form of lowered taxes on farmland, forest lands, historic sites, and so on, are increasingly being offered to protect these lands from intense development pressures.

Currently, more than thirty states offer some form of preferential tax assessments. To be effective, special considerations should be given only to lands that have been used for the specified purpose for at least ten years. One problem of this system is that it often results in higher property taxes for urban landowners in order to maintain tax revenues (Miller, 1979; CEQ, 1974). Several states now compensate local governments for revenue losses resulting from preferential tax assessments.

Another tax-related approach to land use control involves the *donation or purchase of land development rights.* Landowners donate or sell land development rights to a management agency in return for lower property taxes. This approach insures that land will continue to be used only for specified purposes while allowing landowners to retain their land and deduct their donation from federal and state income taxes. For this approach to work properly, great care must be taken in specifying property development rights, especially when land is sold or transferred to heirs. It is also possible that the costs of the rights to develop the lands most in need of protection nearly equal the costs of outright purchase.

Environmental performance standards are also increasingly being used for land management purposes. In this approach, a community sets specific measurable standards for key environmental indicators (e.g., sediment load from a development site) that a developer must meet. The developer is given much greater latitude in this approach than in many others to innovate and experiment with techniques of impact reduction. If after development the project does not meet the performance standards, the developer can be fined and forced to take whatever corrective measures the community has defined in the ordinance (Thurow et al., 1975).

The surest way to guarantee desired land uses is *outright purchase* of the land by federal, state, or local governments, the land then being managed or leased with use restrictions. This approach is widely used in Europe to guarantee open spaces. The drawbacks to public land acquisition are purchase cost, reduction of the tax base, maintenance costs, and the slow rate of acquisition (CEQ, 1974).

Governments frequently use the power of *eminent domain* to obtain private property for public purposes with just compensation. It is commonly used in conjunction with the spending power of government to establish roads, utility rights-of-way, and community facilities and public services such as schools, parks, open spaces, fire protection, and sewers. The design, location, and timing of such *public service investments* are extremely important in determining the timing and location of development.

In addition to the provision of public services, the spending powers of government may be used to attract private investors to a community. Systematic coordination of the spending powers of government with

88 / *Methods of Land Use Planning and Analysis*

the administrative tools of *financial planning and capital budgeting* can contribute substantially to the realization of land use planning goals and objectives (Patterson, 1979).

Between 1970 and 1977 more than three hundred communities attempted to stop or slow land development and population growth. Attempts by some communities to prohibit all further growth and development tend to exacerbate growth and environmental problems elsewhere. For instance, attempts to stop growth by limiting sewer lines and hookups may result in greater use of septic tanks, which can cause groundwater pollution (CEQ 1974). Further, *no-growth policies* are often overturned in the courts for violating or denying landowners constitutional rights to reasonable use of their land (Godschalk et al., 1977).

A more common and successful approach is a long-term program to slow, redirect, and regulate growth. The key is to develop an ecologically sensitive land-use plan and then use an appropriate combination of land management tools to guide the location, timing, and quality of development. Various combinations of tools can be used to accomplish different objectives. For instance, zoning, careful allocation of public services, and tax policies can be most effective in controlling the timing and location of development. Density, cluster, and critical resource zoning; planned unit developments; special use permits; and subdivision ordinances are most effective in protecting unique and sensitive environments and controlling high impact and high density developments.

Recommendations

At the national level there is a need for the development of a national land use management program to encourage growth where it would be most beneficial; to curtail growth where it would place a burden on natural and human resources; and to preserve unique natural environments. A national land use program should provide funding and technical assistance and establish a legislative framework for state and local land use planning activities. A federal program should also carefully monitor and coordinate the interactions between federal, state, regional, and local land use planning agencies.

All states should develop land use plans and policies and coordinate programs affecting land uses within the state. States should take a more active role in guiding planning at all levels of government in mattters of statewide and regional significance. Most state enabling legislation for regional and local planning should be updated, preferably along the lines of the American Law Institute's (1974) model land development code. Local unified development codes should be established having coordinated administrative procedures that integrate land use controls. The codes should be based on long- and middle-term development plans. Further, permission to subdivide and develop should be contingent upon the adequacy of existing community services or those to be provided by the developer. States should also consider enabling innovative land-use control tools such as transferable development rights.

It is essential that local land use controls be strengthened and coordinated for more effective and rational growth guidance. Qualified professional planners should be given more discretionary authority to increase flexibility in administrative processes. Finally, state intervention in regional or local land development should be allowed in instances of extreme growth pressures or development projects too large for local governments to handle or if there is a clear threat to ecological or unique habitats. As land use conflicts increase in scope and scale, federal, state, and local governments need to take a more active role in preserving and enhancing the quality of urban and rural environments.

4 / Natural Resource Management

A "natural resource" can be defined as anything that is useful to an organism, population, or ecosystem. The term "useful" implies that the resource is available and safe and can be obtained at a reasonable cost (Miller, 1979). However, the usefulness of resources often changes with time as social and economic systems grow and develop. For example, more than 90 percent of the energy supply for the United States in 1850 was wood. By 1920 coal had replaced wood as the primary energy source, providing nearly 75 percent of domestic energy. By 1980 U.S. energy demand had quadrupled, and more than 75 percent of it was met by oil and natural gas (Stoker et al., 1975).

Resources are commonly classified as "renewable" or "nonrenewable." Renewable resources are obtained from virtually inexhaustible sources (such as the sun), or they can be readily replenished by natural or artificial cycles. Examples of renewable resources include living organisms, clean air and water, soils, and energy from the sun or from ecological processes. Renewable resource management implies balancing the rate of resource consumption with the rate of replenishment so that the overall resource base is not diminished through time.

Nonrenewable resources are fixed in amount and can be readily depleted to a point where further recovery is either technically or environmentally unfeasible. Examples of nonrenewable resources are metals, minerals, certain building materials, and fossil fuels. Heavy reliance on nonrenewable resources may cause frequent changes in patterns of resource utilization. For example, the ability of nonrenewable petroleum fuels to sustain the world economy through the next century is in serious doubt (Hubbert, 1973); this has stimulated the search both for new petroleum "reserves" or economically developable deposits and for entirely new energy production systems and resources.

This chapter will focus on the flow of material and energy resources through our economic system, using water and energy resources as illustrations of the steps and alternative approaches to resource management.

Table 4-1. Seventy-Year Lifetime Resource Use and Pollution by the Average American.

Direct and Indirect Resource Consumption[1]	Direct and Indirect Waste
623 tons of coal, oil, and natural gas	840 tons of agricultural wastes
613 tons of sand, gravel, and stone	823 tons of garbage, industrial and mining wastes
26 million gallons of water	7 million gallons of polluted water
21 thousand gallons of gasoline	70 tons of air pollution
51 tons of metals	19,250 bottles
50 tons of food	19,000 cans
48 tons of wood	7 automobiles
19 tons of paper	
5.2 tons of plastic, rubber, and synthetic fibers	
5 tons of fertilizer	

[1] Figures assume constant 1975 consumption rates. If per capita consumption continues to increase, the figures would be much higher.

From *Living in the Environment,* 3rd ed., by G. Tyler Miller, Jr. Copyright 1979 by Wadsworth, Inc. Reprinted by permission of Wadsworth Publishing Co., Belmont CA 94002.

Resource Management: Issues and Options

As already stated, the U.S. economy acquires, produces, consumes, and discards resources at an unprecedented rate: Slightly more than 5 percent of the world's population consumes nearly 33 percent of the world's annual production and generates more than 33 percent of the world's pollution (see Table 4-1 for the resource use of the average American). In contrast, the developing nations of the world consume very little of the world's resources. Between 1971 and 1975, Latin America, Africa, and Asia, with more than 75 percent of the world's population, consumed 7 percent of the world's aluminum production, 9 percent of the copper, and 12 percent of the iron ore. By the year 2000, it is predicted that consumption in these regions will have increased only nominally to 8 percent, 13 percent, and 17 percent, respectively (CEQ and U.S. Department of State, 1980).

The most recent projections of world resource supply and demand to the year 2000 indicate no immediate problems of resource exhaustion (see Table 4-2). However, resource use in the United States and other developed nations is expected to rise sharply in the coming decades at the same time that the developing nations hope to expand their economies. Recognition of the combined pressures—of growing demand, higher costs, greater physical and social impacts, and increased technical skills necessary for resource acquisition—has led to speculation that nonrenewable resource shortages may ultimately limit population and economic growth (Ehrlich et al., 1977; Meadows et al., 1972; CEQ and U.S. Department of State, 1980).

Cornucopians Versus Neo-Malthusians

The debate over resource management policy between technical optimists, or "cornucopians," and technical pessimists, or "neo-Malthusians," has heated up considerably in the last decade. The term *neo-Malthusian* is derived from the name of Sir Thomas Malthus (1766–1834), an English economist and clergyman whose landmark "Essay on Population" of 1803 triggered a debate over population growth and resource availability. Malthus contended that the geometrically growing human population would exceed its ability to produce food and that starvation and disease would restore the balance.

Past and present cornucopians (whose name derivation is obvious) are those who believe that technical innovation, discovery, and economic growth will provide the materials, energy, and information resources to continuously improve global welfare. They believe that the competitive free market will continue to function smoothly and properly. They believe that when resource shortages occur, increased prices will stimulate innovation in the acquisition and use of lower grades of ores and the development of product substitutes. However, there are several problems with these beliefs:

1. The market for nonrenewable resources is no longer open and competitive. Individual corporations, unions, and governments exercise increasing control over supply, demand, and prices (Galbraith, 1967).
2. The cost of new raw materials is only a small proportion of the price of finished products. Large increases in the prices of raw materials would only nominally increase the price of finished products and therefore be relatively ineffective in influencing demand (Vogely, 1977).
3. Regardless of what anyone is willing to pay, the total supply of nonrenewable resources is finite.
4. Declines in net production efficiencies associated with the development of progressively lower grades of raw materials, coupled with spiraling energy and materials costs, will make future raw material

Table 4-2. Estimated 1976 World Reserves of Selected Minerals and Life Expectancies at Two Different Rates of Demand (CEQ and U.S. Department of State, 1980).

Mineral Commodity	1976 Reserves	1976 Primary Demand	Projected Demand Growth Rate[2] (%)	Life Expectancy in Years[1] Static at 1976 Level	Life Expectancy in Years[1] Growing at Projected Rates
Fluorine (million short tons)	37	2.1	4.58	18	13
Silver (million troy ounces)	6,100	305	2.33	20	17
Zinc (million short tons)	166	6.4	3.05	26	19
Mercury (thousand flasks)	5,210	239	0.50	22	21
Sulfur (million long tons)	1,700	50	3.16	34	23
Lead (million short tons)	136	3.7	3.14	37	25
Tungsten (million pounds)	4,200	81	3.26	52	31
Tin (thousand metric tons)	10,000	241	2.05	41	31
Copper (million short tons)	503	8.0	2.94	63	36
Nickel (million short tons)	60	0.7	2.94	86	43
Platinum (million troy ounces)	297	2.7	3.75	110	44
Phosphate rock (million metric tons)	25,732	107	5.17	240	51
Manganese (million short tons)	1,800	11.0	3.36	164	56
Iron in ore (billion short tons)	103	0.6	2.95	172	62
Aluminum in bauxite (million short tons)	5,610	18	4.29	312	63

[1] Assumes no increase in 1976 reserves.

[2] Projected growth rates are from CEQ and Department of State, 1980. Global 2000 Technical Report.

development extremely expensive. The cost and availability of energy may ultimately limit resource extraction (Ehrlich et al., 1977).

5. Serious social and environmental consequences would result from more intensive mining and production activities (Ehrlich et al., 1977).

6. Resource managers have been pointing out for years that the market tends to underestimate the value of environmental services and common resources (e.g., the oceans, air, public lands) and fails to incorporate in the price of a good or service the costs of negative externalities and the loss of irreplaceable material and energy resources (Freeman et al., 1973).

In contrast, neo-Malthusians believe that economically affordable supplies of nonrenewable resources are finite and that shortages or adverse impacts from resource production and consumption will ultimately limit resource acquisition. Neo-Malthusians present the following arguments (Ehrlich et al., 1977):

1. Technology does not adequately provide for the present world population, especially in less-affluent nations.

2. Technology and resources cannot be financed or mobilized fast enough to provide for the needs of growing populations, economies, and per capita resource consumption.

3. Haste in developing technological and economic systems may result in serious and irreparable environmental damage, such as poisoned ecosystems, adverse climatic change, or the devastation of war.

Conventional Approaches to Resource Management

Searching the Frontiers

The search for new deposits of nonrenewable resources is becoming progressively more difficult, expensive, and hazardous. The highest quality deposits—those closest to the surface of the earth or those having the largest or highest concentrations—are the first to be developed. As the inevitable progression toward lower quality deposits continues, the amount of waste generated and energy required to obtain the resource increases (a classic example of the second law of thermodynamics) (Ehrlich et al., 1977).

The search for new deposits of resources is moving into more and more sensitive environments. Offshore oil drilling has begun in Georges Bank, one of the most productive fisheries on earth. In April 1984 the United States and Canada went before the International Court in The Hague to establish ownership of Georges Bank. Canada claims nearly half, and the United States claims the entire area. In addition, lease sales have been proposed for environmentally sensitive areas off the

Figure 4-1. Territorial Claims in Antarctica (Jones, 1980).

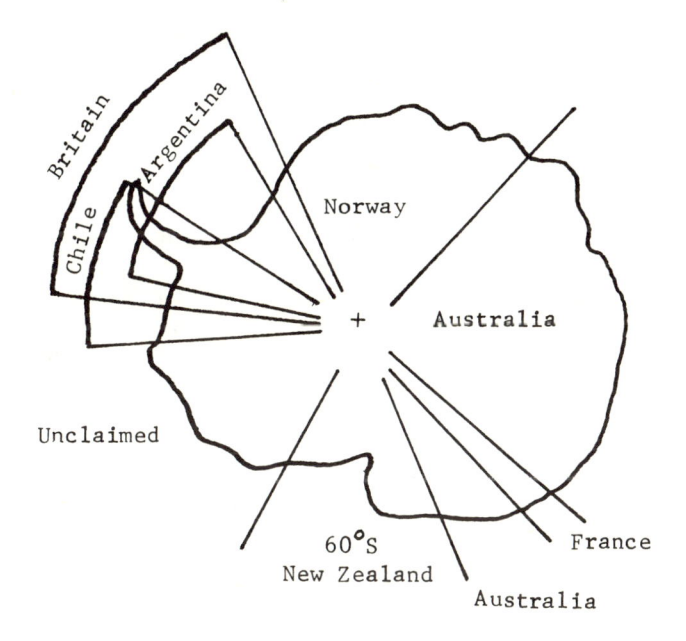

Copyright, 1979, Los Angeles Times. Reprinted by permission.

California coast (CEQ, 1980). Although the Reagan administration's (i.e., former Secretary of the Interior James Watt's) outer continental shelf oil, gas, and mineral lease/sale programs are tied up in the courts, many of the relevant court cases will be resolved and appealed within two to three years. The magnitude of serious ecological damage to coastal areas depends on the outcome of these cases and the 1984 elections, but the potential for damage to these sensitive areas is clearly present (Pope, 1984).

Development pressures are increasing on Alaskan offshore, tundra, and wilderness lands. In addition, the search is extending into two of the world's great commons, the oceans and Antarctica. A heated International debate has developed over resource access and development rights to marine, mineral, and petroleum resources in the Antarctic. Seven nations have made formal territorial claims (some overlapping) to Antarctic lands (see Figure 4-1). Six other nations—the United States, the Soviet Union, Japan, South Africa, Belgium, and Poland—have interests in resource development but have not made formal claims. They also do not recognize the territorial claims of other nations (Jones, 1979; Mitchell, 1980).

The United States is currently developing and investing in seabed mining and seawater resource extraction technologies. Extraction of certain substances, such as magnesium, bromine, and sodium chloride, directly from seawater is possible, but expensive and potentially damaging to other marine resources. Manganese, iron, copper, nickel, and cobalt can be obtained by mining deep seabed nodules, but again only at very high cost (Miller, 1979).

As the ability to exploit ocean resources increases, international negotiations to specify access and development rights have become extremely complex and controversial. The affluent and technically advanced countries are the ones capable of mustering the finances and expertise to exploit seawater and seabed resources. Thus, we are confronted with the classic problem of allocation of commonly held resources (Hardin, 1968; Hardin and Baden, 1977). The tendency is for each nation to take actions that are of short-term benefit to itself (e.g., overexploitation of a resource or using the commons for residuals disposal) but long-term detriment to all nations. In addition, opportunities to improve commonly held resources are overlooked or ignored by individual nations because incremental benefits are shared. Such opportunities require collective investment and management.

Since 1973 more than 150 nations have participated in the United Nation's Law of the Sea Conference (Peterson, 1980). The conflict between developed and developing nations flared when the Reagan administration refused to sign the 440-article Law of the Sea Treaty (Pope, 1984). The Third World bloc of developing nations (called "the Group of 77") accused the United States of favoring unregulated seabed mining. The chairman of the group, Inam Ul Haque of Pakistan, stated (United Press International, 1981), "The seabed area and its resources which are the common heritage of mankind cannot be allowed to be exploited by a few, for the benefit of a few, to the exclusion of the rest of the world."

Any inequitable distribution of resources between the "have" and "have not" nations may have serious consequences in the future. The political and economic clout of the less affluent nations of the world is increasing as the affluent nations become increasingly dependent on them for basic raw materials. The U.S. situation is particularly enlightening. The United States has been second only to the Soviet Union in self-sufficiency in key metal and mineral resources, but the situation is changing. In 1950 the United States imported more than 50 percent of each of four key industrial nonfuel minerals. By the year 2000, the United States could be importing more than 50 percent of each of twelve key minerals, and the cost of raw material imports is expected to triple in real dollars (see Table 4-3).

It is important to note that, in most cases, the United States imports minerals because foreign sources are cheaper than domestic sources. In addition, it is impossible to predict accurately whether interdependencies will foster cooperation or confrontation between nations.

Table 4-3. U.S. Import Dependence for 12 Key Raw Materials.

Raw Materials	Percentage Imported				Major Sources of World Reserves in 2000
	1950	1975	1985	2000	
Chromium	99	91	100	100	U.S.S.R., South Africa, Turkey, Rhodesia, Philippines
Tin	77	75	100	100	Malaysia, Bolivia, Thailand
Manganese	85	98	100	100	U.S.S.R., South Africa, Brazil, Gabon
Nickel	94	71	88	89	Canada, New Caledonia, U.S.S.R., Cuba, Norway
Aluminum (bauxite ore)	40	85	96	98	Jamaica, Surinam, Australia
Zinc	38	64	72	84	Canada, Mexico, Peru
Tungsten	40	54	65	93	China, Canada, Peru, Bolivia
Lead	39	21	62	67	Australia, U.S.S.R., Canada, Mexico, Peru
Iron Ore	8	29	55	67	Brazil, U.S.S.R., India, Canada, Venezuela, Australia
Potassium (potash)	14	49	47	81	Canada, Germany
Copper	31	18	45	75	Chile, U.S.S.R., India, Canada, Zaire, Zambia, Peru
Sulfur	2	0	28	52	Canada, Mexico

Source: *Living in the Environment*, 3rd ed., by G. Tyler Miller, Jr. Copyright 1979 by Wadsworth, Inc. Reprinted by permission of Wadsworth Publishing Co., Belmont CA 94002.

Improving Technology

In the past, improvements in mining and processing technologies, such as the development of machinery for large-scale strip mining, have allowed the acquisition of progressively lower grade deposits or resources without significant cost increases. Neo-Malthusians seriously doubt that this trend can continue, because the mining of progressively lower grade ores is increasingly expensive in terms of money, land, energy, and ecological effects. When the costs of mining and milling inevitably exceed the benefits, argue the cornucopians, substitutes can be found to replace prohibitively expensive resources (Miller, 1979).

Finding Substitutes

Historically, it is true that bronze replaced stone, iron replaced bronze, steel replaced iron, and aluminum and plastics have begun to replace steel for many structural uses. However, finding substitutes for the increasingly scarce resources may be difficult in the future for a number of reasons (Ehrlich et al. 1977; National Academy of Sciences, 1975b; Ophuls, 1977):

1. Considerable research expenditures are required to develop or discover substitutes.
2. Economic hardships frequently occur during periods of transition; for instance, Rifkin (1980) postulated that the Dark Ages were caused, in part, by a lack of wood as a material and fuel resource.
3. Substitutes are often more energy intensive than the resources they replace.
4. Replacements for some materials are currently non-existent or inferior in quality; for instance, there is no known replacement for helium in low temperature superconductors, and substitutes for chromium in stainless steel and for silver in photographic processes are inferior.
5. In many cases, substitute resources are in short supply—for example, cadmium and silver as substitutes for mercury in advanced batteries.
6. Perhaps most importantly, substitutes will need to be found in a number and at a rate unprecedented in human history.

Alternative Approaches to Resource Management

The Materials Balance Model

All approaches to resource management discussed thus far in this chapter have focused on increasing acquisition and production. As mentioned in Chapter 1, the materials balance model provides a useful framework for analysis of alternative methods of resource and residuals management. The model indicates that the production-consumption-waste flow of resources can be managed through the control of throughput (Freeman et al., 1973).

The primary options for reducing resource throughput are (1) limiting resource inputs, (2) increasing the length of time a resource is used, and (3) decreasing the overall level of economic activity. It should be noted that these throughput management approaches can also be influential in reducing energy consumption and waste generation.

Throughput Reduction

The most obvious method of reducing throughput is by *limiting the resource inputs* into the system. Resource inputs can be reduced by improving production efficiency, decreasing the amount of resources used in products, and decreasing the per capita consumption of products.

Production efficiency can be improved through the use of new processes, more efficient machinery, improved maintenance and repair, and recycling or by developing programs to improve worker productivity. Local governments can be very influential in changing production and consumption patterns through taxing, pricing, capital improvements, and regulatory and informational programs.

Resource inputs into an economy can be substantially reduced through resource-efficient product design. For instance, the amount of steel used in the manufacture of cans could be reduced by 25 to 30 percent through the use of two-piece drawn and ironed cans rather than the conventional three-piece soldered cans. This change would annually save enough electricity to meet the needs of 3.5 million people; reduce the consumption of iron ore by 2.3 million tons; reduce the consumption of water by 17 billion gallons; and eliminate 12 thousand tons of air pollution, 68 thousand tons of water pollution, 967 thousand tons of urban solid waste, and 2.8 million tons of mining waste (Environmental Protection Agency [EPA], 1975). Conscious reduction in per capita consumption could provide even greater resource savings. For instance, use of smaller cars or of bicycles can substantially decrease resource and energy consumption without seriously degrading the quality of life of an individual. Automobile manufacturing annually consumes 65 percent of the rubber, 68 percent of the lead, 50 percent of the iron, 33 percent of the zinc, 20 percent of the steel, 13 percent of the nickel, and 7 percent of the copper used in the United States (Miller, 1979).

The goal of *increasing longevity* is to retain the resource in the economy in a useful form for as long as possible. This can be accomplished by improving product quality and reusability and by recycling the resource once the product is discarded (discussed in Chapter 7).

Improving the quality and durability of products can have an enormous impact on resource consumption. For instance, the EPA (1975) estimated that if all cars could be built for a 12-year rather than the current 10-year use life, 6.7 million tons of material resources could be saved by 1990.

Communities can influence the quality and durability of products through the use of taxing, regulatory, and informational programs. For instance, strict design and performance standards can be adopted to prevent shoddy construction and to promote the purchase of durable goods and services. In addition, communities can directly or indirectly influence consumer purchasing behavior by developing quality control and information programs and by providing tax relief for purchasers. Many communities currently offer such incentives to promote the use of solar energy systems.

The useful life of a product can also be enhanced by *improving product repairability*. To promote repair and reuse, manufacturers should simplify and standardize product design and provide the parts and instructions necessary for repair. In addition, information programs can be used to reduce the social stigmas attached to product reuse and to oppose advertising that promotes the style changes in cars and clothes that result in unnecessary consumption.

The most costly method of controlling throughput is the conscious *reduction of overall economic activity*. This can be accomplished by limiting the availability and price of vital resources such as development capital (through high interest rates), land, and permits. Patterson (1979) has provided an excellent review of the opportunities and pitfalls of local growth management. Although this may appear to be a harsh technique to control throughput, it must be noted that one of the probable side effects of real shortages of vital resources is economic stagnation or decline.

Stabilizing the System

In addition to activities to control throughput, resource managers should promote policies and programs to assist in stabilizing the resource base of the local economy. General policies directed toward such stabilization include:

- diversification of the resource base
- limitation of the size (and control capabilities) of public and private entities
- promotion of the sustained-yield use of renewable resources to reduce dependence on nonrenewable resources
- promotion of the development of indigenous resources for local capture of maximum economic benefits
- establishment of reserves of essential nonrenewable resources to reduce the local economic impacts of shortages, cutoffs, or high prices
- development of emergency plans in the event of shortages

Water Resource Management

The availability of uncontaminated water is the single most important factor limiting population growth and determining the quality of human life in much of the world. Water is an important vector for dissolving and transporting nutrients from soils into the bodies of living organisms. It is a raw material for the photosynthesis that provides food for all living organisms. Water vapor created by solar evaporation provides much of the energy that drives world climate and weather patterns. Water is an important factor in world business and commerce and also serves to dilute and dispense many of our wastes.

Although the United States was blessed with ample pure surface and underground water resources, the situation is deteriorating. Surface water and groundwater contamination and the uneven distribution of water resources relative to population and industrial centers have created serious local and regional water supply problems. In the *Second National Water Assessment* in 1978, the U.S. Water Resources Council summarized the major problems:

- inadequate surface water supplies in many areas of the country
- overdraft of groundwater, especially in the High Plains and Arizona and California
- surface water and groundwater pollution, especially in rural areas where drinking water receives little or no treatment
- increasing damage from flooding
- continued erosion and sedimentation

Because flooding and soil erosion problems were discussed in Chapter 3, the following discussion will focus on the provision and protection of an adequate, safe supply of water for a community.

Local Water Resource Management Problems

Water Supply Shortages

The total water supply on earth is estimated at 396 billion billion gallons, or 90 billion gallons per capita. However, only 0.003 percent of this supply is accessible, uncontaminated, fresh water that is suitable for domestic use. This amounts to 2.7 million gallons of usable, fresh water per capita. Yet, in many areas of the world—the Mediterranean Basin, Middle East, Asia, Africa, Australia, and North and South America—severe water shortages are creating enormous agricultural and social problems (Miller, 1979).

The major causes of these shortages are (1) increasing demand for water, especially in the developing nations of the world, (2) uneven distribution of population and industrial centers relative to water supplies, and (3) surface water and groundwater contamination which diminishes the usefulness and increases the health hazards of water supplies.

Today nearly 75 percent of the global rural population and 20 percent of the urban population obtain their drinking water from contaminated sources. Waterborne diseases debilitate one of every three humans and kill an estimated 10 million annually (Miller, 1979). In addition, contamination of the world's supply of fresh water is increasing at a rate of 2 percent per year, and the demand for water by the year 2000 will be at least double the demand today (Handler, 1977; CEQ and U.S. Department of State, 1980).

Although approximately 6,000 gallons of usable fresh water per capita per day are available, the United States will face severe water shortages in the near future. Figure 4-2 indicates the past and projected water use in the United States. If current trends continue, the national water supply limit should be reached within the next twenty to forty years, depending on the accuracy of estimates of the usable supply.

Each day, the average U.S. citizen consumes 60 gallons of water directly for personal use and 1,636 gallons indirectly in the goods and services used. This latter category includes 85 gallons for commercial purposes, 666 gallons to grow food, 608 gallons to cool electric power plants, and 176 gallons for mining and manufacturing processes (Miller, 1979).

Water consumption in a typical municipal water system in the United States averages 150 gallons per capita per day (gpcd). However, community consumption can range from 60 to more than 300 gpcd, depending on (1) culture, (2) climate, (3) extent and nature of industrial and commercial development, (4) water price, (5) presence of meters to detect possible leaks, (6) water quality, (7) distribution system pressure, and (8) the maintenance of the distribution system (Sewell, 1975). Table 4-4 summarizes municipal water use by sector in the United States.

Because of an uneven distribution of population and industry relative to water supplies, several areas of the United States, mainly in the Central Plains and southwestern states, are experiencing chronic or periodically recurring water shortages (see Figure 4-3). Water shortages are currently reported for 28 percent of the land mass and 13 percent of the population of the United States (CEQ, 1978b). Heavy "consumptive" water use (water withdrawn and used but not returned, as in irrigation) is depleting both surface water and groundwater supplies. These problems are exacerbated by growing water demands due to rapid urban and industrial growth in the Sun Belt states. Water shortages are so acute in the lower Colorado River basin that the

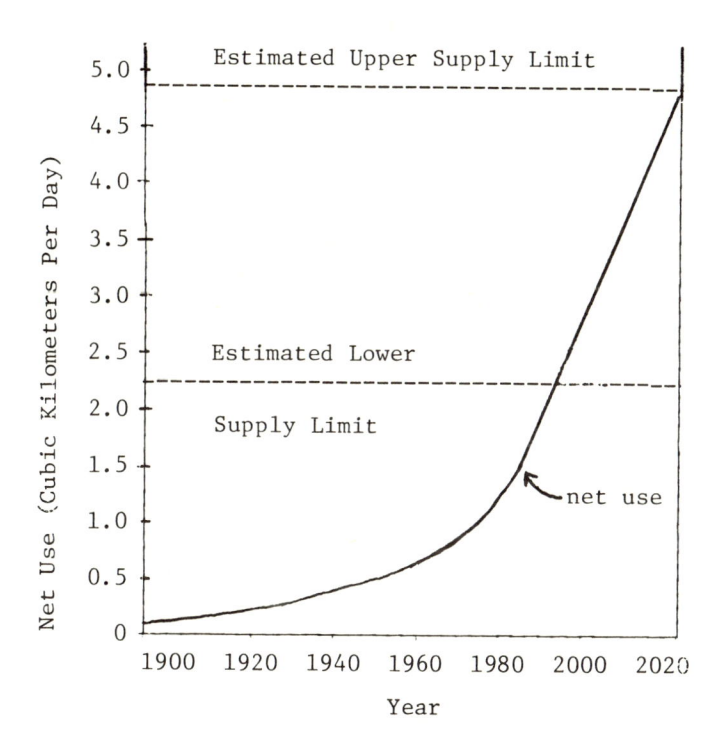

Figure 4-2. Water Supply and Consumption in the United States, 1900 to 2020.

[Graph: Net Use (Cubic Kilometers Per Day) vs. Year, showing Estimated Upper Supply Limit at ~4.9, Estimated Lower Supply Limit at ~2.2, and net use curve rising from near 0 in 1900 to ~4.9 in 2020.]

Source: Modified from *Living in the Environment*, 3rd ed., by G. Tyler Miller, Jr. Copyright 1979 by Wadsworth, Inc. Reprinted by permission of Wadsworth Publishing Co., Belmont CA 94002.

Colorado River no longer reaches its mouth in the Gulf of California. Rather, it ends in a polluted trickle in the Mexican desert south of Yuma, Arizona (CEQ, 1979a).

Between 1970 and 1975, water consumption in larger metropolitan areas in the United States increased more than twice as fast as population. In addition, many eastern and older midwestern metropolitan areas are facing problems both of water contamination from industrial activities and of archaic distribution systems. Repairing these systems could cost as much as $100 million (CEQ, 1979a). The combined problems of increasing demands, contamination, and the need for repairs have already resulted in seasonal and short-term water shortages in Boston, New York, Washington, D.C., and Atlanta (CEQ, 1978b).

Table 4-4. Municipal Water Consumption in the United States.

Sector	Quantity (Gallons per capita per day) Range	Average
Residential	20-100	55
Industrial	20-75	50
Commercial	5-100	20
Public	5-25	10
Losses	5-25	15
Total	60-300	150

Source: Sewell, Granville H. *Environmental Quality Management*, © 1975, p. 86. Adapted by permission of Prentice-Hall, Inc., Englewood Cliffs, N.J.

Figure 4-3. Water Supply Deficiencies in the United States by Watershed Region (U.S. Water Resources Council, 1978).

Current problems

Arizona. New Mexico.
Texas. Oklahoma. Kansas.
Nebraska. Nevada.
Southeastern Wyoming.
Central and Southern California.
Eastern and Central Colorado.
Western Utah

Future problems

Montana. South Dakota.
Wyoming. Southern Idaho.
Southeastern Oregon.
Southern Florida. Northern California.
Eastern Utah. Western Colorado.
Western North Dakota

Finally, legal conflicts and ambiguities over water rights only exacerbate these problems. In the East and Midwest, property owners are, in general, granted "riparian rights" or reasonable use rights to surface water and groundwater sources. The only legal constraint is that an owner may not diminish the water quantity or quality for use downstream. In most eastern and midwestern states that have adequate precipitation, water may not be diverted for use on nonriparian lands.

In the more arid states of the Southwest and West, water use is governed by "appropriate rights." In essence, the first person to use the water for a beneficial purpose is granted the permanent right to that water even if the person is not situated along the waterway (in many states this also applies to groundwater). The water must be used in the same amount for the same purpose in an uninterrupted fashion through time for the use right to be retained (Griggs and Gilchrist, 1983).

Add the myriad federal and state laws and water projects with "benefits" that may be nonexistent, masked, or inequitably distributed, and you have a system of regulation in chaos. To attempt to deal with this situation, many states have developed water rights departments and commissions to adjudicate disputes and new appropriations. All this adds to concerns about a U.S. water crisis that may become the most serious resource limitation experienced in this country in the latter half of the century.

Water Supply Contamination

Approximately 75 percent of the water supply systems in the United States, serving nearly 40 percent of the population, tap groundwater. In the past, groundwater systems were generally preferred because wells could be drilled close to the user, which minimized piping and pumping costs, and the water was relatively pure because of soil filtration (Sewell, 1975). However, water resource managers are becoming increasingly concerned about health hazards associated with groundwater contamination. The cumulative effects on groundwater of leachate from sanitary landfills, septic tanks, sludge storage, road salts, mine wastes, agricultural chemicals, and industrial wastes are creating problems throughout the country. Unlike surface water, groundwater moves very slowly, and once groundwater becomes contaminated, collection and treatment is all but impossible. Even after the original source of contamination is eliminated the water could remain contaminated for centuries (CEQ, 1979a).

In June 1978 the EPA published a report identifying 133,000 ponds, pools, lagoons, and pits that were used for storage, treatment, and disposal of wastes in the United States. The majority of these facilities were unlined, allowing wastes to seep into the ground. The cumulative

Table 4-5. National Interim Primary Drinking Water Standards (source: Environmental Protection Agency, May, 1984, Personal Communication).[1]

Constituent	Maximum Concentration (in mg/l unless specified)
Inorganic chemicals	0.05
Arsenic	0.05
Barium	1
Cadmium	0.010
Chromium	0.05
Lead	0.05
Mercury	0.002
Nitrate (as N)	10
Selenium	0.01
Silver	0.05
Fluoride	1.4-2.4
Organic chemicals turbidity	1 tu up to 5 tu
Coliform bacteria	1/100 mi (mean)
Endrin	0.002
Lindane	0.004
Methoxychlor	0.1
Toxaphene	0.005
2,4D	0.1
2,4,5 TP Silvex	0.01
Radionuclides	
Radium 226 and 228 (combined)	5pCi/l
Gross alpha particle activity	15pCi/l
Gross beta particle activity	4 mrem/year
Total trihalomethanes	0.1
Sodium	20 (recommended)

[1] On October 5, 1983, the EPA issued an Advance Notice of Proposed Rulemaking for the National Revised Drinking Water Regulations.

impact of this contamination will probably not be known for years (Geraghty and Miller, Inc., 1978).

To protect surface water and groundwater systems from contamination, Congress passed in 1974 and amended in 1977 the Safe Drinking Water Act (SDWA). The act requires the EPA to establish federal drinking water standards protecting groundwater sources of drinking water and to establish a cooperative system between the federal and state governments for enforcement (CEQ, 1979a). Table 4-5 lists the maximum allowable levels that have been set for twenty-two contaminants.

The SDWA authorizes states to exercise primary enforc[e]ment [of] drinking water programs, with the EPA assuming the resp[onsibility] when a state is unwilling or unable to meet and enforce the reg[ulations]. To comply, a state must establish drinking water standards a[nd pro]cedures for exemptions at least as stringent as federal regulations, and implement an adequate enforcement program, maintain records and submit reports as required by the EPA administrator, establish an emergency response plan, and develop a program for plan review. As of July 1979, forty-one states had been granted primary enforcement authority and six other states were expected to receive it in the immediate future (CEQ, 1979a).

In 1978 the EPA monitored nearly 62,000 community water systems serving more than 200 million people. Approximately 80 percent of these systems use groundwater. Of the 62,000 systems, approximately 6,745 violated the microbacteriological standard (an increase of 1.6 percent from 1978), 760 surface water systems violated the turbidity standard (an increase of 0.8 percent), and 1,007 systems violated one or more of the chemical-radiological standards (a decrease of approximately 8.4 percent) (EPA, 1980a).

Local Water Resource Management

Supply and Demand

The materials balance model demonstrates that we cannot increase the earth's finite resources, but we can manage what we have much more effectively. The two basic methods of water resource management are input approaches, to increase usable water supplies, and throughput approaches, to reduce demand for usable water. Effective water management should use both and place a much greater emphasis on reducing demand in the United States.

For *input approaches,* water supplies can be augmented by finding new sources, by developing existing sources more intensively and efficiently, by protecting water from contamination, by purifying contaminated water for domestic use, and by encouraging people to move to areas that have plentiful water supplies. The conventional approach to augmenting water supplies is to build dams and diversion systems to store and carry water. Dams and reservoirs prevent flooding, provide flat-water recreation opportunities, and can provide cheap and reliable hydroelectric power.

However, dams and reservoirs have several disadvantages. First, they encourage floodplain development. When floods occur that exceed the control capacity of the dam, the resulting damage can be greater than if the dam had not been built. It should be emphasized that despite the expenditure by federal agencies of nearly $10 billion on flood control projects in the past 30 years, annual flood losses doubled between 1967 and 1977. Damage from flooding can best be controlled through the use of nonstructural floodplain controls (CEQ, 1980; Platt, 1979).

Second, dams only control water flow; they do not increase water supply. Water stored behind a dam is unavailable for downstream use, and often the net basin water supply actually decreases because of accelerated evaporation from the surface. Third, dams and water projects have unpredictable health, economic, and ecological impacts, such as the schistosomiasis problem caused by the Aswan Dam (Bryson and Jenkins, 1972). Fourth, it must be noted that all dams are obstructions to natural drainways and, over geological time, will fail. Thus, the decision to construct a dam commits future generations to pay the costs of inspection, maintenance, and replacement or to bear the burden of deaths and damages when a failure occurs.

Finally, inundation of large areas of land by lakes and reservoirs destroys or disrupts historic and archaeological sites, historic land uses, and natural and scenic habitat and forgoes flowing-water recreational opportunities. Many people have heard about the Tellico Dam in eastern Tennessee where the potential extinction of the seemingly insignificant snail darter (*Percina tanasi*) halted a large Tennessee Valley Authority (TVA) dam project. However, few realize that three independent studies published in 1977 and 1978 concluded that the net benefits of not building the dam and developing the river-based economy would be roughly equal to those of building the dam. The river-based economy had the added advantages of conserving scenic and wildlife habitats (including that of the snail darter) and the native homeland of the Cherokee Indians (General Accounting Office, 1977; TVA, 1978; University of Tennessee, 1978). However, authorization of the dam was approved by Congress, largely through the efforts of the Tennessee congressional delegation, amid charges by conservation groups that the project was a "pork barrel" to visibly channel federal money into the local economy (Cahn, 1979).

A second method of augmenting water supplies is their diversion from areas with ample water to areas of deficiency. The best example is the California water plan where water is diverted from northern California to irrigate agricultural lands in the Imperial Valley and where water from northern California, the Mono Lake Basin, and the Colorado River is used for domestic purposes in the Los Angeles Basin. These diversions have contributed to diminished flow of rivers, destruction of natural ecosystems, problems of soil salinity, and destruction of much of the economy of the Owens Valley (Steinhart, 1980).

The Soviet Union is currently constructing a $100-billion project to divert northern waters which normally flow into uninhabited arctic tundra in Siberia, toward inhabited areas to the south. This 20-year project may, however, cause serious ecological damage through altered arctic climate and ocean currents. In the United States the development of such projects is becoming increasingly difficult because of water rights laws, economics, and a growing realization of the environmental consequences and inequities of such projects.

A third major input approach is to increase the withdrawals from groundwater sources. Groundwater supplies an estimated 20 percent of freshwater use in the United States, mostly in rural areas. The problems involved with continued use of groundwater include (1) depletion of supplies, especially in the Great Plains and Far West, (2) land subsidence, (3) saltwater intrusion into groundwater reservoirs in coastal areas, and (4) contamination.

Finally, saltwater desalinization and climatic modification programs have been proposed to augment freshwater supplies. These are, for the most part, too expensive, energy consuming, or ecologically damaging to be practical for most urban water systems. Perhaps the most practical input approaches in dealing with water shortages are to prevent contamination and to direct population and economic growth to areas that have ample water. Such programs, however, require a national commitment and a coordinated, environmentally sensitive national economic development program.

Throughput approaches to water resource management include (1) decreasing water losses, per capita water consumption, and the amount of water required in consumptive uses, (2) increasing the efficiency of residential, commercial, and industrial water use, and (3) recycling through water purification or by using relatively impure water for certain purposes.

To reduce water losses, scientists have been studying the possibility of reducing evaporation from lakes and reservoirs through the use of thin-film surface coatings. To date, such use has been relatively ineffective and ecologically damaging. Another approach that is quite promising, however, is the use of trickling irrigation systems to reduce the amount of water lost to evaporation. These systems provide water directly to the roots of crops through an underground network of tubes and can reduce irrigation water use by approximately 75 percent.

In addition, agricultural water use can be made much more efficient by preventing unnecessary irrigation, eliminating seepage from irrigation channels, improving crop and climate compatibility, and improving pricing policies to discourage waste. Scientists are also breeding new varieties of crops that require less water.

Industrial and municipal water consumption could be reduced by improving the maintenance of the distribution systems, by individual metering to discourage consumption and to facilitate the tracing of leaks, by pricing water according to the volume used, and by industrial water recycling and treatment. Nearly 40 percent of all water consumed

Table 4-6. Water Conservation Measures.

Activity	Normal Use and Consumption (gallons)	Alternative Use and Consumption (gallons)
Shower	water running - 25	wet and rinse - 4
Brushing teeth	tap running - 10	wet and rinse - 0.5
Bath	full tub - 35	minimal level - 11
Shaving	tap running - 20	fill basin - 1
Dishwashing	tap running - 30	basin wash and rinse - 5
Automatic dishwasher	full cycle - 16	short cycle - 7
Hand washing	tap running - 2	fill basin - 1
Flushing toilet	normal - 6	tank displacement bottle - 5
Washing machine	full cycle, top level - 60	short cycle minimal level - 27
Outdoor watering	per minute - 10	native landscaping - 0

Source: Modified from Living in the Environment, 3rd ed., by G. Tyler Miller. Copyright 1979 by Wadsworth, Inc. Reprinted by permission of Wadsworth Publishing Co., Belmont CA 94002.

in the United States is used for nondegradative cooling purposes and can be reused without significant treatment costs. As a matter of fact, only 2 percent of municipal and industrial effluents are directly polluted; the remainder of the waste stream is generated by diluting the 2 percent with pure drinking water. By separating degradative from nondegradative water uses, a considerable amount of water could be recycled for domestic and agricultural irrigation and industrial processing (Miller, 1979).

Table 4-6 presents some of the individual actions that residents can take to reduce domestic water consumption. Additional water savings can be obtained by (1) using waterless toilets where permitted, (2) installing faucet and shower flow restrictors, (3) composting rather than using a garbage disposal, (4) washing automobiles less frequently and using a bucket rather than a hose, (5) sweeping and raking lawns, walks, and driveways rather than hosing them off, and (6) irrigating in the evenings and early mornings.

It is estimated that between 30 and 50 percent of all water consumption is wasted. In 1977 Marin County, California, residents were able to reduce their water consumption by 65 percent using these and other simple conservation measures (Miller, 1979). These measures can also be useful in reducing energy consumption, especially when the consumption of hot water is reduced. In fact, a well-planned community water conservation and reuse program can contribute significantly to a reduction in demand for both water and energy.

Water Supply Treatment

The treatment required for a municipal water system primarily depends on the quality of water used. Pure water from protected groundwater sources may require no treatment, whereas severely polluted water may require both physical and chemical treatment. The standard treatment processes include storage, use of coagulants, filtration, and chlorination (Sewell, 1975).

Water can be purified through natural physical processes by simple *storage* in a reservoir, lake, or basin. Time, temperature, sunlight, and the lack of motion will tend to reduce levels of suspended solids, hardness, and bacteria and improve color. Depending upon the temperature and chemical conditions, most bacteria can be eliminated by storing water from one to five weeks. However, a retention period of two to three days is most frequently used.

Undesirable materials such as chemicals, suspended particles, and microorganisms are frequently removed from water by precipitating them out through the *use of coagulants* such as aluminum sulfate (alum), sodium aluminate, ferrous and ferric sulfate, ferric chloride, clays, or pulverized limestone or activated charcoal. When coagulant is added to the water in a holding basin, an off-color gelatinous precipitate or floc settles to the bottom. The cleansed water is then drawn off the top and routed to the filtration units.

Filtration units generally consist of tanks that have perforated pipes covered by sand at the bottom. Suspended material, including bacteria, is removed from the water as it moves through the sand into the pipes. The tank is periodically drained and the sand cleaned or replaced.

The final and most critical step in water treatment involves the *chlorination* (by gas or liquid) and holding of the treated water. Between ten and sixty minutes of chlorination is considered adequate; however, longer retention times and higher chlorine concentrations may be required to destroy certain viruses. For instance, four or more hours of contact with chlorine is required to destroy the virus that causes hepatitis. Chlorine concentrations of seven to forty times that required to destroy *E. coli* are required to destroy the Coxsackie viruses that cause some forms of polio, meningitis, and pneumonia. In addition, the chlorine concentration should be adjusted to the water's appearance, pH, temperature, and previous treatment.

Care should be taken to avoid excessive chlorination of water. The chlorine may combine with organic materials in the water to form trihalomethane (THM) compounds, which have been shown to be carcinogenic in animals and may be toxic in extremely low concentrations. The EPA has established an interim maximum concentration level for total THMs (Table 4-5) that applies to all water systems serving more than 10,000 people, and the EPA requires monitoring for

112 / *Natural Resource Management*

THMs in municipal water systems serving more than 75,000 people (CEQ, 1980).

Federal and State Programs

Water supply allocation in arid areas of the United States depends largely on federal and state government investments and developments. Water resource allocation has always been both highly political and subject to abuse because of ambiguous or unsound water rights laws. In addition, the price of water often does not reflect its true value or cost of supply, and water projects have a high political visibility to local constituents (Henning, 1974; Hirshleifer et al., 1960).

For these reasons, water developments in the past—especially those designed to increase supplies—have been supported without real examination of impacts or alternatives (Bruner and Farris, 1969). Cost-benefit analyses were often manipulated by management agencies to justify inefficient allocation of resources for political purposes. In addition, important cumulative, interactive, long-term, or secondary socioeconomic and environmental impacts were overlooked (Spurr, 1970).

In an attempt to rectify the situation, President Carter announced a new comprehensive national water policy on June 6, 1978. The new policy placed emphasis on water conservation, increased attention to environmental concerns, improved water project planning and evaluation, and increased cooperation between federal and state governments in water resource management. The new policy was the result of a one-year review by the U.S. Department of the Interior, the CEQ, and the Office of Management and Budget (OMB), during which it was found that (CEQ, 1978b):

- despite serious water supply problems in several regions of the country, there is no national emphasis on water conservation
- there are wide variations in cost-benefit analysis techniques used by federal agencies
- some water projects were unsafe or unsound economically or environmentally
- there is a lack of integration and cooperation between state and federal programs

In July 1978 President Carter issued a set of directives assigning responsibility for enforcement to the secretary of the interior in consultation with the CEQ and OMB. By June 1980 completed actions included (CEQ, 1980):

- the establishment of eleven criteria for evaluation of policy decisions in federal water projects

Natural Resource Management

- an increase in Water Resources Council emphasis on water servation and nonstructural alternatives such as floodplain management
- the establishment of standard Water Resources Council procedures for evaluation of economic costs and benefits of projects
- the issuance of stronger regulations for the protection of wildlife, historic, and cultural resources in water resource planning
- the establishment of the procedures for independent water project reviews to be done by the Water Resources Council
- proposed legislation for increasing state participation in water resource planning and financing

To promote state primacy in water resource management, the administration proposed to increase the funding for matching grants for state water resource planning from $5 million to $25 million annually. In addition, the president proposed a $25-million matching grant program of technical assistance for water conservation. The administration also proposed to increase the states' share of the cost of structural water control projects to help ensure that federal money was not wasted (CEQ, 1978b).

A U.S. Water Resources Council report (1980) concluded that a lack of state legislation and administrative authority severely inhibits state water resource planning and management. Only twenty-nine states have legislated clear authority to conduct water resource planning, and only a few of these have an agency that provides comprehensive, coordinated management of water quality and quantity (CEQ, 1980).

The Carter administration was working on additional measures to promote water conservation, clarify water rights, and develop procedures for water project evaluation (CEQ, 1980). That administration should be applauded for these efforts to open up and expand water resource planning and management efforts.

Unfortunately, the Reagan administration has chosen a different path for water resource management. In comparing the federal funding requests for fiscal 1983 with actual expenditures in 1981, one finds a 38.9 percent budget cut for the Soil (and Water) Conservation Service, a 100 percent budget cut for the Water Resources Council, and 15.7 percent and 32.5 percent increases for the Bureau of Reclamation's construction and operations and maintenance budgets, respectively. Two of the most controversial projects now receiving funding are the Garrison Diversion project in North Dakota and the Tombigbee Waterway in Tennessee. The latter was termed "economic nonsense" by the *Wall Street Journal* (The Conservation Foundation, 1982).

The 100 percent proposed budget cut for the Water Resources Council reflects the desire of the Reagan administration to eliminate the council (and conceivably, its standards for evaluating water resource development projects). In addition, the U.S. Fish and Wildlife Service

114 / *Natural Resource Management*

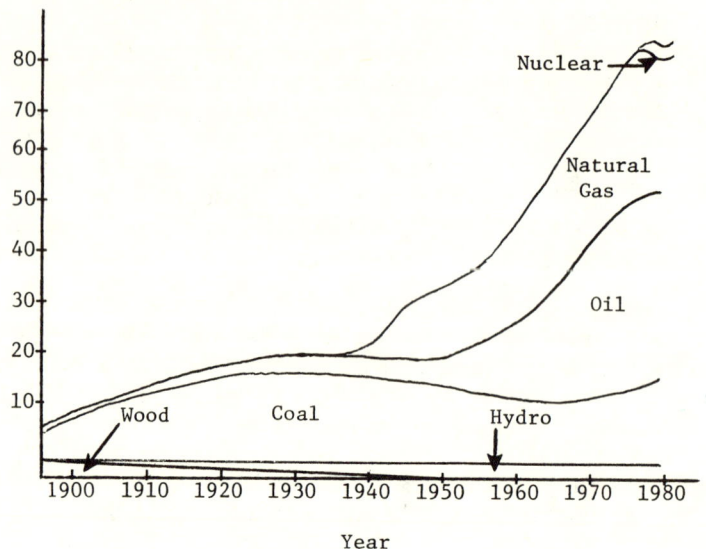

Figure 4-4. Energy Demand and Fuel Supply in the United States, 1900 to 1979 (DOE, June 1980).

is no longer actively involved in the evaluation of water projects (The Conservation Foundation, 1982).

Community Energy Planning and Management

At present, there is a compelling need to reduce U.S. consumption of nonrenewable energy resources. The availability of energy in a usable form at an affordable price with acceptable socioeconomic and environmental impacts is essential to the health and well-being of our economy. Without the expenditure of energy, there is no work; without work, there is no ordering; and without order, there is only entropy.

Figure 4-4 portrays the growth in energy demand in the United States from 1900 to 1979. The United States is currently the world's largest energy consumer and energy waster. We consume 40 to 50 percent more energy per capita than does any other highly industrialized nation, and we waste more energy than is consumed by two-thirds of the population of the world (Hayes, 1976). A recent study by Ross and Williams (1982) found that the U.S. industrial economy could be sustained on nearly 50 percent less energy than is currently consumed. Further, Lovins and Lovins (1982) have contended that from the standpoint of pure economics and national security, policies of decentralization, the promotion of efficient energy use, and the development of renewable resources should have the highest national priority.

Between 1950 and 1970, U.S. energy consumption doubled. This was due, in part, to the tremendous growth in the U.S. economy and the fact that the real price of energy (percent of net income) in the United States actually fell by 28 percent. As a result, the United States built a stock of capital goods (i.e., homes, automobiles, and factory equipment) and an economy based on inefficient uses of energy (Executive Office of the President, 1977).

Conventional Input Approaches

The situation changed, however. Conventional management approaches in the 1970s failed to provide usable energy at affordable prices with acceptable impacts. In essence, the economic system was not functioning properly, or as cornucopians believe it should, for several reasons.

First, there is no free market in energy. A relatively small number of large corporations and utilities control the production and distribution of petroleum, natural gas, coal, nuclear power, and electricity. In many cases, monopolistic practices were encouraged by law to provide affordable energy supplies and to capture economies of scale in the industry. In return for having been granted monopoly rights, these utilities and corporations are subjected to regulation. The tendencies both to abuse monopoly power and to exercise inappropriate and ineffective regulation have exacerbated development problems. Add to this the formation of international producer cartels, conflicts between international economic and religious factions, and international interdependencies for critical resources and you have problems!

In addition to regulatory and management problems, the energy industries have experienced significant technical difficulties. The oil companies were unable to increase domestic production in the 1970s. In fact, domestic production decreased throughout the decade (as first predicted by the U.S. Geological Survey in the late 1950s—see Hubbert, 1973). Rather than invest in progressively less efficient domestic production, the oil industry chose to invest in other fuel sources and nonenergy industries (Stobaugh and Yergin, 1979).

Further, the nuclear power "source of the future" experienced extreme technical and financial difficulties. According to the *New York Times* (1983), between 1979 and 1982 there were no new nuclear reactors ordered in the United States and in each successive year, respectively, there were twelve, fourteen, six, and sixteen plant cancellations. The recent default of the Washington Public Power Supply System on several nuclear projects was the largest in the history of the U.S. bond market. Also, according to the *Energy Digest* (1983), the average post-Three Mile Island (TMI) nuclear power plant will generate power at five times the cost of those nuclear plants constructed before the TMI accident. The average cost of the new nuclear electricity

116 / *Natural Resource Management*

is 11 cents per kilowatt-hour with a range of 5.5 cents to 18 cents per kilowatt-hour.

These management and technical problems combined to produce a number of energy resource difficulties in the 1970s:

1. Energy shortages occurred twice in the decade. The first was created by the Arab oil embargo of 1973 and 1974. The second, in the spring and summer of 1979 (the cause of which is still subject to debate), resulted in long lines, higher prices, and hot tempers.
2. U.S. reliance on imported petroleum increased from an equivalent 12 Q (1 quadrillion BTUs = 1 Q) in 1973 to a peak of 18 Q in 1978. This increase exacerbated problems in balance of payments and national security (CEQ, 1980).
3. The environmental impacts and potential catastrophic effects from energy resource development became much more serious. The U.S. population became aware of the possibilities of climatic changes produced by increasing levels of CO_2 from fuels combustion, of acid rains produced by SO_2 from coal stack gases, and of the hazards associated with a nuclear accident.
4. The price of energy rose dramatically. For instance, in 1974 alone, the world price of oil quadrupled (Executive Office of the President, 1977).

In its policies, actions, and budget proposals, it is clear that the Reagan administration believes that a shortage of conventional supplies of energy rather than a "longage" of demand is the root of past and present energy problems. The Reagan energy policy calls for accelerated development of nuclear power, increased subsidies for petroleum production, and drastic reductions in programs for energy conservation and renewable energy. The third item is reflected in the administration's fiscal year 1983 budget proposals to reduce funding for conservation programs by 98 percent and for renewable energy by 86 percent from 1980 levels (Friends of the Earth, 1982). This failure of the administration to recognize and effectively deal with problems associated with energy production and consumption makes the argument for state, regional, and local energy conservation and renewable energy programs even more compelling.

In summary, the socioeconomic and technical systems of the United States have failed to find an acceptable alternative to nonrenewable oil and natural gas fuels that currently supply over 75 percent of U.S. energy needs and are predicted to be exhausted within the next two or three decades (Hubbert, 1973). What we are faced with is a classic case of entropy as depicted in Figure 4-5.

Figure 4-5. Entropy and Energy. Reprinted from the July 30, 1979, issue of *Business Week* by special permission, © 1979 by McGraw-Hill, Inc.

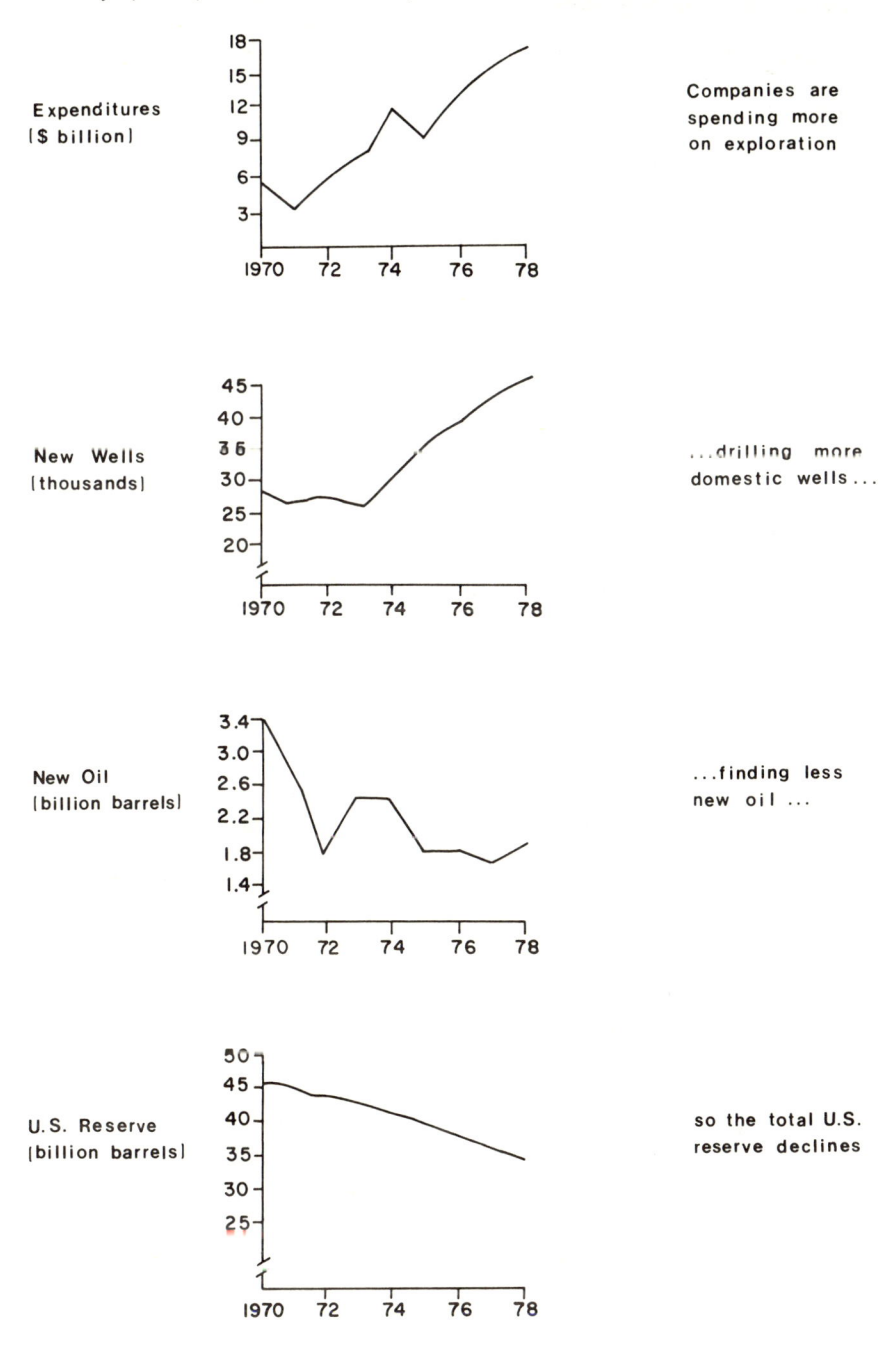

Expenditures ($ billion) — Companies are spending more on exploration

New Wells (thousands) — ...drilling more domestic wells...

New Oil (billion barrels) — ...finding less new oil...

U.S. Reserve (billion barrels) — so the total U.S. reserve declines

Throughput Management

Because energy cannot be recycled, throughput management of energy means using as little as possible, as efficiently as possible. Hayes (1976) enumerated the advantages of energy conservation through the reduction of unnecessary and inefficient uses over the conventional input management approaches:

1. Reducing the impacts from air and water pollution, solid and toxic wastes, and land disruption
2. Reducing the probability of large-scale disasters from energy production
3. Reducing international conflicts and improving our national security and balance of payments by reducing our reliance on foreign oil
4. Extending the lifetime of our nonrenewable fossil fuel resources and allowing more time for the development of acceptable alternatives
5. Reducing the tendencies for energy price escalation by offsetting the need for large capital investments for energy production systems now and in the future when generating capacity would need replacement (additional economic advantages would be realized by reducing operating costs and having programs designed to reduce expensive peak load demands)
6. Increasing the number of jobs in the energy industry
7. Reducing the external costs of energy production borne by noninvolved parties and future generations
8. Improving the safety and stability of international energy systems by marketing technologies and processes that have low weapons potential
9. Improving the net energy output of the energy industry

An energy conservation program can save an enormous amount of energy without serious economic consequences. Several recent studies (CEQ, 1979b; Hayes, 1976; Okagaki and Benson, 1979; Stobaugh and Yergin, 1979) have indicated that the United States could save between 40 and 50 percent of domestic consumption through an energy conservation program. Table 4-7 summarizes by sector the potential fuel savings and some important conservation activities.

In the past few years, U.S. energy demand has fallen significantly below demand forecasts made in the early and middle 1970s. Figure 4-6 shows the significant and progressive decreases in estimates of future U.S. energy demand—the Hudson-Jorgenson forecasts of 1974, 1977, 1978, and 1979. Continued emphasis on energy conservation through education and conservation programs and pricing policies can

Table 4-7. Potential Fuel Conservation by Sector and Activity (revised from Ross and Williams, 1977).

	Potential Savings (10^{15} BTU)	Total Energy Demand in 1973 (10^{15} BTU)
A. Residential and Commercial Sector		
– Use heat pumps	0.60	
– Improve AC efficiency	0.77	
– Improve refrigeration efficiency	0.47	
– Reduce water heating fuel requirements	1.38	
– Improve insulation and reduce ventilation	6.15	
– Use total energy systems in large facilities	0.95	
– Use microwave ovens for 50% cooking	0.31	
	11.58 or 44%	26.13
B. Industrial Sector		
– Increase net energy efficiency	1.67	
– Improve energy management	3.85	
– Use of primary fuels	0.17	
– Cogenerate or regenerate	3.82	
– Recycle aluminum, iron, and steel	0.21	
– Generate fuel from organic wastes	0.70	
	10.42 or 35%	29.65
C. Transportation Sector		
– Improve auto efficiency 150%	5.89	
– Fuel savings other transportation areas	3.20	
	9.09 or 48%	18.96
GRAND TOTAL	31.09 or 42%	74.74

significantly reduce energy consumption and the associated detrimental physical and socioeconomic impacts.

Rationale for Community Planning and Management

Throughout the United States, communities are becoming actively involved in energy planning and management. Many of the tools for the regulation and management of energy are under their direct jurisdiction. These include (1) land use controls, (2) building codes, (3) planning, regulation, and management of transportation systems, (4) planning, siting, and management of public services and facilities, (5)

120 / *Natural Resource Management*

Figure 4-6. Hudson-Jorgenson Total Primary Energy Consumption Forecasts, 1980-2000 (Hudson and Jorgenson, 1974; Uhler and Zycher, 1979).

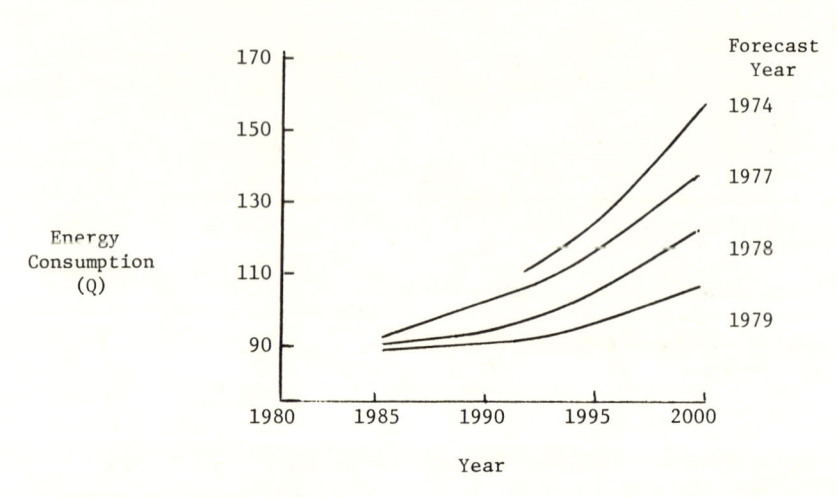

education, (6) utility financing, and (7) control over powerful local ordinances.

Local governments and community groups are also best able to identify and define local problems and to assess the local potential for energy conservation and the development of indigenous nonrenewable and renewable energy resources. Further, local governments tend to have a higher level of citizen accessibility and familiarity and accountability to provide the support and trust necessary for the development of innovative and perhaps restrictive new programs.

There are several additional advantages to producing energy at or near the point of consumption. These include (Corbett, 1981):

- reduced requirements for energy conversion and transmission equipment
- reduced loss of energy in conversion and transmission
- increased energy system stability through the use of many small independent systems rather than large interdependent systems that are vulnerable to failure or sabotage
- localized control over the means of energy production, which one hopes may lead to wiser energy use
- localized environmental impacts of energy production, which reduces externalities

One of the most famous case studies of "localizing" the energy production system was of Franklin County, Massachusetts (U.S. Department of Energy, 1980a). Between 1975 and 1979, the total cost of energy to the county nearly doubled. In addition, a study of its own energy production and consumption system revealed that more than 85 percent of the money the county used to purchase energy was spent outside the county. County residents learned that if they could develop a more self-sufficient energy system, they could develop local resources, diversify the economy, internalize the expenditures for energy, and create local employment opportunities. The localized system presented the added advantages of reducing the vulnerability of the local system to national fuel shortages and rising prices. The county residents learned that they would become nearly independent of "imported" energy supplies by developing alternative local energy resources and by implementing a rigorous energy conservation program.

Community Energy Planning and Management

Community energy planning is a relatively new field. The first comprehensive energy planning and management programs originated in the mid-1970s as results of growing awareness of energy impacts and supply problems and the Arab oil embargo. The following is suggested as a step-by-step approach or template for the formation and implementation of a community energy plan. Included in the sequence are discussions of problems, goals, management strategies, and the range of activities possible in developing a community energy program. Because this is a new field and because communities differ widely in administrative structures, capabilities, aspirations, and energy management problems, considerable variation in this suggested approach is to be expected. For further information see Okagaki and Benson (1979) and Shiffman and Page (1979).

Step 1. Define the Problem

Before the planning activities begin, local perceptions of energy management problems should be surveyed to ascertain the broad goals and objectives of the community energy plan. Some of the most common problems encountered include vulnerability to supply shortages or cutoffs, high capital outlays for energy, and the provision of energy "lifelines" to the poor and elderly. In addition, community leaders and citizens may indicate a desire to promote the development of indigenous and/or renewable energy resources. The end result of this step should be a summary statement of local concerns and goals of the community energy management program.

Step 2. Analyze the Framework for Program Development

The second step should involve an identification of the existing political, economic, legal, and regulatory framework to be included in the formulation and implementation of the community energy plan. Pertinent federal, state, and local regulations and programs should be identified and summarized. This information can be obtained from county, regional, state, or federal energy agencies or from local extension offices. For example, the Oregon Department of Energy (1980) provided a summary of programs to promote weatherization and the development of renewable energy systems in Oregon. These programs include:

- federal tax credits for weatherization and alternative energy use
- state tax credits for alternative energy devices
- state property tax exemptions for alternative energy devices
- state low-cost loans for alternative energy devices
- state veterans' loans for weatherization
- utility weatherization programs
- federal low-income weatherization programs
- consumer tips
- a toll-free number for updated information

In addition, an analysis should be made of the resources locally available for program development, of the local political processes, and of the interplay of citizens, citizen groups, and the local government to assure that the energy program is within the economic and political capabilities of the community.

Step 3. Create an Energy Data Base

A profile of community energy production, consumption, and indigenous energy reserves should be developed to serve as a base for the prediction of local energy production and conservation potential. The data base can be used to (1) identify institutional and physical factors that influence energy production and consumption, (2) compare local patterns of production and consumption with state and national averages, (3) calculate local energy production and conservation potential, (4) assist in formulating specific program goals and activities, and (5) serve as a base line for evaluating program success. Data should be gathered on seasonal, daily, sector, and subsector production and consumption patterns and should be analyzed and summarized in a comprehensible format for presentation in public meetings.

The creation and analysis of the data base should ideally include four major elements (Okagaki and Benson, 1979; McCoy and Singer, 1979):

1. Preparation of a complete inventory of residential, commercial, industrial, and transportation energy consumption. The primary fuel consumed (i.e., coal, natural gas, electricity, etc.) and ultimate work accomplished (i.e., heat, electrical drives, etc.) for major activities in each sector should be calculated and compared in appropriate equivalent

units of measure (e.g., BTUs for technical reports, dollars for public meetings).

2. Projection of energy consumption patterns for two to three decades into the future using conventional assumptions on population and economic growth and per capita energy consumption.

3. Estimation of the potential for energy conservation for each major activity, using the best available technical literature (Okagaki and Benson, 1979) or comparison with national or state averages.

4. Estimation of the potential for the development of new production alternatives. The location, amount, ease of acquisition, cost, and impacts of production of indigenous nonrenewable and renewable energy resources should be analyzed. For example, the annual, seasonal, and daily availability of insolation, wind, geothermal energy, hydroelectric power, and biomass sources should be calculated and mapped (see, for example, Southern Tier Central Regional Planning and Development Board, 1978).

Step 4. Develop Program Objectives

The selection of specific program objectives is extremely important to the planning process because it forms the basis for choice of production and conservation strategies and it establishes the criteria to evaluate their success or failure. The specific problems and issues identified and delineated during analysis of the data base can be used to develop and prioritize program objectives. Widespread community participation is essential in this process to properly develop program objectives and to foster a climate of public support for resulting programs. The resulting objectives should be compatible with other community development goals and should be given official city approval. The objectives can be specific or fairly general in scope, depending on the preferences of the community and the planning team. Some representative objectives include:

- promoting maximum cost-effective utilization of indigenous and renewable energy resources
- promoting maximum cost-effective energy conservation through the elimination of unnecessary and inefficient uses
- improving utility management
- protecting public health, safety, and welfare
- improving the design and siting of new energy facilities
- developing emergency energy plans
- improving public information and participation programs
- improving coordination of energy planning with land use, solid waste, community development, etc., planning

Step 5. Develop Strategies for Achieving Objectives

Strategies for achieving each specific objective should be developed and coordinated in a comprehensive energy management program. For instance, to improve the siting of new energy facilities a community may want to establish procedures for siting review and evaluation. To prepare for emergency situations, fuel reserves can be developed along with procedures to prioritize allocations of fuel or electricity. A sample community program for promoting local solar and conservation objectives is given below.

1. In-House Government
   a. Retrofit public facilities with cost effective renewable energy and conservation devices
   b. Design energy efficient public services (i.e., transportation, sewage, street lighting, etc.)
   c. Promote recycling of materials and use of recycled materials
   d. Encourage reforms in utility rate structures and load management practices
   e. Study the feasibility of developing a municipal solar utility for solar and renewable energy development
2. Public Incentives for Private Actions
   a. Develop one-stop energy centers to provide information on energy conservation and renewable energy systems, energy auditing services, lists of certified manufacturers, and installers and financial assistance
   b. Provide weatherization grants or loans to renters and low-income individuals
   c. Provide commercial and residential property incentives for energy conservation or renewable energy systems
   d. Encourage the development of non–energy intensive industries through municipal economic development expenditures
3. Public Regulation of Private Actions (Brewer and Mackie, 1980)
   a. Amend zoning and subdivision ordinances to promote energy conservation
      - provide density bonuses in energy-conserving designs
      - allow clustering and attached housing
      - promote planned unit developments
      - permit multiple uses of individual buildings
      - develop mixed use zones which would allow energy co generation
      - require energy-efficient landscaping for street and parking
      - study the feasibility of developing energy performance standards in commercial structures
   b. Amend zoning and subdivision ordinances to provide and protect access to renewable energy sources

- properly design and orient streets, buildings, and lots for solar access
- include renewable energy easements in all new deed covenants
- provide density bonuses for developments using renewable energy systems
- develop a solar access recordation ordinance
c. Develop standards and procedures for siting local renewable energy facilities.

Step 6. Plan the Program Implementation and Evolution

With full citizen participation, an implementation plan should be developed, specifying the degree and nature of planned activities. A schedule of activities, budget, and statement of program resource requirements should also be developed. Procedures for monitoring and evaluating program performance should be established for periodic program review and update. Finally, the complete plan (activities, schedule, budget, etc.) should be documented and formally adopted, recorded, and implemented by the appropriate city officials or committees.

Finally, it must be emphasized that citizen support and particpation are essential for the successful development and implementation of a community energy plan. Localized planning and decision making are critical when program emphasis is on solving local problems with local resources. Further, considerable work, sacrifice, or lifestyle changes may be necessary to accomplish program goals and objectives. The motivation to overcome barriers is strongest when generated from within.

5 / Residuals Management

The Materials Balance Model and Pollution Control

According to the law of conservation of mass, all material inputs into the U.S. economy must ultimately leave the system in the form of chemical, physical, and biological wastes. When these wastes, or residuals, are released into aquatic or atmospheric environments, they are air and water pollutants. When released into or onto terrestrial environments, they are solid or toxic wastes. The materials balance model is particularly useful in indicating the four primary residuals control options: (1) reducing the throughput of materials and energy, (2) timing and locating waste releases for maximum dilution and dispersion, (3) augmenting the assimilative capacity of the environment for wastes, and (4) treating residuals (Freeman et al., 1973).

The first pollution control option is to manage the system to *minimize throughput*. As discussed in the previous chapter, this can be accomplished in a number of ways.

The second option involves *choosing the time and place of release* of wastes. For instance, some environments can assimilate waste and pollutant loads larger than the loads that do significant damage in other environments. Larger airsheds or bodies of water or areas of rapid air movement have a greater capacity to dilute and disperse residuals. For instance, a discharger of organic wastes can reduce the degradation of water quality by dispersing the release points of effluents rather than dumping at one location. In addition, discharges can be timed to take advantage of daily or seasonal flow rates and directions (Freeman et al., 1973). Another common practice is the construction of taller smokestacks to increase the rate and area of dispersion of airborne residuals.

Third, various techniques can be used to *increase the ability of the natural environment to accept wastes and pollutants* without significant damage to social or ecological systems. Common approaches to wastewater management include augmenting stream flow to dilute and disperse residuals and using bubblers, agitators, or artificial water cascades to maintain oxygen levels in streams (Freeman et al., 1973).

Finally, *residuals can be treated* biologically, chemically, and physically to concentrate, contain, isolate, detoxify, or recycle them with minimum exposure to social and ecological systems. One example is the concentration, vitrification, encapsulation, and burial of radioactive wastes. Another is the incineration of organic wastes to less toxic forms. In addition, many materials can be recovered and recycled. Practical applications include the recovering and recycling of newspaper, glass, and metals from municipal solid wastes. Even sulfur from stack gases can theoretically be recycled.

In using this last option, however, it is important to remember that although the residual can be converted from one form to another, it seldom disappears. The incineration of materials, for example, may result in air pollution problems, or effluents removed from stack gases may become water pollution or cause waste disposal problems if not handled properly (Freeman et al., 1973).

The Market System and Pollution

The Model of Optimum Levels of Pollution Control

One of the most important concepts in residuals management is the tradeoff of costs and benefits involved in pollution and waste control. Proper decision making involves a comparison of total project costs and benefits in order to choose the alternative that returns the greatest benefit for the least cost, thereby allocating resources in the most efficient way. The ultimate goal of residuals management is to provide the level of protection necessary for the prevention of significant damage to ecological and social systems at a minimal cost.

The relationship between the costs and benefits of investments in residuals control is portrayed in Figure 5-1 (the model of optimum levels of pollution control). The model indicates that as the level of pollution increases, damage to the environment also increases. That is, a small amount of pollution can be tolerated by the environment with little or no ecological or socioeconomic damage. However, as progressively higher levels of pollution are reached, damages rise sharply, especially after the system's capacity to assimilate pollution has been exceeded.

Conversely, as the level of pollution is progressively decreased, the costs of controls increase. For example, primary, secondary, and tertiary sewage treatment can remove 30 percent, 85 percent, and nearly all, respectively, of the oxygen-demanding wastes from sewage. However, tertiary treatment systems in general are nearly twice as expensive to build and four times as expensive to operate as combined primary and secondary treatment facilities (Miller, 1979). In fact, studies of the actual costs of pollution and pollution controls suggest that the shapes of the curves in the model accurately represent the real world situation (Page and Ferejohn, 1974).

The model indicates that, initially, considerable pollution can be eliminated at very low costs. However, in the push to achieve a progressively cleaner environment, costs rise disproportionately fast

Figure 5-1. The Optimum Level of Pollution Control Model (Freeman et al., 1973).

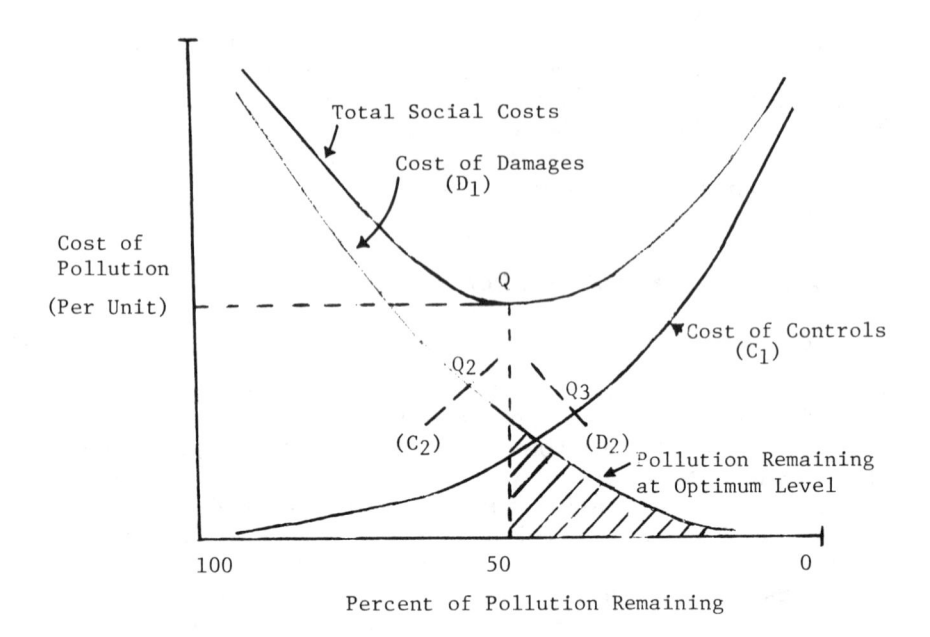

[Figure: Graph with x-axis "Percent of Pollution Remaining" (100 to 0) and y-axis "Cost of Pollution (Per Unit)". Curves shown: Total Social Costs, Cost of Damages (D_1), Cost of Controls (C_1), with points Q, Q2, Q3, and labels (C_2), (D_2), and "Pollution Remaining at Optimum Level" (shaded area).]

Source: Freeman, A. M., et al. *The Economics of Environmental Policy.* Copyright John Wiley and Sons, Inc., New York, 1973.

and benefits begin to level off. Eventually, enormous costs are incurred to clean up pollution that is doing very little real damage. By adding the costs of pollution damage and controls for each level of pollution, the total costs of pollution to society are obtained.

At extremely high and low levels of contamination, the total social costs are high. However, at the point of optimum level of pollution (Q), total social costs are minimized. The benefits of further reductions in the level of pollution are outweighed by the costs of control. It must be noted that, at the optimum level of pollution, some environmental damage does occur (shaded area). Also, levels of pollution higher than the optimum result in damages that are considerably greater than the costs of cleaning up.

The model of the optimum level of pollution control is also useful in indicating the effects of inefficient pollution control strategies and inaccurate estimates of pollution damages. Inefficient pollution controls would increase the control costs from line C_1 to dotted line C_2. Not only would control costs be greater, but the decision maker would be balancing costs and benefits to an optimum level (Q_2) entailing a significantly higher level of pollution. Thus, residuals managers should constantly strive for the least-expensive methods of control. In addition, if the manager fails to incorporate costs for all damages (to health and safety; synergistic, secondary, long-term, and/or intangible damages; etc.), which tends to be the case, the real damage curve would move from line D_1 to dotted line D_2, which indicates further pollution control investments are warranted to the point Q_3 to improve environmental conditions. Thus, failure to incorporate all damage costs results in an underinvestment in pollution controls and an overly polluted environment (Freeman et al., 1973).

It must be emphasized that this is a highly simplified representation of reality. The model assumes perfect knowledge of the costs of damages and controls and that damages and costs of control are proportionate to the level of pollution. The model is difficult to apply to real cases because of the large number of point and nonpoint sources of discharges, the large number of pollutants and cleanup options, the assimilative capacity of the environment through time, and the subjective nature of damage estimates. However, it is extremely valuable in providing a framework for environmental policy and decision making (Freeman et al., 1973).

Market Failures

In recent years, several studies have indicated that, in simple monetary terms, the costs of damages from pollutants and toxic wastes clearly exceed the costs of cleaning up (see Chapter 8). Existing market mechanisms have failed to properly weigh the costs and benefits of pollution control investments in decision-making processes. The major market imperfections that are distorting decision-making processes are failures to recognize externalities and to properly assign rights and prices to resources held in common and public goods.

Externalities are costs of production or consumption that are borne by society and not by the producers' or consumers of the products. The true cost of a good or service is its market price plus the external costs of production or consumption (i.e., for ecological, health, or property damage). A misallocation of resources occurs when producers and consumers base decisions on the market price rather than the true price of a good or service. In addition, the whole system is less efficient because the cleanup and health costs are much higher than those for prevention.

When external costs are added to the price of products, consumers have a more accurate picture of relative value. The higher prices of environmentally harmful products could discourage their purchase and encourage the use of products that require fewer resources and generate less waste and pollution (Mishan, 1971). Most environmental problems are caused by externalities that degrade the environment, a resource held in common. The solution to many environmental problems is cost internalization so that consumers are confronted with the true costs of goods and services.

The second imperfection in the U.S. market system is a failure to assign proper rights and prices to common-property resources and public goods. The price of the use of a resource held in common is zero. No charges are imposed on the power plant that obtains water from a river and discharges pollutants into the water and air. Further, no private claimant exists to charge for the rights to use and abuse a common-property resource. When private claims do arise for the materials and services of a commons, they are often inequitable, as in the claims previously mentioned for Antarctic lands and access to seabed mineral deposits, or are limited by the fact that many types of services are public goods (Shreiber et al., 1976).

A public good is a good or service that cannot be divided. When a public good is available to some, it is by its nature available to all; no one can own and use it exclusively. For instance, the air is a public good; any improvement in air quality is enjoyed by all. Even if exclusive rights were given to manage air quality, charges could not be collected for cleaner air because nonpayers could equally enjoy the benefits. Thus, conventional market approaches of supply, demand, and pricing are not applicable in managing common-property resources and public goods efficiently (Samuelson, 1954; Krutilla, 1967).

The failure of our market system in fairly and efficiently allocating environmental resources is part of Hardin's "tragedy of the commons" (Hardin and Badin, 1977). The absence of proper regulation and management opens the door for individuals or agencies, acting in their own self-interest, to abuse the commons. The benefits of overexploitation and contamination go to the abusers. The costs of the abuse are shared by all. For the same reasons, opportunities to improve the quality of the commons are often overlooked (Freeman et al., 1973; Hardin, 1968). Thus, the regulation and management of environmental resources held in common (air, water, land, and biota) require public or government intervention to ensure that services are allocated fairly and efficiently (Freeman et al., 1973; Hardin and Badin, 1977).

U.S. Pollution Control Policy

The federal and state approach to pollution control has generally been regulatory in nature. Federal and state agencies set standards, develop regulations for compliance, monitor the performance of polluters, and enforce agency actions through the courts. This conventional approach to pollution control has often been criticized as being costly and inflexible.

The goals and objectives of a pollution control program are generally specified in enabling legislation. Such legislation should serve as a legal framework on which policies and programs can be formulated and implemented. However, federal and state legislators, for reasons of political expediency, favor statements that are often ambiguous and unspecified. For instance, the commonly used goal, "to protect public health and welfare," is ambiguous because it does not define the term welfare, nor does it give any indication of the extent of consideration of control costs in decision-making processes. Statements such as these do not specify whether pollution should be controlled regardless of cost or whether control costs can be included and weighed in agency decision making (Freeman, 1978).

The weighing of costs and benefits is a regular, although implicit or hidden, occurrence in agency decision-making processes. For instance, decisions to relax automobile emissions standards involve a balancing of control costs with human health impacts and costs. This has placed a considerable burden on decision makers who must use administrative discretion in setting, regulating, and enforcing standards. This, in turn, has resulted in serious challenges in the courts to agency actions, fueled debates over pollution control policy, and impeded the implementation of pollution control programs. Therefore, to open up decision-making processes and to lay a management framework for pollution control agencies, it is extremely important for federal, state, and local legislative bodies to be more explicit and consistent about the tradeoffs and balances to be considered in formulating control policies (Freeman, 1978).

Because the goals and objectives of pollution control programs are so ambiguous, pollution control agencies have had considerable difficulty in developing regulatory programs. The initial task of setting pollution standards has proved to be extremely difficult, controversial, and time consuming. With no balancing framework for setting standards, agencies often set standards that are enforceable rather than optimal. Current standards are based on technical control capabilities or levels of pollution and not on the optimal level of pollution. Thus, current standards may be too high or too low, resulting in unnecessary expenditures for damages or pollution control systems. In addition, because of agency uncertainty in enacting and enforcing standards and procedures, polluters are often quite successful in using the courts and administrative procedures to delay compliance (Miller, 1979).

The management approach of setting and enforcing standards also has the disadvantage of offering no incentives for polluters to reduce emissions below the standards, even though in many cases they could do so in a cost-effective manner. In addition, requirements for all polluters within a broad category to reduce pollution by an equal

Table 5-1. Waste Discharges and Control Costs of Eight Hypothetical Firms (Freeman et al., 1973).

Firm	Wastes Discharged (lbs/day)	Control Costs (¢/lb)	Wastes Discharged with 4.5¢/lb Effluent Charge
1	100	2	0
2	200	5	200
3	500	10	500
4	400	4	0
5	400	8	400
6	100	4	0
7	200	2	0
8	500	10	500
Total	2,400		1,600

Source: Freeman, A. M., et al. The Economics of Environmental Policy. Copyright John Wiley and Sons, Inc., New York, 1973.

amount ignore the fact that some firms can clean up more cheaply than others. Finally, requiring specified control systems for certain sources of pollution reduces flexibility and forgoes opportunities for innovation.

Alternative Approaches to Residuals Management

For more than a decade, economists have advocated a more flexible and perhaps less expensive economic approach to pollution control. The two types of programs that have received the most attention are effluent charges and pollution rights. Effluent charges are taxes on the volume of effluent discharged per unit time. A pollution rights system involves the sale of marketable permits for the rights to discharge specified amounts of effluent in a given location per unit time (Freeman and Haveman, 1972; Kneese and Schultz, 1975). Both systems function by exerting pressure on firms through the profit motive.

The following hypothetical situation is presented to show how effluent charges function to achieve ambient environmental quality standards at minimum cost. Table 5-1 summarizes the quantity of emissions and marginal control costs of eight hypothetical firms discharging identical types of wastes (with identical impacts) into the natural environment. In order to achieve specified ambient environmental quality standards, a pollution control agency has calculated, the total waste emissions from all eight polluting firms must be reduced by one-third, to 1,600 pounds per day. The agency has three options to attain the necessary reductions. The agency can (1) require each firm to reduce emissions by one-third (uniform percentage), (2) require each firm to reduce emissions by an equal amount of 100 units (uniform reduction), or (3) establish an effluent charge system to attain the necessary reduction (Freeman et al., 1973).

Under the effluent charge system, each firm would be required to pay a cents-per-pound fee for the use of the natural environment to dilute and disperse its wastes. The critical element in this system is setting the charge at the proper level to obtain the necessary 800-pound reduction in emissions. At a charge higher than four cents per pound, firms 1, 4, 6, and 7 would find it cheaper to reduce emissions than to pay the continuing charges. They would invest in pollution control systems to the point where marginal costs would equal the charge. In this case, they would invest to the point of zero discharge. The total cleanup cost to these firms would be the quantity [(2¢ × 100) + (4¢ × 400) + (4¢ × 100) + (2¢ × 200)] or twenty-six dollars. Because their cleanup costs are higher, firms 2, 3, 5, and 8 would elect to pay the charge rather than clean up. The constant payments would provide a continuing incentive for these firms to continually search for least-cost methods of control and, for those that instituted controls, to keep them functioning properly (Freeman et al., 1973).

In contrast, uniform percentage and uniform reduction control strategies would cost more and would allow no freedom of choice to polluting firms. The cost of emissions controls, using a uniform percentage reduction system, would be the quantity [(1/3 × 100 × 2¢) + (1/3 × 200 × 5¢) . . .] or fifty-six dollars. The cost of controls, using a uniform reduction system, would be the quantity [(2¢ × 100) + (5¢ × 100) . . .] or forty-six dollars. An emissions charge system, on the other hand, can achieve a specified level of control automatically, in a flexible manner, and at a minimum cost (Freeman et al., 1973).

In addition, the effluent charge system would generate seventy-two dollars in revenues from the charge levied upon the remaining polluters. These revenues could be used to compensate for any ensuing damages and to finance the management effort. The damage and management costs would thereby be internalized to those creating the problems. Finally, pollution control agency management activities would be relatively simple, involving the setting and collecting of charges and periodic monitoring for compliance (CEQ, 1979a; Freeman et al., 1973).

The other alternative approach to pollution control involves a permit or marketable rights system. Once the maximum permissible total discharge of a pollutant is established, permits to discharge some fraction of this total would be sold or auctioned. The firms with the highest cleanup costs would be willing to pay the most to obtain permits to allow them to pollute. Those with lower costs would elect to clean up rather than purchase the costly permits. In such a manner, marketable permit systems could reduce discharges to a specified level in a cost-effective manner. In addition, the CEQ (1979a) stated that marketable permit systems have several advantages over effluent charge systems, including the fact that

- current legislation already requires discharge permits, although they are nonmarketable at present;
- under the permit approach, the total amount of pollution is fixed by the number of permits—only the price of pollution is controlled under effluent charges;
- a permit system can more easily accommodate economic growth without the deterioration of environmental quality. Under an effluent charge system, new firms could pay the charge, resulting in higher overall levels of pollution. Under the permit system, new firms must purchase the pollution rights from firms with lower cleanup costs.

Although these approaches hold considerable promise for improving the efficiency of pollution control, a number of concerns remain about their actual performance, including (CEQ, 1979a):

- the actual cost savings of the programs
- the ease of imposing sanctions on permit violators
- the actual variation in treatment costs among polluters
- equitable charges so that larger, richer firms will not be given a competitive edge
- the actual response of polluters to the charges
- the response to improper charges
- the adequacy of monitoring systems
- the purchase of marketable permits by industrial competitors to drive a firm out of business
- the possibility of conspiracy on the part of polluters to keep permit prices low

As mentioned in Chapter 1, these alternative economic approaches to residuals control are predicated on the theory that people have no natural right to clean water, land, and air. The air, land, and water quality rights are bought and sold as if the life-sustaining environment were a commodity to be allocated to the highest bidder. Economic efficiency is, indeed, a worthy goal. However, it must be tempered with a sense of fairness and social justice.

For these reasons, it may be prudent not to advocate sweeping reform of pollution control laws and policy. Sweeping reform would require tearing down and rebuilding much of the existing system, which would create uncertainties and delays as new laws and administrative procedures were implemented and tested in the courts. In addition, short of an absolute breakdown in the existing systems, the present political climate is not conducive to reforms of this nature. It is possible, however, to modify existing administrative structures and procedures to capture some of the economic efficiencies of effluent charges and marketable permits (Freeman, 1978).

There are several ways of combining these innovative approaches with existing pollution control programs. Examples include the Environmental Protection Agency's (EPA's) new waiver, offset, and bubble strategy policies for air quality management (discussed in the next chapter). Another alternative that seems promising involves the imposition of a graduated noncompliance fee for discharges above the levels permitted. Such a system would provide a discrete graduated penalty for noncompliance, would be relatively easy to implement and administer, and would provide incentives to minimize costs and stimulate innovation (although not so much as a pure effluent charge system) (Freeman, 1978).

Since taking office, the Reagan administration has frequently stated its intent to deregulate industry and provide incentives to clean up environmental pollution. There has even been speculation that the administration intends to reduce the EPA (beyond its already 50 percent reduction) and/or abandon the entire federal program of environmental regulation in favor of an incentive program (Pope, 1984). Vig and Kraft (1984) commented:

> Asserting that it could "do more with less," the Reagan Administration has radically diminished the institutional resources and capabilities for administering environmental programs. Sheet reductions in budgets and staffs have curtailed many functions, particularly in areas such as research, information gathering and dissemination, monitoring and enforcement. As many experienced officials have been displaced, talent and professional competence have been lost. The capacities for bringing environmental analysis and advice to bear on policy making throughout the government have atrophied. Finally, although many environmental responsibilities have been delegated to the states, these have not been accompanied by additional funding to support state environmental administration.

Such a policy change would penalize responsible municipalities and industries (that are cleaning or have cleaned up), favor the irresponsible (that have previously refused to control their pollution), and throw the door wide open to private influence and manipulation of the public trust. We have already, in the past four years, witnessed a long line of allegation, litigation, legislation, and resignation. Abandonment of the federal environmental regulation program would only accelerate the process. The long-term damage to professional management programs and the health, safety, and welfare of citizens could be significant.

Local Roles in Residuals Planning and Management

Local activities in residuals planning and management are, to a large extent, governed by state and federal rules, regulations, and incentives. These state and federal actions specify the overall goals and the administrative structures and procedures for residuals planning and management. Because residuals management problems tend to be regional in nature (air and watersheds), much of the management authority was given to regional planning commissions that were initially created in the 1960s to coordinate, review, and channel funding for regional planning activities. Local participation in regional agencies was generally through elected or appointed officials (Rowe et al., 1978).

In the 1970s the role of these regional agencies was expanded to include the monitoring and enforcement of federal and state pollution control regulations. Regional planning resulted in a higher level of sophistication and comprehensiveness in planning activities and allowed for the development of regional control strategies and facilities to manage pollution problems more efficiently and effectively. However, because of inadequate funding; the complexity of environmental problems, rules, and regulations; the lack of adequate management and enforcement tools on the regional level; and in many areas, the lack of cooperation from local or country governments, many regional agencies failed to plan properly for and to manage pollution problems. In many cases, the lack of experienced in-house planning personnel resulted in the hiring of engineering consultants who, for the most part, favored technical rather than socioeconomic solutions to pollution problems (Rowe et al., 1978). This management philosophy is changing as regional management agencies evolve and develop coordinated programs for land use, energy, and residuals management; as pollution problems continue and, in some cases (such as toxic waste), actually increase; and as proposed technical control solutions become prohibitively expensive.

As already indicated, the design and function of most regional programs are specified by state or federal governments. For the most part, regional planning and management activities are limited to monitoring and enforcement functions. Regional pollution control agencies, in general, monitor emissions and ambient concentrations of residuals to identify sources and areas in noncompliance with state and federal statutes. Initially, enforcement activities were limited to monitoring and reporting cleanup progress to state and federal pollution control agencies. However, as these agencies introduce flexibility into management procedures, regional agencies are becoming actively involved in designing and implementing programs and plans for residuals management. Some of the activities common to program design and implementation are as follows:

- Develop and adopt management goals and objectives. These should be commensurate with state and federal management goals and objectives. Public participation is essential on the type and nature of residuals, indicators, thresholds, etc.
- Gather information necessary for the management of residuals.
- Monitor emissions and ambient concentrations of residuals.
- Document to the fullest extent possible, the actual and/or theoretical ecological, health, or property damages resulting from improper disposal practices.
- Analyze and test management alternatives.
- Select the favored alternative(s).
- Program implementation—getting the authority, cooperation, support, and resources necessary for the program.
- Evaluate and adjust the program in reaction to internal problems or external changes in policy.
- Establish a continuous public information and participation program.

In developing a local management program, background materials and information should be obtained on federal and state management requirements and incentives; agency jurisdiction; cooperating agencies; program administration from within the home agency; state-of-the-art data on pollution control technologies, techniques, capabilities, and costs (from EPA); and the capabilities and management tools available to each cooperating local jurisdiction. These would include codes, ordinances, standards, capital improvements, public services, land use plans, and so on. All can be extremely useful in curbing pollution and waste management problems. For instance, an inventory of existing and planned land uses can provide the necessary input data for computer simulation of emissions location and dispersal. These simulations can be used in the siting of new emitters (such as power plants) to minimize air quality deterioration or to prevent toxic ambient concentrations of air pollutants (Rowe et al., 1978).

The management agency is also likely to engage in a program of monitoring emissions and ambient concentrations of residuals. Data on emissions sources, types, amounts, timing, spacing, dispersal, assimilation, decay, and avenues of accumulation are all helpful for proper management.

The methods of collecting information on the emissions of pollutants will differ considerably from city to city. Data on emissions can be obtained from the EPA, state management agencies, major offenders, building inspectors, fuel dealers, utility officials, traffic departments, citizens groups, or direct measurement of point and nonpoint sources. The EPA can furnish any number of reports on emissions from local and area sources of pollution such as residences, land fills, and construction sites (EPA, 1972; EPA, 1974a).

The purpose of pollution control is to protect health, property, and natural systems. Therefore, estimates of exposures, not emissions, are most important in defining pollution problems. Exposure estimates can be made by sampling and analyzing the chemical composition of the ambient environment. Great care should be exercised in designing the monitoring program to sample and analyze for the correct pollutants, in the locations and at the times that harmful exposures are likely to occur (Sewell, 1975).

The management agency may also want to gather information on the age and expected lifetime of sources of pollution to determine the applicability and timing of subsidy, tax (e.g., accelerated depreciation), and adjustment assistance programs (discussed in Chapter 8).

The pollution inventory can be extremely useful in reducing the cost and improving the efficiency of a residuals management program. For instance, an area that experiences ambient air pollution levels in excess of federal or state standards is called a "nonattainment area." More often than not there are only a few problem areas within the larger management district that are causing the entire area to be classified as a nonattainment area. The pollution inventory can locate the emission sources and dispersal factors creating the problems. Then management tools, such as emissions controls, emission density zoning (limits on emissions per unit area of land), or alternative control strategies, can be targeted to specific problems. Such procedures reduce the need for broad policies and controls that could be expensive, unnecessary, and unpopular.

The management agency should also fully document the actual and/or theoretical ecological, health, or property damages resulting from improper disposal of residuals. Field studies and interviews can be conducted to document actual or potential problems and public perceptions of their origins and significance. The agency may also want to consult the extensive scientific literature on ecological and health impacts of improper handling of residuals to help develop and build public support for their programs. Because management decisions may be detrimental to special economic interests (to the benefit of the general public), it is important that representatives on all sides of an issue are active and have access to decision-making processes.

Once the goals and objectives are established, and the origin and extent of problems are delineated, the management agency can formulate, analyze, and test management alternatives. Alternative approaches, tools, and techniques of prevention, control, and mitigation of impacts should be studied to determine which combination can achieve the goals with the minimal socioeconomic and environmental costs.

This often involves the development and testing of computer models, using basic systems concepts. These models serve a number of very useful purposes, including (1) providing an understanding of the dynamics of the existing system, (2) creating uniform data collection and analysis processes, and (3) analyzing the impacts of policy alternatives to assist in evaluation and formulation of program elements. A complete discussion of pollution modeling is beyond the scope of this work. However, considerable information on atmospheric and hydrological models can be obtained from the EPA (Metcalf and Eddy, Inc., 1971; Lager et al., 1976).

Residuals models vary from simple static models to complex interactive systems models that can simulate a wide variety of hydrological and meteorological conditions and can accommodate changes in residuals, sources, and discharges. Most models are based on the law of conservation of mass and can be simply stated as

$$Q_i = AO_i + AW_i - LA_i \pm LW_i$$

where Q_i = change in quantity of pollutant i in a carefully defined area
AO_i = quantity of i added from outside the area
AW_i = quantity of i added from within the area
LA_i = quantity of i moved out of the area
LW_i = quantity of i gained from or lost to decay, chemical reactions, etc., within the area

For example, the EPA has developed the AUTO-QUAL model, which can be run either as a steady-state or dynamic model, to estimate concentrations of persistent and degradable residuals in certain rivers and streams. The model calculates concentrations of residuals along a series of evenly dispersed points in the direction of water flow. Hydrologic flow variables are used to calculate the rate of residuals transport between points. Other models such as STORM and SWMM are available for analyzing runoff and hydrologic transport.

Diffusion models are also frequently used by air quality control agencies to estimate the ambient concentration of pollutants downwind from emission sources and to predict the ambient concentrations downwind from future sources. A model similar to the one just described is frequently employed to describe the three-dimensional diffusion of a pollutant. These "Gaussian plume" models can be integrated mathematically through time and summed for multiple emissions sources.

Another commonly used, empirically based dispersion model is the "box" model. In this model, the mixing depth of the atmosphere is roughly equivalent to the vertical extent of a plume, and the layer of air acts as a lid on a box causing pollution to be dispersed internally. Stated formally,

$$c_i = \frac{Q_i}{ud}$$

where c_i = ambient concentration of pollutant i
Q_i = amount of pollutant i emitted per unit time
u = average wind speed
d = mixing depth

Once the spatial distribution of pollutants in the ambient air has been calculated, the level of potential exposure of the general public to the potentially harmful pollutants is estimated. Such estimates should include the number of people and the frequency and duration of exposure. These measurements can then be compared with federal and state standards, which are commonly based on a one-, eight-, or twenty-four-hour period of exposure to harmful ambient levels of air pollution.

The models can then be used to calculate the changes in ambient air quality resulting from various pollution control actions. The hourly and daily variation in ambient pollution concentrations, the impact of spatially separating pollutants, and pollutant impacts on special or disadvantaged groups can also be calculated.

Once the most favorable control activities are selected, the overall program is developed and integrated with existing and future land use, resource management, and economic development plans. The program should be officially adopted by the agency, cooperating governments, and the appropriate state and federal agencies. The home agency should have contingency plans for adjusting the program in reaction to internal problems and successes and external changes in funding and policy. Perhaps the most important factors in agency success or failure are the cooperation of related agencies and the level of political and public support.

6 / Air and Water Quality Management

Air Quality Management

The atmosphere of the earth consists of 78.9 percent nitrogen, 20.94 percent oxygen, 0.95 percent argon, 0.03 percent carbon dioxide, and more than a dozen natural trace elements. Air pollution occurs when chemical, physical, or biological agents are injected into the atmosphere in concentrations high enough to damage property, ecological systems, and human health.

There are two major classifications of air pollution. Primary air pollutants are agents added directly to the atmosphere by human activities. Examples include particulates, hydrocarbons, sulfur oxides, nitrogen oxides, carbon oxides, trace metals, and any number of other chemical agents. Secondary pollutants are harmful chemicals formed in the atmosphere from reactions between primary pollutants and natural constituents of the air. Examples include certain aldehydes, ozone, and smog.

Although there are literally thousands of possible physical, chemical, and biological agents that can be transmitted through the atmosphere, only a few occur in sufficient amounts, concentrations, and toxicities to present a significant threat to life, property, and the natural environment. These pollutants are listed and generally characterized, and the sources are summarized, in Table 6-1. In 1975 transportation accounted for 54.5 percent of the emissions of major pollutants in the United States, followed by stationary fuel combustion at 16.9 percent, industry at 15.8 percent, agricultural burning at 7.3 percent, and solid waste disposal at 4.2 percent. The importance of transportation sources to the air quality of a region is apparent and should not be overlooked in a management plan (CEQ, 1975).

U.S. Air Pollution Control Policy

National Ambient Air Quality Standards

The Clean Air Act of 1970 and amendments of 1977 form the basis of air pollution control policy. The act and amendments direct the Environmental Protection Agency (EPA) to establish national ambient air

TABLE 6-1. Characteristics, Sources, and Health Impacts of Major Pollutants.

Pollutant	Characteristics	Sources	Health Effects
Carbon monoxide	Colorless, odorless, tasteless, toxic gas. Lighter than air.	Combustion and decay of organic matter. Automobiles and cigarette smoking.	Reduces O_2 carrying capacity of hemoglobin. Aggravates heart and lung diseases. May cause death from high exposure.
Carbon dioxide	Colorless, odorless, tasteless gas that traps heat.	Aerobic respiration. Fossil fuel combustion.	Famine from climate moderation.
Sulfur oxides	Heavy acrid, corrosive, toxic gas. Can form acids.	Coal and oil combustion, ore smelting, and volcanoes.	Respiratory system, skin, and eye irritation.
Nitrogen oxides	Yellow-brown irritating gas that can form acids.	High temperature combustion in automobiles, industrial processes, and power plants.	Irritates lungs and aggravates respiratory and heart diseases.
Hydrocarbons	Hydrogen/carbon molecules.	Incomplete combustion of fossil fuels in automobiles, industrial processes, and power plants.	Respiratory damage. Possible cancer from some types.
Inorganic particulates	Solid or liquid particles of inorganic matter in the air.	Combustion, industrial processes, soil disturbance and erosion.	Respiratory and heart diseases.
Organic particulates	Solid or liquid particles of organic matter in air.	Petroleum refining, chemical production, industrial processes, pest controls.	Skin, eye, and respiratory irritation, cancer.
Photochemical oxidants	Secondary pollutants such as smog and ozone.	Combinations of sunlight, hydrocarbons, and nitrogen oxides.	Respiratory system, eye, and skin irritations. Aggravates heart and respiratory diseases.

Radiation	Alpha, beta, and gamma radiation from unstable atomic nuclei.	Natural sources, power generation, nuclear weapons, medical treatments.	Cancer and somatic tissue damage. Genetic defects.
Heat	Long wavelength radiation.	Conversion of available to unavailable forms of energy to accomplish work.	Famine from climate modification.
Noise	Any unwanted sound.	Transportation, industry, construction.	Nervous disorders. Hearing damage.

Sources: Living in the Environment, 3rd ed., by G. Tyler Miller, Jr. Copyright 1979 by Wadsworth, Inc. Reprinted by permission of Wadsworth Publishing Co., Belmont CA 94002. Modifications from Council on Environmental Quality 1975, Environmental Quality; and from Environmental Quality Management, copyright 1975, pp. 165, 166. Adapted with permission of Prentice-Hall, Inc., Englewood Cliffs, N.J.

Table 6-2. The National Ambient Air Quality Standards (CEQ, 1980).

Pollutant	Period of Measurement	Primary Standard µg/m³	Primary Standard ppm	Secondary Standard µg/m³	Secondary Standard ppm
Particulates (TSP)	annual geometric mean	75	—	60	—
	1 day[1]	260	—	150	—
Sulfur oxides (SO$_x$)	annual arithmetic mean	80	0.03	—	—
	1 day[1]	365	0.14	—	—
	3 hours[1]	—	—	1300	0.5
Carbon monoxide (CO)	8 hours[1]	10,000	9	same	same
	1 hour[1,2]	40,000	35	same	same
Nitrogen dioxide (NO$_2$)	annual arithmetic mean	100	0.05	same	same
Ozone (O$_3$)	1 hour[1]	—	0.12	same	same
Hydrocarbons (HC) (nonmethane)	3 hours (6-9 AM)[3]	160	—	same	same
		—	0.24	—	same
Lead (Pb)	3 months	1.5	—	same	—

[1] not to be exceeded more than once a year.
[2] EPA has proposed a reduction of this standard to 29 mg/m³ (25 ppm).
[3] a non-health related standard used as a guide for ozone control.

quality standards (NAAQS) and to develop a program of emissions controls to meet those standards. The Clean Air Act directs the EPA administrator to establish primary NAAQS to protect public health, and secondary NAAQS to protect the public welfare from known or potential adverse effects of air pollution. Table 6-2 summarizes the current primary and secondary NAAQS.

The administration is also allowed to develop NAAQS for any additional pollutants that can be shown to be a threat to public health and welfare. For instance, the EPA is currently considering short-term NAAQS for nitrogen dioxide and sulfur dioxide. In addition, concerns about lung damage from "inhalable particulates" (less than 15 microns in diameter) has stimulated review of the existing particulate standard. The EPA is currently considering changing the standard or developing a separate standard for inhalable particulates (EPA, 1980b; CEQ, 1980).

The Clean Air Act also requires the development of state implementation plans (SIPs) to specify the steps to be followed within each state to comply with the primary NAAQS. States are permitted to adopt standards more stringent than the national standards if they choose to do so. All states have submitted SIPs to the EPA for approval. To date, three plans have been approved, thirteen conditionally approved, and only one (for South Dakota) disapproved (CEQ, 1980).

The 1977 amendments require that the states meet the primary NAAQS for sulfur oxides, nitrogen dioxides, and particulates by 1982. States that cannot achieve the carbon monoxide and ozone standards by 1987 were required to initiate an automobile inspection and maintenance (I/M) program by 1981 or 1982 (depending on the type of program) to control automobile-related sources of these pollutants. As of September 1980 only two of twenty-nine states requiring I/M programs (California and Kentucky) had failed to obtain the necessary authority to implement these programs. The EPA is considering limiting highway and sewage funding to these states. Seven of the I/M programs are currently functioning (CEQ, 1980).

Although the states were permitted to choose any approach to limiting emissions to comply with the NAAQS, all chose the regulation and enforcement strategy. In general, states issue permits to polluters that specify the reduction of emissions to a given level by a certain time. The SIPs also detail monitoring procedures and methods of enforcement to ensure compliance with the provisions of the permits (Freeman, 1978).

Critique of the Standards

By specifying that primary NAAQS be set to protect public health and that secondary NAAQS be established to protect public welfare, Congress rejected the notion of an optimal level of pollution and the tradeoffs involved. Thus, the system could be prone to administrative abuses resulting in unnecessary and expensive controls or in inadequate controls and failure to incorporate all impacts in a judicious weighing of tradeoffs.

For example, the standards are predicated on the assumption that threshold levels exist below which no health or welfare impacts occur. These standards were originally based on studies of the health effects of short-term exposures to high levels of pollution. In addition, these standards were set at a level to protect even the most sensitive people with a "margin of safety." One of the changes being discussed in the process of reauthorization of the Clean Air Act involves changing this criterion for protecting human life to significant health impacts (Arkell, 1981). This change could allow a substantial relaxation of existing standards.

Recent studies, however, have found significant health and ecological damage resulting from long-term exposures to low levels of air pollution (below the standards) and have been unable to verify the existence of a threshold of damage (Lave and Seskin, 1977). If no threshold exists, the primary and secondary standards are inconsistent with a literal interpretation of the purpose and intent of the Clean Air Act because even extremely low levels of air pollution have a detrimental impact on human health and welfare (Freeman, 1978).

Nonattainment Policies

The Clean Air Act forbids the expansion of existing industries or the construction of new industries that would add pollutants in a region where the NAAQS are being violated (a nonattainment area). To introduce some flexibility into these requirements, the EPA proposed and the 1977 amendments authorized a new set of rules to require new or expanded facilities in nonattainment areas to (1) control emissions using best available control technologies (regardless of cost) and (2) offset the additional emissions by reducing existing emissions in the region to achieve compliance with the levels specified in existing permits and plans (CEQ, 1979a; Freeman, 1978).

Under the offset policy, firms entering a region or wishing to expand are responsible for finding additional ways of reducing emissions from existing sources within that region. Thus, existing sources can "sell" emissions reductions to new or expanding sources. New or expanding sources would be willing to buy offsetting reductions as long as the price is less than the advantage or desire to locate in that region. Thus, those sources with the lowest control costs would undertake the largest reductions in emissions. Polluting firms would have incentives to find buyers and minimize control costs as long as any significant amount of pollution is emitted from their facilities (Freeman, 1978).

The EPA is currently considering a related incentive-based control approach, the transferable emissions reduction assessment (TERA) program to improve the ambient air quality conditions in nonattainment areas. The control agency would calculate the amount of emissions reduction necessary to meet the NAAQS in the nonattainment area. Every source of pollution in the region would then be required to reduce its emissions by an equal percentage. However, firms would be free to buy and sell emissions reductions from each other. Thus, those with the lowest cleanup costs would be paid by those with higher costs to reduce emissions. This system is very close in function to a marketable permit system in which a limited number of permits would be auctioned off to the highest bidders. The TERA program, however, has the advantage of directly compensating those who could clean up at least cost (CEQ, 1980).

Nondegradation Policies

As stated in the act, the purpose of the Clean Air Act is to protect and enhance the quality of U.S. air resources. To protect air quality in clean air regions, the EPA developed and Congress authorized regulations controlling the introduction of new sources of the criteria pollutants. The regulations define three general categories of clean air regions.

  Class I: Sensitive national park, wilderness, and other lands where air quality deterioration would have significant impacts. No deterioration of air quality is allowed.
  Class II: Areas where moderate deterioration of air quality would not be considered significant and therefore would be permitted.
  Class III: Areas where air quality could deteriorate to the level of secondary standards to permit concentrated development.

The 1977 amendments to the Clean Air Act designated the areas to be placed in Class I and placed all remaining lands in Class II. States are permitted to reclassify regions and place them in Class I or III (Freeman, 1978). As of 1984, few if any airsheds have been placed in Class III in the Pacific Northwest (EPA, May 18, 1984, personal communication).

Emission Standards

The Clean Air Act requires uniform national emissions standards, based on technical and cost factors, for all new sources of air pollution. However, the act permits differences between and within the states in emissions standards imposed on existing sources of air pollution (Freeman, 1978).

- New Source Performance Standards. The Clean Air Act and amendments require new sources of pollution to adhere to new source performance standards (NSPS), which are much more strict than those for existing sources. This is based on the premise that environmental quality will gradually be increased as existing sources become obsolete. This may, however, result in older plants being operated long past normal retirement to avoid the strict controls on new sources. The Council on Environmental Quality (CEQ) suggested that new sources be allowed to operate under less stringent controls if they can obtain an offset in reductions from other new or existing sources in the same area. Pollution could be reduced by the amount reduced under the NSPS approach, with some of the disincentive to introduce new sources eliminated.

- Control of Hazardous Substances. The EPA administrator is also authorized to establish emissions standards for pollutants that are clearly hazardous to human health. To date, seven substances have been listed: beryllium, asbestos, mercury, vinyl chloride, benzene, radionuclides, and arsenic. Emissions standards have been developed for all but the last three. In addition, several more pollutants are under consideration, including polycyclic organic matter, cadmium, ethylene dichloride, perchloroethane, methylchloroform, toluene, and tri-chloroethylene. In addition, the EPA is currently developing procedures for identifying and regulating airborne carcinogens.

- Economic Incentives and Emissions Controls. The EPA's "bubble" policy is a modest attempt to incorporate economic incentives into the existing regulatory framework for emissions controls. This policy allows a polluter to increase air emissions in one portion of a facility if it will reduce emissions elsewhere in the same facility. It is analogous to placing a bubble over an entire facility with pollution emanating from a single point. A plant can decrease emissions sources that are inexpensive to control in exchange for allowing an increase in emissions from sources that are expensive to control. Thus, total pollution from the plant remains constant while abatement costs are reduced. However, it is important to emphasize that (1) reductions in one type of pollution cannot be used to offset increases in another and (2) the concept cannot be used to delay compliance (CEQ, 1979a).

Using the bubble approach, the Armco Steel Company of Middleton, Ohio, has accomplished six times the required reduction in particulate pollution at only one-fourth the projected costs by planting trees and grass in the plant grounds, by paving or watering company roads, by watering outdoor piles of ore, and by establishing an employee ridesharing program. In another application, a utility in Providence, Rhode Island, has already saved $2.7 million by burning high sulfur oil at one plant and natural gas at another, eliminating the need for expensive low sulfur oil at both and resulting in a net reduction in sulfur dioxide emissions. Similar tradeoffs are planned for the U.S. Steel Corporation, Minnesota Mining and Manufacturing Company, DuPont Corporation, and Coors Brewing Company (*Science,* 1981).

Compliance with Ambient Air Quality and Emissions Standards

The frequency of violations of emissions and ambient air quality standards is an important indication of the location, nature, and degree of air pollution problems and the effectiveness of the management program in attaining its goals. Emissions data are particularly important for certain pollutants (such as ozone) that accumulate in the upper atmosphere and cannot be measured accurately from ground-level ambient air monitoring.

EPA estimates of U.S. human-made emissions of particulates, sulfur dioxide, volatile organic compounds, and carbon monoxide from 1970 to 1978 indicate that they have decreased 46.1 percent, 9.4 percent, 1.8 percent, and 0.5 percent, respectively. However, nitrogen oxides exhibited a 17.1 percent increase over the same period of time. The 46 percent improvement in total suspended particulates is attributed to utility, industrial boiler, and open-burning controls. The sulfur dioxide improvements are attributed to the use of lower sulfur fuels by utilities and smelter and sulfuric acid plant controls. Recent reductions by catalytic converters of emissions of volatile organic compounds from automobiles were nearly offset by increases in industrial emissions. Similarly, increased carbon monoxide emissions from increased automobile travel offset reductions resulting from open burning controls. Finally, the increase in nitrogen oxides is attributed to increased automobile travel (CEQ, 1980).

The problem of automobile emissions has been one of the most important and most difficult to deal with. The original Clean Air Act of 1970 required a 90 percent reduction in carbon monoxide and hydrocarbon automobile emissions by 1975 and a 90 percent reduction in nitrogen oxide emissions by 1976. However, because of pressure from Detroit, the EPA granted one-year extensions of these deadlines in 1973, 1974, 1975, and 1976. In the meantime, the Honda, Peugeot, Mercedes-Benz, and Volkswagen manufacturers managed to meet these standards (and improve gas mileage) (Miller, 1979).

Rather than alter engine design or use new types of engines (actions similar to those of the foreign manufacturers), Detroit chose the add-on approach. To control emissions, afterburners and catalytic converters were installed. In general, these systems were costly, reduced gas mileage, were difficult to maintain and repair, and were, therefore, often tampered with. The result was often increases in certain types of pollution per mile traveled. That is not the case today, however, and tampering with or removing these systems may actually decrease gas mileage as well as increase emissions. For this reason, vehicle I/M programs are essential in states not in compliance with the carbon monoxide and ozone primary ambient air pollution standards.

It is apparent that continued reductions in transportation emissions are warranted, from the standpoint of past performance and the fact that more than 50 percent of U.S. air pollution comes from transportation systems. The automobile continues to be one of the major sources of hydrocarbons, nitrogen oxides, and carbon monoxide in urban areas today. Despite the past record of Detroit in complying with federal air quality standards, proposals for reauthorization of the Clean Air Act include yet another attempt to relax automobile emissions standards (Arkill, 1981).

In addition to maintaining and strengthening emissions controls, greater emphasis needs to be placed on finding new fuels, redesigning engines, improving fuel efficiency, developing mass transit systems and alternative forms of transportation, and redesigning urban environments so that less automobile travel is available, affordable, or necessary.

It is important to contrast the performance of the automobile industry with the compliance record of other U.S. industries. In 1980 more than 27,000 major (emitting more than 100 tons of air pollution per year) stationary sources of air pollution existed in the United States. Table 6-3 summarizes the results of an EPA survey of nearly 6,000 major sources in 13 primary industries. Overall, more than 90 percent of these sources were in compliance with air pollution emissions limitations. Although these numbers are subject to reporting errors, it is apparent that the vast majority of U.S. industries are cooperating and adhering to pollution control regulations. This fact needs to be given greater emphasis in the media, and cooperating industries need to be acknowledged for their activities. The fact that so many are complying can be used to prompt those in violation of the standards (such as the integrated iron and steel industries with a dismal 13 percent compliance record) to comply.

Finally, an analysis by the CEQ of air quality data for counties within federal air pollution control regions in 1978 found that violations in the carbon monoxide and ozone standards were more frequent, widespread, and severe than violations for the particulates, sulfur oxides, and nitrogen oxides. Table 6-4 summarizes the percentages of counties monitoring for a particular pollutant that were in violation of the primary NAAQS for ten or more days of the year. As can be seen, the percentages of violations of the carbon monoxide and ozone standards are considerably greater than for the other pollutants.

Table 6-3. Compliance Status of Major Air Pollution Sources for Industry, 1980 (CEQ, 1980).

Industry	Sample Size	In Compliance (%)	In Violation (%)	Status Unknown (%)
Coal and Oil Power Plants	700	80	18	2
Integrated Iron and Steel	60	13	87	0
Other Iron and Steel	144	71	29	0
Primary Smelters	28	46	43	11
Pulp and Paper	475	87	11	2
Municipal Incinerators	72	83	17	0
Petroleum Refineries	214	79	18	3
Aluminum Reduction	49	76	24	0
Portland Cement	200	88	11	1
Sulfuric Acid	262	94	6	0
Phosphatic Fertilizers	69	90	7	3
Coal Cleaning	409	97	1	2
Grey Iron	433	88	10	2
Asphalt Concrete	2,862	96	2	2
Total	5,977	90	8	2

The Clean Air Act Under Fire

In his campaign for the presidency in 1980, Ronald Reagan made it clear that the Clean Air Act was a principal target of his deregulatory platform. After January 1981, the following draft proposals were leaked from the EPA to Congress, the news media, and environmental groups (Tobin, 1984):

- eliminate air quality standards
- set standards through the use of cost-benefit analysis alone
- eliminate sanctions against regions in noncompliance with air quality standards
- eliminate requirements for the maintenance of automobile pollution control devices
- relax automobile emissions standards
- allow the EPA greater discretion in enforcement of air quality laws
- allow pollution regions to assess their own cleanup programs

Table 6-4. Frequency of Violations of the National Ambient Air Quality Standards for Federal Air Quality Regions by County, 1978 (CEQ, 1980).

Percentage of Counties With Ten or More Days of Violations
Federal Region

Pollutant	1	2	3	4	5	6	7	8	9	10
carbon monoxide	55	21	8	23	28	11	31	53	19	67
photochemical oxidants	29	31	47	12	34	35	31	10	30	0
nitrogen dioxide	0	0	4	0	0	0	20	0	3	0
sulfur dioxide	10	0	1	0	3	0	0	7	7	0
particulates (TPS)	0	2	1	1	5	3	4	2	7	1

Region	States and Territories
1	Maine, N.H., Vt, Mass., R.I., Conn.
2	N.Y., N.J., Puerto Rico, Virgin Islands
3	Pa., Del., Md., Va., W. Va.
4	N.C., S.C., Ga., Fla., Ky., Tenn., Ala., Miss.
5	Ohio, Mich., Ind., Ill., Wis., Minn.
6	Ark., La., Okla., Tex., N. Mex.
7	Iowa, Mo., Nebr., Kans.
8	N. Dak., S. Dak., Mont., Wyo., Colo., Utah
9	Ariz., Nev., Calif., Hawaii
10	Idaho, Oreg., Wash., Alaska

Opposition to these proposals quickly developed from environmental groups and in Congress. A Harris poll (Harris, 1981) found that 80 percent of the respondents felt that the clean air standards were "just about right" or "not protective enough." Thus when the White House in 1981 issued to Congress even basic principles it would use to guide changes in the Clean Air Act, it had little support.

In December 1981 Representative John Dingell introduced HR 5252, a "moderate compromise" bill, in the House. The bill was supported by many business interests and the Reagan administration. Environmentalists, however, called it the "dirty air bill" and pointed out that it would (1) reduce automobile emissions standards, (2) extend the meeting of the NAAQS for eleven years, (3) allow greater air pollution in national parks and wilderness areas, and (4) provide no assistance to clean up acid rain problems (Tobin, 1984). The bill failed to emerge from the House Committee on Energy and Commerce in 1981 and 1982. A bill to effect several changes in the Clean Air Act that was before the Senate Committee on Environment and Public Works met a similar fate (Tobin, 1984).

In his State of the Union message in January 1983, President Reagan once again called for "a more responsible Clean Air Act." However, with a more liberal, Democratic Congress and with well-organized conservation and environmental groups ready to fight against weakening and for strengthening the Clean Air Act, the White House has done little to effect its proposed policy change as of 1984.

Air Quality in the United States

Trends in Ambient Air Quality

Overall, the ambient air quality of the United States is improving. The annual average concentrations of carbon monoxide, sulfur dioxide, and total suspended particulates decreased between 1973 and 1978, while ozone concentrations remained relatively constant (CEQ, 1980).

Air quality in major urban areas is also improving. A study of air quality in twenty-three urban areas of the United States concluded that between 1974 and 1978 the number of days in violation of NAAQS decreased 18 percent. Despite overall reductions, severe air quality problems continue to occur in several major metropolitan areas. For instance, in 1978 New York and Los Angeles experienced 174 and 206 days, respectively, in violation of NAAQS. Other cities, such as Chicago, Houston, and Kansas City, show signs of overall deterioration in air quality (CEQ, 1980).

Health Impacts: The Pollution Standards Index

The pollution standards index (PSI) was created as a means to establish and compare the significance of air pollution levels of the five criteria pollutants: sulfur oxides, nitrogen dioxide, carbon monoxide, ozone, and total suspended particulates. Table 6-5 describes PSI values in terms of pollutant concentrations and health effects. When the levels of all five pollutants are below their primary NAAQS (or the guideline value in the case of nitrogen oxides), the PSI values are between 0 and 99 and rated good (0 to 49) or moderate (50 to 99). As soon as the ambient concentration of one of the five criteria pollutants exceeds its NAAQS, the PSI value registers 100 or more. As more of the criteria pollutants exceed their NAAQS and as ambient concentrations rise, the PSI values increase proportionately (CEQ, 1980).

Data on the PSI values of twenty-three geographically diverse Standard Metropolitan Statistical Areas (SMSAs) from 1974 to 1978 indicate the improving air quality conditions in the United States. Figure 6-1 shows that between 1974 and 1978 the number of hazardous days

Table 6-5. Comparison of PSI Values, Pollutant Levels, and General Health Effects (EPA, 1976a).

PSI value	TSP (24 hr) µg/m³	SO₂ (24 hr) µg/m³	CO (8 hr) mg/m³	O₃ (1 hr) µg/m³	NO₂ (1 hr) µg/m³	Descriptor	Health Effects	Health Warning
400 and above	875 and above	2,000 and above	46.0 and above	1,000 and above	3,000 and above	Hazardous	Premature death of ill and elderly. Healthy people will experience adverse symptoms that affect their normal activity.	All persons should remain indoors, keeping windows and doors closed. All persons should minimize physical exertion and avoid traffic.
300–399	625–874	1,600–2,099	34.0–45.9	900–1,099	2,260–2,999	Hazardous	Premature onset of certain diseases in addition to significant aggravation of symptoms and decreased exercise tolerance in healthy persons.	Elderly and persons with existing diseases should stay indoors and avoid physical exertion. General population should avoid outdoor activity.
200–299	375–624	800–1,599	17.0–33.9	480–899	1,130–2,259	Very unhealthful	Significant aggravation of symptoms and decreased exercise tolerance in persons with heart or lung disease, with widespread symptoms in the healthy population.	Elderly and persons with existing heart or lung disease should stay indoors and reduce physical activity.
100–199	260–374	365–799	10.0–16.9	240–479	NR	Unhealthful	Mild aggravation of symptoms in susceptible persons, with irritation symptoms in the healthy population.	Persons with existing heart or respiratory ailments should reduce physical exertion and outdoor activity.
50–99	75*–259	80*–364	5.0–9.9	120–239	NR	Moderate		
0–49	0–74	0–79	0–4.9	0–119	NR	Good		

NR = No index values reported at concentration levels below those specified by "alert level" criteria.
*Annual primary NAAQS.

Air and Water Quality Management / 155

Figure 6-1. National Trends in Urban PSI Levels, 1974–1978 (for 23 metropolitan areas).

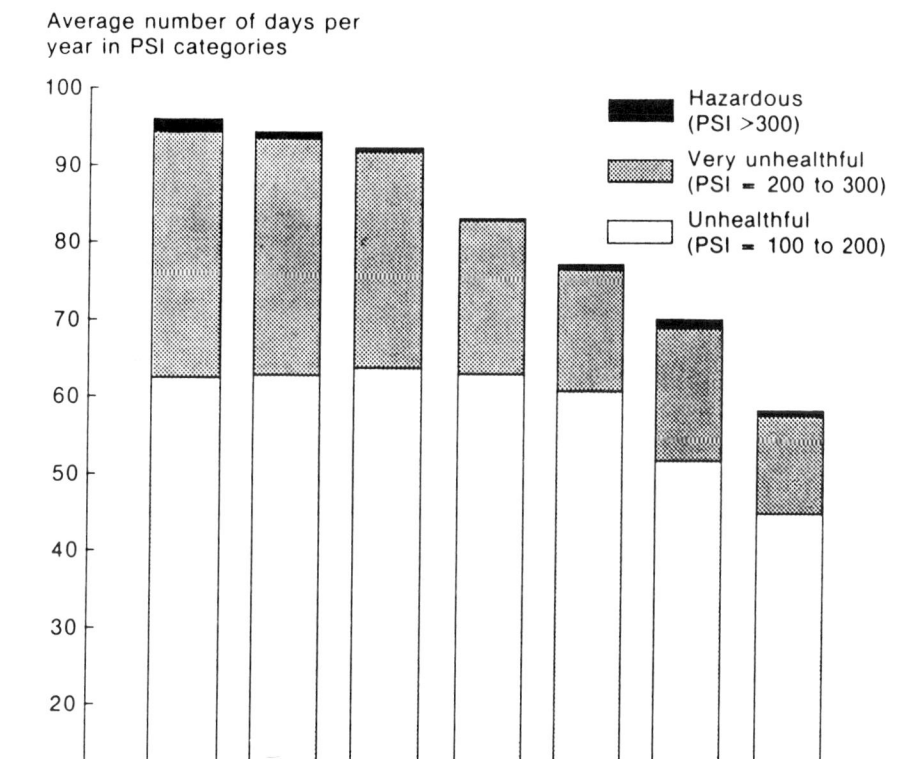

Average number of days per year in PSI categories

Hazardous (PSI >300)
Very unhealthful (PSI = 200 to 300)
Unhealthful (PSI = 100 to 200)

Source: Council on Environmental Quality

decreased 55 percent, the number of hazardous and very unhealthful days decreased 35 percent, and the total number of unhealthful, very unhealthful, or hazardous days decreased 18 percent (CEQ, 1980).

Table 6-6 summarizes and ranks forty SMSAs according to PSI data on the average number of hazardous, very unhealthful, and unhealthful days over a three-year period. The two largest SMSAs in the country, New York and Los Angeles, each averaged more than 200 unhealthful days per year.

Finally, by multiplying national PSI data by 1975 census data on county populations, an estimate of person-days of exposure to un-

Table 6-6. Ranking of 40 Standard Metropolitan Statistical Areas Using the PSI, 1976-78

Severity level (PSI > 100)	SMSA	"Unhealthful," "very unhealthful," and "hazardous" (PSI > 100) (Number of days) 3-yr avg	Min/max annual	"Very unhealthful" and "hazardous" (PSI > 200) 3-yr avg	Min/max annual
More than 150 days	Los Angeles	242	206-268	118	95-142
	New York	224	174-273	51	14-87
	Pittsburgh [a]	168	168	31	168
	San Bernardino Riverside-Ontario	167	145-182	88	68-108
100-150 days	Cleveland	145	60-230	35	17-52
	St. Louis	136	119-164	29	17-44
	Chicago	124	81-150	21	14-31
	Louisville	119	94-160	12	8-14
50-99 days	Washington, D.C.	97	70-147	8	3-15
	Phoenix [b]	84	75-93	10	5-14
	Philadelphia	82	79-87	9	7-10
	Seattle	82	62-95	4	2-5
	Salt Lake City	81	61-110	18	9-25
	Birmingham [b]	75	50-100	19	8-29
	Portland	75	70-81	3	2-5
	Houston	69	50-94	16	11-24
	Detroit	65	62-68	4	2-5
	Jersey City [b]	65	56-74	4	0-8
	Baltimore	60	32-79	12	2-25
	San Diego	52	38-74	6	4-9
25-49 days	Cincinnati	45	30-63	2	1-4
	Dayton	45	32-66	2	1-2
	Gary-Hammond East Chicago	36	27-50	8	1-16
	Indianapolis	36	17-49	2	1-3
	Milwaukee	33	32-34	6	3-8
	Buffalo	31	23-40	5	3-8
	San Francisco	30	22-45	1	0-1
	Kansas City	29	7-56	6	1-9
	Memphis	28	22-37	2	0-3
	Sacramento	28	19-38	2	0-3
	Allentown [a]	27	27	1	27
0-24 days	Toledo	24	15-32	2	1-5
	Dallas	22	6-35	1	1-2
	Tampa	12	5-19	1	0-2
	Akron [b]	10	5-14	0	0-0
	Norfolk [b]	9	9-9	0	0-0
	Syracuse	9	7-12	1	0-2
	Rochester	6	4-8	0	0-0
	Grand Rapids	5	2-8	0	0-1

[a] Based on 1 year of data only.
[b] Based on 2 years of data only.
Source: Council on Environmental Quality.

Air and Water Quality Management / 157

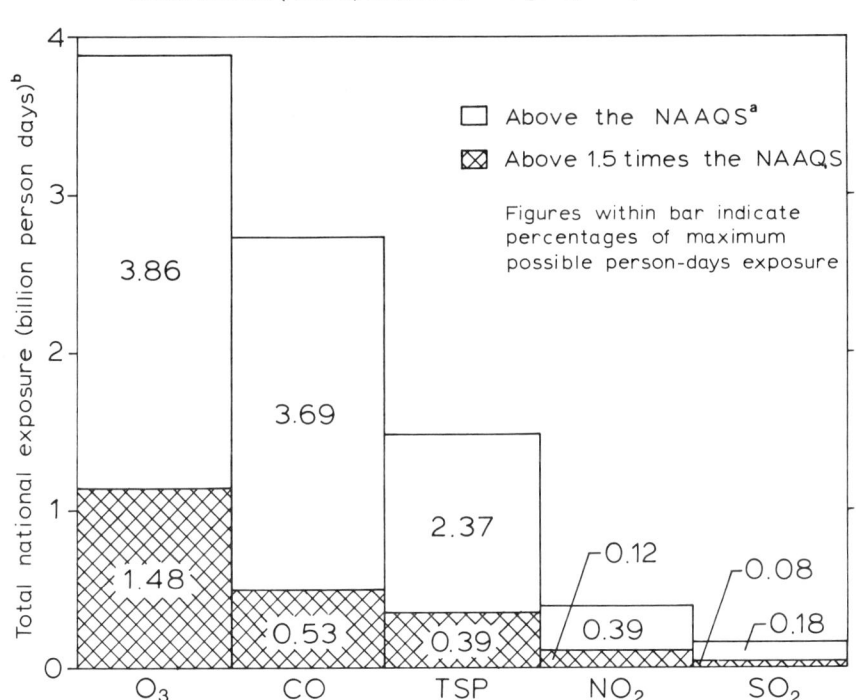

Figure 6-2. Estimated National Exposures to Pollutants Above the Short-Term Ambient Health Related (Primary) Standards, 1978 (CEQ, 1980).

[Bar chart: Total national exposure (billion person days)[b] vs pollutant]
- O_3: 3.86 (Above NAAQS[a]), 1.48 (Above 1.5 times NAAQS)
- CO: 3.69, 0.53
- TSP: 2.37, 0.39
- NO_2: 0.39, 0.12
- SO_2: 0.18, 0.08

Legend:
☐ Above the NAAQS[a]
☒ Above 1.5 times the NAAQS

Figures within bar indicate percentages of maximum possible person-days exposure

[a]NO_2 analysis based on exposures above 0.266 ppm (500 µg/m³).
[b]Maximum national exposure equals 76 billion person days.

Source: Based on U.S. Environmental Protection Agency data.

healthful or worse conditions is possible. Figure 6-2 presents an estimate of national exposures to pollutants above the primary NAAQS for 1978. The figure indicates that the most frequent exposures to unhealthful levels of air pollution were to ozone, carbon monoxide, and total suspended particulates. In 1978 there were nearly 2.9 billion person days of actual exposure to unhealthful ozone levels (approximately 3.9 percent of the maximum possible person-days of exposure) (CEQ, 1980).

These figures and tables indicate the usefulness of the PSI, not only for daily publication of the pollution levels and health impacts, but also for studies of local, regional, and national pollution trends, comparisons of relative pollution levels between regions, and calculations of public exposures to harmful levels of pollution. The PSI is rapidly becoming a valuable tool for public information and awareness and for use in the design and implementation of management programs.

Air Pollution Control

Air pollution control is one of the most difficult tasks of an environmental management agency. The variety of sources and types of air pollutants presents enormous legal and technical monitoring and control problems. For instance, the measurement of airborne residuals, often in parts per billion, requires sophisticated and expensive sampling equipment and the coordination of the activities of a large number of scientists, engineers, and technicians (Sewell, 1975).

If the throughput approach is used, a large number of options are available to manage airborne residuals:

- reduce the consumption of goods and services that generate large amounts of air pollution in their manufacture and use (e.g., improve the efficiency of transportation systems)
- use less-polluting fuels
- improve industrial efficiency and change to less-polluting industrial processes
- remove contaminants from materials inputs
- emissions controls
- use taller stacks to get above inversion layers and to increase dispersion
- use intermittent emissions controls to shut down or change fuels under unfavorable conditions
- spatially isolate and/or separate emitters to prevent toxic pollutant concentrations or exposure
- release chemicals into the air to reduce the production of secondary pollutants such as photochemical smog

It should be evident that several of these approaches are currently overlooked by air pollution control agencies. Industry tends to favor the tall stack approach, and pollution agencies tend to favor the more conventional emissions control approach. The following briefly describes and summarizes several technical emissions control options.

Particulate Control

Particulates consist of various sizes of particles and droplets of a wide variety of chemicals. The health effects of various particulates are a function of the type of material and the size of the particle. The smaller the particle, the greater the ability to remain suspended in the atmosphere and be inhaled into the lungs. Most natural particulate emissions consist of particles that are relatively large in size (greater than 10 microns, or 10 millionths of a meter). However, many man-made pollutants, such as smoke from cigarettes and fuel combustion, photochemical smog, and toxic metal dusts, contain proportionately more inhalable (less than 15 microns) and fine (less than 3 microns) particulates and represent substantially greater health hazards. For instance, automobile emissions, which contribute only 1 percent of the total atmospheric particulates, account for between 60 and 80 percent of all particles less than 2 microns in diameter. Although particulate emissions between 1970 and 1976 dropped 12 percent, the levels of the smallest particles (submicron particles) actually increased. To date, an economical, reliable system for the control of emissions of the smaller particles has not been developed (CEQ, 1979a and 1980).

As already indicated, control agencies tend to favor emissions control systems for airborne residuals. To control particulate emissions, a number of options are available (see Figure 6-3). These include:

- *afterburners*—Afterburners create a secondary combustion of gaseous or particulate pollutants in a hot chamber, commonly containing catalysts, beyond the primary combustion chamber.
- *settling chambers*—Settling chambers are enlargements in the exhaust stream from a primary combustion chamber that reduce the velocity of the exhaust stream (to less than 10 feet per second) to precipitate larger particles. Although settling chambers are inexpensive, they remove only particles greater than 40 microns in diameter.
- *cyclone precipitators*—Cyclone precipitators swirl exhaust gases through a funnellike chamber. Heavier particulates tend to cling to the sides, slow down, and drop into a lower bin. Cyclone precipitators remove 50 to 90 percent of large particulates, but very few of the particles less than 5 microns in diameter.
- *baghouse filters*—In baghouse filters, exhaust gases pass through fiber bags that can catch up to 99.9 percent of the particulates (the very smallest particles pass through) in a manner similar to that of a vacuum cleaner. To prevent clogging, bags must be periodically shaken to remove the accumulated materials. The systems are difficult to maintain, and corrosive materials can quickly destroy the expensive bag filters.
- *wet scrubbers*—In wet scrubbers, exhaust gases pass through a liquid or liquid spray to wash out or dissolve particles and gases. Approximately 99.5 percent of the particulates (excluding the smallest particles) and between 80 and 95 percent of sulfur dioxide are removed. The collected liquid is frequently toxic and corrosive and difficult to handle and dispose of safely.
- *electrostatic precipitators*—Electrostatic precipitators use electrostatic fields to charge particles that are subsequently attracted to electrodes and thereby removed. Approximately 99.5 percent of the particulates (excluding the smallest particles) are removed. However, the systems require considerable maintenance and col-

160

Figure 6-3. Techniques of Particulate Removal From Exhaust Gases of Industrial and Power Plants (Miller, 1979; Sewell, 1975).

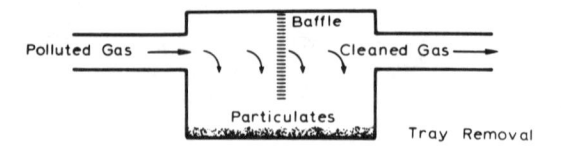

SETTLING CHAMBER

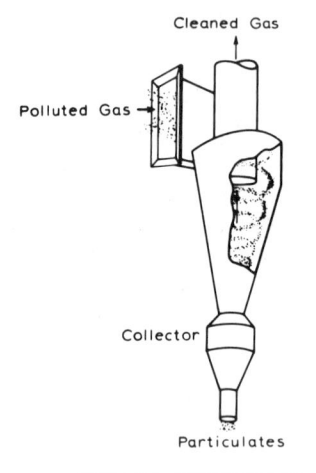

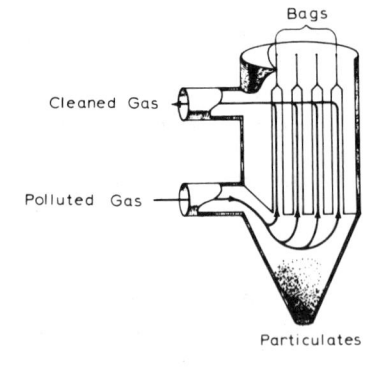

CYCLONE PRECIPITATOR

BAGHOUSE FILTER

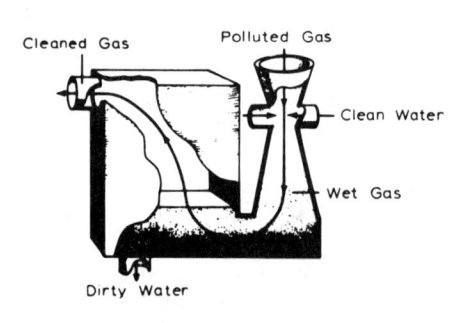

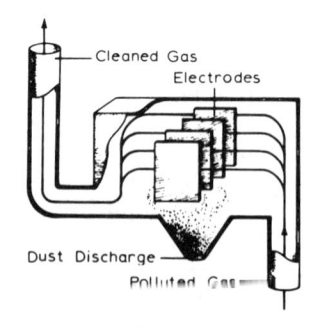

WET SCRUBBER

ELECTROSTATIC PRECIPITATOR

Sources: *Living in the Environment*, 3rd ed., by G. Tyler Miller Jr. Copyright 1979 by Wadsworth, Inc. Reprinted by permission of Wadsworth Publishing Co., Belmont CA 94002. Settling chamber from *Environmental Quality Management*, copyright 1975, p. 192. Adapted with permission of Prentice-Hall, Inc., Englewood Cliffs, N.J.

lector plate replacement and seldom operate to their design specifications.

It should be emphasized that none of these technologies can reduce the levels of fine particulates, the most toxic contaminants, in an efficient and cost-effective manner. All of the systems produce toxic sludges or solid wastes that must be handled and disposed of safely.

As discussed previously, current EPA rules and regulations allow offset of point, nonpoint, natural, and artificial particulate emissions from a given facility to reduce overall ambient particulate concentrations (regardless of size or toxicity). Landscaping, paving, erosion controls, watering, or other chemical and physical controls can be used to reduce the contributions of nonpoint and natural sources of particulates and offset the need for emissions controls of point sources. However, the EPA is expected to issue fine-particulate standards in the near future that would not allow the offset of small-particulate sources for large-particulate natural or nonpoint sources, so care should be taken in developing such a plan (CEQ, 1980).

Gaseous Pollution Control

The emissions control options for gaseous pollutants are few, relatively inefficient, and expensive. The three major options are afterburners for combustible gases, absorption, and adsorption. Absorption systems involve the pumping of gases through chemical or water sprays so that all the molecules of the gas come into contact with the liquid. The process is generally slow, energy consuming, and expensive (Sewell, 1975). In adsorption systems, gas molecules are exposed to adsorbent surfaces, such as those of activated carbon, silicates, aluminas, or special gels. The gas is later removed from the adsorbent, and the adsorbent is reused. The process is relatively inefficient and expensive (Sewell, 1975).

One new approach to controlling the emissions of nitrogen and sulfur oxides, called dry scrubbing, involves the injection of pulverized limestone or sodium bicarbonate into effluent streams or boilers. This and other techniques are rapidly developing and may prove particularly effective in areas of limited water for wet scrubbing (CEQ, 1979a).

The Acid Rain Controversy

A classic confrontation of some consequence to the energy and environmental future of the United States is currently raging over the control of sulfur oxide emissions from coal-fired industrial and electric power plants. Throughout the 1970s the EPA argued that flue gas desulfurization, or "scrubber" systems, is a technically feasible, reliable, and cost-effective method of sulfur dioxide emissions control. However, utilities and industries have resisted adoption of the technology, arguing that scrubbers are not technically feasible, reliable, or cost effective. Because they have been relatively successful in obtaining delays and variances, these utilities and industries have no real incentive to develop and install these systems (Freeman, 1978; CEQ, 1979a).

During the 1970s industries and utilities favored the tall smokestack approach as their most cost-effective solution to pollution. In the 1970s more than 425 tall stacks (more than 200 feet tall) were constructed in the United States, with utilities building more than 96 percent of the stacks taller than 500 feet. The resulting pollution dispersion and acid precipitation became a serious problem in Canada and the eastern United States by the end of the decade (Tobin, 1984).

In response to the problem, in the summer of 1980 the United States and Canada signed a Memorandum of Intent on Transboundary Air Pollution that called acid rain a "serious problem" and both parties agreed to "develop and implement policies, practices and technologies to combat acid precipitation's impact." The Reagan administration, however, developed a policy of "further study—no action." A subsequent report of the National Academy of Sciences (1981) concluded that "continued emissions of sulfur and nitrogen oxides at current or accelerated rates, in the face of clear evidence of serious hazard to human health and to the biosphere, will be extremely risky from a long-term economic standpoint as well as from the standpoint of biosphere protection." Despite this report the administration agreed in 1981 to increase the allowable sulfur dioxide emissions in thirteen states—an increase of more than 1 million tons per year (Tobin, 1984).

In May 1983 when William Ruckelshaus became EPA administrator, he indicated that acid rain would be a priority of his administration. To date, however, proposals to clean up, reduce emissions, and attempt to distribute control costs nationwide have failed to meet with White House approval.

One possible way of providing the necessary incentives for industry cleanup would involve the development of a sulfur dioxide charge system similar to the one first proposed in 1973 by the Nixon administration (Freeman, 1978). If they were paying sulfur oxide emissions taxes, industries and utilities would have little incentive to pressure the EPA for delaying tactics.

Water Quality Management

Water pollution is the presence in water of some contaminant that produces a change in its physical, chemical, or biological characteristics that can harm the health and welfare of living organisms or natural systems. Water pollution is not as difficult to control and manage as air pollution for three reasons (Freeman et al., 1973):

- *damages and costs*—Air pollution creates serious health and property damages that are difficult to avoid. Water pollution damages (primarily to aesthetics and recreation) are limited to areas and individuals in direct contact with polluted waters.
- *location of sources*—A polluter must have direct access to a body of water in order to use it for the dispersal of pollutants, whereas the air can be polluted from any geographical point. Thus the monitoring, detection, and collection of contaminated water is somewhat easier than that of air.
- *treatment*—It is difficult if not impossible to collect and treat discrete units of air or to augment its assimilative capacity. In contrast, water can be collected and treated, and its capacity to assimilate certain types of pollutants can be augmented.

Types and Sources of Water Pollution

Table 6-7 summarizes the major types, sources, and impacts of water pollutants. For management purposes, it is important to make the distinction between degradable and nondegradable types of water pollution. Nondegradable and slowly degradable (or persistent) pollutants, such as heavy metals, DDT, and polychlorinated biphenols (PCBs), remain toxic for long periods of time and, with continued releases, can accumulate, especially when concentrated or magnified by natural physical, chemical, and biological processes. These pollutants can be controlled either by preventing them from entering the environment or by waste treatment.

Degradable pollutants are residuals that are broken down rapidly by natural physical, chemical, and biological processes, as long as they are not in amounts that overload the natural system. Examples include oxygen-demanding wastes, disease-causing agents, and heat. These pollutants can be controlled by (1) preventing their entry into the environment, (2) removing them through waste treatment, (3) storing them until they are less toxic, and (4) timing and spatially separating sources of emissions to allow for sufficient natural degradation of the pollutants to prevent toxic accumulations and system overloads.

For the purposes of regulation, government agencies have divided water pollution emissions into those from point and nonpoint sources. Point sources of pollution are identifiable loci, such as pipes, culverts, or ditches. The most common examples include pipes or culverts from industrial and municipal sewage treatment plants. Nonpoint sources of pollution have no single identifiable outlet. Examples include atmospheric deposition of pollutants in the water, urban runoff from storm sewers and runoff from agricultural, mining, logging, and construction activities (CEQ, 1980).

Urban runoff can contain any number of pollutants, including suspended solids, oxygen-demanding wastes, organic chemicals, heavy

Table 6-7. Types, Sources, and Impacts of Water Pollution (CEQ, 1979a and 1980; Miller, 1979).

Pollutant	Sources	Impacts
Oxygen-demanding wastes.	Domestic, animal and industrial wastes; urban runoff.	Oxygen depletion from bacterial decomposition; foul odors, disruption of aquatic communities.
Disease-causing agents.	Bacteria and viruses from human and animal wastes.	Contagious diseases (i.e., cholera, typhoid fever, dysentery)
Inorganic acids, salts and toxic metals.	Industrial wastes; agricultural irrigation and chemicals/mining, road salts; auto emissions.	Chronic and acute toxicity to living organisms; loss of domestic use of water.
Organic chemicals.	Agricultural chemicals; industrial and domestic wastes; oil spills.	Chronic and acute toxicity to living organisms; foul odor and taste; loss of domestic use of water.
Nitrate and phosphate plant nutrients.	Human, animal and industrial wastes' agricultural runoff.	Eutrophication and oxygen depletion.
Sediments.	Soil erosion from construction, mining, agricultural and forestry activities.	Siltation of waterways; disruption of aquatic communities.
Radioactive substances.	Uranium mining and processing, weapons testing; nuclear power generation.	Somatic tissue damage (including cancer); genetic defects.
Heat.	Industrial and power plant cooling.	Oxygen depletion; disruption of aquatic communities.

metals, petroleum, bacteria, and nitrate and phosphate nutrients. In rural areas the most widespread source of nonpoint pollution is agricultural runoff, which can contain pesticides, fertilizers, oxygen-demanding wastes, pathogens, and dissolved solids (CEQ, 1980).

Sedimentation from topsoil erosion is the largest source of water pollution in the United States. Sediment from nonpoint sources contributes more than 360 times the quantity discharged from industrial and municipal point sources after treatment. Between 1.8 billion and 4.0 billion tons of sediment are washed into U.S. waterways annually, with more than half contributed by agriculture. In the past two centuries, nearly one-third of all agricultural topsoil in the United States has been lost to erosion (CEQ, 1976 and 1980; Miller, 1979; Pimentel et al., 1976). In addition, nitrate, phosphate, and oxygen-demanding wastes

Table 6-8. Thresholds Used in the CEQ Analysis of National Surface Water Quality (CEQ, 1980; EPA, 1976h).

Pollution Indicator	Symbol	EPA threshold level
Fecal coliform bacteria	FC	200 cells/100 ml [a]
Total phosphorus	TP	0.1 mg/l [b]
Dissolved oxygen	DO	5.0 mg/l [c]
Total cadmium	Cd	4.0 µg/l for soft water [d]
		10.0 µg/l for hard water [e]
Total lead	Pb	exp [(1.51 ln (hardness) − 3.37)] [f]
Total mercury	Hg	0.05 µg/l [g]

l = liter; ml = milliliter; mg = milligram; µg = microgram.

[a] EPA criteria level for "bathing waters." There is no uniform national standard for FC concentrations in water used for swimming; standards vary with use and locality. State standards sometimes differ from nationally recommended criteria.

[b] Value discussed by EPA for "prevention of plant nuisances in streams or other flowing waters not discharging directly to lakes or impoundments."

[c] EPA criteria level for "good fish populations."

[d] EPA criteria level for preservation of aquatic life less sensitive than cladocerans and salmonid fishes for water with $CaCO_3$ concentrations of up to 75 mg/l.

[e] Because the EPA Redbook criteria level for preservation of the less sensitive aquatic life for water with over 75 mg/l $CaCO_3$ concentration is 12 µg/l, CEQ has chosen to use the more stringent criteria level "for domestic water supply (health)."

[f] A 1979 EPA proposed criteria level for preservation of aquatic life.

[g] EPA criteria level for preservation of "freshwater aquatic life and wildlife."

from nonpoint sources, such as feedlots, landfills, and agricultural runoff, account for between five and six times the emissions from municipal and industrial point sources (CEQ, 1980).

Because federal water pollution control policy emphasizes controls of point sources of pollution, nonpoint sources of air and water pollution will become increasingly important as federal policy evolves. Given a policy switch to emphasize nonpoint sources of pollution, cleanup would become increasingly difficult and unconventional.

Water Quality in the United States

The quality of surface waters has not changed significantly in the last five years. This is viewed by control agencies as an accomplishment because the U.S. population and economy have grown during that time period. Data from the U.S. Geological Survey, however, indicate that water pollution from some conventional and toxic pollutants is still widespread. This is largely because emissions control systems for point sources take a long time to build, and pollution control agencies have just begun to tackle the problems involved in controlling nonpoint and toxic sources of water pollution. Of the nearly 6,000 sewage treatment projects begun since 1972, only 1,552 were completed by 1980 (CEQ, 1979a and 1980).

Figure 6-4. Violations of EPA Water Quality Criteria in 1978 (CEQ, 1979a).

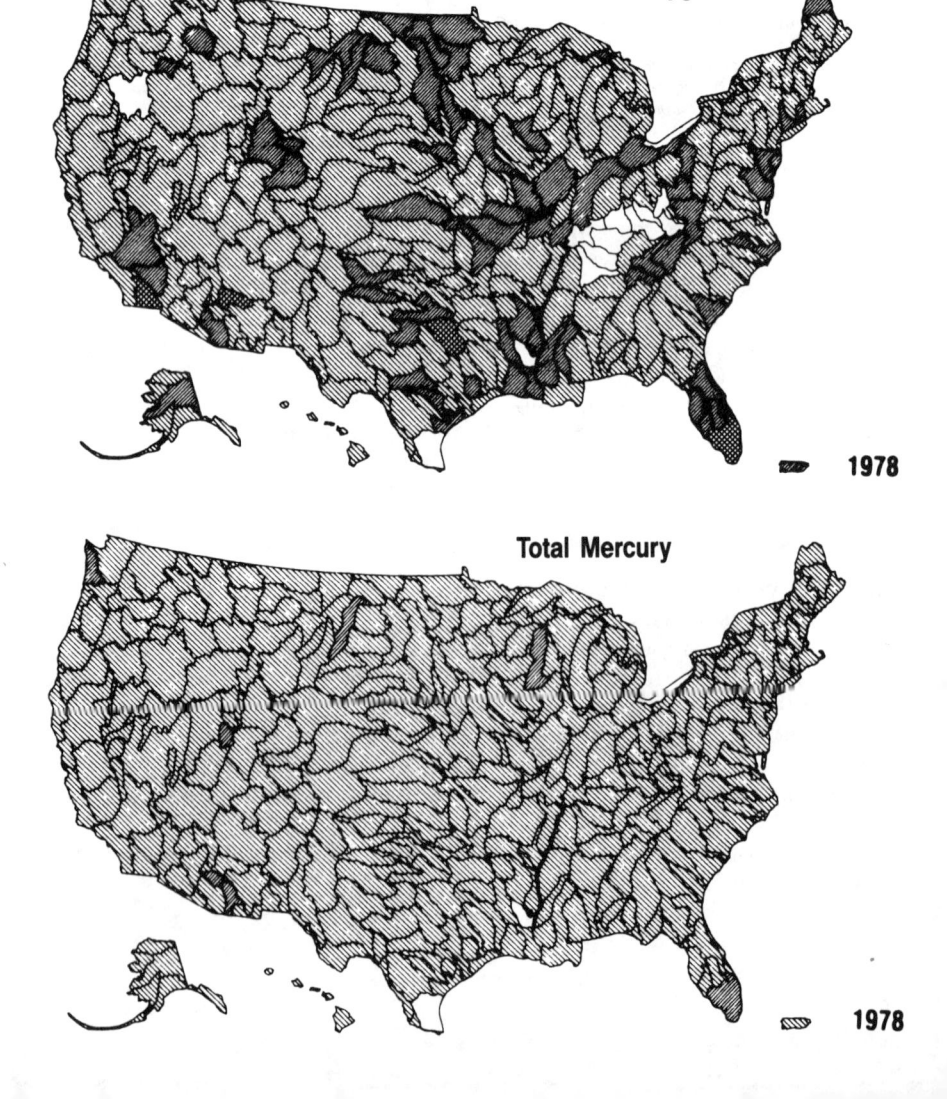

Total Lead

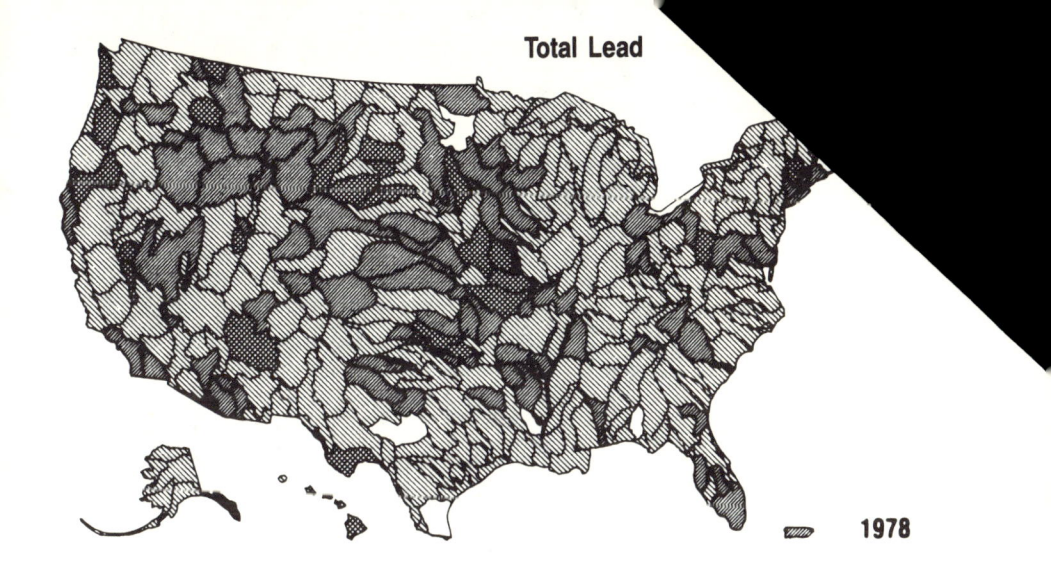

1978

Fecal Coliform Bacteria

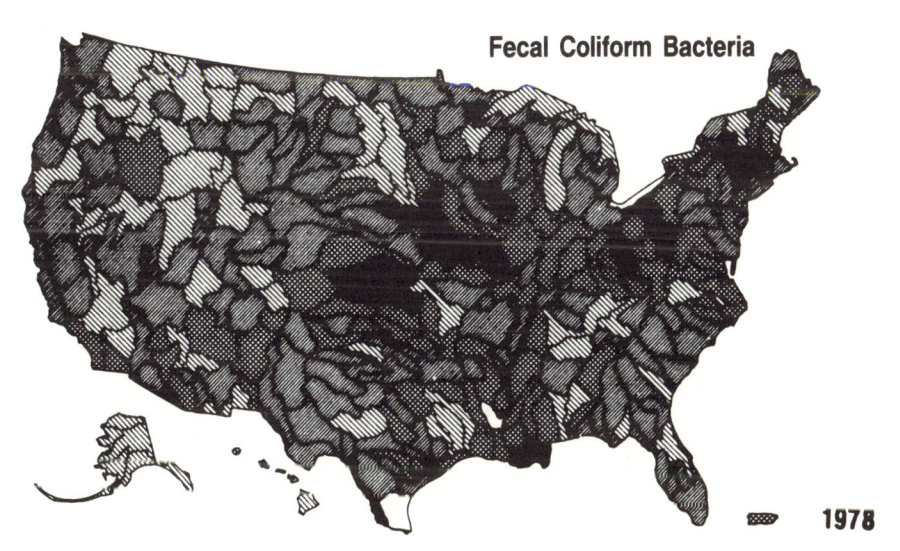

1978

Total Phosphorus

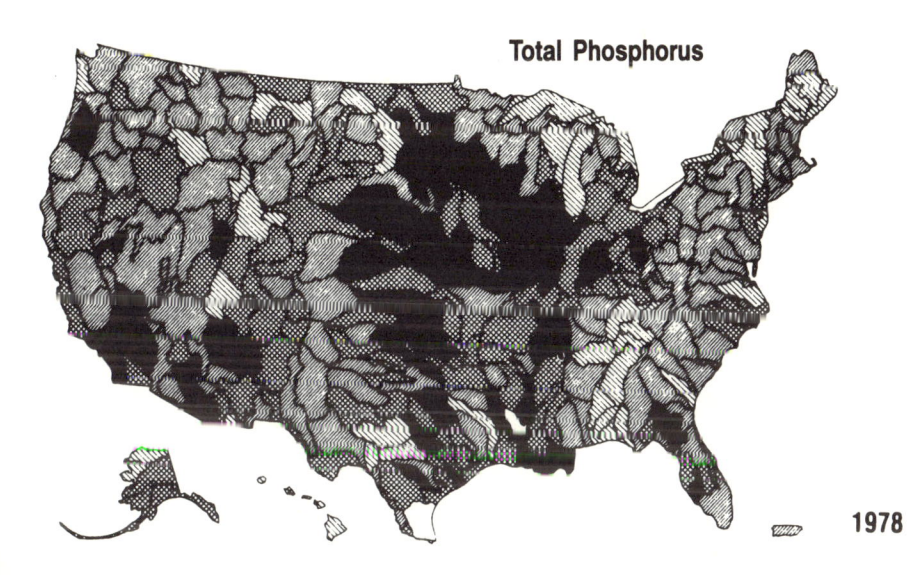

1978

Quality Management

...he EPA water quality criteria, for conventional water ... swimming and preservation of aquatic life. Figure ... EQ analysis of the annual violation rates (percentage ... exceeding the EPA water quality criteria). ...tion of fecal coliform in water is a common measure ... most frequently from domestic human wastes, urban ...d grazing areas. The fecal coliform count indicates ... disease-causing agents in the water. Although the national ...... n 1979 was approximately 90 cells per 100 milliliters (well below the 200 cells per 100 milliliters criterion), 35 percent of the samples taken exceeded the criterion. From 1975 to 1980 the only trend noted in fecal coliform levels was the improvement of the worst waters and the deterioration of the best (CEQ, 1980).

In 1979 phosphorus concentrations were slightly below the 0.1 milligrams per liter criterion, with nearly 50 percent of the samples in violation. In contrast, the dissolved oxygen criterion was violated in only 5 percent of the samples taken. Finally, the criteria for cadmium, lead, and mercury were violated in 10 percent, 25 percent, and 50 percent of the samples, respectively (CEQ, 1980).

Concern is growing, however, about water quality degradation from other toxic substances, such as pesticides, industrial solvents, organic chemicals, acid residuals, and other heavy metals. Thirty-five of thirty-seven states that made Clean Water Reports to Congress in 1978 indicated at least one problem with toxic substances in surface water. The most widely reported problems were toxic metal contamination and pesticide pollution, particularly in Texas, Louisiana, and Arkansas. More than half the states reported pollution problems from cyanides, phenols, PCBs, and other industrial chemicals. These problems may be considerably more widespread than indicated because large-scale monitoring programs for organic toxic pollutants were begun only recently (CEQ, 1980).

The most widely reported problem in a national survey of the water quality of lakes was cultural eutrophication or human-induced nutrient enrichment of lake water. The resulting algal blooms, fish kills, and dissolved oxygen depletion can significantly deter recreational use of lakes. Water quality problems moderately impaired 30 percent of the lakes for aesthetics, 24 percent of fishing, 20 percent for swimming, and 12 percent for boating (CEQ, 1980).

U.S. Water Pollution Control Policy

Control of Point Sources of Pollution

The 1972 Federal Water Pollution Control Act is one of the most comprehensive and controversial pieces of environmental legislation passed by Congress. The act set a goal of making all U.S. waters safe for swimming and aquatic life ("fishable-swimmable") by mid-1983 and called for the elimination of all discharges into navigable waters by 1985. The act also required the EPA to develop a national system of effluent standards and required all point source emitters of pollution to obtain a National Pollution Discharge Elimination (NPDES) permit issued by the EPA or an EPA-approved state agency. As of 1984, more than 64,000 NPDES permits have been issued (Ingram and Mann, 1984).

All municipalities were required to have secondary sewage treatment systems by 1977. All industries were required to use the best practicable technologies (BPT) of pollution control by 1977 and best available technologies (BAT) economically achievable by 1983. To assist in achieving these goals, Congress authorized $24.6 billion for water pollution control between 1972 and 1977, including $18 billion for grants to states for the construction of secondary sewage treatment systems.

In 1977 Congress amended the Clean Water Act. The 1977 act established three categories of water pollution: (1) toxic, (2) nonconventional (pesticides, metal compounds, etc., whose toxicity is not yet established), and (3) conventional, such as sediment, oxygen-demanding wastes, and plant nutrients. The act retained the controversial 1985 zero-discharge goal, but applied it only to toxic pollutants. The deadline for industrial installation of BAT for conventional pollutants was extended to 1984, and the BAT deadline for nonconventional pollutants was extended to mid-1987 with waivers allowed when costs exceed benefits. The deadline for toxic pollutant control was set for 1984 with no waivers allowed (Miller, 1979). The EPA is currently using engineering cost studies to develop BAT toxic pollutant control requirements for twenty-one primary industries, water quality criteria for sixty-five classes of toxic pollutants, new source performance standards, and a pretreatment program for industries dumping toxic wastes into publicly owned treatment works (POTWs) (CEQ, 1979a).

The EPA estimates that more than 87,000 primary industrial facilities use local sewage treatment plants to process their wastes. Toxic industrial pollutants can interfere with normal POTW operations, can cause disposal problems and prevent land application of sludge, or can contaminate receiving stream waters. The EPA's industrial pretreatment program was developed to prevent dumping of incompatible wastes into POTWs. Under this program, industries are required to develop strategies to treat wastes and render them nontoxic before they can be dumped into municipal systems. The EPA requires all larger municipal treatment facilities (more than 5 million gallons of sewage treated per day) to have an approved pretreatment program before complete federal funding is granted. Municipalities will be primarily responsible for enforcement of pretreatment requirements for industries within their jurisdiction (CEQ, 1979a). In addition, municipalities are required to establish a system of user charges to recover the costs of treating residuals from all domestic, commercial, and industrial wastes (Freeman et al., 1973).

Under the 1977 act, construction grants cannot be made unless the municipality demonstrates that innovative and alternative (I/A) wastewater treatment techniques have been fully evaluated. In addition, federal matching funds are increased from 75 to 85 percent for the use of I/A systems (CEQ, 1978b and 1980).

The EPA defines alternative technologies as proven methods of wastewater treatment that reclaim or reuse water, recycle wastewater constituents, or recover energy. Innovative techniques are defined as developed but not fully proven methods that advance the state of the art in wastewater treatment. As of March 1980 the EPA had made twenty-five innovative grants totaling $3.8 million and 188 alternative grants totaling $17.9 million. However, the program is currently suffering from delays in system planning and design and a general lack of funding (CEQ, 1980).

Compliance and Enforcement

The EPA's monitoring and enforcement programs have focused on major dischargers. Approximately 7,500 permit holders have been classified as major dischargers, although the criteria used were often the amount rather than the toxicity or potential harm of the discharges. To rectify this problem, the EPA is in the process of reclassifying all major and minor holders of permits, based on the amount, toxicity, and impact of discharges (CEQ, 1980).

In February 1980 the EPA estimated that 63 percent (2,317 of 3,688) of all major municipal treatment facilities violated the July 1, 1977, deadline for secondary treatment of domestic sewage or more stringent treatment of water to meet quality standards. In 1979 the EPA issued notices of violation of NPDES permits to 85 municipal and 64 nonmunicipal dischargers. Administrative orders were issued for 169 municipal and 347 nonmunicipal dischargers. Of 71 cases referred to the U.S. Department of Justice (10 were municipal dischargers), 52 were resolved, resulting in more than $7.5 million in fines and penalties (CEQ, 1980).

Control of Nonpoint Sources of Pollution

Section 208 of the 1972 Federal Water Pollution Control Act calls for the development and implementation of areawide waste treatment management plans (called "208 plans") specifically refers to nonpoint sources of water pollution. Section 208 assigns state and regional agencies the responsibility (including that for the issuance of NPDES permits) to coordinate the attack on point and nonpoint sources of pollution (CEQ, 1979a; Freeman, 1978).

In 1979 the EPA issued regulations governing the 208 planning process to promote both plan coordination with other environmental management programs and plan implementation, thereby making EPA funding contingent upon state-funded implementation (*Federal Register,* 1979). In recent years, however, state, regional, and local governments have seldom attempted to seriously analyze and manage nonpoint sources of pollution. The 208 plans are not binding and are frequently deficient in funding and data. The underlying causes of the problems are probably the lack of awareness of the seriousness of nonpoint pollution problems and the difficulties and political sensitivities (to land use planning) involved in nonpoint water pollution control (Ingram and Mann, 1984).

The 208 planning process could be an extremely valuable tool for the integration of water quality, land use, and environmental plans. Unfortunately, 208 planning (especially for nonpoint water pollution controls) is seldom used to its full potential.

A Policy Critique

The goal of zero discharge has been attacked as being (1) technically impossible, (2) uneconomical, because it does not consider the cost of controls, (3) unrealistic, because some wastes can be assimilated and degraded by natural systems without damage, and (4) ineffective, because it ignores nonpoint sources of pollution that contribute 92 percent of the suspended solids, 98 percent of the fecal coliform, 79 percent of the total nitrates, 53 percent of the total phosphates, and 37 percent of the oxygen-demanding wastes that enter U.S. waterways (National Commission on Water Quality, 1976). The zero-discharge goal may be justified for very toxic and persistent substances, such as plutonium, DDT, or PCBs. However, in most cases the costs of zero discharge would substantially exceed the benefit (Freeman, 1978).

The goal of making all streams fishable-swimmable also ignores the costs and benefits involved. A careful analysis and weighing of cleanup costs and benefits may reveal that cleaner streams are warranted in some cases and more polluted streams in other cases where costs are inordinately high. Similarly, technology-based emissions standards (BAT and BPT) offset to an extent the need for a case-by-case analysis and weighing of control costs and benefits. In addition, considerable ambiguity exists in defining just what "best practicable," "best available," and "reasonable costs" mean in terms of policy and technology. Finally, technology-based standards actually provide a disincentive to innovate because of the additional investments required throughout an industry when new control systems are developed. As a result, the EPA has been continually in the courts, fighting legal challenges from industry over pollution control objectives, emissions standards, and the extent to which the EPA should allow plant modifications, process changes, recycling, and materials recovery approaches (Freeman, 1978).

Under the current system, dischargers weigh the cost of possible fines against the remote possibility of detection and prosecution. Rather than burden the courts, an effluent charge system or noncompliance charges could easily be developed through the use of the existing NPDES permit system. Effluent charges have been used in Europe for years to control water pollution. For instance, effluent charges have been used to restore the water quality of the heavily industrialized Ruhr Valley in Germany. A cooperative association of management authorities, the Ruhrverband (formed in 1904), has used a system of effluent charges based on treatment costs, waste loads, and industry capabilities to clean up the Ruhr, recycle wastes, and pay for the abatement system (Kneese, 1966).

The 1977 clean water amendments authorized $24.5 billion in grants to be used between 1977 and 1982 to meet the secondary standards. However, these authorizations are small relative to estimated needs. The National Commission on Water Quality estimated that more than $39.2 billion (in 1976 dollars) would be required to meet the standards by 1985. An estimated $47.7 billion would also be required to rehabilitate existing facilities and to provide new collector and interceptor sewers. In addition, an estimated $262 billion would be necessary to separate combined sanitary waste and storm sewers and to control storm waters. The disparity between needs and authorizations would suggest that a substantial increase in funding is warranted (Freeman, 1978).

The lengthy planning and evaluation required to receive federal matching funds have resulted in delays in system design and grant applications, forcing the allocation of funds on a first-come, first-served basis rather than on the basis of need. Larger communities or communities with unusual treatment problems have been at a competitive disadvantage for funding.

Because the federal matching funds can be used only for capital costs of sewage treatment plant construction, municipalities tend to favor systems with high capital and low operating costs. The fact that local governments have to pay the operating costs has resulted in a number of operational deficiencies, including the use of unskilled personnel, lack of chemical supplies and the replacement parts, and a general lack of performance monitoring. For the past several years, inspection surveys by the EPA have revealed that approximately 50 percent of the facilities perform satisfactorily. The EPA is currently developing programs to upgrade facility administration, operation, and maintenance. One suggested solution would involve the expansion of the grant program to provide matching funds for system operation with improved performance monitoring (CEQ, 1980; Freeman, 1978).

As it currently exists, the grant program provides incentives to overbuild facility capacity to accommodate anticipated economic and

Table 6-9. Costs of Water Pollution Controls, 1970 to 1975 (CEQ, 1976).

Sector	Costs of Controls (Billions of Dollars)		
	Capital Investments	Operating Costs	Total Costs
Public	13.9	10.6	24.4
Private	5.3	8.2	13.5
Total	19.2	18.8	38.0

population growth in the service area. The tendency to use a twenty-year design for plants and a fifty-year design for interceptors means that considerable unused capacity exists for many years, tying up valuable resources for unproductive purposes (with state and local governments bearing only 25 percent of the financial burden and all of the future benefits). More work is needed to design facilities for incremental expansion when the service is needed (Freeman, 1978).

Finally, the requirement for secondary treatment systems, whether they are needed or not, reduces the flexibility and increases the costs of public water pollution control systems. Table 6-9 summarizes the costs of water pollution control for public and private facilities between 1970 and 1975. Although domestic wastes equal only 20 percent of the total, cleanup costs for the public sector are nearly double those of private firms. One reason for this disparity is that many private industries use public facilities for the treatment of their residuals. In many communities, more than half the wastes treated in public sewage treatment facilities originate from the private sector (CEQ, 1976).

Table 6-9 also indicates that between 1970 and 1975, capital expenditures exceeded operational costs for public water pollution control facilities, whereas the opposite was true for private facilities. Private firms were relying more on changes in operations and production processes than on capital outlays for treatment systems (CEQ, 1976).

The Battle for the Clean Water Act

Despite its desire to change certain provisions of the Clean Water Act, the Reagan administration has met with little success. As indicated previously, the administration has been preoccupied with changes in the Clean Air Act. One reason for this may be the results of a Harris poll published in 1982 that showed that an estimated 94 percent of U.S. citizens believed that the Clean Water Act should be left intact or made stricter (*Conservation Report*, 1982).

On May 28, 1982, EPA Administrator Gorsuch sent to Congress a list of what she termed minor changes of the Clean Water Act desired by the administration. These changes included (Ingram and Mann, 1984):

1. Making pretreatment standards optional for cities as long as the cities prohibited toxic discharges into municipal sewage systems;
2. Extending BAT deadlines for industrial treatment of toxic pollutants, BPT deadlines for nontoxic industrial pollutants, and EPA effluent guidelines until 1988;
3. Extending the term of an NPDES permit from five to ten years;
4. Giving the EPA administrator more discretion in levying noncompliance penalties, and exempting dams and military facilities from water pollution requirements.

The proposed amendments failed to pass the Congress in 1982, and the Clean Water Act remains relatively unchanged today. Perhaps the most serious threat to water quality control programs by the Reagan administration is the reduction in funding of EPA water quality control programs: Between 1981 and 1983 EPA funding for these programs was reduced by 40 percent. In addition, the 1984 federal budget request proposes a 55 percent reduction in water pollution grants to the states (Ingram and Mann, 1984). If these program reductions are realized, state, regional, and local officials will be saddled with the multiple problems of public health concerns, strict federal mandates, severe noncompliance penalties, a chronically deteriorating federal system, a lack of funding, and a diminished capability to monitor and enforce. With the appointment of EPA Administrator Ruckelshaus, perhaps these policies can be reversed.

Water Quality Planning and Management

Aside from the construction of municipal water treatment facilities, very little water quality planning and management has occurred. The HUD 701 planning grants program that provided funding to local governments for comprehensive planning studies gave some support for integrating water resource, water quality, and water service considerations into land use planning activities (EPA, 1974b). In practice, however, this opportunity was largely ignored, and more recently the program has been discontinued.

The EPA's guidelines for water quality management and the A-95 review process are also important vehicles for the development of areawide water, land use, and economic development programs. "A-95" refers to the OMB's (1976) Circular A-95, which established an areawide review of proposals for federal funding from local jurisdictions for consistency with established areawide planning goals and guidelines.

A-95 review (now termed "intergovernmental program review") has proved to be a very useful tool for areawide water resource planning and management. To a certain extent this program has drawn water quality planning and management away from the narrow focus of conventional local water and sewer departments toward more integrated areawide multipurpose planning. These local, single-purpose departments have traditionally been plagued with a number of problems, including a lack of adequate funding, emphasis on structural solutions to problems, and a hesitancy to change. This last problem generally results from a lack of funding for planning and innovation, the tremendous public investments involved, concerns about public health and safety, and a considerable amount of jurisdictional fragmentation and political uncertainty (EPA, 1974b).

Water resource and water quality planning are important elements in areawide or metropolitan plans. Water quality problems are closely related to air quality, solid waste disposal, and land use considerations. Figure 6-5 summarizes the major elements and issues involved in the development of a water quality management program. At minimum a metropolitan or areawide water quality management plan should consist of the following elements (Berdine and Mariar, 1972):

- *water quality analysis*—standards, water quality, uses, assimilation capacities, problems, probable and achieved water quality levels,
- *wastewater source analysis*—nonpoint and municipal and industrial point sources,
- *existing facilities analysis*—municipal facilities, institutional programs and controls, septic tank use,
- *social, economic, and land use analysis*—demography, economics, land use, and land use planning and controls,
- *planning criteria*—cost-effectiveness criteria; economic impact criteria, federal, state, and local requirements and programs,
- *political and administrative analysis*—existing service areas, agencies, programs, and regulatory powers,
- *resource capability analysis*—federal and state grants, local charges and revenues, implementation schedule,
- *alternatives analysis*—treatment levels, reclamation and reuse, land use control, tradeoff and optimization models,
- *water quality management strategy*—institutions, goals, priorities, alternatives, contingencies, controls, impacts, etc.

Water Pollution Control

Nonpoint Sources

There are many techniques of reducing pollution from nonpoint sources. Because sedimentation is the most serious nonpoint water pollution

Figure 6-5. Water Quality Management System (EPA, 1974a).

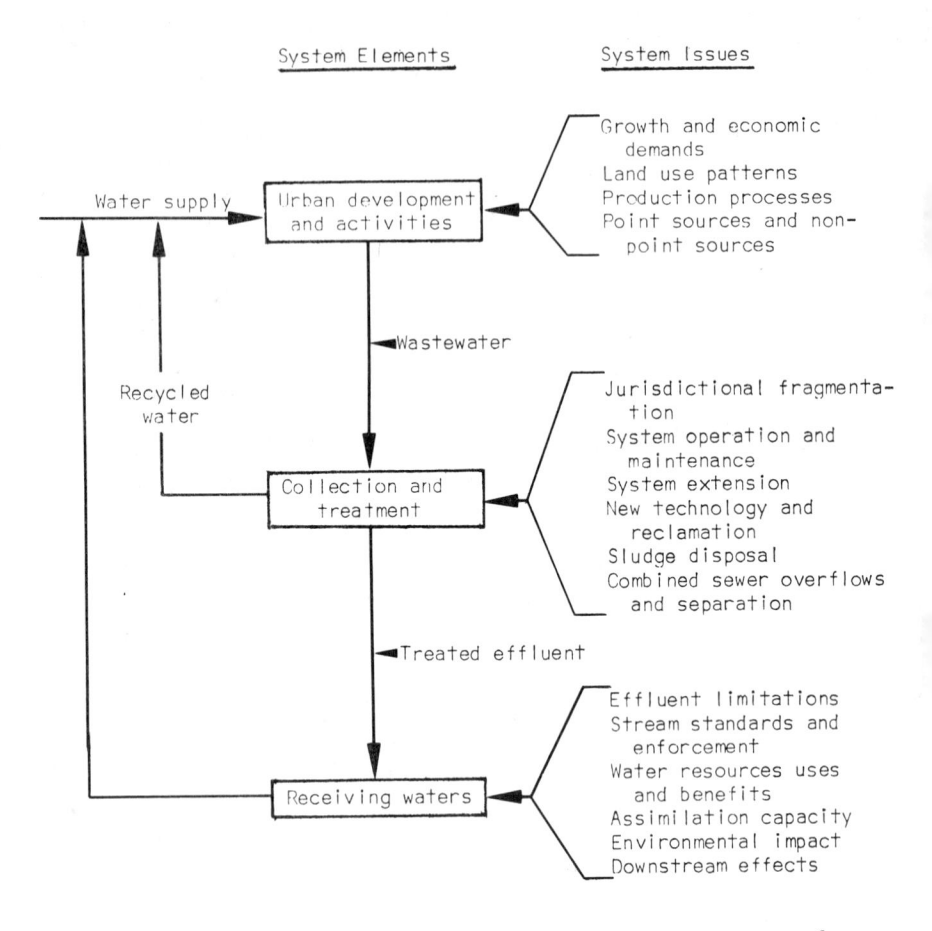

```
             System Elements              System Issues

                                          ┌ Growth and economic
                                          │   demands
                                          │ Land use patterns
  Water supply   ┌─────────────────┐◄─────┤ Production processes
 ───────────────►│ Urban development│     │ Point sources and non-
      ▲    ▲     │  and activities │     └   point sources
      │    │     └─────────────────┘
      │    │              │
      │    │         ◄────── Wastewater
      │    │              │
      │ Recycled           │                ┌ Jurisdictional fragmenta-
      │  water             │                │    tion
      │                    ▼                │ System operation and
      │         ┌─────────────────┐         │    maintenance
      │         │  Collection and │◄────────┤ System extension
      │         │    treatment    │         │ New technology and
      │         └─────────────────┘         │    reclamation
      │                  │                  │ Sludge disposal
      │             ◄────── Treated effluent│ Combined sewer overflows
      │                  │                  └    and separation
      │                  ▼
      │         ┌─────────────────┐         ┌ Effluent limitations
      │         │ Receiving waters│◄────────┤ Stream standards and
      └─────────└─────────────────┘         │    enforcement
                                            │ Water resources uses
                                            │    and benefits
                                            │ Assimilation capacity
                                            │ Environmental impact
                                            └ Downstream effects
```

problem, soil conservation is the most important management focus. In addition, soil conservation practices can reduce particulate air pollution and can help in maintaining the fertility of the land. Soil erosion can be controlled in a number of ways, including (CEQ, 1979; Miller, 1979):

- *stream bank protection*—preservation or planting of native vegetation along waterways can reduce water pollution from runoff. The vegetation filters debris and sediment in runoff, provides wildlife habitat and shade, and the roots bind and hold the soil layers. If vegetative disturbances are minimized within one hundred feet of a waterway, soil erosion problems can be reduced.
- *reduced tillage farming*—planting without removing the existing plant cover (including previous crop residues) can reduce soil

erosion by 95 percent. Shallow plowing and the retention of crop residues and ground litter can also reduce soil erosion.
- *contour and strip cropping*—plowing along the contours of the land can reduce soil erosion by 50 percent. Alternating strips of close-growing crops (e.g., clover) with regular crops can, in conjunction with contour plowing, reduce soil erosion by 75 percent.
- *crop rotation and cover crops*—periodic planting with dense cover crops in rotation or when no crop is being grown can reduce soil erosion.
- *terracing*—building steplike terraces on steep slopes can reduce erosion.
- *windbreaks*—planted windbreaks can reduce wind erosion of soil.
- *land classification*—classifying and allocating land according to its soil suitability for cultivation and construction activities reduces erosion.

Other nonpoint water pollution problems, such as nutrient loading or pesticide contamination, can be minimized by proper timing and application of fertilizer and insecticides. Information on local problems and capabilities can be obtained from the Soil Conservation Service or the nearest office of the U.S. Department of Agriculture.

Point Source Controls

The control of point sources of water pollution strongly depends on the nature and degree of water pollution. Municipal sewage treatment facilities generally employ any number of physical, chemical, and biological processes to remove pollutants from water. Municipal sewage treatment is traditionally broken into three stages: primary, secondary, and tertiary sewage treatment (see Figure 6-6 and Table 6-10).

Primary, or mechanical, sewage treatment involves the use of screens to filter out large debris, a grit chamber where the rate of water flow is decreased to allow the settling of heavier suspended particles, and a sedimentation tank where suspended solids settle out and floating materials are skimmed off the surface. Chemicals can be added to the sedimentation tank to speed up the settling process for suspended matter and bacteria. Depending on the system, primary sewage treatment removes between 50 and 60 percent of the suspended solids and between 30 and 50 percent of the biochemical oxygen demand of the effluent stream (Sewell, 1975).

Secondary sewage treatment traditionally involves bacterial digestion of oxygen-demanding wastes, followed by sedimentation. Bacterial decomposition is accomplished through the use of trickling filter or activated sludge systems. A trickling filter is a large bed of crushed

178 / Air and Water Quality Management

Figure 6-6. Design of a "Typical" Primary, Secondary, and Tertiary Sewage Treatment Plant (modified from Griggs and Gilchrist, 1983).

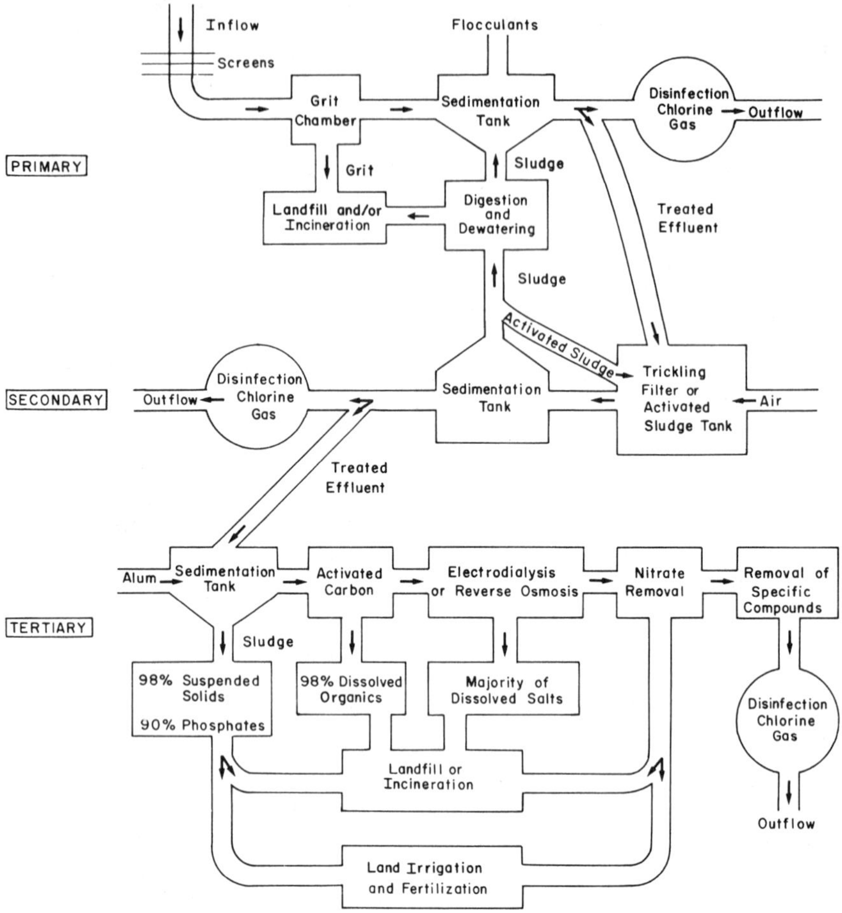

Source: Griggs, Gary B., and John A. Gilchrist. *Geologic Hazards, Resources, and Environmental Planning*, 2nd ed. © 1983 by Wadsworth Inc. Reprinted by permission of Wadsworth Publishing Co., Belmont CA 94002.

stone, gravel, or slag that is coated by a transparent film of microbes. As effluent waters are continuously or periodically sprayed over the beds, the microbes break down the oxygen-demanding wastes and the beds remove some of the suspended solids (Sewell, 1975).

Activated sludge systems "seed" the effluent with microbe-laden sludge, then circulate the mixture for four to six hours in an aerated tank. The microbe community of bacteria, algae, protozoa, and metazoa rapidly oxidize the organic material in the effluent. After the aeration process, the effluent (plus sludge) passes into a sedimentation tank,

Table 6-10. Sewage Treatment Processes and Their Impacts (Chanlett, 1973).

Treatment Action	Process	Sewage Constituent Affected	Cumulative Percentage Removed	Sequential Step Required
Sedimentation	Primary settling	Settleable solids BOD Bacterial count	35–65 25–40 50–60	Sludge digestion, dewatering, and final disposal
Bio-oxidation: each process listed here has been preceded by primary settling	High-rate "trickling filters"	Settleable solids BOD Bacterial count	70–90 65–95 70–95	Secondary settling and digestion, dewatering, and final disposal of the additional sludge
	Activated sludge	Settleable solids BOD Bacterial counts	90–95 85–95 90–95	Secondary settling, thickening, digestion, dewatering, and final disposal
	Intermittent sand filters	Settleable solids BOD Bacterial counts	90–95 85–95 95 and over	None
Disinfection	Chlorination of settled sewage	Settleable solids BOD Bacterial count	35–65 in primary settling 25–40 in primary settling 90–95	None

Source: E. T. Chanlett, Environmental Protection. New York: McGraw-Hill, 1973, p. 151.

where some of the sludge is removed and returned to the aeration tank to activate more raw sewage. It should be emphasized that the biological processes of trickling filter and activated sludge systems are very sensitive to industrial effluents that contain chemicals toxic to the microbial communities.

The sludge from the primary and secondary sedimentation tanks is normally dewatered (with the slurry returned to the incoming wastewater) and digested under alkaline conditions at a temperature of approximately 100°F. Methane, produced by the digestion, is commonly used to heat the process. The digested sludge is commonly dried in drying beds or vacuum filters, then incinerated or disposed of in a landfill (Sewell, 1975).

Primary and secondary sewage treatment removes 85 to 90 percent of the oxygen-demanding wastes, 90 percent of the suspended solids, 50 percent of the nitrogen (leaving mostly nitrates), 30 percent of the phosphorus (leaving mostly phosphates), only 5 percent of the dissolved salts (including toxic metals such as lead and mercury), none of the long-lived radioactive isotopes, and none of the dissolved persistent organic substances such as pesticides (Miller, 1979). In 1977 approximately 50 percent of U.S. sewage was receiving combined primary and secondary sewage treatment, and approximately 25 percent was receiving primary alone (CEQ, 1977).

Tertiary, or advanced, treatment systems are designed to remove many of the remaining materials. Phosphorus compounds and suspended solids can be removed by precipitation. Dissolved organic materials can be removed through the use of activated carbon adsorption processes. Dissolved salts can be removed by electrodialysis or reverse osmosis. These advanced systems are still in the experimental stage of development, are fairly rare, and are prohibitively expensive (twice as expensive to build and four times as expensive to operate as primary and secondary sewage facilities). However, the water emanating from a tertiary system is essentially pure.

Before the treated water is discharged from primary, secondary, or tertiary systems, it is commonly brought into contact with chlorine gas or liquid to remove water coloration and to kill the remaining virulent bacteria and some viruses. A retention time of ten to sixty minutes is sufficient to kill most bacteria, but four hours or more contact can be needed to kill viruses such as those causing infectious hepatitis (Sewell, 1975).

If properly sited, designed, and built, septic tanks can provide a safe and efficient means of sewage treatment. Septic tanks are large steel or concrete containers that hold sewage under anaerobic conditions for at least twenty-four hours and then pass the liquid into a porous drainage or leach field (see Figure 6-7). The undigested solids that collect in the tank should be periodically removed and treated as sludge, but homeowners rarely go to the expense and trouble of having

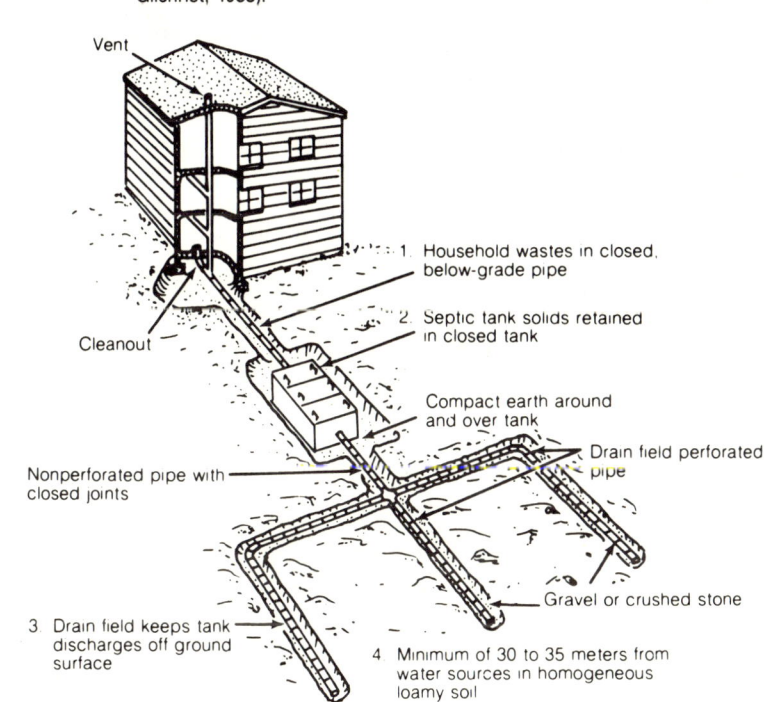

Figure 6-7. The Design of a "Typical" Septic System (modified from Griggs and Gilchrist, 1983).

1. Household wastes in closed, below-grade pipe
2. Septic tank solids retained in closed tank
Cleanout
Compact earth around and over tank
Nonperforated pipe with closed joints
Drain field perforated pipe
Gravel or crushed stone
3. Drain field keeps tank discharges off ground surface
4. Minimum of 30 to 35 meters from water sources in homogeneous loamy soil

Source: Griggs, Gary B., and John A. Gilchrist. *Geologic Hazards, Resources, and Environmental Planning*, 2nd ed. © 1983 by Wadsworth Inc. Reprinted by permission of Wadsworth Publishing Co., Belmont CA 94002.

their tanks pumped. Such neglect results in clogged and seeping drainage fields or sewage backing up into houses (EPA, 1974b; Sewell, 1975).

The rate at which the effluent is absorbed into the leach field is critical for the continued safe operation of the septic tank system. If the soil is too impermeable, the absorption into the leach field will be too slow, thereby causing the effluent to back up into the house or to collect at the ground surface. If the soil is too permeable, the effluent travels through the soil too rapidly, diminishing the natural filtration action of the drainfield and possibly contaminating groundwater and well systems. A simple percolation test should be required before a permit is granted for a septic tank system, the test to be performed preferably during the month when the water table is highest (Griggs and Gilchrist, 1983).

A percolation test is easily performed by the following method (March, 1978).

182 / Air and Water Quality Management

1. Excavate a 2 × 2 × 2-foot pit in the soil (applicable for most areas).
2. Fill the pit with water and allow it to drain completely.
3. Refill with water and determine the average time required for the water level to fall one inch (the percolation rate).

If the percolation rate exceeds 60 minutes, the soil is unsuitable for septic tank use. If the percolation rate is low, such as 30 to 60 minutes, the area of the drainfield should be from 250 to 300 square feet, respectively. If the percolation rate is 10 minutes, the area should be 165 square feet, and for a rate of 3 minutes, the area should be approximately 100 square feet. One additional concern is that the slope of the drainfield ideally should be approximately 3 percent. At slopes of greater than 8 to 10 percent, the effluent moves too rapidly and may accumulate at the foot of the system, causing seepage problems (Marsh, 1978).

Finally, no septic tank system should be placed near a water system (surface water, groundwater recharge area, well, etc.). Minimum parcel sizes of one acre should be established for new septic tank systems, and if a groundwater well is also required, the minimum lot size should be two to three acres. This would appear to be common sense, but an estimated 20 to 30 percent of well systems sampled in the East and Midwest had some septic tank contaminants (Cain and Beatty, 1973; Griggs and Gilchrist, 1983).

The Clean Water Act of 1977 clearly states the intent of Congress to encourage the use of alternative and innovative wastewater treatment systems in the construction grants program. Table 6-11 lists several of the innovative and alternative methods that are currently under consideration by the EPA. These fall into three categories: land application of effluent and sludge, individual on-site systems, and systems that recover and/or conserve energy (CEQ, 1979a).

Land application programs involve spreading wastewater or sludge over agricultural, forest, park, or strip-mined lands to provide nutrients for plants or crops. Such land application has been used in Paris and Berlin since the middle 1800s. In the United States, cities such as Bakersfield, California; Calumet, Michigan; Lake George, New York; and Lubbock, Texas, have found systems of land application economical and dependable (Thomas, 1978). These systems can minimize sewage treatment costs, reduce energy consumption, and provide irrigation water and plant nutrients at very low costs (Thomas, 1978). The principal drawbacks are the considerable land requirements, aerosol transmission of bacterial or viral disease agents, the possibility of groundwater contamination, and the accumulation of heavy metals in crops for human consumption. Careful siting, environmental monitoring, and choice of crops can minimize these problems (CEQ, 1979a).

The system of land application of wastewater in Muskegon, Michigan, has produced an average grain yield of 80 bushels per acre in sandy

Table 6-11. Alternative Wastewater and Sludge Technology (EPA, 1978a).

Effluent Treatment	Sludge Disposal
Land treatment Aquifer recharge Aquaculture * Silviculture Direct reuse (nonpotable) Horticulture Revegetation of disturbed land Containment ponds Treatment and storage prior to land application Preapplication treatment	Land application Composting prior to land application Drying prior to land application

Energy Recovery	Individual and On-Site Systems
Co-disposal of sludge and refuse Anaerobic digestion with $\geq 90\%$ methane Self-sustaining incineration	On-site treatment Alternative collection systems for small communities

* This includes use of natural and artificial wetlands.

soils that normally produced only a few bushels of corn per acre. The total crop income between 1976 and 1978 averaged $900,000 per year, which paid one-third of the costs of operations and debt retirement for the entire wastewater treatment system (CEQ, 1980).

On-site systems, such as septic tank systems, can provide adequate treatment service if system siting, design, construction, and operation are properly managed. The General Accounting Office (1978) concluded that community or state regulation and management could substantially improve system performance.

Composting or waterless toilets (such as the Swedish Clivus Maltrum) can reduce the average household consumption of potable water by nearly 50 percent, recover valuable nutrients for domestic use, and eliminate a large source of water pollution, offsetting the need for new or expanded sewage treatment facilities (CEQ, 1979a).

The EPA estimated that POTWs used 0.142 Q (1 Q = quadrillion BTUs) of energy in 1977 and forecasted that 0.256 Q would be required by 1990 (the U.S. total consumption of energy in 1980 was slightly less than 80 Q). Proposals for federal funds for POTW construction that can provide a savings of an equivalent of 20 percent of the energy used in existing plants may qualify to receive 10 percent additional federal funding (Wesner et al., 1978; EPA, 1978a). Thus, systems that produce large amounts of methane from anaerobic sludge digestion, that employ heat pumps to recover heat from wastewater or exhaust air, that use pump cycling that is energy efficient, that provide energy from sludge incineration, or that employ solar energy designs may be eligible for the 10 percent additional federal funding (CEQ, 1979a).

7 / Hazardous and Solid Waste Management

Hazardous Waste Management

Hazardous wastes are defined as materials that can cause or significantly contribute to serious illness or death or that when improperly managed, pose a substantial threat to human health or the environment. Using this definition, the Environmental Protection Agency has compiled a list of 361 chemicals in 16 categories that pose hazards if improperly discarded (CEQ, 1980). To be classified as a hazardous waste, a material must meet one of the following criteria:

- Flammability—wastes that pose a fire hazard during routine handling,
- Corrosivity—wastes requiring special containers or segregation from other materials,
- Reactivity—wastes that react spontaneously when heated, shaken, or exposed to air and/or water,
- Toxicity—wastes that pose a substantial hazard to human health and the environment.

Examples include acids, bases, heavy metals, solvents, pesticides, phenols, methane, PCBs, disease agents, and radioactive isotopes (CEQ, 1979a).

The Subcommittee on Oversight and Investigations (1979) of the U.S. House of Representatives summarized the problem of hazardous waste management as follows:

> The hazardous waste disposal problems cannot be overstated. The Environmental Protection Agency (EPA) has estimated that 77,140,000,000 pounds of hazardous wastes are generated each year but only 10 percent of that amount is disposed of in an environmentally sound manner. Today, there are some 30,000 hazardous waste disposal sites in the United States. Because of years of inadequate disposal practices and the absence of regulation, hundreds and perhaps thousands of these sites now pose an imminent hazard to man and the environment. Our country presently lacks an adequate program to determine where these sites are; to clean up unsafe active and inactive sites; and to provide sufficient facilities for the safe disposal of hazardous wastes in the future.

In their official listings and formal actions, federal agencies have only scratched the surface of the hazardous waste problem. The EPA recently listed more than 43,000 chemicals as potentially hazardous to human health in an inventory of chemicals in commerce (excluding pesticides, drugs, food additives, and those in cosmetics) subject to regulation under the 1976 Toxic Substances Control Act (Toxic Substances Strategy Committee, 1980). As many as 1,000 new chemicals are being developed annually in the United States alone (Magnuson, 1980). As knowledge of the health and environmental impacts of new and existing chemicals increases, the EPA anticipates the addition of thousands of new chemicals to the list (Toxic Substances Strategy Committee, 1980). In addition, the rapid growth in the use of chemicals provides many new opportunities for human exposure to toxic chemicals (Krieger, et al., 1979).

Approximately 80 percent by weight of the hazardous waste is being disposed of in unsecured ponds, lagoons, and landfills (CEQ, 1979a). An estimated 1,000 to 2,000 of these sites are believed to be significant risks to human health and the environment (Fred C. Hart Associates, 1979). The Health and Scientific Research Subcommittee of the U.S. Senate estimated that as many as 1.2 million U.S. residents are exposed to highly or moderately serious health hazards from dumpsites known to require remedial work (*Washington Post,* 1980).

The magnitude of the health hazard, although not precisely quantifiable, is enormous in light of the number of chemicals involved, routes of human exposure, synergistic effects, and the magnitude of the potential acute and chronic toxicity. The EPA has documented more than 400 cases of health and environmental damage from improper waste disposal and stated that these are only the tip of the iceberg (Maugh, 1979a). In a recent survey of more than 8,221 industrial waste pits, ponds, and lagoons, more than 30 percent were unlined in permeable soils above usable groundwater supplies (EPA, 1980d).

Potential human health effects include cancer, birth defects, reproductive anomalies, neurological and behavioral disorders, kidney damage, lung and heart disease, acute and chronic skin disease, and acute poisoning (Toxic Substances Strategy Committee, 1980). Magnuson (1980) stated:

> In evolutionary terms, the rapidity and scale of . . . chemical creativity is frightening. Through the ages, most of the earth's varied organisms, from single cells to plants, animals, and humans, usually had ample time to adapt to the pace of natural change. They evolved protective mutations to meet the gradual shifts in the earth's vital balance between acids and alkalines, in the salinity of water, in the levels of oxygen in the atmosphere. But man cannot patiently wait through the centuries for his body to develop a genetic defense against these chemicals if, indeed, such a defense is possible.

According to Magnuson (1980), a recent Library of Congress study concluded that toxic chemicals "are so long lasting and pervasive in the environment that virtually the entire population of the nation and indeed the world, carries some body burden of one or several of them."

The greatest health concern is for cancer and birth defects. In 1900 cancer and lung disease had accounted for only 12 percent of the total deaths annually in the United States. In 1980 they accounted for more than 60 percent. Today one in four U.S. citizens will contract some form of cancer. Some scientists believe that nearly 90 percent of all cancers are caused by environmental factors, such as smoking, air pollution, diet, or chemical exposures. An estimated 600 to 800 chemicals of 1,500 tested have exhibited positive evidence of animal carcinogenicity (Toxic Substances Strategy Committee, 1980).

Much less is known about the origins of human birth defects; the cause of more than 80 percent remains unexplained. Approximately 12 percent are linked to genetics (U.S. Department of Health, Education and Welfare [HEW], 1977), and a small percentage have been linked to cigarette smoking, the consumption of alcohol, and chemical contaminants such as aminopterin, thalidomide, carbon monoxide, methyl mercury, and diethylstilbestrol (DES). However, on the basis of the evidence from animal research, it is reasonable to infer that birth defects could result from exposure to any number of toxic chemicals (Toxic Substances Strategy Committee, 1980).

The problem is especially acute in the occupational environment. An estimated one in four workers (more than 20 million people) are exposed to toxic substances on the job (Toxic Substances Strategy Committee, 1980). Although the number of resulting illnesses and deaths is not known, preliminary data suggest the problem is substantial. A 1975 survey of medical conditions in small industries in Oregon and Washington conducted by the National Institute for Occupational Safety and Health found that 28 of 100 workers suffered from a disease of probable occupational origin (Discher et al., 1975). The National Institute for Occupational Safety and Health, the National Cancer Institute, and the National Institute for Environmental Health Sciences recently estimated that in the next two decades 20 percent of cancer cases will result from workplace exposures to toxic chemicals (Toxic Substances Strategy Committee, 1980).

Thus, the case for proper hazardous waste management and the cleanup of old dumpsites is compelling. More than 93 percent of the respondents in a Louis Harris poll conducted in June 1980 wanted stricter hazardous waste regulation, with 86 percent stating that hazardous waste control should be given "very high priority" (Harris, 1980).

The case is also compelling from the standpoint of health and economic benefits. For instance, the cost of proper disposal of the Kepone that was instead dumped into the James River in Hopewell,

Virginia, by the Life Science Product Company in 1975 was estimated at $250,000. Having dumped the Kepone into the river, the company had to pay $13 million in damages, and experts estimated the total cost of cleaning up the river to be $2 billion (Magnuson, 1980).

In another famous case, the cost of proper original disposal of the toxic wastes in the Love Canal in Niagara Falls, New York, was estimated to be $2 million. As of May 1980, more than $36 million have been spent by federal and state agencies to clean up, relocate the residents, and monitor the wastes (CEQ, 1980).

An EPA study of 17 industries found that proper management of hazardous wastes would cost $750 million annually (as opposed to actual annual expenditures by the industries of $155 million). However, the costs of proper management are only 0.25 percent of the value of production of the industries (EPA, 1979). The total cost of cleanup of all inactive hazardous waste sites is estimated to be between $28.4 billion and $55 billion (CEQ, 1979a).

Federal and State Responses to Hazardous Waste Problems

Federal Hazardous Waste Management Programs

In the past several decades Congress has enacted more than two dozen regulatory statutes covering many aspects of chemical production, distribution, use, and disposal. Table 7-1 summarizes the major regulatory legislation. The hazardous substance control regulations form a nearly comprehensive umbrella to regulate hazardous wastes, from extraction or synthesis to ultimate disposal.

Several important principles are embodied in these laws. The statutes call for emphasis on prevention as the key to controlling human health and ecological problems caused by hazardous chemicals. For instance, the legislation requires registration of new drugs and pesticides and the premanufacture testing of toxic chemicals to assess potential hazards before distribution and use. In addition, the legislation mandates action to limit exposure to a potentially hazardous substance when evidence of the hazard is suggested but not completely proven. Because of the subtle or long-term nature of many impacts and the extent of potential chemical distribution, the health and ecological costs of waiting for proof of harm before withdrawing a new chemical could be unacceptably high. The absolute scientific proof, although desirable, is seldom possible and is therefore not required by law. The courts have upheld this precautionary principle (Toxic Substance Strategy Committee, 1980). The three most important federal statutes from the standpoint of management of hazardous wastes are the Toxic Substance Control Act of 1976, the Resource Conservation and Recovery Act of 1976, and the Oil, Hazardous Substances, and Hazardous Waste Response, Liability, and Compensation Act of 1980. The enormity of the task of regulating

Table 7-1. Summary of Major Federal Hazardous Substances Control Legislation (Toxic Substances Strategy Committee, 1980).

Statute	Year Enacted	Agency Responsible	Toxic Substances Covered
Oil, Hazardous Substances, and Hazardous Waste Response, Liability, and Compensation Act	1979	EPA	Abandoned hazardous waste sites and spills of oil, hazardous substances, and hazardous wastes
Toxic Substance Control Act	1976	EPA	Chemical substances except tobacco, nuclear materials, alcohol, pesticides, foods, food additives, drugs, cosmetics, and materials covered by FDA authority
Clean Air Act	1970 amended 1977	EPA	Hazardous air pollutants
Clean Water Act	1972 amended 1977	EPA	Toxic water pollutants
Safe Drinking Water Act	1974 amended 1977	EPA	Drinking water contaminants
Federal Insecticide, Fungicide, and Rodenticide Act	1947 amended 1972, 1975, 1978	EPA	Pesticides
Resource Conservation and Recovery Act	1976	EPA	Solid wastes including hazardous wastes
Occupational Safety and Health Act	1970	OSHA, NIOSH	Workplace toxic chemicals
Hazardous Materials Transportation Act	1975 amended 1976	DOT (Materials Transportation Bureau)	Transportation of toxic substances generally

hazardous wastes will prevent effective implementation of the regulations for several years. At present the implementation effort is in its infancy, suffering from the growing pains of a new system. In a message to the president, the Toxic Substance Strategy Committee (1980) said:

> The magnitude of the toxic substances control problem . . . is staggering in view of the number of substances whose risk should be evaluated, the rate of growth in both number and volume of chemicals, the various routes by which humans and the environment are exposed, possible synergistic or combined effects of the substances, and the effects that they cause—acute and chronic, immediate and delayed. Years of research can be required to determine whether a particular substance is hazardous.

The Toxic Substance Control Act (TSCA) of 1976 gives the EPA broad regulatory powers over chemicals in all phases of their production and use, from acquisition or manufacture to ultimate disposal. The act directs the EPA to inventory the estimated 55,000 chemical substances in commerce. To date, the agency has listed more than 43,000 chemicals as definitely or potentially hazardous to human health or the environment. The act requires premanufacture notice to the agency of all new chemicals in commerce (excluding pesticides, drugs, those in cosmetics, food additives, and radioactive materials regulated by other statutes), about 1,000 annually (CEQ, 1980; Miller, 1979).

Before manufacturing a new chemical, using an old chemical in a new way, or importing a new chemical into the United States, a chemical manufacturer must present information on the nature, use, and toxicity of the chemical to the EPA at least 90 days before manufacture or importation. If the agency believes there is "reasonable risk" of injury to human health or the environment, it can prevent manufacture for 180 days. Importation or manufacture can be prevented by court injunction beyond the 180-day period if there is evidence of risk to health or the environment, if the chemical is expected to enter the environment in large quantities, or if the EPA can prove there are insufficient data to make an informed judgment. Once an injunction is issued, the manufacturer must prove that the compound is safe before it can be imported, manufactured, or marketed.

Implementation of the TSCA has been extremely slow. As of July 1980 only five classes of chemicals—PCBs, chlorofluorocarbons, phthalate esters, chlorinated benzenes, and chloromethane—have been subject to any regulatory actions at all (CEQ, 1980). There are many reasons for the slow implementation. The regulatory effort has suffered from a general lack of funding; industry is hesitant to divulge proprietary information; and the costs of testing for chemical toxicity are high—an estimated $500,000 per chemical. In fact, industry has charged that this could discourage the development and use of new chemicals (Miller, 1979). Perhaps the most significant barrier to implementation of the act is conflict over the testing for chemical toxicity. The EPA is currently not receiving sufficient data from the manufacturers to determine potential risk. In addition EPA efforts to develop policies for issuing test rules have met with stiff opposition. The controversies center on how chemicals are selected for testing, how detailed the testing needs to be to obtain a ruling, what kinds of tests should be conducted, and who should conduct the tests (CEQ, 1980).

The Resource Conservation and Recovery Act (RCRA) of 1976 is the primary tool of the federal government for controlling hazardous wastes. When fully implemented the RCRA will provide cradle-to-grave control of hazardous wastes: Subtitle C establishes a regulatory process that controls hazardous wastes from their acquisition or creation to their final safe disposal. The act calls for the development of criteria for distinguishing hazardous wastes; the creation of a manifest system to label and track wastes through final disposal; and the development of a permit system based on EPA standards to treat, store, and dispose of hazardous wastes. The act clearly defines the responsibilities of the generator, transporter, and disposer of hazardous wastes and requires financial capability to clean up any spills or leachates (CEQ, 1979a).

The manifest system is the central element of the management program. A waste generator is required to prepare a manifest for all wastes listed on the EPA hazardous waste list. The qualifying wastes must be properly packaged and labeled, and the manifest must accompany the wastes from the point of generation to the point of ultimate disposal (CEQ, 1980).

The regulations also provide standards for state waste management programs. A state may operate its own hazardous waste program in lieu of the federal program if it meets the EPA standards. States that meet only the minimum standards or that are lax in listing, regulation, and enforcement may become dumping grounds for the hazardous wastes of industries, so there is a strong incentive for developing a safe program (Lennett, 1980). Failure to comply with the provisions of the act can result in civil action and in certain cases, in fines and imprisonment (CEQ, 1980).

The new regulations have been criticized by both environmentalists and the chemical industry. The chemical industry has said that the tests for chemicals are too expensive and difficult to accomplish (CEQ, 1979a). Environmentalists dislike the provision in the RCRA that exempts nuclear wastes from regulation (Portney, 1978). In addition, generators of less than 2,200 pounds of hazardous wastes per month are allowed, under the regulations, to dump their wastes, no matter how toxic, into municipal landfills without regulation (Lennett, 1980). Finally, the standards for hazardous waste facilities are design standards rather than performance standards. Performance standards would have provided greater incentives to develop more innovative management systems involving incineration, resource recovery, and waste stabilization systems (CEQ, 1979a).

Implementation of the RCRA has been slow and full of controversy. Six years after passage of the legislation, a federal judge ordered the EPA to issue standards for the handling, transportation, and disposal of wastes (Associated Press, 1981). The Reagan administration, citing excessive costs and overregulation of private industry, cut the RCRA budget from $150 million in 1981 to $100 million in 1982 and $87 million in 1983 (*New York Times*, 1983).

Attempts to relax RCRA rules, such as the suspension of a ban on dumping of liquid wastes in landfills (issued on February 25, 1982), were met with a storm of protest and were later withdrawn. Since the departure of Rita Lavelle (EPA's chief of hazardous waste), the resignation of EPA Administrator Anne Gorsuch (Burford), and the appointment of William Ruckelshaus as the new EPA administrator, there appears to be an improvement in the RCRA program (Cohen, 1984).

In reaction to these controversies, Congress is considering amendments to the RCRA to compel the EPA to prohibit the dumping of hazardous wastes in landfills. With the annual increase in the volume of hazardous wastes and no effective management program, more waste may be dumped in the next decade than in all previous years combined (Pope, 1984). With nearly 275,000 waste generators and the need to regulate nearly 30,000 storage, treatment, and disposal facilities, the task is enormous (CEQ, 1979a).

The Oil, Hazardous Substances, and Hazardous Waste Response, Liability, and Compensation Act of 1980, commonly called the superfund law, established a $1.6 billion fund for the cleanup of hazardous substance spills and for the cleanup of inactive hazardous waste sites. The fund can be used to clean up hazardous spills when no responsible party can be identified or if the responsible party is unable to clean up. The government can sue to recover expenses. A tax on oil and certain chemicals will provide 87.5 percent of the funding, with the remaining 12.5 percent appropriated by the federal government (CEQ, 1980). The fund was necessary because the regulatory program of the RCRA does not address abandoned and inactive dumpsites (CEQ, 1979a).

Problems of superfund implementation were exacerbated by the Reagan administration's antiregulatory management policy. Under EPA Administrator Anne Gorsuch, the EPA's Office of Enforcement was reorganized, and the Office of Waste Programs Enforcement was placed under the jurisdiction of Assistant Administrator Rita Lavelle. Lavelle's Hazardous Waste Management Office followed a policy of cooperation rather than confrontation and negotiated a number of cleanup agreements with industry (with little or no public participation). These agreements prohibited the EPA from further enforcement actions at negotiated sites. The nature and pace of these agreements quickly drew the attention of Congress, which requested documentation from the EPA. Gorsuch refused to provide the requested materials (allegedly acting on White House orders) and was cited for contempt of Congress late in 1982. The conflict eventually led to the firing of Lavelle in February 1983 and the resignation of Gorsuch the next month (Cohen, 1984).

After the departure of Gorsuch and Lavelle, the EPA (1983) reported that the superfund program could be substantially improved by (1) streamlining rules and procedures, (2) improving liaison with the states, (3) clarifying enforcement policies, (3) cleaning up hazardous waste sites at federal facilities, and (5) improving EPA internal management. The report concluded that these changes by 1985 could result in an increase of long-term site removal actions from 15 to 43 and short-term cleanups from 253 to 347. At this time it is difficult to assess the impact of the new EPA Administrator Ruckelshaus. Again, with files on more than 15,000 hazardous waste sites, the EPA's task is enormous.

Finally, in a June 1980 report to the president, the Toxic Substances Strategy Committee concluded that the basic approach of the federal statutes that regulate hazardous chemicals is sound. However, the report recommended legislation in four areas to improve regulation:

- Establishing the means to clean up inactive and abandoned hazardous waste sites like the Love Canal (similar to those of the subsequently passed superfund bill),
- Strengthening federal authority over cosmetics,
- Eliminating barriers to the sharing of confidential data with other government agencies and the public,
- Expanding the funding for public participation in hazardous substance regulatory proceedings.

The committee also called for a single centralized information system on hazardous materials to replace more than 220 separate data systems and recommended that the government work to improve public understanding of the testing procedures for toxicity or carcinogenicity of chemicals. The committee emphasized that, measured against need, the number of chemicals that have been analyzed and the number of regulatory actions that have been taken have been disproportionately small.

State Hazardous Waste Management Programs

A recent National Wildlife Federation (Kamlet, 1979) survey of state hazardous substance programs ranked the states according to their "need" for a hazardous waste management program (a function of the amount of wastes generated within the state) and the "response" of the state in developing a comprehensive state hazardous substance program. The evaluation of the state program was based upon responses to forty-three questions by all fifty states, the District of Columbia, and the territories of Guam, the Virgin Islands, and Puerto Rico. Table 7-2 summarizes the results of the needs-response analysis.

Of the ten states generating the largest amounts of hazardous wastes (New Jersey, Ohio, Illinois, California, Pennsylvania, Texas, New York, Michigan, Tennessee, and Indiana), none scored in the bottom twenty of the response rankings. Thus, in the states where wastes are most likely to be a problem, the responses appear to have been more comprehensive than those of states with fewer wastes (Kamlet, 1979). Appearances, however, may be deceiving. Although the management programs compared favorably with those in other states, even those of the highest ranked states in the survey scored no better than C plus in scope and adequacy. The survey found the following:

- More than three-fourths of the states require advance approval both for depositing wastes in a landfill and for landfill initiation and operation;
- Less than half the states regulate the siting of hazardous waste landfills;
- Nearly half the states require no inventory of the chemical content of wastes and less than one-fourth require labeling of wastes;
- Less than one-fourth of the states require water quality monitoring after closing a landfill;
- More than one-third of the states absolve the waste generators of responsibility for hazardous waste after it is turned over to a processor or transporter;
- More than one-fourth of the states exempt on-site storage and disposal of hazardous wastes from some or all regulatory requirements (on-site storage is a common practice in industry).

According to the survey, only seven states have a specific hazardous substance law; only twelve states, the District of Columbia, Puerto Rico, and the Virgin Islands have an official hazardous substance management agency; only nine states have a legally specified list of toxic and/or hazardous substances; and twenty-three states have established procedures for dealing with hazardous chemical emergencies (Kamlet, 1979). Therefore, the risk of serious health impacts and environmental degradation from hazardous materials remains high today in most states. It should be noted, however, that several states have upgraded their laws and programs since the survey in 1979.

Methods of Hazardous Waste Management

The best management option for dealing with hazardous wastes is to minimize the amounts generated by modifying industrial processes, industrial outputs, and consumer purchasing behavior. When waste is generated, the major methods of hazardous waste control can be divided

Table 7-2. Evaluation of State Hazardous Substances Management Programs (Kamlet, 1979).

STATE *	Ranking By Hazardous Waste Generation (1)	Ranking from Survey Results (2)	Need-Response Index** (1) − (2)	Ranking By Need-Response Index
New Jersey	1	12	−11	39
Ohio	2	10	− 8	32
Illinois	3	17	−14	43
California	4	1	3	23
Pennsylvania	5	15	−10	37
Texas	6	13	− 7	29
New York	7	16	− 9	34
Michigan	8	28	−20	47
Tennessee	9	3	6	20
Indiana	10	25	−15	44
North Carolina	11	14	− 3	26
Virginia	12	23	−11	40
Missouri	13	39	−26	50
Louisiana	14	18	− 4	27
South Carolina	15	4	11	12
Massachusetts	16	31	−15	45
Florida	17	9	8	18
Wisconsin	18	30	−12	41
West Virginia	19	43	−24	49
Georgia	20	48	−28	51
Connecticut	21	8	13	10
Kentucky	22	42	−20	48
Alabama	23	19	4	22
Maryland	24	2	22	5
Minnesota	25	32	− 7	30
Washington	26	5	21	6
Iowa	27	35	− 8	33
Kansas	28	20	8	19
Delaware	29	6	23	4
Mississippi	30	45	−15	46
Arkansas	31	22	9	14
Colorado	32	41	− 9	35
Oklahoma	33	21	12	11
Oregon	34	7	27	2
Rhode Island	35	26	9	15
Idaho	36	46	−10	38
Maine	37	44	− 7	31
Nebraska	38	40	− 2	24
Arizona	39	53	−14	42
New Hampshire	40	49	− 9	36
Utah	41	36	5	21
New Mexico	42	33	9	16
Montana	43	29	14	9
Vermont	44	11	33	1
Nevada	45	51	− 6	28
Alaska	46	37	9	17
D.C.	47	27	20	7
Hawaii	48	38	10	13
North Dakota	49	34	15	8
South Dakota	50	52	− 2	25
Wyoming	51*	24	27	3

*The EPA contractor study, from which column (1) is derived, evaluated only the 50 States plus the District of Columbia; the NWF Survey, represented in Column 2, studied an additional three territories (i.e., Guam, Virgin Islands, and Puerto Rico). Only the 51 "States" common to both studies are included in this table.

**The larger the number, the greater the disparity between need and response. Negative numbers indicate that, relative to other state programs, the regulatory effort has fallen short of matching the problem.

into two categories: waste disposal methods and waste storage methods. The three major methods of waste disposal in order of EPA priority are (1) recovery and recycling, (2) waste reprocessing, and (3) incineration. The three major methods of waste storage are (1) deep well injection, (2) solidification and encapsulation, and (3) disposal in a secure landfill. It should be emphasized that a combination of these methods is often used, as no single method is suitable for all wastes and waste mixtures. In addition, before waste control processes are initiated, it is important to separate nontoxic from toxic wastes to reduce the costs of transportation, handling, and disposal.

Waste Disposal Options

The most environmentally sound and thus the top priority option for waste disposal is to recover and recycle the waste materials. An estimated 75 percent of all hazardous wastes could theoretically be used as raw materials for other industries (*Technology Review*, 1980). However, only a small percentage of wastes is currently suitable for exchange because of the process and chemical specificity of recycling, high transportation costs, costs and lack of knowledge of extraction techniques, and a hesitancy on the part of many industries to reveal the amount and types of chemicals they use. Recovery and recycling involves the development of a clearinghouse capable of identifying, handling, separating, treating, and exchanging waste materials and coordinating buyers and sellers. Such clearinghouses have been used in Europe for nearly a decade, and twenty information exchanges and three materials exchanges are now operating in the United States (EPA, 1980c; Maugh, 1979b).

Hazardous wastes can also be reprocessed by physical, chemical, or biological means to render them less toxic, to detoxify them entirely, or to reduce the volume of toxic materials substantially (Maugh, 1979b). Physical processes include carbon or resin adsorption, distillation, centrifugation, flocculation, sedimentation, reverse osmosis, and ultrafiltration. Chemical processes include precipitation, oxidation, neutralization, and ion exchange (to remove heavy metals). Biological processes include activated sludge treatment, trickling filters, composting, and controlled application to land (to degrade organic compounds) (CEQ, 1980). In Europe regional treatment centers provide the necessary treatment materials (e.g., bases to neutralize acids) to reduce costs and volume of hazardous wastes.

If proper controls are used, incineration can destroy the toxicity of certain organic wastes without posing a threat to the environment. EPA standards require that 99.99 percent of the organic wastes be destroyed during incineration—a very costly and energy-intensive undertaking given present technology. To reduce the cost and improve the energy efficiency of the process, the EPA is currently experimenting with heat recovery systems (Maugh, 1979c). One promising experimental approach involves the injection of toxic gases into a microwave plasma that breaks down the gas and retains the breakdown products, such as methane, ethane, or chlorinated hydrocarbons, for recycling or subsequent disposal. This system uses much less energy but is not yet cost competitive (Bailin and Hertzler, 1978).

Waste Storage Options

One of the most controversial methods of hazardous waste disposal is deep well injection, in which wastes are pumped under very high pressures into permeable layers of rock bounded by impermeable strata. Although relatively inexpensive, industry experience with deep well injection has indicated a number of potential problems, including earthquakes, fractured casings and rock strata, back flowing of wastes, and contamination of surface waters and groundwaters (Evans and Bradford, 1969; Forrestal, 1975). Great caution should be exercised in using this alternative.

Encapsulation is a physical process in which a highly impermeable and inert material is used to surround the hazardous waste. Solidification or chemical fixation involves a chemical reaction between a chemical matrix and the waste. Either technique, if properly done, can contain the waste and render it harmless for long periods of time. Solidification is used widely in Europe and Japan, and its use is likely to increase in the United States. The major drawback for such processes is the high cost of pretreatment and solidification or encapsulation (Maugh, 1979b; Pojasek, 1978).

The least acceptable, but often only available, method of disposing of certain hazardous wastes is burial in a secure landfill. This should be the last resort for storage of wastes and residues of wastes from the other processes (Maugh, 1979b). EPA regulations implementing subtitle C of the RCRA require that all landfills be lined with clay, plastic, or other impermeable material to prevent waste from reaching groundwaters or surface waters (*Federal Register,* 1978a). A landfill cannot be located within 500 feet of a water source, and when a site is closed, it must be entirely sealed with clay or impermeable materials. Active sites must be monitored constantly, and closed sites must be maintained and monitored for 20 years after closing to assure the waste is secure. Owners are required to meet a financial responsibility requirement for as much as $5 million per damage incident during operation (CEQ, 1979a).

Costs of Disposal of Hazardous Wastes

The EPA has estimated the costs of several of the methods of waste disposal. The range is from $2 to $25 per metric ton for land spreading

Table 7-3. Costs of Several Methods of Hazardous Waste Disposal (EPA 1980c).

Method	Cost (dollars per metric ton)
Land spreading	2–25
Chemical fixation	5–500
Surface impoundment	14–180
Secure chemical landfill	50–400
Incineration (land based)	75–2,000
Physical, chemical, or biological treatment	varies

to $75 to $2,000 per metric ton for land-based incineration, as indicated in Table 7-3 (EPA, 1980c).

Hazardous Waste Planning and Management

The hazardous waste management system of Oregon, which was rated seventh best in the United States in the 1979 National Wildlife Federation survey (see Table 7-2), serves as a useful case study of waste planning and management. Storage and disposal sites throughout Oregon are required by law to obtain a license from the Oregon Department of Environmental Quality (*Oregon Statute Annotated,* 1979). To date, there is one licensed site in the state, near Arlington, Oregon (east of Portland).

The Chem-Security Systems, Inc., Hazardous Waste Disposal Facility, or CSSI–Arlington facility, is on a high plateau in an area with less than nine inches of annual rainfall. The area is geologically stable. The geological profile is ideal, with gravel surface soils underlain by unsaturated subsoils, followed by tight clay and silt tuffs over impervious basaltic rock. An aquifer lies directly below the site, but it is more than five hundred feet below the surface and two hundred feet into the basalt (CSSI, 1980).

The facility is managed by a private company, Chem Security Systems, Inc., a subsidiary of Waste Management, Inc., which is the largest transporter, treater, and disposer of waste materials in North America. In addition to its waste management program, CSSI can also clean up old waste disposal sites and has the capability to contain major hazardous substance spills. The facility is managed to handle most hazardous wastes except radioactive materials, explosives, biological materials, and poisonous gases. Five waste management systems are employed on site, including land treatment, landfill disposal, surface impoundments (solar evaporation), waste storage, and treatment (detoxification and waste reclamation) (CSSI, 1980).

Wastes are treated through solar evaporation and chemical neutralization. Inorganic liquid wastes are evaporated in large lined impoundments. The sludge is solidified and sent to the landfill facility. Dry bulk wastes and containerized sealed chemicals are placed in the landfill. Organic compounds, such as petroleum wastes, are sent to the treatment facility where they are mixed with soil containing microbes that degrade the wastes (CSSI, 1980).

Electrical transformers contaminated with PCBs are accepted by the facility. Liquid PCBs are drained and flushed from the transformers. Liquid PCBs and flushate are then stored in drums and bulk containers for eventual incineration on one of the two parent company–owned incineration ships. The drained and flushed transformer bodies are disposed of in an approved PCB landfill (CSSI, 1980).

The facility can also solidify certain containerized or bulk wastes. Finally, the CSSI recycles and reclaims as many wastes as possible. In one case, a particular waste stream is being stored in anticipation of future markets (CSSI, 1980).

The hazardous materials are routinely picked up throughout the state from individual industries or at centralized facilities when a number of small waste producers are involved. Toxic wastes are transported to the Arlington facility by special trucks or tankers. All shipments are inspected upon arrival and chemically analyzed to confirm they can be handled at the facility. Above ground and subsurface monitoring are used to detect leakage of wastes. No problems have as yet developed.

It is important to note that before CSSI can accept wastes, it must have prior approval from the Oregon Department of Environmental Quality. Such approval includes a detailed listing of chemical content and assurances by the generator that the waste cannot be beneficially reused. Also, the state of Oregon is the owner of the site. This assures that the waste permanently residing at the site will always be under careful control by governmental agencies irrespective of any change in operator or other business impacts.

The Arlington facility has not always been the only operational disposal site in Oregon. A survey by the Oregon Department of Environmental Quality published in 1980 found thirty-eight abandoned hazardous disposal sites within the state. In the survey, each site was characterized as to:

- Source of wastes
- Location
- Type of disposal
- Hazards represented
- Findings on the hazards
- Current status of the site
- Type of investigation (interviews, phone calls, etc.).

The survey resulted in the publication of an official list of sites and concluded that "no immediate threat to public health or the environment existed."

Local participation in such a program involves cooperation with state agencies in developing hazardous chemical lists, formulating regulatory strategies, identifying waste producers, and inventorying existing and abandoned waste disposal sites. Local governments may want to designate safe local sites for waste collection, storage, and pickup. Local communities should develop emergency plans to evacuate areas, notify the proper authorities, and clean up spills along major transportation routes and around industries where hazardous substances are generated, handled, and stored. Information on the location of old dump sites should be readily available to citizens and public and private agencies to prevent improper development or disturbances of the site and to promote periodic monitoring for groundwater and surface water contamination.

Solid Waste Management

Before the early 1970s, municipalities either burned solid waste in an incinerator or took it to an open dump. However, as the volume of wastes increased and existing sites were filled, communities experienced mounting opposition to the development of new sites, especially near residential developments and in ecologically significant lands. In response to these problems, federal and state agencies have recently made significant changes in the requirements and management systems for municipal solid wastes. William Ruckelshaus, former and current EPA administrator, said that solid waste management is "a fundamental ecological issue. It illustrates, perhaps more clearly than any other environmental problem, that we must change many of our traditional attitudes and habits. It shows us very directly and concretely that we must work to adjust our institutions, both public and private, to the problems and opportunities posed by our traditional disregard for the pollution effects of disposal, and particularly for our misuse of natural resources" (Ruckelshaus, 1972).

Figure 7-1 indicates the amount and composition of municipal solid waste from 1960 to 1977. In this period the rate of waste generation increased at an average of 5 percent per year. From 1970 to 1977 the rate of increase slowed to approximately 2 percent, due in part to a recession in 1974 and 1975. In 1978 the total U.S. municipal waste was estimated at 154 million tons, or approximately 1,400 pounds per person (CEQ, 1979a).

Most solid waste in the United States is produced indirectly by agriculture (56 percent), mining (34 percent), and industrial activities (5 percent) (see Table 7-4). Municipal solid waste is only 4 percent of the total solid waste generated annually in the United States. However,

Figure 7-1. Generation of Residential and Commercial Solid Waste in the United States, 1960 to 1977 (CEQ, 1979a).

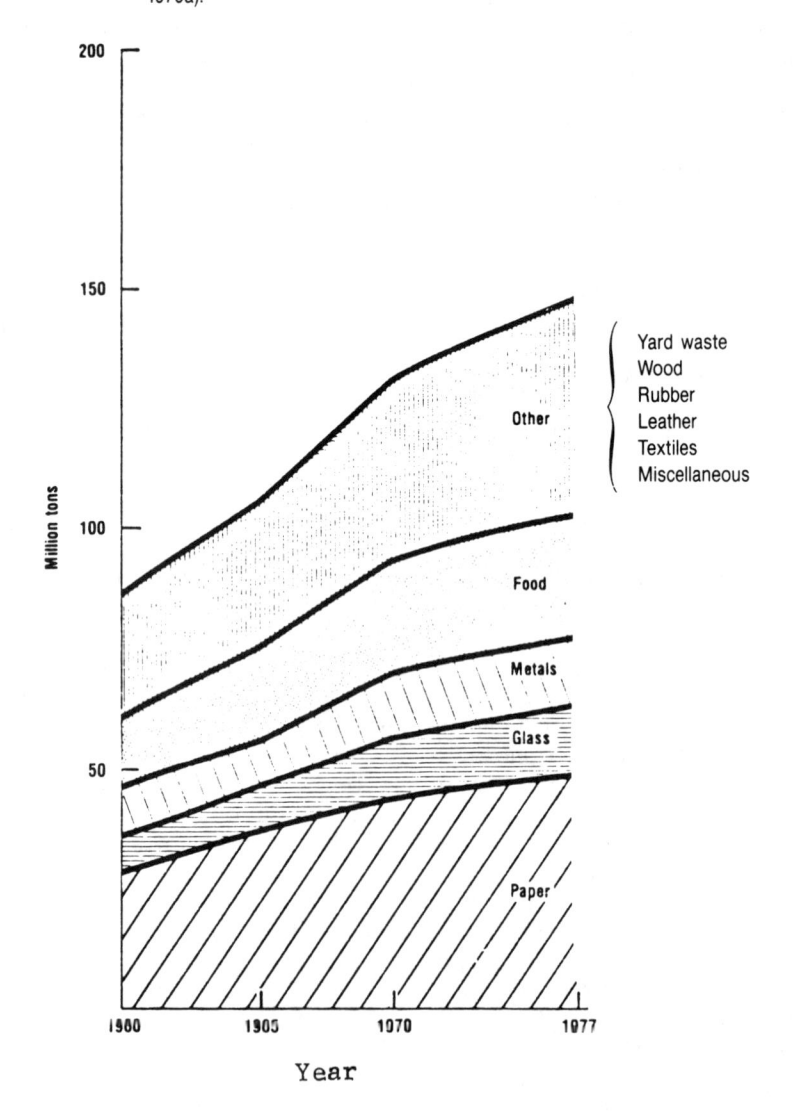

Table 7-4. Estimated Solid Waste Production of the United States in 1975 (Miller, 1979).

Type of Waste	Total Wet Weight Production Trillions of Kilograms	Total Wet Weight Production Billions of Tons	Average Wet Weight Production per Person Kilograms	Average Wet Weight Production per Person Pounds
Indirect				
Agricultural	2.1	2.3	10,000	22,000
Mining	1.3	1.4	6,200	13,640
Industrial	0.236	0.260	1,125	2,476
Direct				
Urban (residential and commercial)	0.124	0.136	645	1,418
Total	3.8	4.1	17,970	39,534

Source: *Living in the Environment*, 3rd ed., by G. Tyler Miller Jr. Copyright 1979 by Wadsworth, Inc. Reprinted by permission of Wadsworth Publishing Co., Belmont CA 94002.

for a number of reasons, policy emphasis has focused on municipal solid waste (EPA, 1977):

- The wastes are concentrated in urban areas,
- Municipal wastes potentially pose a health hazard and must be removed quickly and efficiently,
- Present methods of disposal of municipal wastes are inadequate,
- More information exists on the amount and composition of municipal solid waste because more than two-thirds is collected,
- The expenditures for municipal solid waste collection and disposal are one of the largest budget items of a municipality.

The last point is of considerable importance. In 1975, local governments spent more than $4 billion to collect and dispose of solid waste, more than 80 percent of which was spent for labor to collect the wastes. Between 1975 and 1985 collection and disposal costs are expected to double or triple (EPA, 1977).

Federal and State Responses to Solid Waste Problems

The 1976 Resource Conservation and Recovery Act called for a national effort to promote safe solid waste management practices and to promote resource conservation and recovery. The act regulates waste solids, sludges, liquids, and contained gases (excluding domestic sewage, return irrigation flows, industrial discharges into waterways, and radioactive wastes regulated through other legislation). The main solid waste management provisions of the act are (CEQ, 1978b):

- Federal financial and technical assistance to state and local governments for the development of comprehensive solid waste management programs,
- Stringent environmental controls on all land disposal of solid wastes,
- Provisions for resource conservation and recovery,
- A cabinet-level interagency study of resource conservation policies,
- Research and development on solid waste problems,
- Public participation in the development of all policies, regulations, and programs.

Appropriations to the EPA for implementation of the act were $17.3 million in 1977, $39.8 million in 1978, and more than $70 million in 1979 (CEQ, 1978b). The Council on Environmental Quality (1975) estimated that compliance with the provisions of the act will double the cost of disposal of solid wastes in the United States, an increase of $4.50 per ton of waste. Much of this increase is attributable to new landfill regulations. The new expenses will be incurred gradually as the planning and regulation mechanisms are promulgated in the 1980s.

The act requires states to develop solid waste management plans, including development of environmental controls for land disposal of solid wastes and resource conservation and recovery activities. Federal grants for development of state management programs totaled $3 million in 1977, $14.3 million in 1978, and more than $26 million in 1979. To receive federal funding, state solid waste management plans must meet the following criteria (CEQ, 1979a):

- Define boundaries for regional solid waste management and identify state, regional, and local agencies responsible for implementing the state plan,
- Prohibit new open dumps or other environmentally unacceptable disposal facilities,
- Require that all solid wastes either be processed through resource recovery or be disposed of in an environmentally sound manner,
- Set compliance schedules for closing or upgrading all existing facilities that do not meet acceptable environmental standards,
- Develop the regulatory powers needed to implement the state solid-waste management plan,
- Remove impediments for supplying solid wastes to resource recovery facilities,

- Include resource recovery, conservation, and disposal programs for environmentally acceptable management.

The criteria for determining the acceptability of a solid waste disposal facility are based on the nature of impacts to surface water and groundwater, air quality, and public safety and use of a cover material. Facilities that allow open burning or facilities in wetlands, floodplains, endangered species habitats, or drinking water recharge zones would be defined as unacceptable and would have to be phased out (CEQ, 1979a; *Federal Register,* 1978b).

The combined effects of the increased cost of solid waste disposal and, in many cases, the lack of acceptable landfill sites may stimulate the development of resource conservation and recovery systems (CEQ, 1979a).

Solid Waste Planning and Management

Conventional Approaches

Until recently, the costs of solid waste disposal were low enough and suitable sites were sufficiently plentiful that local governments had little incentive to change their waste management practices. In 1978, for instance, the average cost of collection and disposal of municipal solid wastes was $43 per ton (or approximately $25 per capita per year) (CEQ, 1979a).

Municipal solid waste in the United States in 1978 was being sent to 18,500 land disposal sites with a total land area of more than 50,000 acres (CEQ, 1979a). The typical municipal solid waste management system remains rudimentary compared with systems of resource acquisition, processing, and marketing. The typical system involves laboriously picking up and emptying garbage cans each week into the rear hopper of a garbage truck. Material, typically weighing 100 to 200 pounds per cubic yard, is compacted in the truck to between 500 and 600 pounds per cubic yard. When the truck is full, it is driven to a municipal landfill where the material is dumped. The municipal landfills are often poorly sited from the standpoint of air and water pollution and are often poorly managed. In addition, the whole system is unnecessarily labor intensive. Many of the tasks could be performed more safely and efficiently by machines (Sewell, 1975).

Because collection and transportation of refuse account for 80 to 90 percent of the cost of solid waste disposal, innovation in these systems can realize substantial savings. One innovation, which is saving Scottsdale, Arizona, more than $350,000 annually, is the use of a collection truck with a long mechanical arm that picks up 80-gallon hard plastic containers placed on curbsides. Phoenix, Arizona, began using a similar system in 1978 (Miller, 1979).

Pneumatic tube collection systems are, perhaps, the most advanced and efficient systems commercially available. Trash is dumped into a chute and sucked through a vacuum-powered pipeline to a centralized incinerator. Valuable metal and glass materials can be separated before or after incineration and the heat generated by combustion can be captured for useful purposes. These systems are currently in use in a number of hospitals and apartment and housing complexes, especially in Sweden, England, West Germany, and France, where more than 400 were operating in 1978 (Miller, 1979).

As already related, the 1976 Resource Conservation and Recovery Act forbids the siting and operation of new open dumps and requires that all existing open dumps in the United States be upgraded or closed. The most technically simple and inexpensive disposal alternative to open dumping is the sanitary landfill. The costs of controlled burial of wastes in a sanitary landfill are from $2 to $4 per ton, excluding land costs (Sewell, 1975).

A sanitary landfill should be situated in a well-drained site away from major bodies of surface water or groundwater. To avoid problems with rodents, insects, and blowing material, wastes are compacted to a depth of 6 to 8 feet then covered daily with 6 inches of compacted soil. When the landfill is full, it should be covered with a minimum of 2 feet of compacted soil (see Figure 7-2) (Sewell, 1975).

When a sanitary landfill is closed, it is important to cap the site with a layer of relatively impermeable soil. This reduces the downward movement of precipitation and surface water through the refuse and reduces the problem of leaching of contaminants. Areas that have high water tables and permeable substrata should be avoided to prevent leaching by and to groundwater sources.

If a landfill is located at the base of a hill, soil for covering and compaction can be obtained from the hillside. If located in a flat area, a trench is usually dug and the fill covered by the excavated earth. Some sites may require special drainage systems including techniques of removal of leachate to a sewage treatment plant. Gas vents are frequently used to prevent explosive concentrations of methane gas from the decomposition of organic materials. Several systems (e.g., a garbage-to-methane gas system in the San Fernando Valley) have been designed to collect the methane gas and use it as fuel. As the wastes decompose, considerable subsidence is possible, especially within the first five years after filling. This can damage structures built over the landfill, so most landfills are used for open space or recreational purposes. In addition, submarginal lands can be reclaimed by developing a landfill. The major problems that plague most landfills are (Sewell, 1975):

- Inadequate soil coverage and compaction,
- The generation of methane gas,

Figure 7-2. A "Typical" Sanitary Landfill. A thin layer of wastes is compacted by a bulldozer, then covered daily with a fresh layer of soil by a scraper (Miller, 1979).

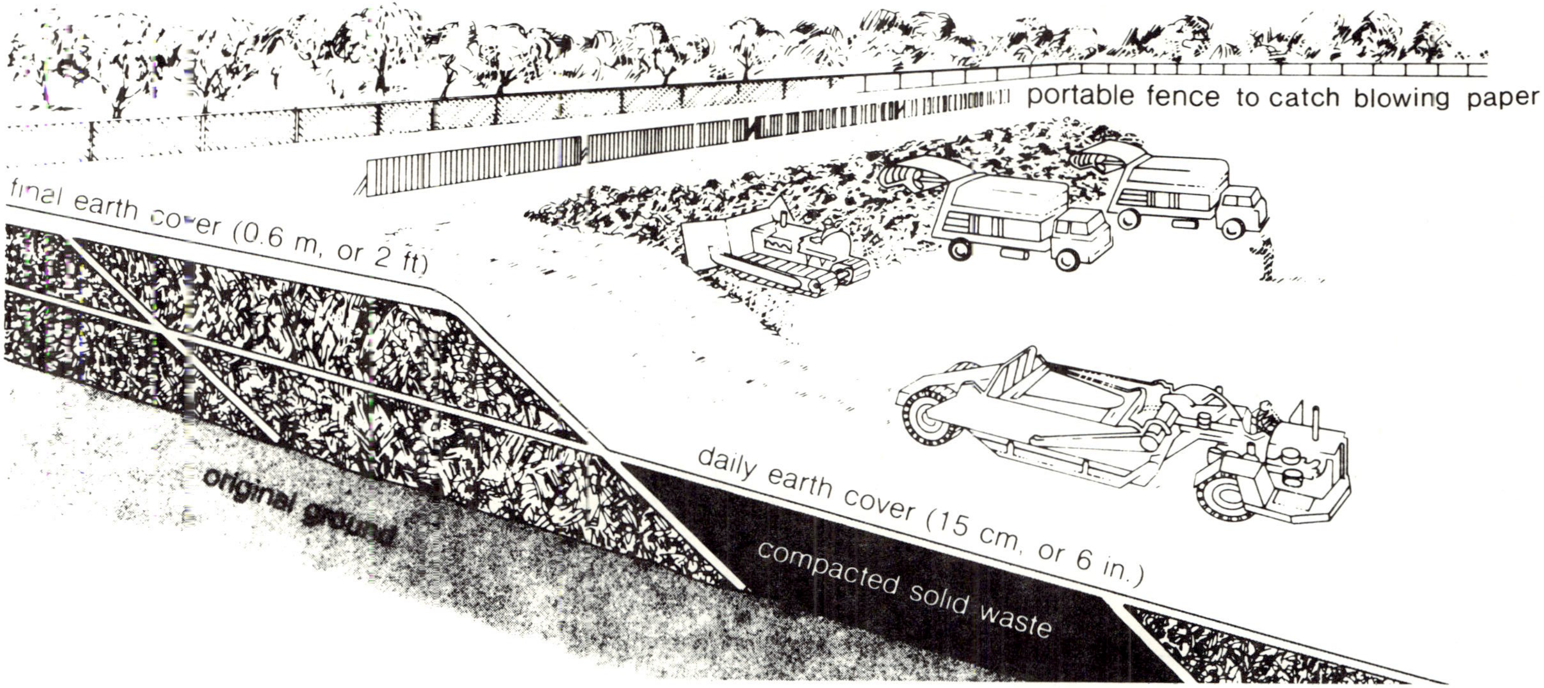

portable fence to catch blowing paper

daily earth cover (15 cm. or 6 in.)

compacted solid waste

final earth cover (0.6 m, or 2 ft)

original ground

- Land subsidence,
- Water quality problems due to poor original siting,
- Control of blowing materials,
- Diminished adjacent land uses and values.

Incineration, or the burning of wastes under carefully controlled conditions, is a second, somewhat more expensive (cost: $9 to $17 per ton) alternative to the open dump. Incinerators can reduce the volume of waste by more than 80 percent (extending the life of a landfill); remove odors and disease-causing agents; allow recycling of some metals and glass; and allow recovery of some of the energy generated. However, incineration systems require skilled operators; have high capital, operational, and maintenance costs; and may cause air and water pollution if the emissions and residue are improperly controlled (Miller, 1979; Sewell, 1975).

The air pollution problem is an unusually difficult one. Because municipal wastes contain virtually every chemical produced by modern industry, the combination of these materials produces a large number and volume of toxic gases and particulates that pose a threat to human health and tend to corrode equipment. To overcome the problem, engineers have been testing a number of new systems, including (Sewell, 1975):

1. High temperature incineration—burning wastes at temperatures higher than 300° F, which promotes rapid and complete combustion (nearly 97 percent of the volume of waste can be eliminated). Problems have been encountered, however, with molten residue "freezing" in the bottom of the furnace, with metal stain, and with the production of nitrous oxide air pollution.
2. Fluidized-bed incineration—forced air suspends a hot bed of materials that engulfs and burns injected particles of waste. The system requires expensive waste shredding and the fluidized bed may become unstable if the wastes are not distributed evenly.
3. Pyrolysis—destructive distillation of wastes by heating under anaerobic conditions. The resulting mixture of organic liquids, gases, and charcoal residue can be recovered and sold to offset high capital investment and operating costs (of $5 to $13 per metric ton) (EPA, 1976c). Large amounts of energy are required for shredding the wastes and for the pyrolysis reaction. Pyrolysis systems are sensitive to the composition of entering wastes and can result in air pollution problems.

Innovative Solid Waste Management

Municipal efforts to dispose of increasing amounts of solid waste have usually resulted in programs to conserve resources or to promote the recycling of useful materials, such as paper, glass, aluminum, and rubber, in the municipal waste stream. Because recycling requires the expenditure of resources and energy to collect and reprocess materials, it is less efficient than many of the programs that promote resource conservation and reuse (CEQ, 1979a).

Recycling programs can provide a number of benefits to a community, which include reducing the demand for raw materials, reducing the volume of solid wastes, diminishing pollution and land disruption, and promoting the conservation and recapture of valuable sources of energy. For instance, the recycling of scrap iron requires 74 percent less energy, and 97 percent fewer raw materials and generates more than 90 percent less air pollution than does obtaining and processing iron ore (Staff of *Environmental Science and Technology*, 1975).

In 1975 the United States recycled 15.5 percent of the paper (compared to 50 percent in Japan), 4.7 percent of all the metals (including 8.7 percent of the aluminum), 6.9 percent of the rubber, 2.7 percent of the glass, and 0 percent of the plastics from residential and commercial wastes or, in total, only 5.9 percent of these wastes (EPA, 1977). Overall, the amount of wastes recycled as a percent of consumption actually fell between 1950 and 1970 (Ehrlich et al., 1977). In recent years, recycling has become increasingly attractive as resource prices increase, pollution and solid waste control prices rise, and recycling processes improve in cost and efficiency (Freeman et al., 1973).

The physical limit to recycling is ultimately determined by the amount of material and by the impact and cost of energy required to locate, collect, and reprocess materials. In economic terms, the main barrier to recycling is its cost relative to that of raw material inputs. The true economic value of recycling in the United States is underestimated for a number of reasons, including the six listed below (Miller, 1979; Sewell, 1975; Staff of *Environmental Science and Technology*, 1975).

- The U.S. government offers direct subsidies, tax write-offs, and resource depletion allowances to raw materials production industries. On the average, ore mining companies pay income taxes of 25 to 30 percent of their profits, compared to 48 percent for recycling industries.
- Railroad and truck shipping rates are commonly higher for recycled materials (often 50 to 100 percent higher) than for raw materials.
- The cost of disposal of a product is not reflected in its price.
- U.S. manufacturing systems are oriented toward raw materials processing and are poorly prepared for recycling. For instance, the German and Japanese steel industries are physically capable of processing more scrap iron than is the U.S. steel industry.

- Complex mixtures of resources, characteristic of many of the products of U.S. industry, are expensive and technically difficult to recycle.
- Market fluctuations in the price of recycled products prevent the development of an efficient market system.

The two principal approaches to recycling are source separation and resource recovery systems. Most of the recycled materials in the United States are obtained through source separation. In a source separation program, recyclable waste materials are separated and either collected by a private or public collection service or taken to a neighborhood recycling center by individual businesses or homeowners. The collected materials are then transported and sold to manufacturers or scrap dealers. The EPA (1977) estimated that more than 25 percent of all urban wastes could be recycled through source separation by 1990.

The key to successful source separation programs is the requirement that homes and businesses segregate trash into glass, metal, paper, and organic components. In addition, a local government could promote source separation by providing incentives for public or private collection and by strengthening the market for recycled materials through the purchase of recycled products.

In 1978 more than 40 cities in the United States had a separate collection program for recyclable materials, and an additional 196 cities recycled newspapers. In total, more than 3,000 voluntary community recycling centers were in operation (CEQ, 1979). These programs have found that source separation is the only proven method to recycle newspaper, office paper, corrugated cardboard, glass sorted by color, plastics, and rubber from municipal wastes. In addition, source separation remains the best method for recycling aluminum (CEQ, 1979a).

Source separation programs require only minimal capital investments for warehouses and collection vehicles and require only minimal paid labor because most of the separation is done voluntarily by the participants. However, source separation programs are rarely profit-making enterprises because the cost of collecting, sorting, and repackaging recyclables often exceeds their market value. In most towns that have initiated such programs, however, they are economically viable when the alternative costs of incineration or disposal in a landfill are incorporated into the calculations (EPA, 1977).

In a resource recovery system, municipal wastes are collected and transported to a waste processing facility rather than a landfill, incinerator, or recycling center. At the processing facility, ferrous metals and other materials can be recovered from the waste before or after incineration (CEQ, 1979a). Nearly 100 resource recovery facilities are now in operation or under construction in the United States (EPA, 1977).

The advantages of resource recovery systems over conventional landfill or incineration systems include the following (CEQ, 1979a):

- Waste volume is reduced from 75 to 90 percent, and the residue is sanitary and relatively inert.
- The EPA estimated that more than 75 percent of municipal wastes could be used to generate energy equivalent to more than 424,000 barrels of oil per day (EPA, 1975).
- The potential is great for recycling iron, steel, aluminum, and glass. The recovery efficiency of ferrous metals is from 90 to 97 percent; of aluminum, 65 percent; and of glass, from 50 to 70 percent (Office of Technology Assessment, 1978). Glass and aluminum recovery systems, however, are plagued with technical difficulties.
- If systems are designed and operated properly, little air and water pollution is emitted.

The most popular incineration and recovery systems are waterwall incinerators, which produce steam in pipes in the side walls, and modular incinerators, which capture heat from the exhaust gases. Waterwall systems must be fairly large (in the 1,000-ton-per-day range), whereas modular incinerators can function at 20 to 40 tons per day (CEQ, 1979a).

A second proven technology for energy recovery is the refuse-derived fuel (RDF) system, which converts trash into a fuel that can be burned in the incinerators just mentioned or industrial and utility boilers. The incoming solid waste is shredded and noncombustible materials removed by physical manipulation (see Figure 7-3). Ferrous metals (i.e., iron and steel) are removed through the use of electromagnets. Paper and plastic can be removed by blowing them into chambers. Mechanical screens, aluminum magnets, and flotation are used to extract organic materials, nonferrous metals, and glass. The incinerator residues (grit, stone, concrete, sand, etc.) are sent to a landfill (Miller, 1979). In practice, only a few of the planned or existing facilities actually separate ferrous and nonferrous metals and glass for recovery. The majority of resource recovery systems are primarily or exclusively concerned with energy recovery for municipal and industrial uses (EPA, 1977).

There are several disadvantages to resource recovery facilities, including (CEQ, 1979a):

- Emission of measurable amounts of fine particulates, hazardous organic compounds, toxic metals, and disease agents.
- Unhealthful working conditions due to noise, fires, and explosions.
- The difficulty of finding markets for the RDF. A 1,000-ton-per-day system could handle the trash of more than 600,000 people, yet generate only 3 percent of their energy.

210 / *Hazardous and Solid Waste Management*

Figure 7-3. Flow Diagram of a Typical Resource Recovery System.

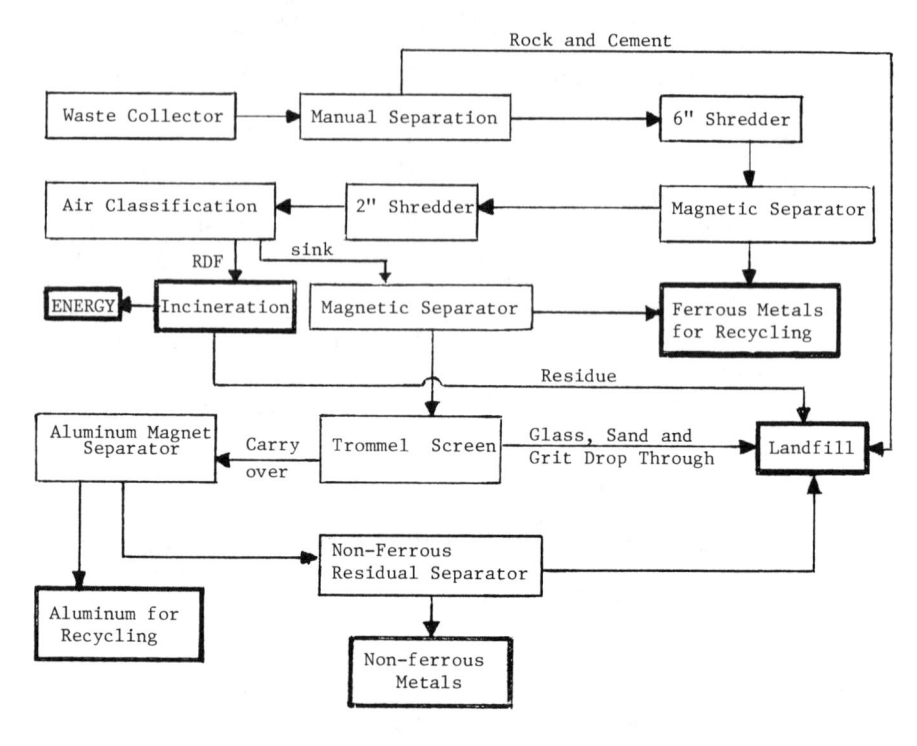

```
                                    Rock and Cement
                        ┌──────────────────────────────────────────────────┐
                        │                                                  │
┌───────────────┐   ┌──────────────────┐        ┌──────────────┐          │
│Waste Collector│──▶│Manual Separation │───────▶│ 6" Shredder  │          │
└───────────────┘   └──────────────────┘        └──────┬───────┘          │
                                                       │                   │
┌──────────────────┐   ┌─────────────┐        ┌────────▼─────────┐        │
│Air Classification│◀──│ 2" Shredder │◀───────│Magnetic Separator│        │
└────────┬─────────┘   └─────────────┘        └────────┬─────────┘        │
     RDF │       sink                                  │                   │
┌────────▼──┐ ┌─────────────┐ ┌──────────────────┐  ┌──▼──────────────┐   │
│  ENERGY ◀─┤ Incineration│ │Magnetic Separator│─▶│Ferrous Metals   │   │
└───────────┘ └─────────────┘ └────────┬─────────┘  │ for Recycling   │   │
                     │                 │            └─────────────────┘   │
                     │                 │   Residue                        │
┌───────────────────┐│       ┌─────────▼──────┐ Glass, Sand and ┌─────────▼┐
│Aluminum Magnet    ││ Carry │                │ Grit Drop Through│          │
│   Separator       ││──────▶│Trommel  Screen │─────────────────▶│ Landfill │
└────────┬──────────┘│ over  └────────┬───────┘                  └──────────┘
         │           │                │                                ▲
         │           │       ┌────────▼─────────┐                      │
         │           └──────▶│   Non-Ferrous    │──────────────────────┘
         │                   │Residual Separator│
         │                   └────────┬─────────┘
┌────────▼──────┐                     │
│  Aluminum for │            ┌────────▼─────────┐
│   Recycling   │            │   Non-ferrous    │
└───────────────┘            │     Metals       │
                             └──────────────────┘
```

- The greater value of many of the resources that are used as fuel if they were recycled. For instance, recycled paper is worth between $10 and $200 per ton, whereas its energy value is only $5 to $8 per ton (Seldman, 1976).
- The reluctance of the utilities that are the best potential market for RDF and prime candidates for owning and operating facilities to "get into the garbage business."
- The lack of economical competitiveness of resource recovery systems. They break even or turn a profit, however, when the costs for alternative methods of waste disposal are incorporated into the calculations.

A typical 1,000 ton per day facility costs approximately $25 million to build. At the Saugus, Massachusetts, 1,200-ton-per-day waterwall incinerator system, processing costs are an estimated $17.85 per ton. The Ames, Iowa, RDF System costs an estimated $22.69 per ton (Gordian Associates, Inc., 1977). However, these figures do not include revenues. Table 7-5 summarizes a theoretical analysis of possible resource recovery options for the Kansas City area. The total annual cost for larger facilities

Table 7-5. Projected Costs and Revenues for Energy Recovery Systems in the Kansas City Area in 1978 (dollars per processed ton) (Black and Veatch and Franklin Associates, Ltd., 1978).

Type of System	Annual Cost [a] Ownership	Annual Cost [a] Operating and Maintenance	Annual Cost [a] Total	Revenues	Net Cost
Modular Combustion Units [b]					
25 tons/day	$17.50	$23.41	$40.91	$18.00[c]	$22.91
50 tons/day	15.48	15.08	30.56	18.00[c]	12.56
100 tons/day	12.38	11.93	24.31	18.00[c]	6.31
200 tons/day	10.85	10.14	20.99	18.00[c]	2.99
Waterwall Combustion Unit [d]					
200 tons/day	16.27	12.68	28.95	18.00[c]	10.94
500 tons/day	14.34	8.75	23.09	18.00[c]	5.09
1500 tons/day	13.25	7.15	20.40	18.00[c]	2.40
Refuse-Derived Fuel System [e]					
500 tons/day	12.09	10.78	22.87	10.02[f]	12.85
1000 tons/day	10.78	9.33	20.11	10.02[f]	10.09

[a] Annual costs include interest on land, amortization of equipment, insurance, and operating and maintenance costs.

[b] Plants are assumed to operate at 95 percent of rated capacity, 5 days a week, 50 weeks a year.

[c] The plants are assumed to sell steam at $3 per thousand pounds in competition with fuel oil.

[d] Plants are assumed to operate at 78 percent of rated capacity, 7 days a week, 50 weeks per year. Capital investment was calculated at $43,370 per ton at 200 tons/day capacity; $38,157 per ton for 500 tons/day; and $35,187 per ton for 1500 tons/day.

[e] The system is assumed to operate at 85 percent of rated capacity, 6 days per week, 50 weeks per year. Capital investment includes modification of an existing boiler, and was calculated to be $32,102 per ton at 500 TPD capacity and $26,819 per ton at 1000 TPD capacity.

[f] The plants are assumed to sell RDF at $8.00 per ton. Ferrous and aluminum scrap are assumed recovered and sold.

is slightly more than $20 per ton, but revenues from the sale of energy substantially reduce the net costs of a facility. The net costs are, in most cases, substantially lower than the cost of operating future landfills, and considerable land would be saved.

Local governments can assist in overcoming the high capital costs of resource recovery facilities by offering loan guarantees, tax exemptions for municipal industrial development, pollution bonds, or outright construction grants. Many larger facilities have been financed with tax-exempt municipal bonds. In addition, the Energy Tax Act of 1978 allows businesses to take an additional 10 percent investment tax credit for installing alternative energy systems, including recycling equipment (CEQ, 1979a).

In summary, if properly designed and constructed, a resource recovery facility can simultaneously achieve the multiple objectives of

Table 7-6. Comparison of Source Separation and Centralized Waste Processing for Municipal Waste Disposal (CEQ, 1975).

	Source Separation	Centralized Waste Processing
Typical size of processing facility	10 tpd	1000 tpd
Typical capital investment (dollars)	low (50,000)	high (25,000,000)
Net cost per ton processed (after revenues)	$0-7	$3-15
Reduction in waste stream (percent)	10 to 50	75 and up
Products recovered	glass, paper, iron, aluminum	energy, iron
Environmental impact	negligible	some air pollution and worker health hazards

tpd = tons per day

reducing the volume of the waste stream, recycling valuable resources, and generating energy from previously underutilized resources. The EPA (1977) estimated that a national network of resource recovery facilities could increase the volume of the municipal waste stream recycled from the present 6 percent to 26 percent.

Superficially, it would appear that source separation and resource recovery systems are mutually exclusive. If recyclable materials are removed from the waste stream before processing in a resource recovery system, surely the value of materials and energy generated at the central facility would be seriously diminished. Plant revenues would drop, rendering the recovery system uneconomical. However, because the systems for resource recovery of recyclables, except those for ferrous metals, are in their initial stages of development, many existing facilities do not recover a significant amount of recyclables. Therefore, removal of metals and glass from the waste stream would not impose significant economic impacts (CEQ, 1979a).

In addition, the EPA estimated that an effective newspaper recycling program would reduce the energy content of the waste stream by only 3.5 percent. Further, an effective bottle and can source separation program would actually increase the energy content per unit weight of solid waste by 6 percent (CEQ, 1979a).

Table 7-6 summarizes the major characteristics of source separation and resource recovery systems. The source separation program is better suited for smaller communities because of the limited capacity of a local facility. In addition, smaller communities where citizens are more closely and actively involved in decision making are more likely to have the cooperation essential for a successful program. The higher capital and operating costs and the large waste volume necessary to make a recovery system economical favor larger cities and metropolitan areas. In addition, the large amount of energy generated seems best suited for industrial facilities or district heating systems. Resource recovery systems appear, therefore, to be best suited for urban areas with populations larger than one hundred thousand. However, smaller modular units can be developed for smaller communities (CEQ, 1979a).

Past experience with these systems indicate that a cautious step-by-step approach can prevent major technical or economic problems. In the development of a source separation program, the following prerequisites should be met (CEQ, 1979a): negotiated long-term contracts for recycled materials that specify floor prices; enthusiastic support of participants in the separation programs before program initiation; and the development of an ordinance that integrates the program into the waste disposal system and that mandates separation at the household level.

The following can facilitate the successful implementation of a resource recovery system (CEQ, 1979a): use of a simple, proven system; location of a user and negotiation of a long-term contract for the energy generated; and resource recovery of only a portion of the waste to avoid waste shortfalls and to facilitate the development of complimentary waste reduction or source separation programs.

It must be emphasized that the key to any successful recycling program, be it a high technology resource recovery system or a low technology source separation program, is to establish a consistent long-term market for recovered energy and wastes. Market fluctuations in the prices and demand for recovered materials are very difficult to contend with, especially for the relatively inflexible and expensive resource recovery systems. Despite the popularity of resource recycling programs, federal, state, regional, and local economic and political systems continue to be oriented toward the use of primary raw materials. However, impending shortages, high prices, and damage to ecological systems in the coming decades may rapidly alter this picture.

Federal Incentives For Waste Reduction and Recycling

Beverage container deposits. A recent Resource Conservation Committee (1979) report paid special attention to a national *bottle bill* that would require a system of deposits and refunds on beverage containers. The report concluded that the national legislation would:

- Reduce the volume of litter by 35 percent,
- Reduce solid waste by 0.5 to 1.5 percent annually,
- Save $25 million to $50 million annually in disposal costs,
- Save between 5 and 10 percent of the annual production of aluminum in the United States,
- Reduce steel consumption by 1 to 2 percent annually,
- Reduce air pollution by 0.75 billion to 1.2 billion pounds annually,

- Reduce water pollution by 140 million to 210 million pounds annually,
- Reduce national energy consumption by 0.1 percent annually,
- Save consumers between $660 million and $1.76 billion annually in reduced retail price of beverages,
- Inconvenience consumers,
- Eliminate between 4,900 and 10,400 jobs in the glass container production industry and between 14,200 and 22,000 jobs in the metal can production industry over a 5-year period,
- Create between 80,000 and 100,000 new jobs in the beverage distribution and retail sectors.

The committee recommended that any container legislation should apply to all sealed beer and soft drink containers, regardless of the material used, and that the deposit should be a minimum of 5 cents, beginning at the level of the distribution wholesaler. This proposal is quite similar to Oregon's now famous bottle bill, which has been extremely successful in realizing many of the previously mentioned benefits for nearly a decade. However, efforts to pass a national bottle bill have met with well-funded lobbying efforts by can and bottle manufacturers, aluminum and steel industries, metal worker unions, supermarket chains, brewers, and soft drink bottlers. Yet, surveys by the Federal Energy Administration indicate that more than 70 percent of the U.S. population favors the legislation (Miller, 1979).

Solid waste disposal charges are paid by consumers to cover the waste management costs for products, based on product weight or volume or unusual disposal costs. The intent is to provide a financial incentive for manufacturers and consumers to avoid excess packaging and to use recycled materials (CEQ, 1979a).

Local user fees are charges per household for waste pickup according to volume or weight of trash collected: the greater the volume or weight, the higher the fee. By having to pay such a fee, consumers have an incentive to conserve resources. If fees are set too high, however, illegal dumping may occur (CEQ, 1979a).

Virgin resource industries enjoy a number of *tax advantages* over recycling industries, which places recycled materials at a competitive disadvantage. Many of these advantages were originally intended to stimulate economic growth through the development of indigenous resources. The advantages include depletion allowances for certain minerals, tax advantages in royalty income from iron ore and coal mining, and allowing sales income to be taxed as capital gains. These and other provisions amount to a subsidy to the nonfuels mineral production industry of $375 million and to the timber industry of between $275 million and $550 million annually (Resource Conservation Committee, 1979).

In addition, railroad *freight rates* discriminate in favor of virgin resources at the expense of recycled materials. The Resource Conservation Committee (1979) study of the freight rates concluded that rate reductions of 38 percent for waste paper, 34 percent for recycled glass, between 1 and 2 percent for scrap iron, and 9 percent for recycled aluminum are warranted.

One way government can promote recycling is to *emphasize purchase of recycled products.* This can bolster the market considerably by stabilizing and increasing the demand. Government can thus promote recycling and conserve resources, reduce dependence on nonindigenous resources, reduce pollution, and conserve energy. The 1976 Resource Conservation and Recovery Act requires the EPA to develop guidelines for federal agencies to "procure items composed of the highest percentage of recovered materials practicable." However, the EPA, confronted with more than 45,000 federal product and material specifications, has been unable to do more than scratch the surface in developing legally defensible guidelines (CEQ, 1979a).

The 1983 Oregon legislature passed a recycling bill that contains many new innovative elements (Oregon Senate Bill 405). Key provisions of the bill include the following:

- All commercial garbage haulers that dump refuse in licensed sanitary landfills must provide an "opportunity to recycle" to their customers.
- "Opportunity to recycle" is defined as minimally a place for collecting source-separated recyclable materials at the disposal site or a more convenient location, a public education program including a notice to each customer of the opportunity to recycle, and, for communities with a population of 5,000 or more, collection at least once a month of source-separated recyclable materials from each customer serviced.
- A person who source-separates recyclable material may be charged less, but not more, for these collection services.
- "Recyclable material" is defined as material that can be collected and sold for recycling at a cost equal to or less than the cost of collection and disposal.
- After July 1, 1986, every person in Oregon shall have the opportunity to recycle.

8 / Economic Impacts of Environmental Controls

Are environmental controls hurting the economies of industrialized and developing nations? It has been asserted that environmental controls are expensive and inflationary, contribute to unemployment, and inhibit economic growth and development. Conversely, proenvironment forces argue that environmental controls create jobs, conserve valuable resources and energy, and provide a very valuable service by promoting health, safety, welfare, peace, and permanence.

These arguments deserve serious consideration because the stakes are high. The U.S. economy is becoming increasingly unstable and insensitive to conventional management tools. Improper growth and development of the economy is directly or indirectly creating a myriad of noneconomic problems.

Despite the importance of the economy-vs.-environment debate, very few reliable economic analyses have been done of the economic impacts of environmental controls. According to Haveman and Smith (1978), there are several reasons for this lack: (1) the economic effects of environmental controls are many and often subtle or hidden; (2) the benefits of environmental controls are difficult to quantify in economic terms—for example, try to put a dollar value on the health and safety of your children; and (3) the costs of environmental controls are often underwritten, subsidized, or hidden. Such obstacles are not insurmountable. In the detailed studies that have been completed of the economic costs of environmental controls (Haveman and Smith, 1978; CEQ, 1979a; Data Resources Inc., 1979; Chase Econometrics Associates, Inc., 1976), the results are quite interesting.

This chapter provides a discussion of the economic costs and benefits of environmental controls. Some recent findings on the distributive effects of costs and benefits are provided, followed by critique and discussion of analytical and management tools. The intent of this chapter is to provide ammunition for the promotion and defense of environmental quality control programs; to pinpoint real problems to promote more effective resolution; and to indicate several of the more important policy tools available for efficient management.

The Costs and Benefits of Environmental Controls

The Costs of Pollution Controls

Environmental problems often result indirectly from failure to include the total cost of production or consumption in the price of goods or services. If these external costs could be included in the price of a good or service, consumer purchasing behavior would more accurately reflect the true costs of production or consumption. Demand for higher-priced "high-polluting" goods and services would be reduced, and the relatively low prices of "low-polluting" goods and services would increase the demand for them.

Estimates of the economic impacts of environmental controls are made annually by the Council on Environmental Quality. The estimate for 1980 is given in Table 8-1. The CEQ reported that the total cost of compliance with all existing federal environmental quality programs in 1979 was $36.9 billion, most of which was for air and water pollution abatement programs. Air pollution expenditures totaled $22.3 billion, with $10.4 billion spent on capital costs and $11.9 billion on operations and maintenance. It is important to note that 93 percent of the air pollution expenditures came from the private sector. The predominance of operation and maintenance expenditures indicates the preferences of the private sector for changes in processes rather than large capital expenditure programs.

Water pollution expenditures in 1979 were approximately $12.7 billion, with 47 percent of the expenditures by the public sector (which accounts for only 20 percent of the wastes). Approximately 58 percent of the expenditures were for capital costs, reflecting the reliance of the public sector on large capital expenditure programs for sewage treatment. The private sector's ability to treat a greater amount of waste at a reduced cost is indicative of the inefficiencies in capital-intensive municipal and regional water treatment programs.

The total 1979 expenditure of $36.9 billion represents approximately 1.5 percent of the GNP (gross national product) in that year. Total annual environmental quality expenditures are estimated to be $69.0 billion (in 1979 dollars) by 1988. Total spending between 1979 and 1988 is estimated at $518.5 billion, of which approximately 58 percent will go for air pollution controls, 33 percent for water pollution controls, and only 9 percent for control of all other environmental problems (see Figure 8-1).

It should be noted that these environmental quality control expenditures have resulted in many new industries and employment opportunities. There are currently more than 600 companies producing emissions control equipment. Air and water quality control firms had more than $1.8 billion in equipment sales in 1977, and their sales

Table 8-1. Estimated Incremental Pollution Abatement Expenditures,[a] 1979-1988 (billions of 1979 dollars) (CEQ, 1980).

Program	1979 Operation and mainte- nance	1979 Annual capital costs[b]	1979 Total annual costs	1988 Operation and mainte- nance	1988 Annual capital costs[b]	1988 Total annual costs	Cumulative (1979-1988) Operation and mainte- nance	Cumulative (1979-1988) Capital costs[b]	Cumulative (1979-1988) Total costs
Air pollution									
Public	1.2	0.3	1.5	2.0	0.5	2.5	15.8	3.7	19.5
Private	10.7	10.1	21.8	14.3	20.8	35.1	120.2	159.4	279.6
Subtotal	11.9	10.4	22.3	16.3	21.3	37.6	136.0	163.1	299.1
Water Pollution									
Public	1.7	4.3	6.0	3.3	10.0	13.3	25.1	59.2	84.3
Private	3.7	3.0	6.7	5.7	5.4	11.1	44.9	40.5	85.4
Subtotal	5.4	7.3	12.7	9.0	15.4	24.4	70.0	99.7	169.7
Solid Waste	<0.05	<0.05	<0.05	1.3	1.0	2.3	9.0	6.4	15.4
Toxic substances	0.1	0.2	0.3	0.5	0.6	1.1	3.6	4.6	8.2
Drinking water	<0.05	<0.05	<0.05	0.1	0.3	0.4	1.3	1.4	2.7
Noise	<0.05	0.1	0.1	0.6	1.0	1.6	2.6	4.3	6.9
Pesticides	0.1	<0.05	0.1	0.1	<0.05	0.1	1.2	<0.05	1.2
Land reclamation	0.3	1.1	1.4	0.3	1.5	1.5	3.8	11.5	15.3
Total	17.8	19.1	36.9	28.2	40.8	69.0	227.6	291.0	518.5

[a] Incremental costs are those made in response to federal legislation beyond those that would have been made in the absence of that legislation.

[b] Interest and depreciation.

Figure 8-1. The Estimated Amount of Spending for Environmental Protection, 1979 to 1988 (CEQ, 1980).

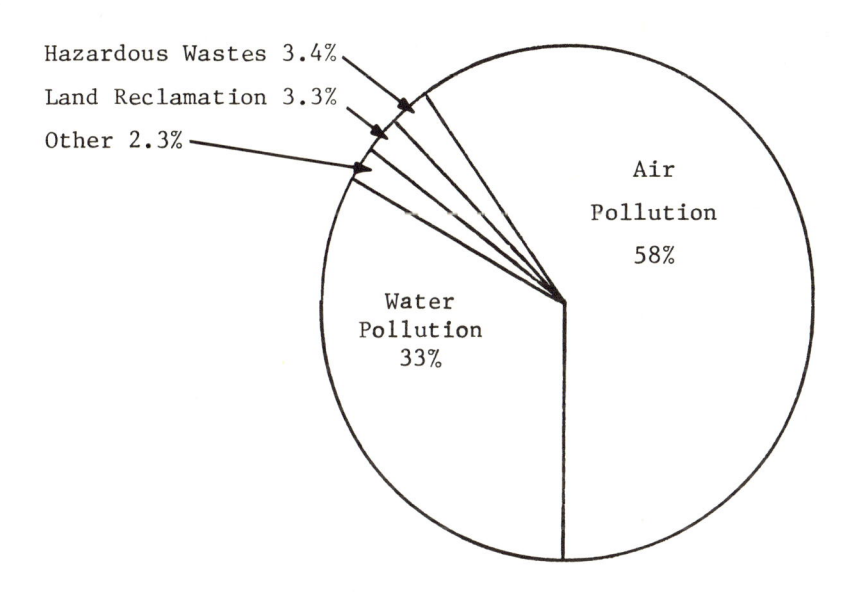

- Hazardous Wastes 3.4%
- Land Reclamation 3.3%
- Other 2.3%
- Water Pollution 33%
- Air Pollution 58%

growth rate is twice that of the rest of U.S. industries. By 1985 their sales are expected to triple. In addition, business opportunities have resulted in recycling, mass transit, building design, and renewable energy systems (McCloskey, 1981).

To define more precisely the economic impacts of environmental controls, data are needed on the regional and industrial impacts. Table 8-2 summarizes the CEQ projections of the impacts of environmental controls from 1971 to 1983 on the investment and operations and maintenance of individual industries. Note the high air pollution abatement costs for the pulp and paper; chemicals; petroleum; stone, clay, and glass; primary nonferrous metals; and electricity industries. High water pollution abatement costs were predicted for the pulp and paper, chemicals, petroleum, machinery, and electricity industries (Chase Econometrics Associates, Inc., 1976). Table 8-3 indicates the estimated impacts of environmental quality controls on the prices, output, and employment of selected industries. The greatest price increases were predicted for the paper, chemicals, nonferrous metals, auto, and utilities industries. The highest decline in output was predicted to be in the auto industry (5.6 percent) by 1983. In many industries, employment was predicted to rise due to environmental quality programs. It is important to emphasize that the actual economic impacts on prices or

Table 8-2. Estimated Incremental Pollution Control Expenditures, 1976-1983, (billions of 1974 dollars)(Chase Econometrics Associates, Inc., 1976).

Industry	Air Pollution Abatement Costs (1976-1983) Investment	Air Pollution Abatement Costs (1976-1983) Annual Operating and Maintenance	Water Pollution Abatement Costs (1976-1983) Investment	Water Pollution Abatement Costs (1976-1983) Annual Operating and Maintenance
Food and Beverages	0.33	0.89	0.54	1.77
Textiles	0.0	0.0	0.23	0.38
Pulp and Paper Products	1.11	4.25	4.10	3.48
Chemicals	1.27	3.54	7.61	10.74
Petroleum	0.57	3.29	2.36	4.51
Rubber and Misc. Plastics	0.25	0.64	0.0	0.0
Stone, Clay, and Glass	1.37	3.32	0.03	0.53
Iron and Steel	1.88	6.17	1.81	1.80
Primary Nonferrous Metals	1.25	6.67	-0.20	0.39
Machinery	0.69	2.20	8.19	4.59
Motor Vehicles	0.01	0.29	0.0	0.0
Other Transportation	0.06	0.28	0.80	1.57
Electricity	11.03	28.95	2.53	7.49
Utilities	0.26	0.61	0.0	0.0

output of individual industries rarely exceed 5 to 6 percent by 1983. The most serious impacts were predicted in the prices of the utilities (increases of 27.8 percent) and nonferrous metals (increases of 8.1 percent) industries and in the output of the auto industry (decreases of 5.6 percent). In summary, these figures indicate relatively insignificant impacts for the majority of U.S. industries (Haveman and Smith, 1978).

Because such figures can be controversial, the Environmental Protection Agency (EPA) in 1980 conducted a study of the accuracy of its estimates of the cost of compliance with federal environmental laws (Putnam, Hayes and Bartlett, Inc., 1980). The study found that the EPA was quite accurate and slightly better at estimating compliance costs than were the affected industries.

Finally, it has been suggested that adverse localized effects of environmental controls may be severe despite relatively modest national and general industrial impacts. This would appear to be true, especially in areas of heavy reliance on the metals, petroleum, chemicals, and electricity industries. The impact generally appears to be most serious

Table 8-3. Estimated Impacts on Individual Industries (percentage change)(Chase Econometrics Associates, Inc., 1976).

	By 1983		
Industry	Prices	Output	Employment
Agriculture	0.6	-1.3	+1.3
Mining	0.7	-2.5	-0.4
Construction	0.2	-3.5	-0.2
Food	1.2	-1.5	+1.2
Tobacco	0.4	-2.7	+0.9
Textiles	0.9	-2.5	-0.2
Apparel	0.5	-2.2	-0.6
Lumber	1.5	-4.4	-0.6
Furniture	0.5	-3.1	-1.3
Paper	6.2	-2.9	-1.0
Printing	0.3	-3.1	-1.3
Chemicals	4.8	-2.8	-1.1
Petroleum	2.3	-2.0	+0.7
Rubber	1.0	-4.2	-1.4
Leather	0.9	-1.4	-0.3
Stone, clay and glass	3.2	-3.4	-1.0
Iron and steel	4.1	-2.9	-0.3
Nonferrous metals	8.1	-2.4	+0.3
Fabricated metals	0.8	-3.1	-0.6
Nonelectrical machinery	2.8	-1.6	+0.3
Electrical machinery	1.2	-3.5	-0.1
Autos	5.5	-5.6	-2.4
Other transportation equipment	0.6	-0.9	+0.8
Instruments	0.4	-2.7	-0.4
Misc. manufacturing	0.4	-1.7	-0.7
Transportation services	0.5	-2.7	+0.5
Communications	0.4	-4.0	-1.5
Utilities	27.8	-1.8	+0.6
Travel	0.6	-2.7	-0.8
Finance, insurance and real estate	0.8	-2.4	-1.0
Other services	0.7	-2.6	+1.6

Employment

Industrialists tend to assert that environmental quality controls force plant closings, causing undue hardships and unemployment. The real evidence suggests that such impacts are quite minimal. Through 1982, an estimated 118 plants were closed because of environmental quality controls, causing a loss of approximately 22,000 jobs. In 60 percent of the cases, the plants were old or obsolete. The majority of the businesses relocated to more economically efficient facilities or locations (McCloskey, 1981).

Table 8-4 presents a breakdown of actual and threatened job losses (1971–1976) from environmentally related causes. Haveman and Smith (1978) pointed out that approximately 25 percent of the actual and 90 percent of the threatened job losses occurred in the Great Lakes Region of the United States (EPA Region V). These closures occurred mainly in the primary metals, chemicals, and heavy industrial plants of the region that could generally be characterized as older and relatively inefficient. Therefore, it would seem that a program carefully targeted to provide assistance to selected industries in certain regions of the country could alleviate many of the negative economic and employment impacts that are actually experienced by the imposition of environmental quality controls.

This view, however, focuses only on the negative employment effects of environmental controls. It was predicted that environmental quality expenditures could actually reduce the total U.S. unemployment rate by 0.8 percent and result in the creation of 400,000 jobs in 1980 and 1981 (CEQ, 1979a). Figure 8-2 indicates the rate of unemployment between 1970 and 1986, with and without environmental quality controls. Overall, it is believed that well over 1 million new jobs have been created due to environmental quality controls between 1971 and 1977 (Miller, 1979)—each billion spent on environmental quality programs results in 67,000 to 85,000 jobs. The estimated expenditures for pollution control between 1978 and 1987 of $477 billion could result in more than 40 million new jobs. Even if this estimate is off by a factor of ten, it is apparent that environmental regulations result in significantly more jobs than are lost (Miller, 1979).

Inflation

Whether environmental programs are managed by government or industry, ultimately the consumer pays the costs through taxes or prices. The question then must be asked, What effect are environmental quality

Table 8-4. Jobs Affected: Actual and Threatened Closings Where Pollution Control Costs Were Alleged To Be a Factor, January 1971 to December 1976 (EPA, 1978c).

Regions	Primary metal industries	Food & kindred prods.	Chemicals & allied prods.	Paper & allied prods.	Stone, clay, glass & concrete prods.	Fabricated metal prods.	Other industries[a]	Totals
I								
Actual	0	0	0	0	0	30	700	730
Threatened	0	0	0	0	0	0	74	74
II								
Actual	124	252	1,505	1,677	0	750	924	5,232
Threatened	0	0	0	0	0	0	0	0
III								
Actual	94	105	590	0	0	102	1,021	1,912
Threatened	0	204	38	0	0	0	533	775
IV								
Actual	942	0	0	217	0	0	0	1,159
Threatened	0	0	0	0	0	0	0	0
V								
Actual	670	165	2,230	500	210	0	1,778	5,553
Threatened	24,250	0	435	200	228	0	3,100	28,213
VI								
Actual	1,440	0	43	0	0	0	0	1,483
Threatened	0	0	400	0	0	0	0	400
VII								
Actual	70	272	0	0	0	0	0	342
Threatened	0	25	0	0	0	0	0	25
VIII								
Actual	0	0	0	0	0	0	0	0
Threatened	0	0	0	0	0	0	0	0

Table E.4 (continued)

Regions	Primary metal industries	Food & kindred prods.	Chemicals & allied prods.	Paper & allied prods.	Stone, clay, glass & concrete prods.	Fabricated metal prods.	Other industries[a]	Totals
IX								
Actual	438	165	46	103	748	0	35	1,535
Threatened	1,800	0	0	0	0	0	0	1,810
X								
Actual	0	190	0	833	0	83	510	1,616
Threatened	0	0	0	0	0	0	0	0
Total								
Actual	3,778	1,149	4,414	3,330	958	965	4,968	19,562
Threatened	26,060	229	873	200	228	0	3,707	31,297
Grand Total	29,918	1,378	5,287	3,530	1,186	965	8,675	50,859
Percentage	59	3	10	7	2	2	17	100

Notes: Economic dislocation information is compiled and reported by EPA regional offices. Dislocations involving fewer than 25 jobs are not reported.

[a] Includes all dislocations where the combined "actual" and "threatened" plants amount to fewer than five.

Region   States and Territories
I   Maine, N.H., Vt, Mass., R.I., Conn.
II   N.Y., N.J., Puerto Rico, Virgin Islands
III   Pa., Del., Md., Va., W.Va.
IV   N.C., S.C., Ga., Fla., Ky., Tenn., Ala., Miss.
V   Oh., Mich., Ind., Ill., Wis., Minn.
VI   Ark., La., Okla., Tex., N. Mex.
VII   Iowa, Mo., Nebr., Kans.
VIII   N. Dak., S. Dak., Mont., Wyo., Colo., Ut.
IX   Ariz., Nev., Ca., Hawaii
X   Id., Or., Wash., Alaska

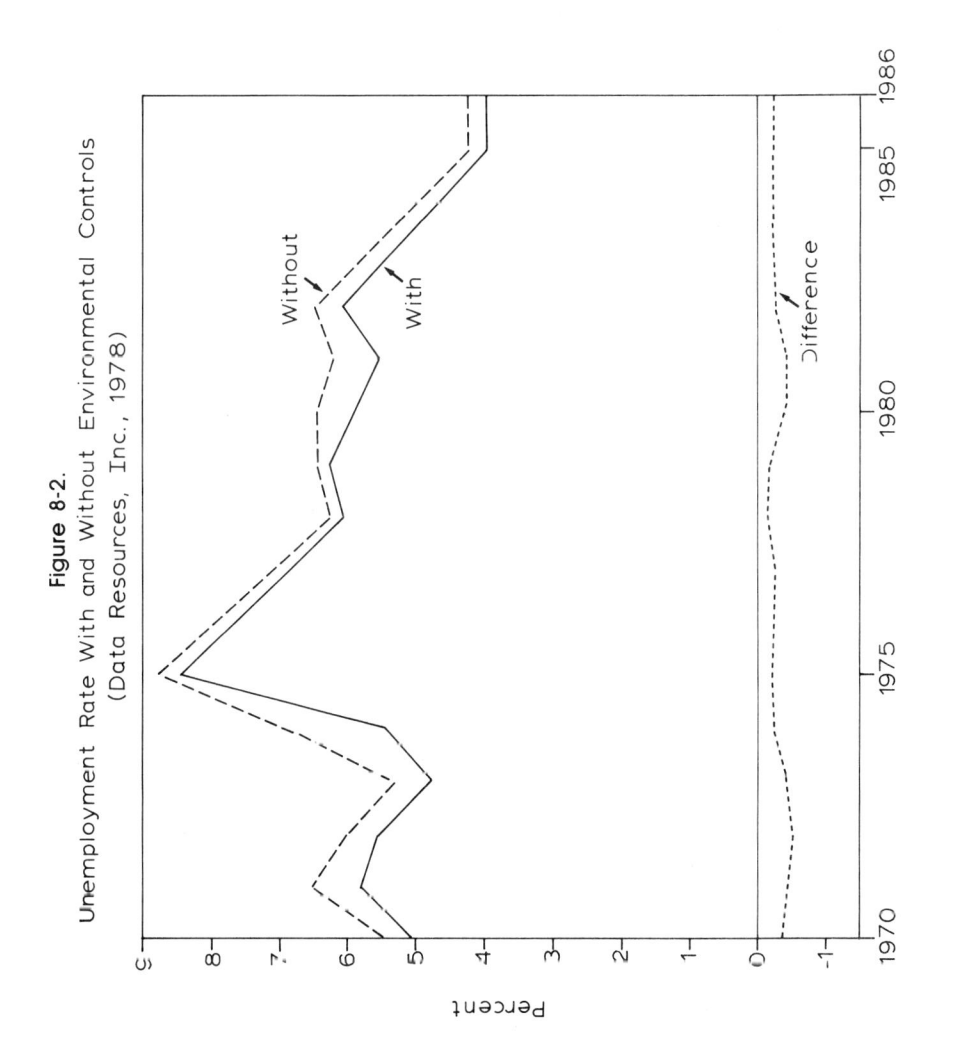

Figure 8-2.
Unemployment Rate With and Without Environmental Controls (Data Resources, Inc., 1978)

Figure 8-3.
Percent Annual Increase in Consumer Price Index With and Without Environmental Controls.
(Data Resources, Inc., 1978)

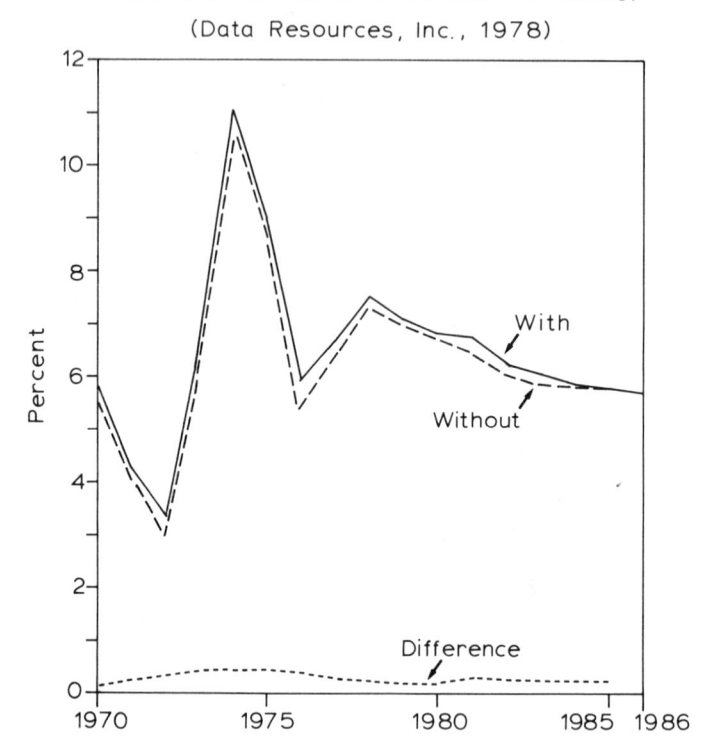

controls having on inflation? Conventionally, inflation is defined as an increase in the consumer price index (CPI), a composite measure of the average price of a fixed market basket of goods and services. Between 1960 and 1965, the CPI increased annually at a rate of 1.3 percent. Between 1970 and 1978, this rate increased to 6.5 percent annually (CEQ, 1979a). More recent figures indicate an annual increase of approximately 7 percent.

How much have environmental quality controls contributed to this inflationary spiral? According to several estimates (CEQ, 1979a; McCloskey, 1981; Speth, 1978), the annual contribution of environmental quality controls to inflation in the 1970s was approximately 0.3 percent (see Figure 8-3). Because most of the pollution control technology is now in place, this is expected to drop to between 0.2 and 0.1 percent between 1979 and 1986 (CEQ, 1979a).

Two additional comments on inflation are warranted. The first is that the CPI is a very poor measure of true inflation. Expenditures to improve the environment greatly increase the general welfare (improvements in public health, property values, resource yields, recreation, etc.). However, such important benefits are inadequately represented in the CPI. Moreover, as the prices of high-polluting goods and services increase, substitution of cleaner products will occur. To the extent that some substitution will take place, the CPI will overstate the impacts of price changes because it is assumed in computing the CPI that the market basket remains the same (Speth, 1978).

The second comment is on the true causes of inflation. Two notable characteristics of current inflation are that it is common throughout the industrial nations of the world and it continues despite repeated recessions. Lester Brown, the director of the Worldwatch Institute, believed that the roots of current economic problems lie in the deteriorating relationship between the world's population and the world's resources and natural systems. Brown cited increasing food, fuel, and forest products prices as an example of too many people seeking too large a share of the world's dwindling resource base. Although he did not believe that all inflation has its base in competition for resources, it is important to note that wise stewardship through natural resource and environmental regulation may be the best economic investment possible in the future of industrialized societies (Speth, 1978).

Productivity

Since the early 1960s the rate of growth of productivity, measured by the dollar value of output per hour of paid employment in the private sector, has been steadily declining. In 1979 and 1980 productivity actually dropped in the United States by 0.9 percent and 1.7 percent, respectively (CEQ, 1980). Regulations, including environmental controls, can reduce productivity through the diversion of labor and capital from the production of goods to the production of safe workplaces or clean land, water, or air. Environmental regulations can also reduce productivity through delays in construction and uncertainties of administration. Numerous studies have attempted to quantify the relative effects of various factors on productivity. The typical estimate of the role of environmental regulations in the decrease in productivity is a mere 0.05 to 0.3 percent (CEQ, 1980).

Economic Growth

Unfortunately, the GNP, like the CPI, is often misinterpreted as a measure of national welfare, and there are serious shortcomings in so using it. The GNP is a measure of goods and services produced annually, rather than those consumed. In pure economic terms, satisfaction or "well being" is regarded as the direct result of the consumption of goods and services. The GNP does not indicate what types of goods or services are produced nor account for the equity issues of income group, ethnicity, or number of people involved in consumption. The sales of cigarettes increase the GNP as well as the potentially resulting expenditures for lung cancer. Further, housepersons and people who choose to reduce the hours they work are considered to be of no or reduced value to the overall GNP. But perhaps most importantly, the enjoyment citizens obtain from a cleaner, safer, and more pleasant environment is not reflected in the GNP (CEQ, 1979a).

For these reasons, many economists and environmentalists have called for a more accurate measure of national well being. The economic council of Japan has developed a net national welfare measure that reflects many of these concerns. The Bureau of Economic Analysis of the U.S. Department of Commerce is studying the possibility of such a measure for the United States (CEQ, 1979a).

Environmental programs have a mixed effect on real GNP (see Figure 8-4). Between 1970 and 1977 the GNP was actually higher because of the production of goods and services for environmental controls. In 1972 the difference due to such production was $14.4 billion or approximately 1 percent of GNP. After 1977 environmental control expenditures began to exert a drag on the economy, and by 1986, the GNP is predicted to be approximately 1 percent lower because of environmental controls (CEQ, 1979a).

One reason for the nominal impact of GNP is that environmental control investments often increase the efficiencies of industrial processes and stimulate technological innovation. McCloskey (1981) found that pollution control investments cut operating costs at one division of the Dow Chemical Company by $2 million, reduced energy consumption in Alcoa plants by 30 percent, and saved $11 million from process changes for the 3M Company.

The Benefits of Environmental Controls

The cost of protecting the environment is ultimately borne by consumers through increased prices or taxes. Yet, failure to prevent environmental contamination could cost citizens even more in health, physical, and environmental damage.

The annual cost for monitoring air pollution in the United States is estimated at $20 billion. Water pollution results in costs of approximately $10 billion annually. Damages would be much higher without environmental quality controls (Miller, 1979). For instance, the EPA (1974b) estimated that the Clean Air Act saved an estimated 25,000 lives and prevented more than 6 million cases of acute respiratory disorders in the United States between 1973 and 1980.

Figure 8-4.
Real Gross National Product With and Without Environmental Controls (Data Resources, Inc., 1978)

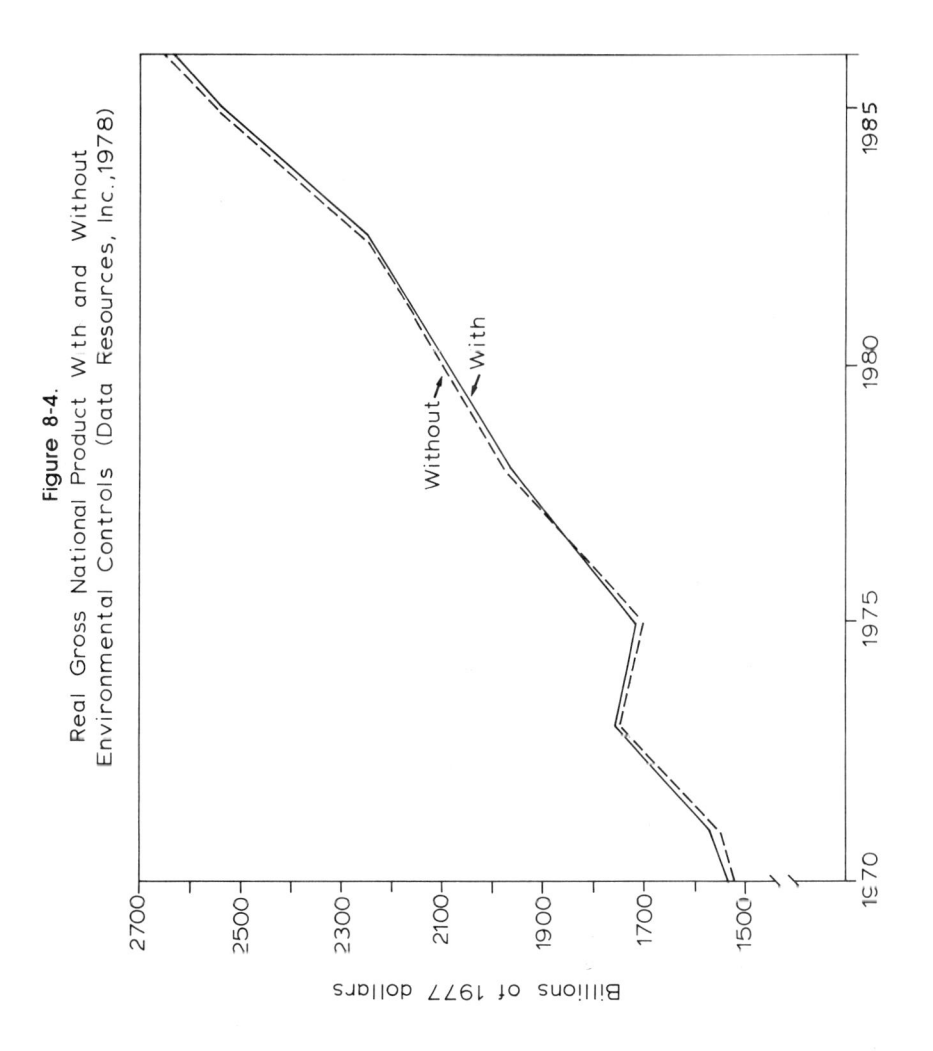

In addition, land use controls that reduce geologic hazards to life and property have been shown to be extremely cost effective. Figure 8-5 summarizes a thorough study of the expected damage, possible loss reduction, and program costs from 1970 to 2000 involved in a California program to implement state-of-the-art controls in managing geologic hazards (Alfors et al., 1973). Overall, approximately $6 billion would be required to reduce the total damages from $55 billion to $17 billion. It must be emphasized that these figures reflect only the monetary costs and ignore the nonmonetary costs, such as risk, anxiety, or suffering, associated with geologic hazards.

It is very important to emphasize that environmental quality programs improve the living conditions of all citizens. For instance, air pollution can reduce longevity, curtail physical activities, and reduce human resistance to disease. If industry were to achieve the national air quality standards, mortality losses to the economy would be reduced by $36 billion annually.

Further, the national incidence of cancer is increasing at 2 percent annually, and an estimated 60 to 90 percent of all cancer is induced by environmental factors. It has been shown that the incidence of cancer in crowded city centers is double that of the suburbs.

Environmental quality controls can offer more subtle benefits. Environmental controls reduce the need for defensive products, such as medical care, health and life insurance, burglar alarms, and so on, by improving the health and living conditions of the general population. Environmental controls can improve the quality, longevity, and safety of commercial products. Conservation of energy and natural resources can substantially reduce operating costs and reduce our dependencies on foreign suppliers of natural resources. Mass transit can reduce the cost and improve the speed of and increase public access to adequate transportation. By forcing price increases in high-polluting goods and services, production can be shifted toward cleaner industries and municipalities.

In summary, the economic, health, physical, and social benefits of environmental quality controls clearly outweigh the costs. In the true economic sense, environmental controls provide a valuable service to U.S. citizens by promoting health, safety, welfare, peace, and permanence.

The Distributive Effects of Environmental Controls

In the public forum, environmentalists are often accused of being elitist—of being unconcerned about the health, safety, and welfare of the poor and minority groups. Until recently few real data existed to support the charges or the defense. The task of identifying the benefits and burdens, much less the individuals affected, has been a formidable one. Several studies have been published, providing some interesting insights into the debate over the distributive effects of environmental

Figure 8-5. Estimated Losses, Savings, and Costs for Managing Geologic Hazards in California from 1970 to 2000 (Alfors et al., 1973).

Explanation
- Total losses, 1970–2000, under current practices
- Loss-reduction possible, 1970–2000
- Cost of loss-reduction measures, 1970–2000

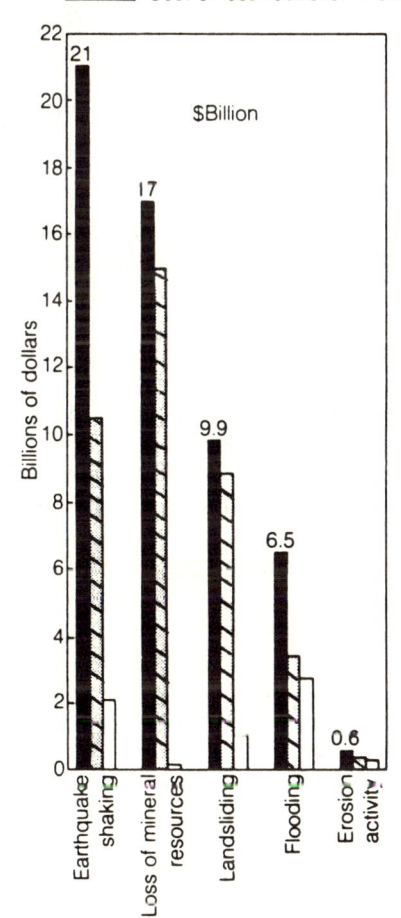

Hazard	Total losses ($Billion)
Earthquake shaking	21
Loss of mineral resources	17
Landsliding	9.9
Flooding	6.5
Erosion activity	0.6

programs (see Baumol, 1974; Gianessi, Peskin, and Wolff, 1977; and Peskin, 1978). For our purposes we will focus on an analysis of the distributive effects of the Clean Air Act of 1970.

Peskin (1978) studied the relative costs and benefits of pollution control programs for families within county or Standard Metropolitan Statistical Areas of the United States. As seen in Table 8-5, residents of the heavily industrialized Northeast gain the most from air pollution control programs, those in the Southwest and West gain the least. Note that the benefits are heavily concentrated in a very few regions. More than 30 percent of the national benefits go to the five dirtiest SMSAs with only approximately 8 percent of the U.S. population.

As seen in Table 8-6, the costs are much more widely distributed because prices and taxes are relatively evenly distributed throughout the country. Table 8-7 provides a summary of the net benefits of air pollution control programs. Only 24 of 274 SMSAs with only 28 percent of the population indicate a net benefit from air pollution control programs (Peskin, 1978). It must be emphasized, however, that these citizens suffer a disproportionately large share of the physical and social costs of air pollution and that much of the rest of the nation enjoys the products produced by the heavy industries in these areas.

A subsequent analysis of the population of each statistical area provides an insight into the racial and income distribution of costs and benefits of environmental controls. For the purposes of analysis, two categories of air pollution sources were established: (1) industry and government and (2) household, which is represented by the number of automobiles per family. The two categories are markedly different when broken down into income groups. Table 8-8 summarizes the net benefits of air pollution control for industry and government and for households by income and racial group.

It is interesting to note that all ethnic and income groups benefit from industrial air pollution controls except the wealthy white group, which can avoid the effects of the pollution by living in wealthier suburbs. Note that in most categories, the benefits increase as income increases. This is believed to be a result of decreased benefits to the very poor rural population (Peskin, 1978). Conversely, all groups lose from household (automobile) controls. Nonwhites lose proportionately less than whites, and poor nonwhites lose the least, probably because they bear a much greater burden of the costs of automotive air pollution in central city areas and they own fewer automobiles per family. In total net benefits, the white population loses, and losses increase with income. All categories of nonwhites gain except for the wealthy.

To summarize, the damages of air pollution are disproportionately borne by the minority and low-income communities. Thus air pollution controls are most beneficial to these groups.

Table 8-5. Areas with Highest and Lowest Per Family Gross Benefits Under the 1970 Clean Air Amendments (Peskin, 1978).

Rank	County Group or SMSA	Dollars per Family
	Ten Highest	
1	Jersey City SMSA	2,547.29
2	New York, N.Y. SMSA	1,169.94
3	Erie SMSA	1,040.37
4	Newark SMSA	864.41
5	Paterson SMSA	782.99
6	Detroit SMSA	762.77
7	Chicago SMSA	660.71
8	Cleveland SMSA	652.12
9	Providence SMSA	631.39
10	Gary SMSA	622.94
	Ten Lowest	
1	Alaska	0.32
2	Nevada, S. Utah	1.42
3	Montana	2.53
4	S. New Mexico, W. Texas	2.98
5	Wyoming, W. Nebraska	2.98
6	N. New Mexico	3.79
7	Arizona	3.85
8	S.W. Texas	4.09
9	N.W. Texas	4.15
10	C. Texas	4.63

Source: P. R. Portney (ed.). Current Issues in U.S. Environmental Policy. Published for Resources for the Future by The Johns Hopkins University Press, 1978.

Table 8-6. Areas with Highest and Lowest Per Family Costs Under the 1970 Clean Air Amendments (Peskin, 1978).

Rank	Area	Dollars per Family
	Ten Highest	
1	Oxnard-Ventura SMSA	438.96
2	Bridgeport SMSA	422.86
3	Anaheim SMSA	416.95
4	Paterson SMSA	405.04
5	San Jose SMSA	401.18
6	S.W. Texas	400.22
7	Columbia SMSA	396.73
8	Alaska	396.11
9	Lansing SMSA	395.76
10	Dayton	395.30
	Ten Lowest	
1	S. Arkansas, W.C. Mississippi	254.56
2	Jersey City SMSA	263.18
3	N.W. Mississippi	270.16
4	N. West Virginia	274.14
5	N.W. Florida	279.63
6	Central S. Carolina	279.63
7	N.C. Missouri	282.08
8	New York, N.Y. SMSA	284.11
9	N. Mississippi, W. Tennessee, E. Arkansas	286.77
10	C. Tennessee	289.23

Source: P. R. Portney (ed.). Current Issues in U.S. Environmental Policy. Published for Resources for the Future by The Johns Hopkins University Press, 1978.

Table 8-7. Areas with Highest and Lowest Per Family Net Benefits Under the 1970 Clean Air Amendments (Peskin, 1978).

Rank	County Group or SMSA	Net Benefit (Dollars per Family)
	Ten Highest	
1	Jersey City SMSA	2,284.11
2	New York SMSA	885.83
3	Erie SMSA	700.85
4	Newark SMSA	509.59
5	Detroit SMSA	385.15
6	Paterson SMSA	377.95
7	Chicago SMSA	317.87
8	Providence SMSA	283.91
9	Cleveland SMSA	278.80
10	Gary SMSA	264.09
	Ten Lowest	
1	S.W. Texas	-396.13
2	Alaska	-395.79
3	Nevada, S.W. Utah	-379.42
4	Santa Barbara SMSA	-362.08
5	Wyoming, W. Nebraska	-350.35
6	S. New Mexico, W. Texas	-349.71
7	Tucson SMSA	-347.52
8	C. Nebraska	-345.12
9	E.C. California	-343.57
10	N.E. Colorado	-342.23

Source: P. R. Portney (ed.). Current Issues in U. S. Environmental Policy. Published for Resources for the Future by The Johns Hopkins University Press, 1978.

Table 8-8. Annual U.S. Per Family Air Pollution Control Costs and Benefits by Income, Class, and Race (dollars) (Peskin, 1978).

Costs and benefits	Less than 3,000	3,000 to 3,999	4,000 to 5,999	6,000 to 7,999	8,000 to 9,999	10,000 to 11,999	12,000 to 14,999	15,000 to 19,999	20,000 to 24,999	25,000+
Industry and gov't. net benefits										
Whites	40.48	41.59	36.32	46.92	72.50	80.48	84.10	86.68	77.38	-64.72
Nonwhites	106.34	134.52	183.68	206.60	235.39	221.69	280.08	243.60	201.08	38.47
Total	52.78	56.86	57.70	65.01	86.29	89.60	96.50	95.10	82.88	-62.07
Household net benefits										
Whites	-65.87	-97.67	-117.54	-135.03	-145.68	-159.43	-169.92	-185.89	-197.41	-190.87
Nonwhites	-8.64	-23.26	-16.12	-49.11	-52.47	-61.90	-67.68	-90.54	-122.19	-140.96
Total	-55.00	-85.45	-102.75	-125.25	-137.77	-153.13	-163.42	-180.75	-194.07	-189.58
Total net benefits										
Whites	-23.39	-56.08	-81.23	-88.11	-73.18	-78.95	-85.82	-99.21	-120.03	-255.59
Nonwhites	97.70	111.16	167.56	157.49	182.92	159.79	212.40	153.06	78.89	-102.49
Total	-2.22	-28.59	-45.05	-60.24	-51.48	-63.53	-66.92	-85.65	-111.19	-251.65

Source: P. R. Portney (ed.). Current Issues in U. S. Environmental Policy. Published for Resources for the Future by The Johns Hopkins University Press, 1978.

Techniques of Analysis

Cost-Benefit Analysis

The cost-benefit analysis is the most used and abused technique for public works project and environmental impact evaluation. Too frequently, the decision maker is presented a list of cost-benefit ratios for project alternatives and has no option but to choose the alternative with the highest return on investment. The mechanics of cost-benefit analysis are well developed and beyond the scope of this work. However, the planner or manager should be aware of the serious flaws or deficiencies in the calculation and application of cost-benefit analysis.

Deficiencies of Simple Quantifiable Categories. Cost-benefit analyses typically involve reducing a myriad of complex physical and socioeconomic variables to simple, quantifiable categories of costs and benefits. Complex methodologies are used to calculate the value in current monetary terms of future costs and benefits. The intent is to achieve maximum benefits at minimal costs. This simplied black-and-white view of project impacts can be greatly misleading. Benefits are commonly defined by a person's willingness to pay for project outputs. Costs are often defined as the monetary expenditure required (or the monetary value of forgone opportunities) for using resources in one manner rather than another (Peskin and Seskin, 1975).

Important variables often ignored include the distributive costs and benefits of the project and costs associated with low probability catastrophic events (e.g., reactor meltdown or dam failure). Intangible cost and benefits that cannot adequately be assigned monetary value (e.g., aesthetics, ecological diversity and stability, justice, the value of present and future health and life) are often omitted (Ophuls, 1977). A classic example of the latter is the standard calculation for the monetary value of human life. The loss of your life, in a conventional analysis, is roughly worth the wages lost from your working from the date of your death until the date you would be expected to retire. Under these criteria nonearning people (those retired, raising children at home, etc.) have no value, and older workers have less value than younger. One final problem is the tendency to undervalue the nonrepresented. For example, future generations are not represented in the decision to build nuclear power plants, yet they may pay significant costs to clean up facilities used to generate electricity today. Because of these shortcomings, it is important to stress that cost-benefit analysis is a means to an end, not an end in itself. The tangible dollar values of costs and benefits are only a few of the variables that should be considered in project evaluation. Others include long-term, distributive, and intangible effects. No criterion should be explicitly or implicitly offered as the single most important criterion in project evaluation (Erickson, 1979).

Analytical Deficiencies. An evaluator or decision maker must learn to identify deficiencies that are commonly found in cost-benefit analyses that prevent an accurate representation of the true economics of a project. Several of the recurring deficiencies include failure to study the impacts of all project phases, failure to identify all the major assumptions inherent in the analyses, comparison of the project with improper alternatives, failure to give proper value or weight to project impacts, and use of an inordinately low interest rate to discount future cost and benefits of the project.

Perhaps the most common analytical deficiency is the use of a low interest rate. Most public works projects have high capital and low operating costs. By discounting the future operating cost and total benefits of a project with a low interest rate, the benefit/cost ratio of the project will be inordinately high. In essence the lower the interest rate used to calculate the benefit/cost ratio, the higher the ratio will be. The use of interest rates below the prevailing rate for private investments means that tax money is being used very inefficiently relative to private investments.

Government and industry analysts have used several legal and policy instruments to allow the use of less than prevailing interest rates in calculating benefit/cost ratios. Techniques include tying interest rates to those of long-term bonds with interest ceilings (Carlin, 1973). The literature is rich with examples of the use of low interest rates. The original analysis of the Florida Barge Canal used an interest rate of 2⅞ percent (Roberts, 1971). The analysis of the proposed Tocks Island Dam used a 3⅞ percent interest rate at a time when interest rates in the private sector were approaching 10 percent (Brown, 1972).

The Tocks Island Dam analysis is classic in its failure to properly weigh and evaluate project impacts. Brown (1972), in a review of the analysis, concluded that overestimates were made of the recreational, water supply, power, and flood control benefits of the project. The number of stormy days, impacts of drought on recreation, and costs of recreational development were all underestimated.

The classic example of the use of improper alternatives is in the analysis by the Bureau of Reclamation of the Marble Gorge and Bridge Canyon Dams in the Grand Canyon (Carlin, 1973). The bureau compared the cost of the dams with the "most likely" alternative, expensive fossil-fueled thermal plants. Further, the bureau insisted on equal transmission costs even though the thermal plants could be located much closer to demand centers. Finally, the analysis was done using an interest rate of 3⅛ percent as allowed under U.S. Senate Document 97, which establishes a formula for calculating interest rates based on the average rates paid by the treasury on long-term bonds. Congress established the interest ceiling on such bonds in 1918 (Carlin, 1973).

Alternative Techniques of Analysis

From the previous discussion, it should be apparent that cost-benefit analyses warrant scrutiny for accuracy and objectivity. The benefit/cost ratio should be only one of several carefully established categories of impact and value used in project evaluation. In evaluating alternative actions, similar categories of impacts (e.g., loss of genetic diversity, aesthetics, benefit/cost ratio, distributive impacts, etc.) could be analyzed in a manner similar to that for a scaled checklist analysis of project alternatives often found in environmental impact statements. The decision maker is thereby provided several categories of impacts for each alternative where the relative impacts between alternatives for each category can be compared. The decision maker, with public and expert input, should then be responsible for the relative weighing of categories. Such a system would not guarantee more objective or better decisions, but it would reduce many of the abuses of the past.

Cost Subsidies and Adjustment Assistance

On the rare occasions when an industry or community is experiencing economic difficulties in complying with environmental regulations, a program of economic assistance could be established to assist in overcoming the difficulty. Such programs are generally classified in one of two categories, cost subsidies or adjustment assistance.

Cost subsidies can be either direct or indirect. Direct subsidies consist of grants or cash payments to communities or industries to partly reimburse them for pollution control costs. An example would be the federal subsidies for municipal water treatment plants. Indirect cost subsidies include accelerated depreciation allowances and/or exemption from sales or real property taxes on pollution control equipment. Both direct and indirect cost subsidies have two major drawbacks. First, cost subsidies relieve dischargers of the responsibility of paying the full costs of treating their wastes. The costs of their products will probably not reflect the total costs of production. Second, where cost subsidies go to individual industries, it is unlikely that their benefits will be passed on to consumers in the form of lower prices (Freeman et al., 1973).

Adjustment assistance programs involve temporary support, redirection, and relocation of firms or workers experiencing economic hardships due to environmental controls. Loans, loan guarantees, conversion incentives, or technical assistance can assist firms in converting to new activities where market conditions are better. However, obsolete or poorly managed firms would be allowed to fail, thus retaining a measure of competition.

Adjustment assistance could also be provided to low-income workers hardest hit by a closing in the forms of unemployment benefits, retraining, and relocation allowances. Adjustment assistance programs can thereby deal directly with the problem by easing the plight of those who bear a disproportionate share of the total costs of environmental controls (Freeman et al., 1973).

A word of caution on both subsidy and assistance programs is warranted. As previously noted, industries experiencing financial difficulties because of environmental controls are often old, obsolete, or poorly managed. Further, firms may prematurely threaten to close or exaggerate impacts if subsidies or the postponement or relaxation of compliance requirements may result. The industries in question should be carefully studied before any form of assistance is offered (Haveman and Smith, 1978). Finally, funding for an assistance program should be obtained in an equitable manner. If the federal or state tax systems are more progressive than those of local property or sales taxes (which they normally are), the use of federal or state monies benefits lower-income groups at the expense of higher-income groups (Freeman et al., 1973).

Rather than supporting the addition of programs to existing environmental quality programs, Haveman and Smith (1978) suggested the use of existing mechanisms for regional assistance, such as the Economic Development Administration. Through a coordinated program, this administration could offer regional assistance in the event that plant closings create local or regional economic hardships. Such assistance would begin after closing and could be coordinated with existing environmental, regional, and local economic development programs.

Economic Development and the Environment

On the whole, it is apparent that the benefits of environmental controls to the health, safety, and welfare of human and nonhuman systems clearly outweigh the costs. Some minor problems are created in the economy: however, these can easily be overcome through thoughtful management.

A strong economy and a healthy ecology can be highly mutually beneficial. In this age of growing awareness of amenities, a clean, healthy environment can be a major drawing factor for economic development. However, it is important that the economy does not grow to a level that exceeds the resource and residuals carrying capacity of the environment. When the carrying capacity is exceeded, the economy begins to cannibalize its own foundation.

In the last two decades of the twentieth century, a fundamental reevaluation is occurring of what truly constitutes economic development and what is its true role in human development. People are beginning to realize that the "American dream" cannot be realized in a garbage heap. Words such as quality, sufficiency, stability, and sustainability and even ecological terms such as diversity and stability and carrying capacity are slowly creeping into the vocabularies of the business schools and chambers of commerce of the nation.

A fundamental reevaluation of community economic development policies is also occurring. Local officials are beginning to evaluate critically rather than simply encourage economic growth. In many cases they are finding that the conventional processes of wooing industries and providing incentives often cost the community more than it receives from increased tax revenues and employment (Morris, 1981). They have found a spiraling subsidy of private industry at the expense of the taxpayer. In addition, the desired benefits of increased employment for local citizens are often not realized because of the importation of workers from outside the community for most of the skilled (high-paying) jobs.

In addition, local economic development planners are becoming aware that small businesses, not large corporations, are the key to future economic development. In a seven-year study of 5.6 million firms (that include 82 percent of the private jobs in the United States) Birch (1979) found that the largest source of employment was the small business. Approximately two-thirds of all new employment created from 1971 to 1978 came from small firms employing fewer than twenty people. Most of these new jobs resulted from the development of new businesses or the expansion of existing ones. It is also interesting to note that the top one thousand firms on the *Fortune* list generated only 1 percent of the new employment created from 1970 to 1976. Such a new focus for economic development has the additional advantages of (1) helping to diversify the local economy, (2) preventing large industries from unduly influencing local officials, (3) reducing the threat of severe socioeconomic impacts due to a major plant closing, and (4) reducing the leakage of capital and resources out of the local economy. Small businesses tend to rely more on local labor and resources. The result is a reduced reliance on "foreign" sources of raw materials and accelerated economic activities locally from the use of indigenous resources, from the increased recycling of activities within the economy, and from the reduced flow of capital and resources out of the local economy. By internalizing the flow of resources (or maximizing the use of indigenous resources), a greater level of economic activity can be generated by the local government per dollar or unit resource consumed. This, in turn, reduces the environmental impacts of the local economy by reducing the resource demands and residuals generated per unit of economic activity.

In conclusion, history is rich with examples of civilizations that flourished at the expense of the natural environment. The destruction of the natural environment hastened their decline, and "civilization" simply moved on to a new frontier to flourish and perish again. Today, as the human race expands and increases the "development" of the surface of the earth, we are faced with the stark realization that there is no new frontier. If we exceed our global carrying capacity, like the Kaibab Plateau deer herd, we may temporarily thrive. However, we may ultimately destroy the foundation of the living systems on the earth.

9 / Environmental Impact Assessment

Public officials are frequently involved in developing and reviewing environmental impact statements, especially when planning for public services and protecting valuable resource areas. The following survey of the National Environmental Policy Act (NEPA) and the environmental impact statement (EIS) protocol should familiarize the reader with the processes of EIS formulation, analysis, and review. More detailed information on EIS development, analysis, and review can be found in Canter (1977), Erickson (1979), and Jain et al. (1981).

The need to incorporate environmental services and amenities in public decision-making processes has long been recognized. One of the earliest statements addressing this need was made in 1864 by George Perkins Marsh in *Man and Nature:*

> But it is certain that man has reacted upon organized and inorganic nature, and thereby modified . . . the material structure of his earthly home. We cannot always distinguish between the results of man's actions and the effects of purely geological or cosmical causes. But man is everywhere a disturbing agent. Wherever he plants his foot, the harmonies of nature are turned to discords. Man extends his actions over vast spaces, his revolutions are swift and radical, and his devastations are, for an almost incalculable time after he has withdrawn the arm that gave the blow, irreparable. But our inability to assign definite values to these causes of the disturbance of natural arrangements is not a reason for ignoring the existence of such causes in any general view of the relations between man and nature, and we are never justified in assuming a force to be insignificant because its measure is unknown, or even because no physical effect may be traced to its origin.

The following discussion of environmental impact analysis focuses mainly on the requirements of the NEPA and the regulations for EIS preparation issued by the Council on Environmental Quality. However, because nonfederal environmental assessment requirements closely parallel those of the NEPA and the CEQ, the information presented should also be relevant to state and local environmental analyses.

The NEPA

The NEPA of 1969 was the first piece of recent federal legislation directed toward environmental management (see the Appendix). The purpose of this legislation as stated in the act was "to declare a national policy which will encourage productive and enjoyable harmony between man and his environment; to promote efforts which will prevent or eliminate damage to the environment and biosphere and stimulate the health and welfare of man; to enrich the understanding of the ecological systems and natural resources important to the Nation; and to establish a Council on Environmental Quality."

Section 101 of the act formally establishes a national policy for environmental quality restoration and protection. Section 102 requires federal agencies to make a full and adequate analysis, of the environmental effects of their programs or actions. Section 102(2)(c) states the requirements and guidelines for preparing an EIS. The primary purpose for preparing EISs is to disclose the environmental consequences of a proposed project or action to alert decision makers, the public, and ultimately the president and the U.S. Congress of the environmental consequences involved. The intent was to build into the decision-making processes of federal agencies an awareness of environmental considerations.

Federal agencies are required to produce an EIS for all "major federal actions significantly affecting the quality of the human environment." According to the NEPA, an EIS should contain the following elements:

1. The environmental impact of the proposed actions
2. Any unavoidable adverse environmental effects
3. Alternatives to the proposed action
4. The relationship between local short-term uses of man's environment and the maintenance and enhancement of long-term productivity
5. Any irreversible and irretrievable commitments of resources resulting from the implementation of the proposed action

Many of the court cases resulting from the NEPA involve interpretation of the terms *major, federal actions,* and *significant impacts.* *Major* has been defined as not minor, or requiring substantial planning, time, resources, or expenditures (CEQ, 1973). Similar ambiguity arises in the definition of *federal action.* Federal construction projects, expenditures, and regulatory programs clearly qualify, but partial federal participation in a project is more problematic. Partial participation has generally been sufficient to "federalize" a project, with the notable exception of revenue-sharing grants with no federal strings attached (Rowe et al., 1978; CEQ, 1973).

Similar ambiguity exists in the definition of *significant environmental impact.* There is general agreement that the term *significant* represents a threshold, but disagreement over whether that threshold is high or low. The CEQ (1973) stated that if a project is "controversial," then an EIS should be prepared. Thus, an agency can account for community attitudes in making threshold decisions (Rowe et al., 1978).

Section 102(2)(A) and (B) of the act requires that an agency use "a systematic, interdisciplinary approach" to identify and develop procedures and methods such that "presently unquantified environmental amenities and values may be given appropriate consideration in decisionmaking," along with conventional technical and economic considerations (NEPA, 1969).

Section 103 of the act requires all federal agencies to review their statutory authority, administrative regulations, and current policies and procedures for the purpose of determining whether there are any deficiencies or inconsistencies that prohibit full compliance with the purposes and provisions of the NEPA.

The second major section of the NEPA, often referred to as Title II, establishes the CEQ as an environmental advisory body for the executive branch of government. According to the NEPA (1969), the duties and functions of the CEQ are to:

1. Assist and advise the president in the preparation of an annual environmental quality report that contains the following:
    a. The status and condition of the major natural and altered ecological systems of the nation,
    b. Current and future trends in the quality, management, and utilization of such environments and socioeconomic impacts of these trends,
    c. The adequacy of available natural resources,
    d. A review of governmental and nongovernmental activities on natural resources and the environment,
    e. A program for remedying the deficiencies and recommending appropriate legislation.
2. Gather, analyze, and interpret information concerning the conditions and trends in environmental quality.
3. Review federal programs and activities for their compatibility with environmental protection and enhancement.
4. Develop and recommend to the president national policies to promote environmental improvement.
5. Conduct research related to ecological systems and environmental quality.
6. Accumulate the necessary information for a continuing analysis of environmental change and its underlying causes.

7. Report annually to the president on the condition of the environment.
8. Conduct studies and furnish reports and recommendations requested by the president.

It must be emphasized that the powers of the CEQ are advisory in nature. It has no regulatory or enforcement responsibilities (Jain et al., 1981).

Finally, an EIS is an official document submitted by a federal agency to the CEQ, proposing to support, regulate, or fund an action or project. The EIS is the official statement of the responsible or "lead" federal agency of the environmental impacts, alternatives, or tradeoffs of the proposed project or action. After indicating the environmental consequences of alternative actions, the lead agency can recommend a favored alternative. Selection of the final project or action, however, may be based on a number of decision-making tools and may not always adhere to the recommended alternative in the EIS. In addition, agencies are subject to the conventional legal tests of arbitrary and capricious decision-making processes (Canter, 1977).

The CEQ Regulations for EIS Preparation

The NEPA gives the CEQ authority to administer the EIS process (see Appendix). CEQ responsibilities include serving as a central repository for final EISs, formulating federal regulations for EIS preparation, reviewing draft EISs when necessary, analyzing the impact statement process, and advising the president on project development (Canter, 1977).

One of the most important functions of the CEQ is the development of federal agency regulations for EIS preparation. The first CEQ guidelines were published on August 1, 1971 (CEQ, 1971). These advisory guidelines were designed to coordinate the EIS process and to clarify procedures for review of draft EISs. The guidelines added two sections to the five basic requirements specified in the NEPA. The first new section, coming before the five basic items, requires a complete description of the proposed project or action. The second new section, coming after the five, requires a discussion of the concerns and objections of EIS reviewers (Canter, 1977).

The second set of advisory guidelines, issued on August 1, 1973, called for two further additions to an EIS and the expansion of the section describing the proposed project or action to include a complete description of the existing environmental conditions (an "environmental inventory") at the proposed project site (CEQ, 1973). The first new section pertained to the interface of the proposed action to proposed or adopted federal, state, and local land use plans, policies, and controls at the affected site. The second section required an open discussion and specification of the importance of any nonenvironmental influences that affected the final decision on the proposed action (Canter, 1977).

The 1978 CEQ Regulations for EIS Preparation

To accommodate concerns about needless delays, excessive paperwork, the proliferation of individual agency regulations for EIS preparation, and improper decisions, President Carter directed the CEQ in 1977 to issue new regulations to implement more effectively the procedural requirements of the NEPA. These new regulations, issued for public comments in June 1978 and promulgated in final form on November 29, 1978, replaced the CEQ's previous advisory EIS guidelines and are binding on all federal agencies (thereby replacing more than seventy different sets of agency regulations). All federal agencies were required to adopt procedures implementing these regulations by July 30, 1979. (For a copy of these regulations see 40 CFR Parts 1500–1508.)

The three principal goals of the new CEQ regulations were to reduce paperwork and delays, to streamline the EIS process, and to produce better decisions to further the national policy of environmental enhancement and protection.

To reduce paperwork and make EISs more readable, the new CEQ guidelines require that an EIS be analytic rather than encyclopedic and normally not exceed one hundred fifty pages, although a maximum length of three hundred pages is set for complex proposals. The EIS should contain a summary section and be clearly written (free of technical jargon) in a precise format.

One of the most significant innovations in the new regulations is the "scoping process." At an early stage in EIS preparation, federal agencies must identify and eliminate unimportant or insignificant matters from the EIS. In essence, impacts should be discussed in proportion to their importance. This scoping process eliminates unnecessary information and is important in identifying additional legal considerations and political entities that should participate in the assessment process.

To eliminate duplication between NEPA and state and local environmental policy laws, the new regulations require federal agencies to cooperate with state and local jurisdictions to the fullest extent possible. The regulations encourage joint planning and research and the use of a single document for complying with both state and federal laws. An EIS must discuss any conflicts between a proposal and state or local laws and must indicate the extent to which the agency will reconcile the conflict (CEQ, 1979a).

To reduce delay, the new regulations call for (1) time limits on the NEPA process at the request of the applicant, (2) integration of the NEPA into early planning to reduce delays and have meaningful input, (3) emphasis on interagency cooperation before a draft is produced, (4) swift and fair resolution of interagency conflicts, (5) encouragement of "tiering" or the use of a program EIS for broad federal actions followed by more specific EISs describing site-specific consequences and alternatives for individual actions under the program, (6) simultaneous rather than consecutive integration of EIS requirements with other review and consultation requirements, and (7) acceleration of procedures for legislative proposals (CEQ, 1978a).

Several changes were made in the new regulations to improve EIS decision-making processes. The first was to eliminate a potential conflict of interest when applicants for federal funding or permit approval participate in the environmental assessment of their activity. Under the new guidelines, private entities may submit information to be incorporated into an EIS, but the information must be independently evaluated by the federal agency involved. Contractors wishing to do EISs must sign disclosure statements specifying that they have no financial or other interest in the outcome of the project or action (CEQ, 1979a).

The new regulations also require a written record of the decision on the project or action, specifying the alternatives considered, the decision, the rationale for the decision, and the mitigation and monitoring measures to be implemented. The lead agency is required to implement all mitigating measures indicated in the chosen alternative of the EIS and must provide sufficient monitoring to assure that these requirements are carried out. Finally, before the final decision, agencies are prohibited from committing resources to the project, that might prejudice selection of alternatives (CEQ, 1979a; Jain et al., 1981).

EIS Development

Administrative Procedures. The new CEQ regulations were designed to streamline and standardize the EIS process. Figure 9-1 illustrates the steps agencies must follow to comply with the new CEQ guidelines. The first step is to identify the project or action proposed by the agency. If the project or action is a routine or recurring agency action or if it clearly has no impact on the environment, it may be "categorically excluded" from the requirement to produce an EIS. For actions not excluded, the agency assuming the major responsibility for producing the EIS may either go through a process to determine whether an EIS is required or, if project impacts are clearly significant, may commence EIS preparation. If the first approach is taken, the lead agency must prepare an environmental assessment (EA) to determine whether an EIS is required. If not, a statement of the finding of no significant impact (FONSI) is prepared, summarizing the reasons for not preparing an EIS (Kitto and Burns, 1980).

When an EA or early preliminary analyses indicate that a project or activity requires an EIS, a notice of intent to prepare an EIS must be sent to the Environmental Protection Agency to be published in the *Federal Register.* The next step involves the formation of an

Figure 9-1. EIS Development Steps (Kitto and Burns, 1980)

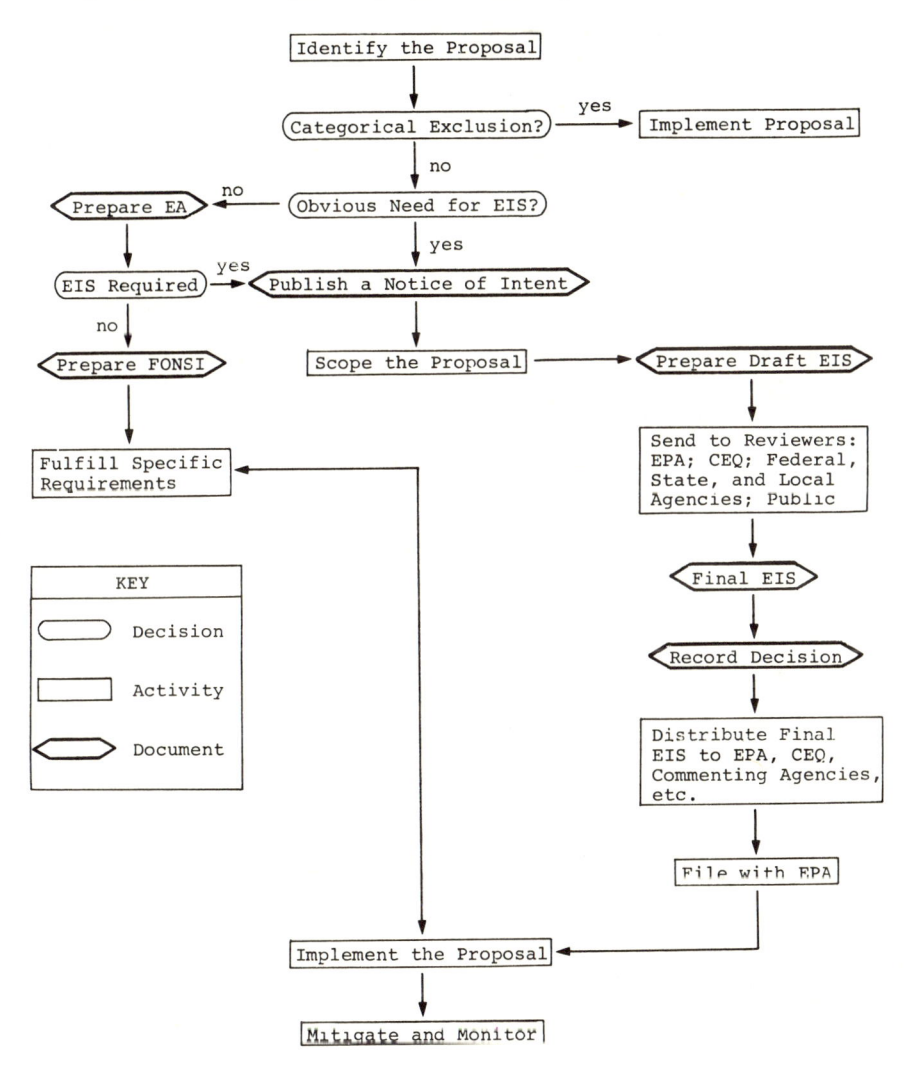

interdisciplinary team to identify significant issues related to the proposal. This scoping process narrows the focus of study early in the planning stage to relevant environmental issues and often specifies the content and timing of the EIS (Kitto and Burns, 1980).

The draft EIS is prepared, which specifies the environmental consequences of the proposed project or activity, and is sent to the EPA and other interested organizations and individuals for review. After receiving comments on the draft EIS, the lead agency must prepare a final EIS, which must contain its decision along with a summary of the reviews and changes made to accommodate reviewer concerns. A record of decision must be prepared and sent to the EPA, specifying alternatives considered in the analysis, the decision, and the rationale for the decision. Finally, the lead agency is responsible for developing and monitoring the mitigation measures specified in the EIS.

EIS Documents. The new CEQ regulations require that a number of documents be prepared during the EIS development process. This section will briefly identify and discuss each of these documents (Jain et al., 1981; Kitto and Burns, 1980).

The *notice of intent* is a notice published in the *Federal Register* by the EPA, stating that an EIS will be prepared and considered by a specified lead agency. The notice of intent should include a description of the proposed action, possible project alternatives, the proposed scoping process, and the name and address of a person in the lead agency who can answer questions about the EIS and the proposed action.

The EA (*environmental assessment*) is a document prepared by a federal agency to determine whether an EIS is necessary. An EA must specify the need for the proposed project or activity, alternatives to the proposal, and the environmental impacts of the proposal and alternatives. Individuals and agencies contacted in preparing the EA must be listed. Although quite similar to the EIS in format, an EA should be brief and require much less preparation than an EIS. EAs must be circulated to other agencies and available to the public.

The FONSI (*finding of no significant impact*) is a formal statement prepared by a federal agency, indicating that no significant impact will occur from proposed projects or activities. The FONSI is based on data in the environmental assessment, which should be clearly stated in the document. A FONSI is required if no EIS is to be produced.

The draft EIS (*draft environmental impact statement*) is a detailed written statement and analysis of project impacts required by the NEPA and the CEQ. The draft EIS is sent to the EPA (for formal review), federal agencies, interested parties, and the general public for review and comment.

The final EIS (*final environmental impact statement*) is a modified draft EIS that accommodates and incorporates the comments and concerns of reviewers. If substantive concerns are not accommodated, an explanation must be made in the document. Copies of the final EIS must be sent to the EPA (which will send one to the CEQ) and should be sent to all commenting agencies and individuals if possible.

A *record of decision* should be prepared at the time an agency decides on which alternative to choose. This record should include:

- the final decision,
- identification of all alternatives considered including specification preferable,
- identification and an indication of the importance given to all economic, technical, national policy, and so on, factors that were balanced by the agency in arriving at its decision,
- a statement of practicable mitigation measures to be taken to reduce project or activity impacts,
- identification of the monitoring and enforcement program to be used to assure proper mitigation measures and project activities are followed.

The Timing of Procedures. Each week, the EPA publishes the notices of intent filed with that agency in the preceding week. The minimum time periods established by the new CEQ guidelines should be calculated from the date of publication of this notice. No decision on a proposed project or activity should be completed or recorded by a lead agency within ninety days after publication of the notice of intent. A minimum of forty-five days must be allowed for comments on the draft EIS (usually sixty days is allowed). The lead agency must wait thirty days after filing the EIS with the EPA before the proposed action may be initiated. The lead agency may extend these periods or petition the EPA under compelling or certain prespecified circumstances to reduce them. In addition, other federal agencies may petition the EPA to extend the deadlines. The EPA must notify the CEQ of any schedule changes (CEQ, 1978a; Jain et al., 1981; Kitto and Burns, 1980).

Suggested EIS Format

The new CEQ regulations call for changes in the form and content of EISs. The CEQ has provided a streamlined standard format for all agencies to follow unless an agency determines that there is a compelling reason to do otherwise. A summary of the required EIS format and content is given in Table 9-1.

Cover Sheet. The cover sheet should not exceed one page and should present the title of the proposed action; state the precise location of that action; list the lead and cooperating agencies; provide the name, address, and telephone number of the person at the lead agency who can provide further information; designate whether the statement is draft, final, or supplemental; provide a one-paragraph abstract of the statement; and present the deadline for receipt of comments (CEQ, 1978a).

Summary. The major conclusions of the EIS should be summarized in less than fifteen pages. The summary should stress major conclusions,

Table 9-1. CEQ-Prescribed EIS Format (CEQ, 1978a).

1. Cover sheet (1 page)
2. Summary (not to exceed 15 pages)
3. Table of contents (unspecified)
4. Purpose and need for the action
5. Alternatives including the proposed action
    - Describe all alternatives (including "no action")
    - Describe and discuss alternatives eliminated from the analysis
    - Compare the environmental consequences of the alternative
    - Indicate the preferred alternative and mitigation measures
6. Affected environment
    - Describe the affected environment
    - Emphasis on environmental parameters should be proportionate to potential impacts
    - Summarize, integrate or reference information to reduce length
7. Environmental consequences
    - Document and determine significance of direct and indirect effects
    - Conflicts with other federal, state, local, or Native American plans.
    - Energy requirements and conservation potential
    - Depletable resource requirements and conservation potential
    - Impacts on urban quality, historic or cultural resources
    - Mitigation measures not covered under "alternatives section"
8. List of preparers (not to exceed 2 pages)
9. Appendix (unspecified)

(Items 5–7: not to exceed 150 pages normally or 300 pages in special cases) controversies (including issues raised by agencies and the public), and issues to be resolved (including the choice among alternatives) (CEQ, 1978a).

Table of Contents. Although the CEQ guidelines do not specify the length or content of the table of contents, it is suggested that it include a list of all headings and subheadings, a list of figures, a list of tables (all with appropriate page numbers), and a summary of all symbols and abbreviations used. This would normally not exceed five to six pages.

Purpose and Need for the Action. The EIS should briefly specify the underlying purpose or need to which the agency is responding in proposing the action and alternatives.

Alternatives. According to the CEQ, the identification and analysis of alternatives is the heart of the EIS. Considerable information on the affected environment and environmental consequences of the proposed action and each alternative is required for proper analysis, so it may be necessary to develop these sections simultaneously. The analysis of alternatives should clearly present the environmental impacts of the proposal and alternatives in a comparative form to define the issues and provide a clear basis for choice.

It is important that the "no action" alternatives and all reasonable alternatives outside the jurisdiction of the lead agency be considered in the alternatives identification and selection process. The reasons for eliminating alternatives from further consideration should be carefully documented (CEQ, 1978a).

Mitigation measures for the preferred alternatives may be included in this section. A plan and an implementation strategy for integrating the mitigation measures into project activities should be developed. Finally, to fully comply with the CEQ requirements, a statement should be prepared indicating how the identification and analysis of alternatives complies with the purpose and intent of the NEPA, the EIS process, and other relevant environmental laws and policies (CEQ, 1978a).

Affected Environment. The EIS should succinctly describe the environment of the area(s) affected by the proposed activity. This environmental inventory or base line analysis should be limited to factors necessary for the comprehension of the effects of the proposed activities, and the detail of study should be proportionate to the significance of the impact. To reduce bulk, the CEQ recommends that information be summarized, consolidated, or referred to whenever possible (CEQ, 1978a).

The purposes of the environmental inventory are to provide a base line from which impacts of proposed actions can be assessed, to assist in assuring that significant environmental factors are not overlooked in the analysis, to assist in identifying critical environmental parameters that warrant study emphasis, and to provide reviewers with an understanding of the overall environmental setting of the activity site(s) (Canter, 1977).

Environmental factors often mentioned in studies of the affected environment include climate, air quality, noise levels, aesthetics, water quality, groundwater and aquifers, aquatic and terrestrial ecology, contamination and disruption of chemical cycles, rare and endangered species, soils, geography, topography, geology, land uses, historic sites, economics, public services, and governmental jurisdictions. These environmental factors can be scoped to determine which ones should be included in analysis by asking two questions. Will the proposed activity have a significant positive or negative impact on the environmental factor? Will the environmental factor exert a significant influence on project scheduling, construction, or operation? If the answer to either is "yes," the factor should be included in the analysis (Canter, 1977).

Environmental Consequences. The study of environmental impacts forms the scientific and analytic basis for the comparison and selection of alternatives. The analysis should include

- significant direct and indirect environmental impacts of all alternatives
- any unavoidable adverse effects
- any irreversible and irretrievable commitments of resources
- the relationship between short-term use of man's environment and the maintenance and enhancement of long-term productivity
- conflicts between the proposed action and federal, state, local, and native American land use plans, policies, and controls
- energy, natural resource, and depletable resource requirements and conservation potential
- urban quality, historic preservation, and cultural resource impacts
- mitigation measures not discussed in the alternatives section of the report

List of Preparers. The names and qualifications of those persons primarily responsible for preparing the EIS or background papers or analyses used in the EIS should be included. Where possible, persons responsible for a particular study or section of the report should be identified. The intent of this list is to assist in evaluating whether a systematic, interdisciplinary approach was used; to increase the accountability and professional responsibility of those preparing an EIS; and to give credit and enhance professional standing (CEQ, 1978a).

Appendix. The appendix should contain only materials prepared in support of the EIS or those substantiating important sections of the report. The methods and computations of significant impacts should be included. Material available in other documents should be referenced. The appendix can be circulated with the EIS or made available upon request (CEQ, 1978a).

Environmental Impact Assessment

Environmental impact assessment requires a systematic interdisciplinary analysis of the physical, chemical, biological, cultural, and socioeconomic impacts of a proposed project or activity. The three elements involved are (1) determining agency activities associated with implementing the action or the project; (2) determining the probability, nature, magnitude, duration, and location of impacts resulting from agency actions; determining the significance of impacts. Figure 9-2 presents a systematic approach to the development of an environmental impact analysis. Actual analyses vary considerably from this suggested approach because of individual preferences and differences in the nature, scope, and magnitude of project activities.

Step 1. Identify Action or Alternatives. All reasonable alternatives, including the "no action" alternatives, to the proposed project or activity that could have significant environmental impacts should be analyzed. The CEQ requires federal agencies to prepare and publish lists of actions that normally require EISs or EAs or are categorically excluded. Proposed activities and alternatives should be compared with the list to determine their status.

Step 2. Identify Activities That May Have Impacts. Once the proposed activity is clearly defined and it is determined that significant impacts may occur, agency activities should be categorized into functional areas (such as preplanning, site preparation and construction, and operation categories). For each functional category, detailed project activities should be listed. Federal agencies have lists of categories and activities for specific types of projects. Examples can also be found in EISs of activities similar to the one proposed.

Step 3. Inventory the Affected Environment. Initially, all existing environmental, socioeconomic, and cultural conditions in the affected area should be studied. As the assessment team becomes familiar with the project, its impacts, and the affected area, it can begin scoping the inventory to existing factors that are pertinent to the nature and degree of potential impacts. The EIS should contain only those factors significantly affected and emphasize those most seriously impacted.

256 / *Environmental Impact Assessment*

Figure 9-2. Procedure for Developing an Environmental Impact Analysis (modified from Jain et al., 1981).

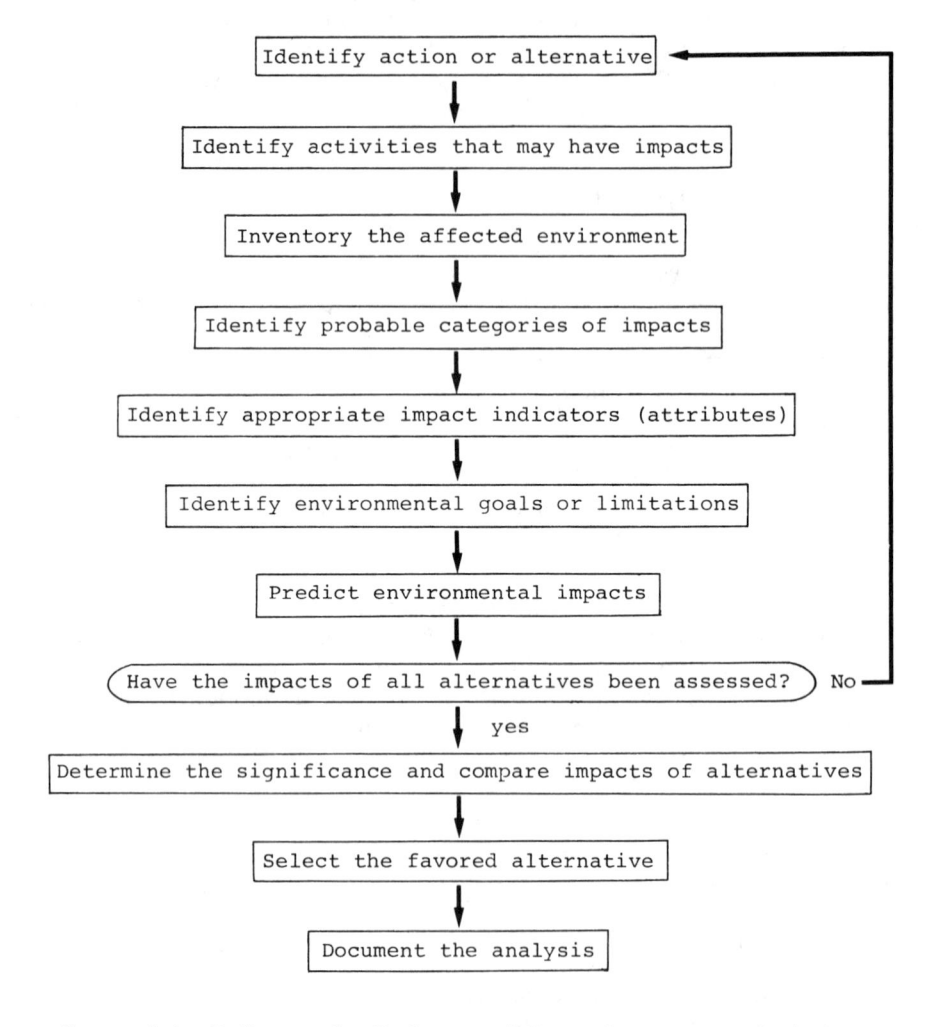

```
        ┌─────────────────────────────────────┐
        │   Identify action or alternative    │◄──────┐
        └──────────────────┬──────────────────┘       │
                           ▼                          │
        ┌─────────────────────────────────────┐       │
        │ Identify activities that may have impacts │  │
        └──────────────────┬──────────────────┘       │
                           ▼                          │
        ┌─────────────────────────────────────┐       │
        │   Inventory the affected environment │      │
        └──────────────────┬──────────────────┘       │
                           ▼                          │
        ┌─────────────────────────────────────┐       │
        │  Identify probable categories of impacts │  │
        └──────────────────┬──────────────────┘       │
                           ▼                          │
        ┌─────────────────────────────────────┐       │
        │ Identify appropriate impact indicators (attributes) │
        └──────────────────┬──────────────────┘       │
                           ▼                          │
        ┌─────────────────────────────────────┐       │
        │  Identify environmental goals or limitations │
        └──────────────────┬──────────────────┘       │
                           ▼                          │
        ┌─────────────────────────────────────┐       │
        │     Predict environmental impacts    │      │
        └──────────────────┬──────────────────┘       │
                           ▼                          │
     ( Have the impacts of all alternatives been assessed? )── No ──┘
                           │ yes
                           ▼
   ┌──────────────────────────────────────────────────────┐
   │ Determine the significance and compare impacts of alternatives │
   └──────────────────────────┬───────────────────────────┘
                              ▼
            ┌─────────────────────────────────────┐
            │     Select the favored alternative   │
            └──────────────────┬──────────────────┘
                               ▼
            ┌─────────────────────────────────────┐
            │         Document the analysis        │
            └─────────────────────────────────────┘
```

Source: Jain, R. K., et al. *Environmental Impact Assessment.* Academic Press, New York, 1981. Reprinted by permission.

Step 4. Identify Probable Categories of Impacts. Probable significant project impacts should be assigned to appropriate categories. The most common assignments are air, land, water, ecological, socioeconomic, and cultural categories. Subcategories can then be established according to project impacts. For example, the air category can be divided into climate, air pollution, noise, and visual effects subcategories.

Step 5. Identify Appropriate Impact Indicators. Appropriate indicators or attributes for the various categories of environmental, socioeconomic, and cultural impacts should next be developed. A listing of a representative attribute package is given in Table 9-2. This is a very important step because the indicators will be used to describe, measure, predict, and assess the significance of impacts. These attributes should accurately reflect impacts, be readily measurable and quantifiable, and be capable of comparison against some threshold or standard to determine the significance of the impact. An excellent summary of environmental attributes is given in Jain et al. (1981).

Step 6. Identify Environmental Goals or Limitations. The appropriate standards, goals, rules, regulations, or scientifically developed and recommended exposure or threshold limits for each environmental attribute should be clearly defined. These will be used at a later point in the study as a base line for the analysis of impact significance. The threshold of significance for certain categories of impacts may vary widely by geographic region and/or be difficult to ascertain. For instance, at what point does urban encroachment onto agricultural lands become significant? When in doubt, keep in mind that if a controversy is likely to develop, that level of impact could be interpreted in the courts as significant (Jain et al., 1981).

Step 7. Predict Environmental Impacts. One of the most critical steps in the analysis is the prediction of the nature, probability, magnitude, duration, and affected area of the positive and negative impacts of the proposed activity. Most of this information can be obtained from an analysis of the detailed design specifications of the project, consultation with technical experts, socioeconomic surveys, site surveys, and EISs of similar projects. Special attention should be given to indirect, long-term (such as the consequent future economic growth), and cumulative or interactive impacts. In certain cases, laboratory or field experiments or computer models can be employed to ascertain the impacts of previously unstudied actions or to estimate cumulative or interactive impacts. The resulting impacts are most frequently compared with those of the "no action" alternative as a measure of the benefit of or harm caused by the proposed activity. Considerable attention should be paid to documentation of information sources.

Step 8. Determine the Significance and Compare Impacts of Alternatives. Several methodologies have been developed to organize, present, evaluate, and compare the impacts of project activities and alternatives. The following section contains a brief summary of each of the major techniques. A much more detailed evaluation can be found in Warner and Preston (1974).

Table 9-2. A Sample Attribute Package.

Air
1. Particulates
2. Sulfur oxides
3. Hydrocarbons
4. Nitrogen oxides
5. Carbon monoxide
6. Photochemical oxidants
7. Odors
8. Noise

Water
1. Temperature
2. Nutrients
3. Biological oxygen demand
4. Dissolved oxygen
5. Suspended solids
6. Toxic chemicals
7. Fecal coliforms

Land
1. Soil stability
2. Flood hazards
3. Land use patterns
4. Toxic waste disposal sites

Ecology
1. Nutrient cycles
2. Biological diversity
3. Food chain integrity
4. Rare or endangered species

Socioeconomic
1. Life styles
2. Consumption patterns
3. Income distribution
4. Economic development
5. Employment
6. Community services
7. Governance

Cultural
1. Cultural integrity
2. Historic sites
3. Archaeological sites

The *ad hoc technique* more frequently involves a team of specialists that meet and "brainstorm" about project impacts. This technique can be used in suggesting broad areas of possible impacts or is used in lieu of more formal analysis when one alternative is clearly favored (Canter, 1977; Jain et al., 1981).

Overlay techniques use overlay maps of land features and environmental factors to produce composite maps of characteristics of environmental impacts and development suitability. The severity of impacts or limitations is most frequently indicated by shading and coloring systems. There are several drawbacks to using such techniques, as discussed in Chapter 3.

Networks chart a series of impacts triggered by a project action through an analysis of cause and effect relationships. The analysis defines a series of probable events from which a user can identify impacts from specific project actions (Jain et al., 1981).

Checklists are frequently used to determine and compare impacts from proposed actions or alternatives. The first step is to develop a list of environmental factors pertinent to the proposed actions and alternatives. Project impacts can be characterized in a number of ways. A simple checkmark can be used to indicate that an action will impact a given environmental parameter. Descriptive checklists list and discuss the relevance, indicators, measurement, and so on, of environmental parameters. Scaling checklists are used to determine quantitatively the magnitude of project impacts (see Adkins and Burke, 1974). Scaling-weighting checklists are used to determine the magnitude and importance of project impacts (see, for example, Dee et al., 1972).

The process of scaling involves the comparison of project impacts with environmental quality standards, goals, rules, regulations, or scientifically established threshold levels. The point of using the scaling process is to express impacts in commensurate units for comparison. To establish commensurate units, the expected values are converted into an environmental quality (EQ) scale. Such a conversion is based on the fact that there is a certain range of possible values for each attribute and the project impact is proportional to the anticipated attribute value. Dee et al. (1972) used value function graphs to transform attribute values into an EQ scale. Attribute values are shown in the abscissa and the EQ scale in the ordinate. EQ values generally range from 0 (low environmental quality) to 1 (high environmental quality).

Two examples of value function graphs are given in Figure 9-3. These graphs state the professional opinions of the assessment team. In the species diversity graph, the assumption is that environmental quality improves in linear proportion to species diversity. The dissolved oxygen graph assumes a sigmoidal relationship. At the upper and lower ends of the scale, changes in dissolved oxygen concentration have little impact on environmental quality. To ascertain the EQ value corresponding to a given attribute value, a perpendicular line is drawn

Figure 9-3. Value Function Graphs (Dee et al., 1972).

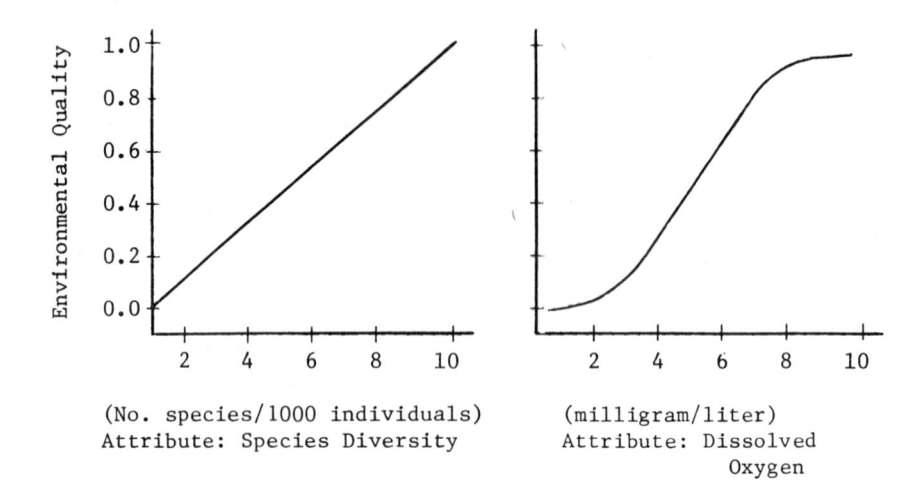

(No. species/1000 individuals)
Attribute: Species Diversity

(milligram/liter)
Attribute: Dissolved Oxygen

from the given attribute value on the abscissa. From the point of intersection of the perpendicular line with the graph, a horizontal line is drawn to the ordinate, where the corresponding EQ value is marked.

The second step in assessing the overall significance of impacts is to develop a method to compare the relative importance of the environmental factors studied. For instance, now that the water quality impacts are known to be significant, how important are those impacts relative to other environmental, socioeconomic, and cultural impacts? One easy method of accomplishing such weighting is to use a modified version of one of the many existing weighting schemes that have been developed by agencies and independent consultants for a variety of projects and environments.

Another commonly used procedure for weighting environmental factors involves a modified "Delphi technique," a procedure for eliciting and analyzing the opinions of experts. The experts, through a pairwise ranking procedure, prioritize the environmental factors according to relative impacts. After several iterations of group analysis, feedback, and study, a stable consensus is achieved (Jain et al., 1981). The parameters are then assigned a relative numeric weight, which when multiplied by the scaling factor provides a number that represents both the degree and importance of the impacts of the proposed activity. This information can be displayed in numeric form in a checklist or matrix or used to determine the degree of shading for overlay analyses.

Matrices combine a list of project activities with a checklist of environmental variables to assess the impacts of project activities or phases. In essence a matrix can indicate which activities impact which

Table 9-3. A Simplified Matrix Analysis.

	Project Activities				
Environmental Attribute	Project Planning	Site Preparation	Construction	Operation	Impact on each Attribute
Water Quality	0 / 2	5 / 10	5 / 10	2 / 5	110
Air Quality	0 / 1	5 / 8	5 / 8	2 / 4	88
Species Diversity	0 / 1	2 / 6	2 / 6	0 / 3	24
Land Use	1 / 1	10 / 6	3 / 6	3 / 3	88
Aesthetics	1 / 1	3 / 4	3 / 4	1 / 2	27
Impacts of Each Activity	2	174	132	29	337

Key: Magnitude / Importance

Total Impact of the Proposed Activity
0 = Nil; 10 = Greatest Impact or Importance

environmental attributes. The major use of matrices is to assist in identifying those activities with the greatest impacts. Once the most harmful activities are identified, it can be determined whether the activity can be avoided or mitigated. Table 9-3 presents a simplified sample format of a matrix of the impacts of activities of a hypothetical project. The matrix indicates that water quality, air quality, and land use impacts are the most important, with the majority of impact occurring during the site preparation and construction phases. It must be emphasized that actual matrix analyses contain many more categories of environmental attributes and project activities.

Step 9. Select the Favored Alternative As previously mentioned, check lists are frequently used to compare impacts of proposed actions and

Table 9-4. Checklist Analysis for a Proposed Activity and Alternatives

Environmental Attribute	Proposed Activity	Alternative A No Action	Alternative B Reduced Action	Alternative C Increased Action
Water Quality	110 [1]	0	132	107
Air Quality	88	361	143	0
Species Diversity	24	222	360	221
Land Use	88	153	25	152
Aesthetics	27	64	0	90
Impact of Each Activity	337	800	660	570

[1] The Higher the Number, the Greater the Impact.

alternatives. Table 9-4 contains a simplified checklist comparison of a proposed action and three alternatives. In actual analyses, the list of attributes would be considerably more extensive. Note that in this analysis, the proposed activity is clearly the most environmentally benign. Socioeconomic, cultural, and technical considerations are absent from this analysis, so a decision maker can weigh additional information on benefit/cost ratios, public preferences, technical difficulties, and so on, in arriving at a final decision. Great care should be exercised in documenting all decision processes and factors, especially when an alternative other than that favored is chosen.

Step 10. Document the Analysis. The processes and results of the impact analysis should be carefully recorded in the resulting environmental document (i.e., EA, FONSI, draft or final EIS). The analytical conclusions should be presented in an overlay, matrix, or checklist to enable a reviewer to quickly comprehend the relative impacts of the proposed action and alternatives.

Local Roles in EIS Development

One of the principal goals of the NEPA is to open federal agency evaluation and decision-making processes to the public. Public participation in the development of an EIS is necessary and highly desirable to ensure both public support for the favored alternative and that there are no major omissions or inaccuracies in the analysis. The assessment team should encourage public participation as early as possible in the EIS planning process. If the lead agency waits for public input until distribution of the draft, the agency will tend to resist changes in the document because of the amount of time and effort already expended. In addition, citizens and community groups would tend to be more critical of the analysis because of a perceived lack of consideration for their needs and desires. It must be emphasized that the general public can perform a number of beneficial functions in the development of an EIS, which include (Erickson, 1979):

1. Providing assessment data and information,
2. Identifying individuals and groups with useful special expertise,
3. Identifying relevant local environmental issues,
4. Providing historical information on the affected area,
5. Helping to generate and verify field data,
6. Providing criteria for evaluating impact significance,
7. Assisting in identifying project alternatives,
8. Assisting in developing public participation programs,
9. Monitoring the accuracy and relevancy of the assessment process,
10. Reviewing interim reports,
11. Assisting in analyzing and evaluating secondary, interactive, long-term, and irreversible impacts,
12. Helping to scope and schedule the assessment,
13. Providing liaison between the assessment team and organizations and the general public,
14. Evaluating and recommending consultants,
15. Identifying and evaluating integration and project monitoring activities.

EIS Review

At various stages in the development process, the assessment team is required to solicit comments from the lead agency, other federal and state agencies with legal jurisdiction or special expertise, conservation groups, community organizations, local officials, citizens, and ultimately, agency decision makers. A review should assess whether all procedural and substantive EIS requirements have been fulfilled, including:

1. The completeness, organization, clarity, and conciseness of the document,
2. An accurate description of the proposed activity and the affected area,

3. The need for the proposed activity,
4. The selection of reasonable alternatives,
5. The use and explanation of an appropriate impact assessment methodology,
6. The consideration of long-term, secondary, cumulative, interactive, and irreversible impacts,
7. An objective determination of the nature and significance of impacts,
8. The proper choice of alternatives,
9. The overall merits of the project.

In-house Review

Most federal agencies require an in-house review prior to the release of the draft EIS. These reviews generally cover legal and administrative compliance, objectivity, statement clarity, and technical content. If deficiencies are apparent, the lead agency can rectify the problems before public release of the document (Jain et al., 1981).

By the time the lead agency releases the draft for outside review, the agency has invested a considerable amount of time and effort in the assessment. Therefore, the lead agency is hesitant in most cases to make changes in the assessment requested by other agencies, organizations, or the general public. This can be minimized by maintaining open channels of input and dialogue between the lead agency, other government entities, and the general public (Erickson, 1979).

Interagency Review

When the draft EIS is released, the lead agency is required to solicit comments from any federal agency with legal jurisdiction or special expertise related to the project or the impacts. In addition, the lead agency must request comments from other federal or state agencies with specific statutory obligations requiring council or coordination, from state and local agencies authorized to develop and enforce environmental standards, and from native American tribes if impacts occur on a reservation (Jain et al., 1981).

Draft and final EISs, as well as comments and responses, must be filed with the EPA. This agency follows a formal review process and publishes its results in the *Federal Register*. Categories of EPA classifications for draft and final EISs are given in Table 9-5. The EPA is required to review the final EIS if the draft is rated in categories 2, 3, ER (environmental reservations), or EU (environmentally unsatisfactory). If the final EIS is rated environmentally unsatisfactory by the agency, the project is referred to the CEQ. The CEQ must either reject the EPA contentions, resolve the conflict, or rule that the lead agency is not in compliance with the NEPA. The CEQ then publishes its

Table 9-5. EPA Draft and Final EIS Review Classification (Jain et al., 1981).

Draft EIS Classifications
- a. Environmental Impacts of the Action
  Lack of Objections (LO) - The EPA has no objections to, or only minor changes in the proposed action.
  Environmental Reservations (ER) - The EPA has reservations about activity impacts. Further study or reassessment is required.
  Environmentally Unsatisfactory (EU) - The EPA is not satisfied with the proposed action. The project is potentially harmful to the environment and proposed safeguards are inadequate. EPA recommends further analyses.
- b. Adequacy of the EIS
  Category 1. Adequate
  Category 2. Insufficient Information - Additional information is required to fully assess the impacts of the proposed action even though a preliminary determination of the impacts is possible from the information presented.
  Category 3. Inadequate - More information and analysis is needed to determine the impacts of the proposed action. A substantial revision is necessary before a rating is possible of the proposed activity.

Final EIS Classifications
  Lack of Objections - The lead agency has responded satisfactorily to EPA's comments on the draft EIS. The EPA does not object to the proposed action.
  Environmental Reservations - The EPA believes further study is required and requests the lead agency to reassess the proposed action.
  Unresponsive Final Impact Statement - The lead agency has not responded to comments made by the EPA on the draft EIS or new environmental concerns brought to the attention of the EPA after the review of the draft. The EPA is unable to assess the environmental impact of the proposed action.
  Environmentally Unsatisfactory - The proposed activity is unsatisfactory from the standpoint of public health, or environmental quality. The proposed activity is referred to the CEQ for action.

Source: Jain, R. K., et al. Environmental Impact Assessment. Academic Press, New York, 1981. Reprinted by permission.

findings and makes a recommendation for action to the president (Jain et al., 1981).

Public Review

The lead agency must also request comments from the general public. This may be accomplished through public hearings, publication of notification of the availability of draft EISs in the newspaper, and developing and using mailing lists of interested groups and individuals.

To facilitate public review of draft and final EISs, the Office of Management and Budget maintains a system of state and regional clearinghouses.

When commenting on a draft EIS, a reviewer should always request a copy of the final EIS. Upon receipt of the final EIS, the reviewer should check the comments section to determine whether his or her statements were acknowledged and concerns satisfactorily accommodated. If not, a formal letter of protest should be sent to the lead agency, the EPA, and the CEQ. The reviewer should look in the comments section for other individuals or agencies with similar or related concerns to form a group to fight implementation of the project. Such a group can fight through the actions of public officials or can seek legal council to stop the project in the courts for noncompliance with the purpose and intent of the NEPA (Canter, 1977).

The NEPA and the Courts

After passage of the NEPA, the courts moved quickly to establish judicial review of its implementation. In the early 1970s several important court cases helped to define and interpret the procedural and substantive requirements of the act. The earliest cases focused primarily on procedural requirements, but by 1973 it became evident that emphasis in litigation was shifting toward substantive issues, such as the quality and intent of the EIS and agency decision-making processes.

One of the first major cases dealing with the adequacy of an EIS was *Natural Resources Defense Council v. Grant* (1972). The court held in this case, involving a Soil Conservation Service project in North Carolina, that the EIS inadequately assessed or omitted many of the project impacts and alternatives. The court concluded that the EIS did not meet the NEPA's full disclosure requirements. In a similar case, *Sierra Club v. Froehlke* (1973), a federal district court enjoined the Army Corps of Engineers from proceeding with the Wallisville Dam project because the EIS was found to be lacking in scope, detail of analysis, discussion of alternatives, and adequate mitigation procedures (Anderson, 1973).

The most famous case dealing with the purpose and intent of the NEPA was *Calvert Cliff's Coordinating Committee v. Atomic Energy Commission* (1972). In this case an appellate court concluded that agency decision making must comply with the intent of Congress in implementing legislation (Anderson, 1973).

In addition, courts began ruling on agency decision making for compliance with the substantive provisions of the NEPA. In *Environmental Defense Fund v. Froehlke* (1972), the court declared that a "formal impact study supplies a convenient record for the courts to use in reviewing agency decisions on their merits to determine if they are in accord with the substantive policies of NEPA" (Anderson, 1973).

Affirmation of the judicial role in reviewing the substance of agency decision making came in *Environmental Defense Fund* v. *Corps of Engineers* (1972), or the Gillham Dam case, in which the Court of Appeals concluded that there was a judicial responsibility to assure that agency decision making was not "arbitrary and capricious." The most notable example of court intervention in NEPA agency decision making was *Burger* v. *County of Mendocino* (1975). In this case, the court, addressing the purpose and intent of the NEPA, held that an agency had illegally approved a motel project in a sensitive environment. The EIS had concluded that the proposed project had the most serious environmental impacts of the seven alternatives analyzed.

In addition to judicial review of agency compliance with the NEPA, the new CEQ (1978) guidelines have added considerable weight to the substantive requirements of the act (Jain et al., 1981).

Between 1970 and 1979 more than 12,000 EISs were filed for federal agency actions. Citizens, environmental groups, governments, and private entities filed lawsuits and obtained injunctions involving approximately 10 percent and 2 percent, respectively, of the EISs. In 1979 approximately 1,400 EISs (evenly divided between drafts and finals) were prepared and filed with the Environmental Protection Agency. During the same period 139 lawsuits were filed challenging federal actions under the NEPA. In 61 percent of the cases, the suit was filed to force an agency to do an EIS for a proposed action, and 25 percent of the cases alleged inadequacies in the EISs. The remaining 14 percent of the cases involved miscellaneous NEPA issues, such as international impacts and failure to implement mitigation measures (CEQ, 1980).

The five federal departments that were sued most frequently were: Transportation (24 percent of the cases), Housing and Urban Development (17 percent), Interior (14 percent), Agriculture (10 percent), and Defense (10 percent). The other most common types of federal actions litigated were highway and road construction (11 percent of the cases), public lands (10 percent), mass transit (9 percent), energy projects (9 percent), water and sewage treatment (7.4 percent), and subsidized housing (7.5 percent) (CEQ, 1980a). Environmental groups were among the plaintiffs in 20 percent of the cases; citizen groups and individuals in 20 percent; business and industry in 19 percent; property owners and residents in 17.5 percent; local and state governments in 16 percent; and unions, native American tribes, and other plaintiffs in 6 percent (CEQ, 1980).

State Environmental Policy Acts

Several states have adopted environmental policy acts (or "little NEPAs") that require consideration of the environmental impacts of projects supported by the state that are not covered by the provisions of the NEPA. As of 1978 twenty-seven states and Puerto Rico had

Table 9-6. State Environmental Impact Statement Requirements, June 1, 1979 (CEQ, 1979a).

States With Comprehensive Statutory Requirements

Source	Guidelines	State Contact
California		
California Environmental Quality Act of 1970, Cal. Pub. Res. Code, Section 21000-21176 (Supp. 1972), as amended by: Ch. 1154, Statutes of 1972, December 5, 1972; Ch. 895, Statutes of 1973, September 28, 1973; Ch. 56, Statutes of 1974, March 4, 1974; Ch. 276, Statutes of 1974, May 21, 1974 Ch. 1187, Statutes of 1975, September 30, 1975; Ch. 593, Statutes of 1976, August 27, 1976; Ch. 753, Statutes of 1976, September 7, 1976; Ch. 1312, Statutes of 1976, September 29, 1976; Ch. 854, Statutes of 1977, eff. Jan. 1, 1978; Ch. 1045, Statutes of 1977, eff. Jan. 1, 1978; Ch. 1200, Statutes of 1977, Sept. 30, 1977, eff. Jan. 1, 1978; Ch. 308, Statutes of 1978, eff. June 30, 1978; Ch. 291, Statutes of 1978, eff. Sept. 15, 1978; Ch. 760, Statutes of 1978, eff. Jan. 1, 1978; Ch. 356, Statutes of 1978, eff. July 5, 1978; Ch. 1075, Statutes of 1978, eff. Sept. 25, 1978; Ch. 1091, Statutes of 1978, eff. Jan. 1, 1979; Ch. 1113, Statutes of 1978, eff. Sept. 25, 1978; Ch. 1271, Statutes of 1978, eff. Jan. 1, 1979.	California Administrative Code, Title 14, Division 6, Ch. 3 (Sections 15000 through 15192) and appendices adopted February 3, 1973, as amended December 14, 1973, January 18, 1974, March 26, 1974, December 30, 1974, January 30, 1975, February 18, 1975, January 6, 1976, October 8, 1976, December 8, 1976, December 23, 1976, February 4, 1978. Guidelines prepared by the Resources Agency of California (under revision).	Norman E. Hill, Assistant to the Secretary for Resources, The Resources Agency, 1414 Ninth Street, Sacramento, Calif. 95815 (Phone: 916-445-9134).
Connecticut		
Connecticut Environmental Policy Act of 1973, Pub. Act 73-562 (approved June 22, 1973), Conn. Gen. Stat. Ann. Ch. 439, Section 22a-1 et seq. (Cum. Supp. 1974-1975), effective February 1, 1975, as amended by: Pub. Act 77-514, effective October 1, 1977.	Regulations of Connecticut State Agencies. Section 22a-1(a)-1 to 22a-1(a)-12.	Jonathan Clapp, Principal Environmental Analyst, Office of Planning and Coordination. Department of Environmental Protection. State Office Building, Room 114, Hartford, Conn. 06115 (Phone: 203-566-3740).
Hawaii		
Governor's Executive Order of August 21, 1974, as supplemented by Act 246, Sess. Laws of Hawaii (approved June 4, 1974), Hawaii Rev. Stat. Ch. 343 (1974), as amended June 1979.	"Rules and Regulations Pertaining to Chapter 343," promulgated in September 1975 by the Hawaii Environmental Quality Commission (under revision).	Richard O'Connell, Director, Office of Environmental Quality Control, Office of the Governor, 550 Halekauwila Street, Room 301, Honolulu, Hawaii 96813 (Phone: 808-548-6915).

Indiana

IC 1971, 13-1-1-10-3, added by Pub. L. 98, 1972, Ind. Stat. Ann. Section 1-301(c) (effective July 1, 1975).

EMB-2; "The Definition of Actions of State Agencies Which Have a Significant Environmental Impact," effective August 7, 1975.

Ralph Pickard, Technical Secretary, Environmental Management Board, 1330 W. Michigan Street, Indianapolis, Ind. 46206 (Phone: 317-633-8405).

Maryland

Maryland Environmental Policy Act of 1973, Ch. 702, Md. Acts of 1973, 41 Ann. Code of Md., Section 447-451 (Cum. Supp. 1973), and Ch. 703, Md. Acts of 1973 Natural Res. Art., Ann. Code of Md., Section 1-301 et seq. (1974 Volume) as amended by Ch. 129 of the Md. Acts of 1975.

"Revised Guidelines for Implementation of the Maryland Environmental Policy Act," issued by the Secretary of the Department of Natural Resources, June 15, 1974.

Joseph Knapp, Administrator, Clearing House Review, Department of Natural Resources, Tawes State Office Building, Annapolis, Md. 21401 (Phone: 301-269-3548).

Massachusetts

Ch. 747, Acts of 1977, Mass. Gen. Laws; Ch. 30, Section 61, 62 a-h.

Massachusetts Environmental Protection Act (MEPA) regulations, Massachusetts Register 142 (January 25, 1979), 301 CMR 10.00.

Samuel G. Mygatt, Director, MEPA Programs, Executive Office of Environmental Affairs, 100 Cambridge Street, Room 2000, Boston, Mass. 02202 (Phone: 617-727-5830).

Minnesota

Minnesota Environmental Policy Act of 1973, Ch. 412, Laws of 1973, Minn. Stat. Ann. Ch. 116D (Cum. Supp. 1974).

"Rules and Regulations for Environmental Impact Statements," issued by the Minnesota Environmental Quality Council on April 4, 1974, as amended February 13, 1977.

Joe Sizer, Director, Environmental Planning, Environmental Quality Council, Capital Square Building, 550 Cedar Street, St. Paul, Minn. 55101 (Phone: 612-296-2712).

Montana

Montana Environmental Policy Act of 1971, Title 75, Ch. 1, Mont. Code Ann. (MCA).

Montana Environmental Quality Council, "Revised Guidelines for Environmental Impact Statements Required by the Montana Environmental Policy Act of 1971," issued September 19, 1975 (under revision).

Ron Fenecs, Staff Attorney, Montana Environmental Quality Council, Capitol Station, Helena, Mont. 59601 (Phone: 406-449-3742).

Table 9-6 (Continued)

States With Comprehensive Statutory Requirements—Continued

Source	Guidelines	State Contact
New York New York State Environmental Quality Review Act, Art. 8, New York State Environmental Conservation Law, effective June 1, 1976, as amended and added by Section 8-0117 (May 28, 1976), as amended by Ch. 228 of 1976 Session laws, Ch. 252 of 1977 Session laws, Ch. 460 of 1978 Session laws.	6 N.Y.C.R.R., Part 617, effective November 1, 1978.	Jerome W. Jensen, CEQRA Coordinator, New York State Department of Environmental Conservation, 50 Wolf Road, Albany, N.Y. 12233 (Phone: 518-457-2224).
North Carolina North Carolina Environmental Policy Act of 1971 (1971, c. 1203, s.1), N.C. Gen Stat. Ch. 113A (Cum. Supp. 1973).	North Carolina Department of Administration, "Guidelines for the Implementation of the Environmental Policy Act of 1971," issued February 18, 1972, updated March 1, 1975.	A. F. McRorie, Director, Division of Management, Dept. of Natural Resources and Community Development, P.O. Box 27687, Raleigh, N.C. 27611 (Phone: 919-733-7015).
South Dakota South Dakota Environmental Policy Act, SL 1974, Ch. 245 (approved March 2, 1974), S.D. Comp. Laws 1967, Ch. 11 1A (Supp. 1974).	Department of Environmental Protection, 1974 Informal Guidelines.	Warren Neufeld, Secretary, South Dakota Department of Water and Natural Resources, Foss Building, Pierre, S.D. 57501 (Phone: 605-773-3151).
Virginia Virginia Environmental Quality Act of 1973, Ch. 384, Laws of 1973 (approved March 15, 1973) and Ch. 774, Laws of 1972, Va. Code Anr. Sections 10-17.107 through 10-17.112 and 10-177 through 10-186 (Supp. 1973), as amended by Ch. 354, Laws of 1974 (approved April 4, 1974), Va. Code Ann. Section 2.1-51.9, Section 10.181, Section 10.183, and Section 10.185, as amended by Ch. 404, Acts of Assembly, 1977.	*Procedures Manual for Environmental Impact Statements in the Commonwealth of Virginia*, issued by the Council on the Environment (December 1973; revised June 1978).	Reginald Wallace, Environmental Impact Statement Coordinator, Governor's Office, Council on the Environment, Eighth Street Office Building, Richmond, Va. 23219 (Phone: 804-786-4500).

Washington

State Environmental Policy Act of 1971, Rev. Code Wash. Ch. 43.21C (Supp. 1973), as amended by Sub. Senate Bill 3277 Ch. 179, Laws of 1974 (May 5, 1974).

"Guidelines for Implementation of the State Environmental Policy Act of 1971," prepared by the Department of Ecology, as revised by "State Environmental Policy Act Guidelines" (WAC 197-10) issued by the Council on Environmental Policy, January 16, 1976, revised by Department of Ecology, January 21, 1978.

Tom Elwell, Environmental Review Section, Office of Comprehensive Programs, State of Washington, Department of Ecology, Olympia, Wa. 98504 (Phone: 206-753-6890).

Wisconsin

Wisconsin Environmental Policy Act of 1971, adding Wisc. Stat. Ann. Ch. 1 Section 1.11 et seq. (Cum. Supp. 1974-1975), as amended by Ch. 204, Laws of 1973.

"Revised Guidelines for the Implementation of the Wisconsin Environmental Policy Act," issued by the Governor's Executive Order No. 26 (February 1976) (under revision).

Caryl Terrell, State WEPA Coordinator, Wisconsin Citizen's Environmental Council, Rm. 415, 110 East Main St., Madison, Wisc. 53702 (Phone: 608-266-9338).

Puerto Rico

Puerto Rico Environmental Policy Act, 12 Laws P.R. Ann. Section 1121, et seq. (1977), as amended Art. 11 § 24 (July 10, 1978).

"Guidelines for the Preparation, Evaluation, and Use of Environmental Impact Statements," issued by the Environmental Quality Board on December 19, 1972.

Roberto Rexach, Executive Director, Environmental Quality Board, 1550 Ponce de Leon Avenue, 4th Floor, Santurce, P.R. 19910 (Phone: 809-725-5140).

States With Comprehensive Executive or Administrative Orders

Michigan

Michigan Executive Directive 1971-10, as superseded by Michigan Executive Order 1973-9, as superseded by Michigan Executive Order 1974-4 (May 1974).

Interim Guidelines, prepared by the Environmental Review Board and issued June 24, 1974. Revised guidelines were adopted in November 1975.

Boyd Kinzley, Executive Secretary, Environmental Review Board, Department of Management and Budget, Lansing, Mich. 48913 (Phone: 517-373-6491).

New Jersey

New Jersey Executive Order No. 53 (October 15, 1973).

"Guidelines for the Preparation of an Environmental Impact Statement," issued by the Office of the Commissioner, Department of Environmental Protection, in 1973 and updated in February 1974.

Lawrence Schmidt, Chief, Office of Environmental Review, Department of Environmental Protection, P.O. Box 1390, Trenton, N.J. 08625 (Phone: 609-292-2662).

Table 9-6 (Continued)

States With Comprehensive Executive or Administrative Orders—Continued

Source	Guidelines	State Contact
Texas		
Policy for the Environment, adopted by the Interagency Council on Natural Resources and the Environment on March 7, 1972, and published in "Environment for Tomorrow: The Texas Response," subsequently updated by "The Environment Policy—Guidelines and Procedures for Processing EISs," developed and adopted by the Interagency Council on Natural Resources and the Environment, published November 1975.	Paul T. Wrotenbery, Director, Governor's Budget and Planning Office, Executive Office Building, 411 W. 13th Street, Austin, Tex. 78701 (Phone: 512-475-6156).
Utah		
State of Utah Executive Order, August 27, 1974.		William C. Quigley, Assistant Attorney General, State Capitol Building, Office of the Attorney General, Salt Lake City, Utah 84114 (Phone: 801-533-7643).

States With Special or Limited EIS Requirements

Source	Guidelines	State Contact
Arizona		
Game and Fish Commission Policy of July 2, 1971.	Memorandum by the Arizona Game and Fish Commission, "Requirements for Environmental Impact Statements," issued June 9, 1971.	Robert D. Curtis, Chief, Wildlife Planning and Development Division, Arizona Game and Fish Commission, 2222 W. Greenway Rd., Phoenix, Ariz. 85023 (Phone: 602-942-3000).
Delaware		
a) Delaware Coastal Zone Act, Ch. 175, Vol. 58, Laws of Del. (June 28, 1971), adding Del. Code Ann. Section 7001 et seq. (Supp. 1973), ard b) Delaware Wetlands Law of 1973, adding 7 Del.Code Ann. Ch. 66 (Supp. 1973).	a) Del. Code Ann. Ch. 66, Section 6604 (Supp. 1973), and "Permit Application Instructions and Forms and Information Material on Required Procedures for the Coastal Zone Act," prepared and published by the Delaware State Planning Office (effective July 1, 1977); this office will be known as the Delaware Office of Management, Budget, and Planning, and b) "Department of Natural Resources and Environmental Control, Wetlands Regulations," adopted pursuant to Section 6607 of the Wetlands Act, effective December 23, 1976.	a) For the Coastal Zone Act—David Hugg, Manager, Coastal Zone Program, Delaware Office of Management, Budget, and Planning, Dover, Del. 19901 (Phone: 302-678-4271). b) For the Wetlands Act—William Moyer, Wetlands Manager, Department of Natural Resources and Environmental Control, Division of Environmental Control, Dover, Del. 19901 (Phone: 302-678-4761).

Georgia

Ga. L. 1972-179 (March 10, 1972), Ga. Code Ann. Ch. 95A-1, Section 241(e)(1) (1973).

Policy and Procedures Manual: State Tollway Authority, prepared by Georgia's Tollway Administrator's Office in May, 1972 and revised in February, 1973.

Robert L. Austin, State Location Engineer, Division of Preconstruction, Department of Transportation, 2 Capitol Square, Atlanta, Ga. 30334 (Phone: 404-656-5312).

Kentucky

Ch. 278.025 Ky. Rev. Stats (April 1, 1979) (requires statement of environmental compatibility before a power plant may be built.)

None.

Office of Policy and Program Analysis, Kentucky Department for Natural Resources and Environmental Protection, Capital Plaza Tower, Frankfort, Ky. 40601 (Phone: 502-564-7320).

Mississippi

Title 49 Chapter 27, Mississippi Code of 1972, Section 49-27 1-49-27:69, amended in 1974 to include 49-27-7(s), relating to Wetlands.

Rules and Regulations written by the Mississippi Marine Resources Council, July 10, 1973, revised April 15, 1975 (under revision).

Joe Gill, Jr., Marine Projects Manager, Mississippi Marine Resources Council, P.O. Drawer 959, Long Beach, Miss. 39560 (Phone: 601-864-4602).

Nebraska

Nebraska Department of Roads, *Department of Road's Action Plan*. *Environmental Action Plan*, prepared by the Nebraska Department of Roads and approved by the Federal Highway Administration, June 24, 1975.

Mark Glaess, Acting Comprehensive Planning Coordinator, Office of Planning and Programming, Box 94601, State Capital, Lincoln, Nebr. 68509 (Phone: 402-471-2414).

Nevada

Ch. 311 Laws of 1971, 58 N.R.S. Ch. 704 (1971).

No guidelines have been issued.

Hardy Heber, Public Service Commission, Capitol Complex, Carson City, Nev. 89710 (Phone: 702-885-4180).

New Jersey

a) Coastal Area Facility Review Act P.L. 1973, Ch. 185 (approved June 20, 1973), N.J.S.A. 13: 19-1 et seq. (Cum. Supp. 1974-1975).

b) The New Jersey Wetlands Act of 1970, Ch. 272, Laws of 1970, N.J.S.A. 13:9A-1 et seq. (Cum. Supp. 1974-1975).

c) Waterfront Development Permit Program, N.J.S.A. 12:5-3.

a) "Procedural Rules for the Administration of the Coastal Area Facility Review Act," prepared by the Department of Environmental Protection in 1974 and adopted April 1, 1977, and

b) "New Jersey Wetlands Order: Basis and Background," issued by the New Jersey Department of Environmental Protection, April 1972, "Procedural Rules and Regulations to

a) David N. Kinsey, Chief, Office of Coastal Zone Management, New Jersey Department of Environmental Protection, P.O. Box 1889, Trenton, N.J. 08625 (Phone: 609-292-8262), and

b) Thomas F. Hampton, Supervisor, Office of Wetlands Management, Division of Marine Services, Department of Environmental Protection, P.O. Box 1889, Trenton, N.J. 08625 (Phone: 609-292-8202).

Table 9-6 (Continued)

States With Special or Limited EIS Requirements

Source	Guidelines	State Contact
New Jersey—(Continued)	Implement the Wetlands Order," N.J.A.C. 7A-1 et seq., adopted September 2, 1976. Rules on Coastal Resource and Development Policies, N.J.A.C. 7:7E-1.1 et seq., Sept. 28, 1978 (applies to all).	
Rhode Island Section 10-20-8B of General Laws of R.I. (1978) Environmental Rights Act.	None.	R. Daniel Prentiss, Chief Legal Counsel, Office of Environmental Management, 83 Park St., Providence, R.I. 02903. (Phone: 401-277-2771).

City NEPA's

Source	Guidelines	City Contact
Bowie, Maryland The Bowie, Maryland, Environmental Policy and Impact Statement Ordinance, passed by the City Council of Bowie, Maryland on May 3, 1971, and Ordinance 0-2-73 of the City Council of Bowie, Maryland, Declaring an Environmental Policy and Providing for Environmental Impact Statements, passed July 16, 1973, and Ordinance 0-14-76, Changing Notification and Referral Requirements under the Ordinance, passed September 8, 1976.		Glen Garber, Planning Director, Office of Planning and Community Development, City Hall, Bowie, Md. 20715 (Phone: 301-262-6200).
New York City Executive Order No. 91, June 1, 1977. New York City is currently working on a replacement policy which will incorporate the Executive Order and the requirements of the New York State Law. This order is being amended to conform with CEQRA amendment of November 1978.	A "City Environmental Policy Executive Order Environmental Information Form" is utilized for environmental analysis. The Information Form was prepared by the City of New York Environmental Protection Administration in 1973.	Francis Caroll, Director, Office of Environmental Impact, New York City Department of Environmental Protection, Room 2344, Municipal Building, New York, N.Y. 10007 (Phone: 212-566-4107).

enacted environmental policy acts, the requirements of which are summarized in Table 9-6. States with comprehensive statutory provisions generally require an EIS for the majority of state-supported activities. States with special or limited provisions require an EIS for only a few categories of state projects. In most cases state impact analysis procedures are quite similar to those required under the NEPA (Jain et al., 1981; CEQ, 1979a).

To reduce conflicts and duplication between federal and state procedures, the CEQ has drafted a model statute for states to use in amending their laws. The model legislation has been adopted by the Council of State Governments and submitted to the states. It directs federal agencies to cooperate with state and local agencies in eliminating conflicts and duplication (CEQ, 1979a).

The Evolution of the EIS

To date, the NEPA has experienced three primary development phases. In the first phase, roughly between 1970 and 1973, the assessment process consisted of superficial observations of physical impacts in the affected area and was used primarily to justify decisions already made. Between 1972 and 1975 the assessment process became more ordered and standardized. However, the process in this second phase became little more than the massing of voluminous technical and scientific data. More recently the assessment process has evolved into a third phase, with emphasis on physical and social relationships, early assessment of impacts, better decision making, and the use of quantitative and qualitative models to predict impacts. Erickson (1979) outlined current trends in the development and refinement process as follows:

1. Increasing emphasis on secondary, cumulative, and social impacts,
2. The development of quantitative and qualitative models for social and physical impact assessment,
3. Increasing emphasis on public participation,
4. The development of more interdisciplinary assessment teams,
5. The development of guidelines for assessing the significance of impacts,
6. The development of improved decision-making guidelines,
7. Decreasing emphasis on the procedural and increasing emphasis on the substantive requirements of the NEPA,
8. Increasing emphasis on streamlining EISs,
9. Increasing emphasis on assessing alternatives rather than justifying decisions,
10. Increasing emphasis on mitigation and monitoring impacts,
11. The development of curricula, workshops, training programs, and so on that focus on interdisciplinary problem solving,

12. The development of regulations and guidelines to avoid conflicts of interest,
13. The development of programmatic assessments that can later be adapted to specific site conditions,
14. Increasing recognition in the courts of the purpose and intent as well as the procedural requirements of the NEPA,
15. Increasing public awareness of the goals and legal requirements of the NEPA.

Although more than a decade old, the NEPA is continually being refined and adapted to socioeconomic and political conditions. The continued vitality of the NEPA is indicative of public support for its purpose and intent. The NEPA is now embodied in a dynamic system of case law, agency regulations, executive directives, and public rights and obligations, and it is doubtful that the NEPA can or will diminish in influence in the foreseeable future. However, because the NEPA involves such a dynamic process, it is virtually impossible to predict the nature and degree of future changes.

10 / Local Environmental Planning and Management

The purpose of this final chapter is to describe and summarize the information requirements, analyses, and planning and information processes necessary for proper local environmental management. Traditionally, local environmental management consisted of water, domestic wastewater, solid waste, land use, and recreation planning. The programs were generally administered through engineering or public works departments that tended to emphasize structural solutions to environmental problems. The approach to environmental management was, therefore, fragmented, narrow in focus, and unnecessarily mechanistic (EPA, 1974). Even now, the tendency is to deal with problems individually as if they were unrelated to other problems. Important relationships and social and ecological goals are often ignored or overlooked. As René Dubos (1974) put it:

> Planners are primarily concerned with the technological efficiency of the urban system with regard to industrial, economic, and political activities. They pay less attention to the psychological and emotional needs of city dwellers or to the relation between city life and civilization. While the technological aspects of the urban system are fairly well understood and can be manipulated, little is actually known about the influence that cities have exerted on the development of human potentialities and therefore on the emergence of civilized life. Civilizations have flourished in cities for more than 5,000 years, but they have difficulty in surviving the huge urban agglomerations of the contemporary world.

The failure of conventional environmental management programs has resulted, in many cases, in serious problems of land use, health, pollution, and resource depletion. This in turn has stimulated public awareness and concern for the integrity of the natural and urban environment, providing substantial public support for environmental control programs.

To properly integrate human and natural systems, a multitude of social and natural factors should be considered. Natural features, such as climate and landforms, are extremely important in determining the suitability of a site for certain land uses, such as agriculture, forestry, mining, development, or preservation. For instance, climate and landforms influence water and renewable and nonrenewable material resource availability, energy consumption, and pollution dispersion.

In addition, a number of socioeconomic factors are important in determining the location, nature, and extent of development. For instance, community size may be limited by the ability of the local economy to utilize indigenous resources, the proximity to other settlements, population densities, transportation patterns, the history of the site, educational institutions, technical systems, the capability to govern, and the aspirations of local inhabitants (Corbett, 1981).

The integration of all these factors into an effective and harmonious development or redevelopment plan requires knowledge, sensitivity, and creativity. The natural and human history of the locality, the ecosystem structure and function, and a sense of time, space, line, proportion, pattern, and symbolism should all play a part. This is extremely important because the manner in which human and natural systems are integrated ultimately influences the beauty, health, safety, economy, security, and stability of human settlements.

Local Planning and Management

It is evident that the key to successful local environmental planning and management is areawide coordination and planning to integrate the jurisdictional and functional elements of local environmental systems. This integration is essential in relating environmental objectives and alternatives to other sectors, such as housing and economic development, both to reduce adverse external impacts and to create more efficient environmental management. According to the EPA (1974), the following activities are necessary to properly integrate urban and environmental systems:

- Multiple objectives must be met, based on local and regional needs and jurisdictions.
- A wide range of alternative courses of action should be evaluated, including structural and nonstructural, leading to projects and actions that accomplish multiple objectives.
- Public and private actions must be coordinated, and citizen input into program formulation, implementation, and evaluation should be encouraged.
- Monitoring and research programs should be developed to provide the necessary information for program evaluation and evolution.
- Environmental planning must be integrated into local and metropolitan planning processes.

- A framework must be established for coordination of local, metropolitan, regional, state, and federal environmental planning and management.

Local governments are currently the weak link in the intergovernmental environmental management framework because of underutilization by higher levels of government and a lack of technical skills and funding. Local governments tend to have a strong sense of environmental responsibility when encouraged to become more involved in environmental management (EPA, 1974).

Approaches to Local Planning and Management

Communities can take an additive or a comprehensive approach in incorporating environmental considerations into local planning processes. The additive approach is the addition of an environmental planning agency or process to the more traditional elements of community planning, such as transportation, social service, or economic development planning.

Federal and state governments have favored the additive approach in developing their environmental management programs. One of the first communities to use this approach was Huntington, New York. In 1972 Huntington established a local environmental protection agency to review environmental impact statements on all public and certain private (industrial and subdivision) development projects. The agency acts as an environmental advocate for the city in negotiations between developers and the community (EPA, 1974).

The additive approach is a popular one because it is administratively easy to accomplish and it produces a tangible, visible entity. However, the creation of a new agency or process does not guarantee that environmental goals will be achieved. Often the new agency or process is at odds with conventional community development goals or agencies that have been part of creating the problems in the first place. The failure to resolve the inherent conflicts may result in inefficient and ineffective management programs. Effective resolution of such conflicts requires a more comprehensive, fundamental approach to environmental planning and management.

The second approach to local environmental planning and management is a fundamental realignment of community planning processes. In this approach the concepts of proper resource and residuals management are integrated with other community development goals as an important aspect of the quality of life in a community. For example the Wayne County (Michigan) Planning Commission in 1970 adopted its *Comprehensive Planning Process for Wayne County*, which incorporated environmental quality considerations as an important element in overall community planning processes. The commission recommended that the county

- establish an optimum population range
- gradually adjust the economy of the county to that range
- promote the development of energy sources other than fossil fuels
- promote recycling
- prevent soil erosion and the sedimentation of waterways
- increase awareness of the nonfiscal costs of pollution
- require reporting of the public and private monetary costs of pollution
- promote preservation of open lands

A similar approach was taken by the Albuquerque–Bernalillo County Planning Department. Their *Comprehensive Plan, Metropolitan Environmental Framework* (1972) assessed two alternative growth strategies. The first would require more stringent public controls in urban development to modify the trends in environmental degradation. For instance, this approach would limit population growth and promote stricter land development standards. The second strategy involved changes in the planning and management framework to promote long-term environmental quality goals. The intent was to make urban development compatible with ecological processes. This approach would promote a population level based on the concept of regional carrying capacity. In addition, development codes would be developed to improve environmental quality (e.g., air and water quality) and resource utilization patterns (e.g., energy use, replenishment of renewable resources, and protection of topsoil).

The real difference between the additive and comprehensive approaches to local environmental management lies in the intent of the program. The intent of the additive approach is to achieve specific environmental objectives, such as air and water quality goals. The approach is fragmented, the time frame is short, and conventional land use and population growth planning are not questioned. The intent of the second approach is to develop an understanding of the relationships of human and natural systems and to integrate these systems in a compatible manner. The two approaches need not be mutually exclusive. The additive approach can be used to achieve immediate short-term goals while the more comprehensive realignment of planning processes is developed to promote long-term harmony between human and natural systems. Both approaches are necessary, and they can be used together if properly balanced and integrated (EPA, 1974).

The Environmental Plan

Environmental planning and management involves, then, the integration of urban and environmental systems. To accomplish this integration

Figure 10-1. The Cycle and Relationships of Land Use, Residuals, and Resources.

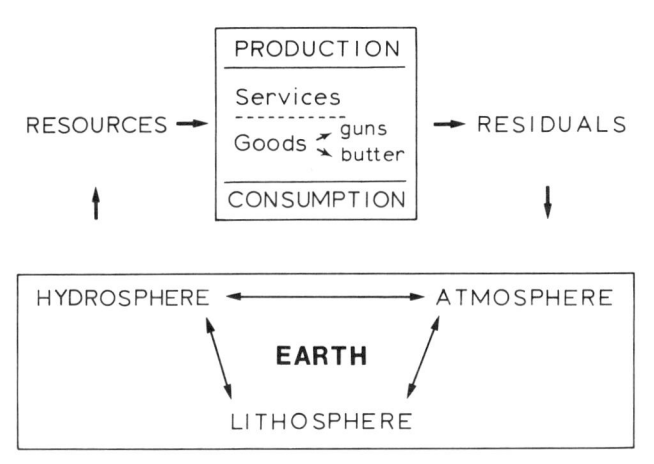

```
                    ┌──────────────┐
                    │  PRODUCTION  │
                    │   Services   │
      RESOURCES ──► │ ──────guns   │ ──► RESIDUALS
                    │  Goods⦃butter│
                    │              │
          ▲         │  CONSUMPTION │         │
          │         └──────────────┘         ▼

      ┌──────────────────────────────────────────┐
      │  HYDROSPHERE ◄──────────► ATMOSPHERE     │
      │              \            /              │
      │               \  EARTH   /               │
      │                \        /                │
      │                 LITHOSPHERE              │
      └──────────────────────────────────────────┘
```

the plan of action must be in accord with the cycles and flows of both natural and human systems. This requires a proper program design, adequate information, and careful program implementation.

Plan Design. Integrated management has three major areas of concentration: land use, resources, and residuals. The cornerstone of management and of the environmental plan should be the use of land, for the land is the platform, source, and sink for the activities of all natural and human systems. Figure 10-1 indicates the relationship between land use, resources, and residuals and the cycle of materials as they flow through our economy. The major features of a local environmental plan design and implementation are given below.

1. Land Use Plan
   A. Suitability for land development—opportunities and constraints.
   B. Resource lands such as forests, agricultural lands, open space, recreation and aesthetic lands.
   C. Ecologically significant lands such as forests, wetlands, wilderness, wildlife.
2. Resource Plan
   A. Efficiency of development and use of renewable and non-renewable resources.
   B. Sustained yield management of renewable resources.
   C. Multiple use of resources and use of multiple resources.
   D. Preservation of unique and significant natural resources.
   E. Promotion of the use of indigenous renewable resources.

F. Soil conservation and land reclamation.
G. Protection of valuable resources from pollution damage.
3. The Residuals Plan
   A. Identify the nature, location, and timing of all point and nonpoint sources of residuals. Emphasis should be placed on nonpoint sources of pollution and their relationship to land use patterns.
   B. Assess the costs, benefits, and external effects of alternative residuals management strategies.
4. Plan Implementation: The plan should address:
   A. Local educational and informational (media) programs.
   B. Overall community goals and objectives including the economic development goal.
   C. Political environment and capabilities of the community.
   D. Local capital improvement and infrastructure investment programs.
   E. The needs of as many neighborhood and citizen groups as possible.

Traditional land use plans are based on achieving efficiency in urban development and systems. The plans evaluate the demand and suitability of lands for development based on the size, location, accessibility, availability of utilities, slope, and soil characteristics of the parcel. This has often resulted in unwise siting of developments (e.g., on floodplains), the loss of valuable resource lands (e.g., forests and fields), and the despoliation of air, land, and water through improper residuals disposal practices (EPA, 1974).

A physical world view of land use broadens this perspective to accommodate concerns over resource development, residuals disposal, and the integrity of the natural environment. Thus, conventional land use planning has expanded to include consideration of (1) valuable resource lands such as agricultural and forest lands, (2) lands set aside for recreation, open space, or aesthetics, and (3) ecologically important lands, such as estuaries, wetlands, watersheds, coastal zones, and wildlife refuges. In addition, this expansion is promoting a more enlightened weighing of positive and negative aspects of urban growth.

Modern resource planning is also expanding to accommodate a wider range of environmental concerns. In the past, resource planning existed for the sole purpose of promoting the maximum rate of resource acquisition without regard for the socioeconomic or environmental consequences. The additional concerns of environmental quality and integrity of natural systems have created a greatly expanded set of resource management objectives, including preservation of unique and significant natural resources, efficient use of resources, promotion of the use of indigenous and/or renewable resources, land reclamation and soil conservation, pollution control, and promotion of economic diversification. The last policy enhances economic stability and is based on the ecological concept of diversity and stability. One way to promote economic diversification involves inventorying and then properly using and reusing as many indigenous resources as possible.

To inventory and manage local resources effectively, it may be useful to assign them to renewable and nonrenewable material and energy categories. Nonrenewable material (e.g., land, metals, minerals) and energy (e.g., fossil fuels) resources should be managed for efficiency of use to prolong their economic lifetimes without damaging natural ecosystems. The same is true of renewable material (e.g., crops, forests, wildlife, water) and energy (e.g., sunlight, geothermal energy, hydropower, wind, biomass) resources, but the emphasis is not to exceed the harvest capacity.

Once the resources are assigned to categories, the management area (airshed, watershed, jurisdictional boundary) should be defined and the resources inventoried for amount, location, and where appropriate, quality. For instance, water can be classified as a renewable resource, and the appropriate management area is the watershed. The amount and location of water at any time can be learned from records and/or predictive models of precipitation patterns and major waterways. The uses of water should be characterized (e.g., domestic purposes, cooling, dilution of pollution, aesthetics, recreation), and the quantity and quality of supply for each use characterized. Water resource problems, such as flooding, sedimentation, and contamination, should be identified to develop policies for protection and priorities for allocation. The information could then be integrated into management strategies or flexible packages of policies and alternative courses of action, such as the guidance system approach to land use and environmental management.

Residuals planning involves many of the processes of resource planning. All point and nonpoint sources of air, land, and water pollution should be inventoried. Alternative methods of residuals collection, recycling, containment, and disposal should be identified and analyzed for cost, effectiveness, external effects, and practicality.

Local planning and management should emphasize nonpoint sources of residuals in order to complement state and federal management efforts that concentrate primarily on point sources. Local governments can be influential in residuals management because (1) emissions are concentrated in urban areas, (2) many pollution problems are directly related to land use patterns, proximity of generators to receptors, and demands for urban growth, and (3) many of the land use controls are under their jurisdiction (EPA, 1974).

Local governments will become increasingly involved in land use, resource, and residuals management as they develop data bases and expertise and as higher levels of government refuse or fail to accomplish the environmental quality and health and safety goals of local citizens.

Information Requirements: The Environmental Inventory. The environmental inventory system is more than a data file. At minimum it should contain (1) a detailed data file of existing environmental conditions, (2) a summary of site preparation, construction, and operation actions, (3) a system to relate and project the environmental consequences of urban activities, and (4) a specified set of outputs (maps, tables, overlays, etc.). The quality of analysis and presentation and the effectiveness of the planning and management program are ultimately determined by the scope and detail of information collected.

The specific components of the information system vary according to community goals and objectives, management agency responsibilities and capabilities, the type of plan and guidance system utilized (e.g., environmental impact assessment, land suitability analysis, and the availability of data for the specified geographic area (Chapin and Kaiser, 1979). However, certain basic elements are commonly found in local environmental information systems, including local (1) land uses, (2) natural ecosystems, (3) demographics, (4) resources, (5) residuals, (6) economics, and (7) governmental regulatory and management practices (Rowe et al., 1978). The following summarizes some of the important information useful for environmental planning and management.

The land use inventory should include three categories of information: factors influencing land use, past and present land uses, and the influence of land use on other important environmental factors. The first category includes land availability, ownership, and value, as well as traditional land uses. The inventory of past and present land uses should include data on urban, agricultural, forest, wetland, park, open space, wilderness, and archaeologic and historic lands. Coastal communities may also want to designate special areas of particular concern, which may include productive estuaries, natural hazard zones, industries (such as refineries), and public facilities (such as ports and airports). Finally, information should be obtained on the relationship of various land uses to other environmental factors, such as air quality, water quality (especially sedimentation), and flooding (Rowe et al., 1978).

To properly assess the consequences of possible human activities, data are needed on the structure, function, and key components of local ecosystems. These data are particularly useful in environmental impact analyses and studies of constraints and opportunities for development. The inventory should minimally include plant and animal communities, climatic conditions (such as inversion patterns), physiography (soils, slope, geology, minerals, etc.), and hydrology. The hydrologic system in particular is important as a hazard, a resource, and a medium for residuals dispersal, so it is necessary to characterize fully the drainage patterns; significant waterways, such as lakes and streams; floodplains; and groundwater resources, recharge zones, and rates of flow. Particular attention should be paid to seasonal variation in climate and hydrology.

Demographic data are extremely important for predicting demand for urbanization. The most important demographic info for environmental planning and management is the size and age structure of the local population, including selected ethnic groups; birth, death, and net migration data; and data on family size, income, water and material consumption, and housing requirements.

The resource inventory should include the best possible assessment of the amount, availability, cost, and present and future demand for indigenous renewable and nonrenewable material and energy resources. The socioeconomic and environmental impacts of resource development should be characterized. In addition, the socioeconomic impacts of resource availability should be studied. One important interface is that of energy with transportation systems, land use, building design, and urban development.

The residuals inventory involves many different studies. The federal Water Pollution Control Act amendments (40 CFR Part 31) require a water quality inventory of lakes and streams to determine the location, nature, and extent of water pollution. At minimum, analyses of water temperature, turbidity, dissolved oxygen, nitrogen, phosphorous, and organic carbon should be done. In addition, an inventory of the location, nature, and extent of all sources of water pollution is required (Rowe et al., 1978). A similar analysis of air quality and an inventory of air pollution sources are required by the Clean Air Act. Much of this information is currently available from state environmental management agencies, but calculations of the contributions of nonpoint sources may have to be done on the local level. Finally, the local management agency should inventory all sources of toxic and solid wastes as well as all past, present, and future disposal sites.

Data on the local economy can be very useful in determining patterns of urban development, urban growth rates, and immigration and for formulating strategies for guided growth, economic diversification, and economic stabilization. The most important elements of this economic inventory are the nature and interrelatedness of the local industrial, commercial, and agricultural economic base; the origins of raw materials and destinations of products; employment characteristics and opportunities; the size and training of the work force; and the future plans of existing or incoming industries.

The goals, program activities, and capabilities of local governments are important in formulating and implementing an environmental plan. Information should be obtained on governmental mandates, jurisdictions, statutory limits, operational capabilities, and regulatory practices (e.g., building codes and zoning and subdivision ordinances).

The existing and planned levels of community services (schools, libraries, fire protection, parks, etc.), transportation, and utility systems should be analyzed carefully because of their role in determining the location and nature of development. Maps should be developed of all forms of intracity and intercity transportation. Data should be obtained on seasonal, daily, and hourly transportation patterns in relation to system capacities. Utility systems (water, sewer, storm drainage, natural gas, and electricity) should be mapped, and data on service demand and system capacity should be acquired (Chapin and Kaiser, 1979).

The environmental plan should be carefully integrated with existing plans for capital improvements, economic development, transportation, and so on, to avoid conflicts and facilitate the achievement of multiple objectives (Rowe et al., 1978). Finally, local decision makers and decision-making processes, such as review of and comment on development and/or redevelopment plans, should be characterized (Rowe et al., 1978).

Chapin and Kaiser (1979) proposed the following primary steps involved in the development of an environmental information system:

- Identification of important elements to be included in the information system (discussed previously).
- Determination of the variables or attributes to be measured. This involves the identification of variables and the location and nature of measurements (technique, timing, accuracy, and data storage for measurements).
- Data collection, including literature studies and field research.
- Data storage and retrieval. The system should allow easy access to information in a usable form, allow rapid storage and retrieval of information without loss, and be sufficiently flexible to allow modification over time. Computer-based information systems (supplemented by figures, tables, and maps) are particularly well suited for these purposes.
- Design and calibration of analytic models. This task involves organizing, analyzing, and presenting data to provide for the information needs of the system. These needs may range from simple descriptions and statistical analyses to complex computer statistical and simulation models.
- Presentation and communication. The outputs of the system should provide the required information in a format as comprehensible (to the user), attractive, and simple as possible.

Implementation. To date, there is no clear consensus on the most effective approach to accomplishing community environmental quality goals, especially given the tremendous variation in community resources, problems, goals, and controls. Therefore, it is suggested that an environmental guidance system, similar to the land use guidance system discussed in Chapter 3, can provide a comprehensive, coordinated, and systematic approach for the formulation and implementation of a local environmental plan. A guidance system involves a series of planning steps with corresponding decision guides and action instruments (see Figure 10-2). EPA's (1974) suggested planning steps include:

- Problem identification and analysis, including an inventory and analysis of relevant environmental attributes;
- Formulation of goals and objectives to define the future form and quality of the environment, with emphasis on citizen input;
- Formulation of alternatives to achieve the goals and objectives;
- Testing and evaluation of alternatives using explicit criteria;
- Selection and implementation of the favored alternative, including monitoring, feedback, and system change.

The actual guidance system consists of two components—decision guides and action instruments. Decision guides can include background studies, impact analyses, information summaries, budgets, laws and regulations, and officially adopted policies and plans (comprehensive, land use, transportation, etc.). Their purpose is to ensure the formulation of the management program in as effective and efficient a manner as possible. Action instruments are the means by which government intervenes in community processes to accomplish environmental quality goals.

The three major types of action instruments are regulations, incentives, and public investments. Among the most effective are regulations such as emissions standards; environmental quality standards; subdivision and planned unit development regulations; housing, building, and health codes; and zoning (EPA, 1974).

Two often overlooked, yet potentially effective, tools of local environmental management are building codes and subdivision codes, covenants, and restrictions. For instance building codes can require that structures be energy efficient or use solar space or water heating. One example is the San Diego (California) County's building code, which requires solar water heating in all new construction where electric heating is the only alternative. Subdivision codes, covenants, and restrictions have been used by innovative homeowner associations, such as the Village Homes subdivision in Davis, California, to promote community gardens, recreational developments, open spaces, and other neighborhood improvement projects (Corbett, 1981).

Incentive and disincentive tools, such as preferential taxation, bonus and penalty provisions in zoning and subdivision regulations, and pricing policies (e.g., for electricity, water, and solid waste disposal), can also be quite effective.

Public investments for highways, utilities, sewers, open space, public housing, schools, and urban renewal play an indirect but important role in influencing private and public actions. When properly coordinated, incentive and public investment action instruments can be quite

Figure 10-2. Interrelationships Among Components of an Environmental Guidance System. Planning activities and the political process determine decision guides and action instruments (modified from Chapin and Kaiser, 1979).

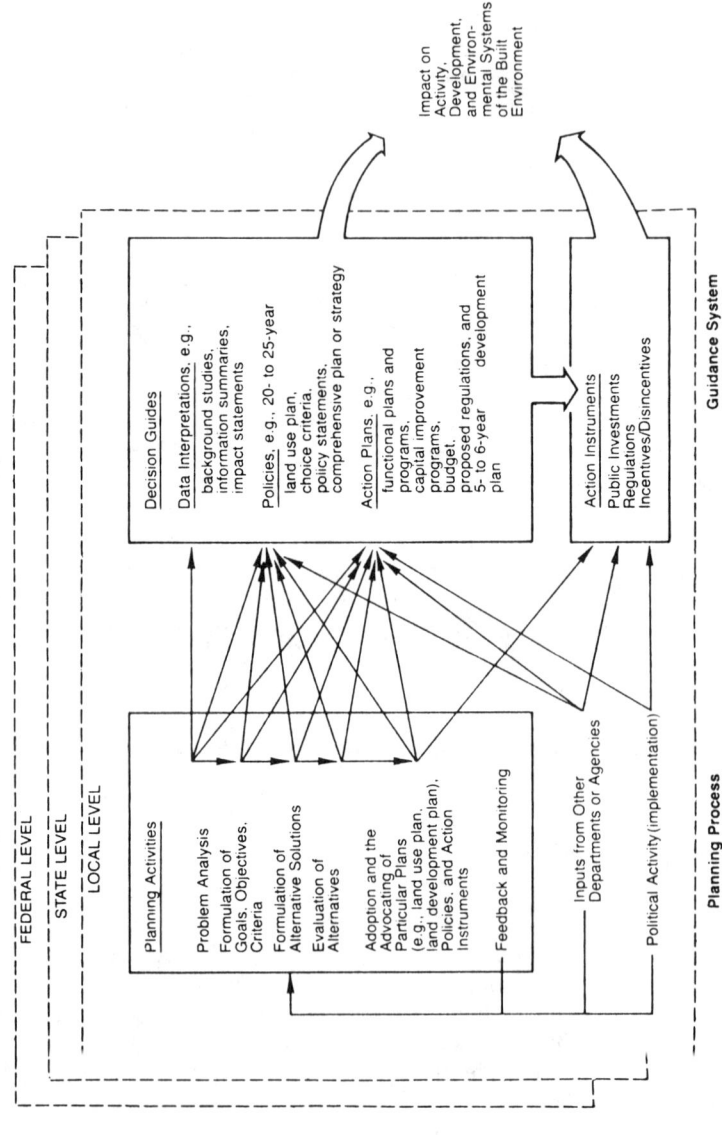

Source: *Urban Land Use Planning.* F. Stuart Chapin Jr. and Edward J. Kaiser. Third edition, 1979. University of Illinois Press. © by the Board of Trustees of the University of Illinois.

effective in influencing and guiding the proper growth and development of a community (Chapin and Kaiser, 1979).

To provide the information necessary for the proper development and coordination of action instruments, the management agency should develop and continuously update information files on regulations, incentives, and public investments that relate to environmental quality management. The files should have the type, extent, jurisdiction, and/or location of all relevant laws, regulations, policies, plans, and public services.

Citizen Participation

Public participation in the formulation and implementation of an environmental plan is highly desirable to promote public support for agency actions and to ensure that no major omissions or inaccuracies occur in the planning process. The key to a successful public participation program is effective communication of the goals and activities of the management agency and feedback from individuals and organizations to agency decision makers. To promote effective communication, the management agency should be careful to present information in a timely and appropriate manner and should be open and receptive to criticisms (Canter, 1977).

Purpose of the Public Participation Program

Canter (1977) delineated an active public participation program, which, depending on the stage of plan development, can help to

- Provide the public with information on environmental problems and agency goals and proposed activities,
- Develop a strong liaison between the agency and the general public,
- Assist the agency in identifying environmental problems and needs, potential solutions, and relevant local values,
- Assist the agency in identifying relevant alternatives and mitigation measures,
- Insure that the agency receives feedback from the public on the significance of impacts, the evaluation of alternatives, the identification of tradeoffs, and the value of unquantifiable environmental amenities,
- Resolve conflicts through information sessions, negotiation, and mediation to avoid costly and unnecessary litigation.

Advantages and Disadvantages

There are several advantages and disadvantages associated with public participation in environmental planning and management. The major benefits include the provision of useful information to decision makers, the enhancement of public confidence and support for agency planning processes, decisions, and actions, and the enhancement of agency accountability.

The disadvantages of a public participation program include the receipt of possibly confusing and erroneous information and the potential delays and increased costs. Proper planning and design of the public participation program can maximize the benefits while minimizing the costs (Canter, 1977).

Developing the Program

Public participation programs most commonly involve public hearings and formal and informal public information sessions. However, there is considerable variation in such programs. Erickson (1979) stated that in selecting and implementing a program of public involvement, a management agency must carefully consider the objectives of the analytical and integrative tasks, the physical setting, timing, and public groups involved, the nature and degree of management activities, the monitoring and enforcement actions involved, the attitudes and previous experiences of the involved public, and the resources assigned to the public participation program.

The management agency should carefully coordinate its public participation program with other federal, state, and local agencies that have interests and responsibilities in the same geographic or technical areas of study to avoid public confusion. In communicating with the public, the management agency should use all forms of news media and publish and distribute a planning newsletter. A list of all interested individuals and organizations should be compiled and used for information dissemination and feedback solicitation.

When conducting a public information program, the management agency should keep its presentations informative, precise, interesting, and free of technical jargon. The location, nature, timing, and socioeconomic and environmental impacts of project alternatives should be clearly presented. Finally, to promote a proper dialogue and to foster a climate of mutual trust and public support for agency actions, the attitude of the management team should be friendly, interested, honest, and sincere (Canter, 1977).

The Role of Government

Optimally, local, regional, state, and federal agencies involved in environmental planning and management should be hierarchically arranged so that each level of government would have the expertise, funding, and legal authority to manage resources and residuals of significant concern to them. In addition, each level of government should have the authority to compensate for the inadequacies and to resolve the problems of and conflicts between lower levels of government within their jurisdiction.

The purpose of this hierarchical arrangement is to allow the decision making to take place at the level that is closest to the problem, allowing maximum access of the public to the decision makers. This would produce decisions more closely reflecting the needs of the people and would foster a more democratic approach to decision making. The local public support for environmental quality could thereby become a force to counter the opposition of groups with special interests (Corbett, 1981).

Federal

Many resource and residuals problems transcend state and national boundaries. For instance, acid rains affect much of the northeastern United States and eastern Canada, and the waters of the Great Lakes and the St. Lawrence flow between two nations and several states. Such problems and management regions can only be dealt with effectively at the federal level. However, heavy reliance on the federal level for planning and management may result in an inflexible management program unable to recognize and compensate for the variations, inadequacies, or opportunities that exist at the local level. For instance, stringent air pollution controls on automobile emissions, designed to curb air quality problems in large metropolitan areas, may be unnecessary and unwanted in remote areas of the country.

The federal government should formulate flexible national policies to protect legitimate national interests of economic development and environmental protection. The standards and administrative procedures established should be sufficiently flexible to allow for regional differences, yet have sufficient enforcement powers to accomplish the national goals and objectives. If national environmental quality and emissions standards are developed, clear procedures and standards for variances should be stipulated. In addition, the federal government should sponsor activities where economies of scale can be achieved (e.g., technical and methodological research). Finally, the federal government should assume leadership in promoting long-term planning, coordinating the planning and management activities of lower levels of government, and promoting citizen participation in decision-making processes (Rowe et al., 1978).

State and Regional

The role of states in environmental planning and management varies widely with the nature and degree of environmental problems, the capabilities of the state, and the relationships between the state and regional and local governments. Some states have highly centralized management structures, whereas others rely heavily on regional and local management. In either case, the state government should coordinate its management activities to be consistent with and complimentary to the programs of higher and lower levels of government (retaining some flexibility in its procedures to reflect regional and local needs).

In addition, the state should identify environmental concerns of statewide significance and work with higher and lower levels of government to improve, preserve, or protect them. States without centralized controls can coordinate or review regional and local activities to assure that statewide interests are protected. Finally, state governments should provide the legal, financial, and technical tools necessary for regional and local environmental planning and management.

Regional organizations, such as river basin commissions and councils of government, have generally assumed the major responsibility for coordinating local actions with federal and state requirements and for preparing long-range regional development plans. They are often intimately involved in the planning of waste treatment facilities, transportation systems, and other public investments, such as housing and health care programs, and are primarily responsible for maintaining and disseminating specific regional information for public and private decision making (Rowe et al., 1978).

Local

Local governments should have a major role in environmental planning and management because they are in direct contact with the people who may help create and/or are affected by environmental problems and controls. In addition, local governments have the necessary role of monitoring and enforcing through the use of potentially powerful local management tools, including the following (EPA, 1974):

- Advice and review—local monitoring programs, information systems, environmental and land use planning, plan review procedures, etc.;
- Regulations—environmental quality and emissions standards, zoning, subdivision regulations, building codes, planned unit developments, transfer of development rights easements, eminent domain, etc.;
- Incentives or disincentives—differential tax policies (property taxes, accelerated depreciation, depletion allowances), effluent or emissions fees, etc.;
- Public investments—direct land purchase, utility or highway development policies, public facilities, planned industrial parks, urban renewal, etc.

Because federal and state governments establish many of the ground rules for environmental management (e.g., they develop standards and management strategies and provide financial, technical, and enforcement assistance), the local management agency should be certain that its actions comply with current federal and state laws, rules, and regulations.

Local governments are often involved in a myriad of activities to implement specific rules, regulations, and enforcement procedures in addition to attacking the roots of environmental problems through comprehensive land use planning and growth guidance systems. The EPA's 1974 report enumerated the most common activities of local management agencies:

- Maintaining and updating information systems (usually in conjunction with a regional information base),
- Documenting and characterizing local environmental problems,
- Promoting citizen participation programs for information and decision-making programs,
- Formulating management goals and objectives,
- Developing and evaluating program alternatives in achieving goals and objectives,
- Selecting a preferred management program, including implementation procedures and tools,
- Implementing the tools,
- Monitoring environmental quality and effluent emissions,
- Mitigating impacts of program development,
- Enforcing standards and procedures.

Case Study: Village Homes, Davis, California

Perhaps the best example of a conventional (e.g., privately and individually owned, with single family homes, noncommunal) ecologically planned neighborhood is the Village Homes subdivision in Davis, California (Corbett, 1981). The seventy-acre subdivision was initiated in 1972 and completed in 1980 (see Figure 10-3). The subdivision features energy efficient passive-solar homes and a transportation network based on walking and the bicycle rather than the automobile. Every house in the subdivision faces a street. However, fences and shrubs have been placed between streets and homes to form private courtyards that turn front yards into usable space. The back yards are used for common open spaces as drainage ways, gardens, bike paths, parks, and so on. Children tend to play collectively in the commons areas rather than on the streets.

The innovation that created the most difficulty in winning approval for the subdivision was the natural drainage system. The developer was able to save more than $800 per house in construction costs by developing surface drainage swales and existing natural waterways.

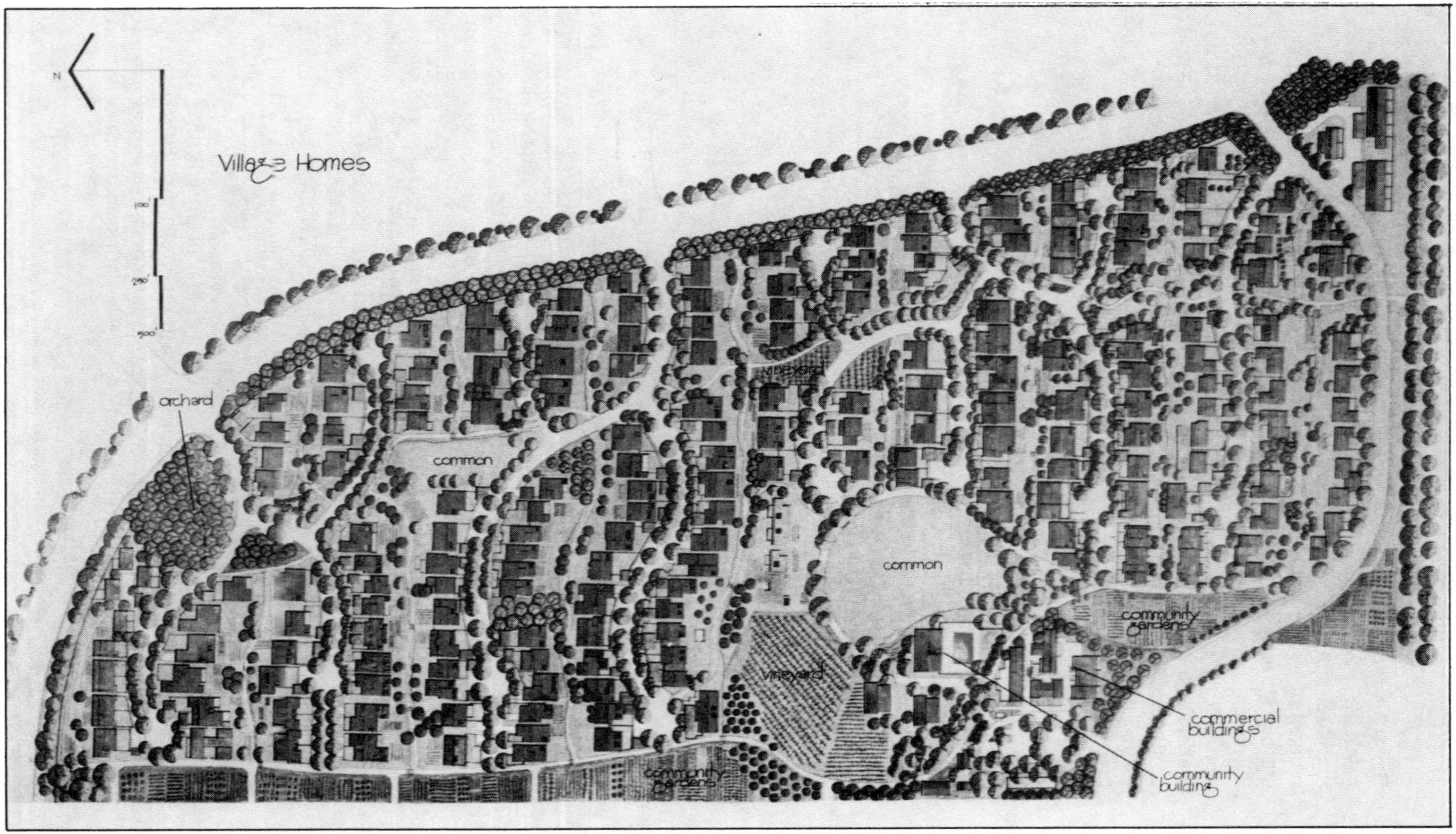

Figure 10-3. The Layout of the Village Homes Subdivision in Davis, California. Note the street pattern, runoff corridors, common areas, and community gardens (Corbett, 1981).

The swales run through the common areas, where checkdams and landscaping create a parklike atmosphere. By retaining more surface water on the site, there is greater habitat diversity, more groundwater recharging, and less flooding downstream. The natural system is cheaper and easier to operate than a conventional storm sewer system. The system requires no pumping and any obstructions are easily detected and removed (Corbett, 1981).

The subdivision is landscaped with native vegetation to provide needed shade in the summer. The streets, parking lots, patios, and bikeways and/or walking paths are also shaded in the summer to reduce the ambient temperature.

Landscaping and community gardens were designed to provide the residents with food and fuel. The need for private lawns was reduced by providing a large community playing field. The subdivision also features its own recycling center for source separation.

Finally the transportation system for automobiles is designed so that all streets feed outward to a peripheral road. Bikeways and walking paths all feed inward toward the community center, where the commercial and civic facilities are located. The paths tend to follow the natural corridors formed by the commons and natural drainage systems, so residents can bike or walk safely to markets or playing fields without coming into contact with automobiles. To accomplish the identical trip by automobile would be more costly, indirect, and time consuming. The result has been extensive use of the walkways (Corbett, 1981).

In conclusion, as citizens demand better environmental quality at home, subdivisions and urban renewal projects that incorporate many of the innovative features of the Village Homes subdivision will become the norm. It is important for planners, managers, and local governments to anticipate and facilitate this movement because it is cost effective and can enhance the environmental quality of all.

Conclusions

Proper planning and management of our residuals and natural resources are becoming increasingly important to the health and perpetuation of the socioeconomic systems of the United States. The environmental planning and management field is soberingly complex and still in its early stages of development. Thus, the public is only now becoming aware of the problems associated with the overconsumption of resources and demanding that resource allocation decisions reflect to the fullest extent possible the total costs involved.

The emphasis of this book has been on general processes and concepts of environmental planning and management. The intent is to provide the information for local communities to develop plans to meet their own needs and capabilities. To do so requires a basic understanding of the interrelationships of ecological and social systems, the "rules of the game," and decision-making processes. It is hoped that this book provides sufficient information to be a valuable first step for local governments to design and implement sound environmental management programs.

Appendix: The National Environmental Policy Act of 1969, as Amended*

An Act to establish a national policy for the environment, to provide for the establishment of a Council on Environmental Quality, and for other purposes.

Be it enacted by the Senate and House of Representatives of the United States of America in Congress assembled, That this Act may be cited as the "National Environmental Policy Act of 1969."

PURPOSE

SEC. 2. The purposes of this Act are: To declare a national policy which will encourage productive and enjoyable harmony between man and his environment; to promote efforts which will prevent or eliminate damage to the environment and biosphere and stimulate the health and welfare of man; to enrich the understanding of the ecological systems and natural resources important to the Nation; and to establish a Council on Environmental Quality.

TITLE I

DECLARATION OF NATIONAL ENVIRONMENTAL POLICY

SEC. 101. (a) The Congress, recognizing the profound impact of man's activity on the interrelations of all components of the natural environment, particularly the profound influences of population growth, high-density urbanization, industrial expansion, resource exploitation, and new and expanding technological advances and recognizing further the critical importance of restoring and maintaining environmental quality to the overall welfare and development of man, declares that it is the continuing policy of the Federal Government, in cooperation with State and local governments, and other concerned public and private organizations, to use all practicable means and measures, including financial and technical assistance, in a manner calculated to foster and promote the general welfare, to create and maintain conditions under which man and nature can exist in productive harmony, and fulfill the social, economic, and other requirements of present and future generations of Americans.

(b) In order to carry out the policy set forth in this Act, it is the continuing responsibility of the Federal Government to use all practicable means, consistent with other essential considerations of national policy, to improve

---

*Pub. L. 91–190, 42 U.S.C. 4321–4347, January 1, 1970, as amended by Pub. L. 94–83, August 9, 1975.

and coordinate Federal plans, functions, programs, and resources to the end that the Nation may—

(1) Fulfill the responsibilities of each generation as trustee of the environment for succeeding generations:

(2) Assure for all Americans safe, healthful, productive, and esthetically and culturally pleasing surroundings;

(3) Attain the widest range of beneficial uses of the environment without degradation, risk to health or safety, or other undesirable and unintended consequences;

(4) Preserve important historic, cultural, and natural aspects of our national heritage, and maintain, wherever possible, an environment which supports diversity, and variety of individual choice;

(5) Achieve a balance between population and resource use which will permit high standards of living and a wide sharing of life's amenities; and

(6) Enhance the quality of renewable resources and approach the maximum attainable recycling of depletable resources.

(c) The Congress recognizes that each person should enjoy a healthful environment and that each person has a responsibility to contribute to the preservation and enhancement of the environment.

SEC. 102. The Congress authorizes and directs that, to the fullest extent possible: (1) the policies, regulations, and public laws of the United States shall be interpreted and administered in accordance with the policies set forth in this Act, and (2) all agencies of the Federal Government shall—

(A) Utilize a systematic, interdisciplinary approach which will insure the integrated use of the natural and social sciences and the environmental design arts in planning and in decisionmaking which may have an impact on man's environment;

(B) Identify and develop methods and procedures, in consultation with the Council on Environmental Quality established by title II of this Act, which will insure that presently unquantified environmental amenities and values may be given appropirate consideration in decisionmaking along with economic and technical considerations;

(C) Include in every recommendation or report on proposals for legislation and other major Federal actions significantly affecting the quality of the human environment, a detailed statement by the responsible official on—

(i) The environmental impact of the proposed action,

(ii) Any adverse environmental effects which cannot be avoided should the proposal be implemented,

(iii) Alternatives to the proposed action,

(iv) The relationship between local short-term uses of man's environment and the maintenance and enhancement of long-term productivity, and

(v) Any irreversible and irretrievable commitments of resources which would be involved in the proposed action should it be implemented.

Prior to making any detailed statement, the responsible Federal official shall consult with and obtain the comments of any Federal agency which has jurisdiction by law or special expertise with respect to any environmental impact involved. Copies of such statement and the comments and views of the appropriate Federal, State, and local agencies, which are authorized to develop and enforce environmental standards, shall be made available to the President, the Council on Environmental Quality and to the public as provided by section 552 of title 5, United States Code, and shall accompany the proposal through the existing agency review processes;

(D) Any detailed statement required under subparagraph (C) after January 1, 1970, for any major Federal action funded under a program of grants to States shall not be deemed to be legally insufficient solely by reason of having been prepared by a State agency or official, if:

    (i) the State agency or official has statewide jurisdiction and has the responsibility for such action,

    (ii) the responsible Federal official furnishes guidance and participates in such preparation,

    (iii) the responsible Federal official independently evaluates such statement prior to its approval and adoption, and

    (iv) after January 1, 1976, the responsible Federal official provides early notification to, and solicits the views of, any other State or any Federal land management entity of any action or any alternative thereto which may have significant impacts upon such State or affected Federal land management entity and, if there is any disagreement on such impacts, prepares a written assessment of such impacts and views for incorporation into such detailed statement.

The procedures in this subparagraph shall not relieve the Federal official of his responsibilities for the scope, objectivity, and content of the entire statement or of any other responsibility under this Act; and further, this subparagraph does not affect the legal sufficiency of statements prepared by State agencies with less than statewide jurisdiction.

(E) Study, develop, and describe appropriate alternatives to recommended courses of action in any proposal which involves unresolved conflicts concerning alternative uses of available resources;

(F) Recognize the worldwide and long-range character of environmental problems and, where consistent with the foreign policy of the United States, lend appropriate support to initiatives, resolutions, and programs designed to maximize international cooperation in anticipating and preventing a decline in the quality of mankind's world environment;

(G) Make available to States, counties, municipalities, institutions, and individuals, advice and information useful in restoring, maintaining, and enhancing the quality of the environment;

(H) Initiate and utilize ecological information in the planning and development of resource-oriented projects; and

(I) Assist the Council on Environmental Quality established by title II of this Act.

SEC. 103. All agencies of the Federal Government shall review their present statutory authority, administrative regulations, and current policies and procedures for the purpose of determining whether there are any deficiencies or inconsistencies therein which prohibit full compliance with the purposes and provisions of this Act and shall propose to the President not later than July 1, 1971, such measures as may be necessary to bring their authority and policies into conformity with the intent, purposes, and procedures set forth in this Act.

SEC. 104. Nothing in section 102 or 103 shall in any way affect the specific statutory obligations of any Federal agency (1) to comply with criteria or standards of environmental quality, (2) to coordinate or consult with any other Federal or State agency, or (3) to act, or refrain from acting contingent upon the recommendations or certification of any other Federal or State agency.

SEC. 105. The policies and goals set forth in this Act are supplementary to those set forth in existing authorizations of Federal agencies.

TITLE II

COUNCIL ON ENVIRONMENTAL QUALITY

SEC. 201. The President shall transmit to the Congress annually beginning July 1, 1970, an Environmental Quality Report (hereinafter referred to as the "report") which shall set forth (1) the status and condition of the major natural, manmade, or altered environmental classes of the Nation, including, but not limited to, the air, the aquatic, including marine, estuarine, and fresh water, and the terrestrial environment, including, but not limited to, the forest, dryland, wetland, range, urban, suburban and rural environment; (2) current and foreseeable trends in the quality, management and utilization of such environments and the effects of those trends on the social, economic, and other requirements of the Nation; (3) the adequacy of available natural resources for fulfilling human and economic requirements of the Nation in the light of expected population pressures; (4) a review of the programs and activities (including regulatory activities) of the Federal Government, the State and local governments, and nongovernmental entities or individuals with particular reference to their effect on the environment and on the conservation, development and utilization of natural resources; and (5) a program for remedying the deficiencies of existing programs and activities, together with recommendations for legislation.

SEC. 202. There is created in the Executive Office of the President a Council on Environmental Quality (hereinafter referred to as the "Council"). The Council shall be composed of three members who shall be appointed by the President to serve at his pleasure, by and with the advice and consent of the Senate. The President shall designate one of the members of the Council to serve as Chairman. Each member shall be a person who, as a result of his training, experience, and attainments, is exceptionally well qualified to analyze and interpret environmental trends and information of all kinds; to appraise programs and activities of the Federal Government in the light of the policy set forth in title I of this Act; to be conscious of and responsive to the scientific, economic, social, esthetic, and cultural needs and interests of the Nation; and to formulate and recommend national policies to promote the improvement of the quality of the environment.

SEC. 203. The Council may employ such officers and employees as may be necessary to carry out its functions under this Act. In addition, the Council may employ and fix the compensation of such experts and consultants as may be necessary for the carrying out of its functions under this Act, in accordance with section 3109 of title 5, United States Code (but without regard to the last sentence thereof).

SEC. 204. It shall be the duty and function of the Council—

(1) To assist and advise the President in the preparation of the Environmental Quality Report required by section 201;

(2) To gather timely and authoritative information concerning the conditions and trends in the quality of the environment both current and prospective, to analyze and interpret such information for the purpose of determining whether such conditions and trends are interfering, or are likely to interfere, with the achievement of the policy set forth in title I of this Act, and to compile and submit to the President studies relating to such conditions and trends;

(3) To review and appraise the various programs and activities of the Federal Government in the light of the policy set forth in title I of this Act for the purpose of determining the extent to which such programs and activities are contributing to the achievement of such policy, and to make recommendations to the President with respect thereto;

(4) To develop and recommend to the President national policies to foster and promote the improvement of environmental quality to meet the conservation, social, economic, health, and other requirements and goals of the Nation;

(5) To conduct investigations, studies, surveys, research, and analyses relating to ecological systems and environmental quality;

(6) To document and define changes in the natural environment, including the plant and animal systems, and to accumulate necessary

data and other information for a continuing analysis of these changes or trends and an interpretation of their underlying causes;

(7) To report at least once each year to the President on the state and condition of the environment; and

(8) To make and furnish such studies, reports thereon, and recommendations with respect to matters of policy and legislation as the President may request.

SEC. 205. In exercising its powers, functions, and duties under this Act, the Council shall—

(1) Consult with the Citizens' Advisory Committee on Environmental Quality established by Executive Order No. 11472, dated May 29, 1969, and with such representatives of science, industry, agriculture, labor, conservation organizations, State and local governments and other groups, as it deems advisable; and

(2) Utilize, to the fullest extent possible, the services, facilities and information (including statistical information) of public and private agencies and organizations, and individuals, in order that duplication of effort and expense may be avoided, thus assuring that the Council's activities will not unnecessarily overlap or conflict with similar activities authorized by law and performed by established agencies.

SEC. 206. Members of the Council shall serve full time and the Chairman of the Council shall be compensated at the rate provided for Level II of the Executive Schedule Pay Rates (5 U.S.C. 5313). The other members of the Council shall be compensated at the rate provided for Level IV of the Executive Schedule Pay Rates (5 U.S.C. 5315).

SEC. 207. There are authorized to be appropriated to carry out the provisions of this Act not to exceed $300,000 for fiscal year 1970, $700,000 for fiscal year 1971, and $1 million for each fiscal year thereafter.

Approved January 1, 1970.

Acronyms

BAT	best available technologies
BPT	best practicable technologies
CEQ	Council on Environmental Quality
CPI	consumer price index
CSSI	Chem-Security Systems, Inc.
CZMA	Coastal Zone Management Act
DES	diethylstilbestrol
EA	environmental assessment
EIS	environmental impact statement
EPA	Environmental Protection Agency
EQ	environmental quality
FONSI	finding of no significant impact
GNP	gross national product
HEW	U.S. Department of Health, Education and Welfare
HUD	U.S. Department of Housing and Urban Development
I/A	innovative and alternative
I/M	inspection and maintenance
IPR	intergovernmental program review
NAAQS	national ambient air quality standards
NEPA	National Environmental Policy Act
NPDES	National Pollution Discharge Elimination System
NSPS	new source performance standards
OMB	Office of Management and Budget
OSM	Office of Surface Mining
PCBs	polychlorinated biphenols
POTWs	publicly owned treatment works
PSI	pollution standards index
RCRA	Resource Conservation and Recovery Act
RDF	refuse derived fuel
RPA	Forest and Rangeland Renewable Resources Planning Act
SCS	Soil Conservation Service
SDWA	Safe Drinking Water Act
SIPs	state implementation plans
SMSAs	Standard Metropolitan Statistical Areas
TERA	transferable emissions reduction assessment

THM	trihalomethane compounds
TMI	Three Mile Island
TSCA	Toxic Substance Control Act
TVA	Tennessee Valley Authority
WRC	Water Resource Council

Bibliography

Adkins, W. G., and D. Burke, Jr. 1974. "Social, Economic, and Environmental Factors in Highway Decision Making." Research Report 148-4, Texas Transportation Institute, Texas A&M University.
Albuquerque–Bernalillo County Planning Dept. 1972. *Comprehensive Plan, Metropolitan Environmental Framework.* County Planning Dept., Albuquerque, N.M.
Alfors, J. T., J. E. Burnett, and T. E. Gay, Jr. 1973. "Urban Geology Master Plan for California: The Nature, Magnitude, and Costs of Geologic Hazards in California and Recommendations for Their Mitigation." *California Division of Mines and Geology Bulletin* 198.
Allen, D. L. 1976. "Pressures on Outdoor Space." *National Parks and Conservation Magazine* 50:5:2, 31.
American Law Institute. 1974. *A Model Land Development Code.* American Law Institute, Philadelphia, Penn.
Ames, S. 1981. "Sustainable Portland." In: *Knowing Home: Studies for a Possible Portland* (RAIN Staff Report), RAIN, Portland, Ore.
Anderson, F. R. 1973. *NEPA in the Courts—A Legal Analysis of the National Environmental Policy Act.* Johns Hopkins University, Baltimore, Md.
Andrews, R. (ed.). 1979. *Land in America.* Lexington Books, Lexington, Mass.
Arkell, D. 1981. "Proposed Changes in Clean Air Act Could Effect Lane County." *Monitor,* July/Aug. Lane Regional Air Pollution Control Authority, Eugene, Ore.
Associated Press. 1980. "Judge Orders EPA to Issue Regulations." *Eugene Register-Guard,* Nov. 14, p. 10B.
Atwood, G. 1975. "The Strip Mining of Western Coal." *Scientific American* 233:6:23–29.
Bailin, L. J., and B. L. Hertzler. 1978. "Development of Microwave Plasma Detoxification Process for Hazardous Wastes." *Environmental Science and Technology* 12:6:673–678.
Barnes, P. 1971. "Land Reform in America." *The New Republic,* June 5, 12, and 19.
Barnes, P., and L. Gasalino. 1972. "Who Owns the Land." *Clear Creek,* Dec., no. 18, pp. 17–31.
Baumol, W. J. 1974. "Environmental Protection and Income Distribution." In: *Redistribution Through Public Choice,* H. M. Hochman and G. E. Peterson (eds.), Columbia University Press, New York.
Beatley, T. 1981. "The Need for Equity as a Planning Rationale." *Oregon American Planning Association Newsletter,* Jan./Feb., 7:1:1.
Berdine, S., and J. Mariar. 1972. "Water Quality Management Planning in Metropolitan Areas." Environmental Protection Agency, Boston, Mass.
Bergen, T. F. 1978. "Needed. A New Theory of Land-Use Planning." In. *Toward a New Ethic of Land Use,* Piedmont Environmental Council.

Birch, D. 1979. *The Job Generation Process.* MIT Press, Cambridge, Mass.

Black and Veatch and Franklin Associates, Ltd. 1978. "Detailed Technical and Economic Analysis of Selected Resource Recovery Systems." Prepared for the Mid-American Regional Council.

Brewer, D., and M. Mackie. 1978. *Implementing Energy Efficient Land Use.* Oregon Department of Energy, Salem, Ore.

Briggs, R. P., J. S. Pomeroy, and W. E. Davies. 1975. "Land-Sliding in Allegheny County." *U.S. Geological Survey Circular,* no. 728.

Brown, G. 1972. "Economic Evaluation of the Proposed Tocks Island Project." Environmental Defense Fund. Mimeo.

Bruner, J. M., and M. T. Farris. 1969. "The Conventional Wisdom in Water Philosophy." Proceedings of the 8th Annual Meeting of the Westen Regional Science Association, Newport Beach, Calif.

Bryson, R. A., and S. Jenkins. 1972. "The Environmental Impact of the Aswan High Dam." Institute for Environmental Studies, University of Wisconsin, Madison, Wis.

Burger v. County of Mendocino. 1975. 45 Cal. App. 3d 322, 119, Cal. Rptr. 568 (Cal. Ct. of App., 1975).

Business Week. 1979. "The Oil Crisis Is Real This Time." Special Report, July 30, pp. 44–60.

Cahn, R. 1979. "The God Committee." *Audubon,* May, p. 16.

Cain, J. M., and T. M. Beatty. 1973. "Disposal of Septic Tank Effluent in Soils." *Journal of Soil and Water Conservation* 20:101–105.

Calvert Cliff's Coordinating Committee v. Atomic Energy Commission. 1972. 404 U.S. 942 (1972).

Canter, L. 1977. *Environmental Impact Assessment.* McGraw-Hill, New York.

Carlin, A. 1973. "The Grand Canyon Controversy, or How Reclamation Justifies the Unjustifiable." In: *Pollution, Resources, and the Environment,* A. C. Enthoven and A. M. Freeman III (eds.), W. W. Norton, New York.

Carter, L. J. 1973. "Land Use Law (I): Congress on Verge of a Modest Beginning." *Science,* Nov. 16, pp. 691–697.

Chanlett, E. T. 1973. *Environmental Protection.* McGraw-Hill, New York, p. 151.

Chapin, F. S., Jr., and E. J. Kaiser. 1979. *Urban Land Use Planning.* 3d. ed. University of Illinois Press, Urbana, Ill.

Chase Econometrics Associates, Inc. 1976. *The Macroeconomic Impacts of Federal Pollution Control Programs: 1976 Assessment.* Prepared for the Council on Environmental Quality and the Environmental Protection Agency, New York.

Chassie, R. G., and R. D. Goughnour. 1976. "States Intensifying Effort to Reduce Highway Landslides." *Civil Engineering* 46.

Chem-Security Systems, Inc. (CSSI). 1980. Promotional Materials. CSSI, Arlington, Ore.

Clark, C. 1963. "Agricultural Productivity in Relation to Population." In: *Man and His Future,* Churchill, London, pp. 23–35.

Coates, G. J. (ed.). 1981. *Resettling America: Energy, Ecology, and Community.* Brick House Publishing Co., Andover, Mass.

Cohen, S. 1984. "Defusing the Toxic Time Bomb: Federal Hazardous Waste Programs." In: *Environmental Policy in the 1980's: Reagan's New Agenda,* N. Vig and M. Kraft (eds.), Congressional Quarterly Inc., Washington, D.C.

Committee on Interior and Insular Affairs. 1972. *National Land Use Policy.* U.S. Government Printing Office, Washington, D.C.

Conservation Foundation. 1982. *State of the Environment: 1982.* Conservation Foundation, Washington, D.C.

Corbett, M. 1981. *A Better Place to Live.* Rodale Press, Emmaus, Penn.

Costle, D. 1979. "Dollars and Sense." *Environment* 21:8:25–27.

Council on Environmental Quality (CEQ). 1971. "Guidelines for Statements on Proposed Federal Actions Affecting the Environment." *Federal Register* 36:7724–7729.

———. 1973. "Preparation of Environmental Impact Statements, Guidelines." *Federal Register* 36:147:20550–20562.

———. 1974. *Land Use.* U.S. Government Printing Office, Washington, D.C.

———. 1975. *Environmental Quality.* U.S. Government Printing Office, Washington, D.C.

———. 1976. *Environmental Quality.* U.S. Government Printing Office, Washington, D.C.

———. 1977. *Environmental Quality.* U.S. Government Printing Office, Washington, D.C.

———. 1978a. *Regulations for Implementing Procedural Provisions of NEPA.* Federal Register 43:55978–56007.

———. 1978b. *Environmental Quality.* U.S. Government Printing Office, Washington, D.C.

———. 1979a. *Environmental Quality.* U.S. Government Printing Office, Washington, D.C.

———. 1979b. *The Good News About Energy.* U.S. Government Printing Office, Washington, D.C.

———. 1980. *Environmental Quality.* U.S. Government Printing Office, Washington, D.C.

Council on Environmental Quality and the U.S. Department of State. 1980. *The Global 2000 Report to the President.* vol. 1. U.S. Government Printing Office, Washington, D.C.

Dasmann, R. 1966. *Environmental Conservation.* John Wiley and Sons, New York.

Data Resources Inc. 1979. *The Macro-Economic Impact of Federal Pollution Control Programs: 1978 Assessment.* Prepared for the Council on Environmental Quality and the Environmental Protection Agency.

Dee, N., et al. 1972. *Environmental Evaluation System for Water Resource Planning* (Final Report). Prepared by Battelle–Columbus for the Bureau of Reclamation.

Diman, B. D. 1976. "The SO_2 Ambient Air Quality Standard, with Special Reference to the 24-Hour Standard—An Inquiry Into the Health Bases." In: *Statistics and the Environment,* Proceedings of the 4th Symposium of the American Statistical Association, Washington, D.C.

Dingham, L., and R. Platt. 1977. "Floodplain Zoning: Implications of Hydrologic and Legal Uncertainty." *Water Resources Research* 13:3:519–523.

Discher, D. P., G. P. Kleinman, F. J. Foster, and P. Lot. 1975. *Study for Development of an Occupational Disease Surveillance Method.* HEW Publication no. (NIOSH) 75-162.

Dregne, H. E. 1977. "Desertification of Arid Lands." *Economic Geography* 33:4:329.

Dubos, R. 1974. *Beast or Angel: Choices That Make Us Human.* Charles Scribner's Sons, New York, p. 92.
Dunne, T., and J. B. Leopold. 1978. *Water in Environmental Planning.* W. H. Freeman, San Francisco, Calif.
Duscha, J. 1981. "How the Alaska Act Was Won." *The Living Wilderness* 44:152:4–9.
Eckholm, E. P. 1976. *Losing Ground: Environmental Stresses and World Food Prospects.* W. W. Norton, New York.
Eckholm, E. P., and L. R. Brown. 1977. *Spreading Deserts—The Hand of Man.* Worldwatch Paper no. 13. Worldwatch Institute, Washington, D.C.
Ehrlich, P. R., and A. H. Ehrlich. 1974. *The End of Affluence.* Ballantine Books, New York.
Ehrlich, P. R., et al. 1977. *Ecoscience: Population, Resources, and Environment.* W. H. Freeman, San Francisco, Calif.
Environmental Defense Fund v. Corps of Engineers. 1972. 470 F 2d 289, 2 ELR 20740 (8th Cir., 1972).
Environmental Defense Fund v. Froehlke. 1972. F 2d 346, 3 ELR 20001 (8th Cir., 1972).
Environmental Policy Division. 1973. *National Land Use Policy Legislation: 93rd Congress.* U.S. Government Printing Office, Washington, D.C.
Environmental Protection Agency (EPA). 1972. *Guide for Compiling a Comprehensive Emissions Inventory.* Research Triangle Park, N.C.
――――. 1974a. *Promoting Environmental Quality Through Urban Planning and Controls.* Office of Research and Development, Washington, D.C.
――――. 1974b. *The Economic Damages of Air Pollution.* U.S. Government Printing Office, Washington, D.C.
――――. 1974c. *Compilation of Air Pollution Emission Factors.* Research Triangle Park, N.C.
――――. 1975. *Resource Recovery and Waste Reduction.* Third Report to Congress, Office of Solid Waste Management Programs, Washington, D.C.
――――. 1976a. "Guidelines for Public Reporting of Daily Air Quality–Pollutant Standards Index." EPA-450/2-76-013, Washington, D.C.
――――. 1976b. *Quality Criteria for Water.* U.S. Government Printing Office, Washington, D.C.
――――. 1976c. *Decision-Makers Guide in Solid Waste Management.* U.S. Government Printing Office, Washington, D.C.
――――. 1977. *Resource Recovery and Waste Reduction.* Fourth Report to Congress, Washington, D.C.
――――. 1978a. *Innovative and Alternative Technology Assessment Manual.* EPA-430/4-4-78-009, U.S. Government Printing Office, Washington, D.C.
――――. 1978b. *National Water Quality Inventory, 1977 Report to Congress.* EPA-440/4-4-78-001, U.S. Government Printing Office, Washington, D.C.
――――. 1978c. *Quarterly Report to the Secretary of Labor on the Economic Dislocation Early Warning System.* Fourth Quarter, Attachment C, Sheet 2.
――――. 1979. "Hazardous Waste Fact Sheet." *EPA Journal,* Feb.
――――. 1980a. *A Preliminary Analysis of Drinking Water Regulation Compliance.* Office of Drinking Water, Washington, D.C.
――――. 1980b. *Air Quality Criteria for Particulate Matter and Sulfur Oxides* (External Review Draft).

———. 1980c. *Everybody's Problem: Hazardous Waste.* Office of Water and Waste Management, U.S. Government Printing Office, Washington, D.C.

———. 1980d. *A Preliminary Report on the Potential Groundwater Contamination from Liquid Waste Storage: Treatment and Disposal in Surface Impoundments.* U.S. Government Printing Office, Washington, D.C.

———. 1983. *Superfund Initiatives.* Office of Emergency and Remedial Response, Washington, D.C. Internal Briefing Book.

Erickson, P. A. 1979. *Environmental Impact Assessment.* Academic Press, New York, pp. 246–258.

Erwin, D. E. et al. 1977. *Land Use Control.* Ballinger, Cambridge, Mass.

Evans, D. M., and A. Bradford. 1969. "Under the Rug." *Environment* 11:8:2–13.

Executive Office of the President. 1977. *The National Energy Plan.* Office of Energy Policy and Planning, U.S. Government Printing Office, Washington, D.C.

Federal Register. 1978a. "Hazardous Waste Guidelines and Regulations." *Federal Register* 43:58946.

———. 1978b. *Federal Register* 43:4492–4955.

———. 1979. *Federal Register* 44:30016–30042.

———. 1980. *Federal Register* 45:12722, id. p. 33066.

Flawn, P. T. 1970. *Environmental Geology.* Harper and Row, New York.

Foin, T. C., Jr. 1976. *Ecological Systems and the Environment.* Houghton Mifflin, Boston, Mass.

Forrester, J. 1971. "Counterintuitive Behavior of Social Systems." *Technology Review* 73, no. 3.

Forrestal, L. 1975. "Deep Mystery." *Environment* 177:322–329.

Fred C. Hart Assoc. 1979. *Preliminary Assessment of Cleanup Costs for National Hazardous Wastes Problems.* Prepared for the Environmental Protection Agency, Washington, D.C.

Freeman, A. M., III. 1978. "Air and Water Pollution Policy." In: *Current Issues in U.S. Environmental Policy,* P. R. Portney (ed.), Johns Hopkins University Press, Baltimore, Md.

Freeman, A. M., III and R. H. Haveman. 1972. "Residual Charges for Pollution Control: A Policy Evaluation." *Science* 177:322–329.

Freeman, A. M., III, R. H. Haveman, and A. V. Kneese. 1973. *The Economics of Environmental Policy.* John Wiley and Sons, New York.

Friends of the Earth. 1982. *Ronald Reagan and the American Environment.* Friends of the Earth Books, San Francisco, Calif.

Frome, M. 1984. *The Forest Service.* 2d ed., Westview Press, Boulder, Colo.

Galbraith, J. K. 1967. *The New Industrial State.* Houghton Mifflin, Boston, Mass.

General Accounting Office (GAO). 1977. *The Tennessee Valley Authority's Tellico Dam Project—Costs, Alternatives, and Benefits.* Report to Congress.

———. 1978. *Community Managed Septic Systems—A Viable Alternative to Sewage Treatment Plants.* CED 78-168, Washington, D.C.

Geraghty and Miller, Inc. 1978. *Surface Impoundments and Their Effects on Ground-Water Quality in the United States—A Preliminary Survey.* EPA-570/9-78-004, U.S. Government Printing Office, Washington, D.C.

Gianessi, L. P., H. M. Peskin, and E. Wolff. 1977. "The Distributional Effects of the Uniform Air Pollution Policy in the United States." Resources for the Future Discussion Paper. Unpublished.

Godschalk, D. R., and F. H. Parker. 1975. "Carrying Capacity: A Key to Environmental Planning." *Journal of Soil and Water Conservation,* July/Aug., pp. 160–165.

Godschalk, D. R., et al. 1977. *The Constitutional Issues of Growth Management.* American Society of Planning Officials, Chicago, Ill.

Gordian Associates, Inc. 1977. *Overcoming Institutional Barriers to Solid Waste Utilization as an Energy Source.* Prepared for the U.S. Department of Energy, Washington, D.C.

Griggs, G. B., and J. A. Gilchrist. 1983. *Geologic Hazards, Resources and Environmental Planning.* Wadsworth Publishing Co., Belmont, Calif.

Haar, C. M. 1959. *Land Use Planning.* Little, Brown and Co., Boston, Mass.

Handler, B. 1977. "The Politics of Water." *Saturday Review,* May 14, pp. 16–19.

Hansen, W. R. 1965. "Effects of the Earthquake of March 27, 1964 at Anchorage, Alaska." *U.S. Geological Survey Professional Paper* 542A, U.S. Government Printing Office, Washington, D.C.

Hardin, G. 1968. "The Tragedy of the Commons." *Science* 162:1243–1248.

———. 1974. "Living in a Lifeboat." *BioScience* 24:561–568.

Hardin, G. and J. Baden. 1977. *Managing the Commons.* W. H. Freeman, San Francisco, Calif.

Harris, L. 1980. "Toxic Chemical Dumps: Corrective Action Desired." Press release, July 7.

———. 1981. "Substantial Majorities Indicate Support for Clean Air and Clean Water Acts." *The Harris Survey,* June 11.

———. 1982. "Harris Reports the Voice of the People." *National News Report* (May), Sierra Club.

Haveman, R. H., and V. K. Smith. 1978. "Investment, Inflation, Unemployment, and the Environment." In: *Current Issues in U.S. Environmental Policy,* P. R. Portney (ed.), Resources for the Future, pp. 164–200.

Hayes, D. 1976. *Energy: The Case for Conservation.* Worldwatch Institute, Washington, D.C.

Healy, R. G. 1979. *Land Use and the States.* 2d ed. Johns Hopkins University Press, Baltimore, Md.

Henderson, H. 1981. *The Politics of the Solar Age.* Anchor Press, Garden City, N.Y.

Henning, D. H. 1974. *Environmental Policy and Administration.* American Elsevier Publishing Co., New York.

Hirshleifer, J., J. C. DeHaven, and J. W. Milliman. 1960. *Water Supply: Economics, Technology, and Policy.* University of Chicago Press, Chicago, Ill.

Hubbert, M. K. 1973. "Survey of World Energy Resources." *Canadian Mining and Metallurgical Bulletin* 66:735:37-54.

Hudson, E. A., and J. A. Jorgenson. 1974. "U.S. Energy Policy and Economic Growth, 1975–2000." *Bell Journal of Economics and Management Science,* pp. 461–514.

Hughes, J. D. 1975. *Ecology in Ancient Civilizations.* University of New Mexico Press, Albuquerque, N.M.

Ingram, H. M., and D. E. Mann. 1984. "Preserving the Clean Water Act: The Appearance of Environmental Victory." In: *Environmental Policy in the 1980's: Reagan's New Agenda,* N. Vig and M. Kraft (eds.), Congressional Quarterly Inc., Washington, D.C.

Interagency Task Force. 1979. *Our Nation's Wetlands.* U.S. Government Printing Office, Washington, D.C.
Jain, R. K., L. V. Urban, and G. S. Stacey. 1981. *Environmental Impact Assessment.* Academic Press, New York.
Jones, D. E., Jr., and W. G. Holtz. 1973. "Expansive Soil—The Hidden Disaster." *Civil Engineering* 43:49-51.
Jones, R. A. 1979. "The World Eyes Antarctica's Resources." *Los Angeles Times,* Oct. 25.
Kamlet, K. S. 1979. "Toxic Substance Programs in the U.S. States and Territories: How Well Do They Work?" National Wildlife Federation, Scientific and Technical Series, no. 4.
Kazmann, R. G. 1972. *Modern Hydrology.* 2d ed. Harper and Row, New York.
Kellogg, C. 1966. "Soils Surveys for Community Planning." In: *Soils Surveys in Land Use Planning,* Bartelli, L. J. et al. (eds.), Soil Science Society of America, American Society of Agronomy, Madison, Wis., pp. 19-31.
Kephart, G. S., 1977. "Problems in the Smokies." *American Forest,* Aug., pp. 28-31.
Kitto, W. D., and A. F. Burns. 1980. "The ABC's of NEPA Regs." *Planning,* June, pp. 17-18.
Kneese, A. V. 1966. "The Ruhr and the Delaware." *Journal of the Sanitary Engineering Division* (ASCE), Oct., pp. 83-92.
Kneese, A. V., and C. L. Schultz. 1975. *Pollution, Prices and Public Policy.* Brookings Institution, Washington, D.C.
Knott, J. M. 1973. *Effects of Urbanization on Sedimentation and Flood Flows in Colma Creek Basin, California.* U.S. Geological Survey Open-File Report.
Kormondy, E. J. 1969. *Concepts of Ecology.* Prentice-Hall, Englewood Cliffs, N.J.
Krieger, J., et al. 1979. "Facts and Figures for the U.S. Chemical Industry." *Chemical and Engineering News* 57:32-68.
Krutilla, J. V. 1967. "Conservation Reconsidered." *American Economic Review* 57:4:777-786.
Lager, J. A., et al. 1976. *Development and Application of a Simplified Storm Water Management Model.* Environmental Protection Agency, Cincinnati, Ohio.
Lave, L., and E. Seskin. 1977. *Air Pollution and Human Health.* Resources for the Future, Johns Hopkins University Press, Baltimore, Md.
Lennett, D. L. 1980. "Handling Hazardous Waste: An Unresolved Problem." *Environment* 22:8:6-15.
Leopold, A. 1966. *A Sand County Almanac.* Ballantine Books, New York.
Leopold, L. B. 1968. "Hydrology for Urban Land Planning: A Guidebook on the Hydrologic Effects of Urban Land Use." *U.S. Geological Survey Circular,* no. 554.
Leopold, L. B., et al. 1971. "A Procedure for Evaluating Environmental Impact." *U.S. Geological Survey Circular,* no. 645.
Lovins, A., and H. Lovins. 1982. *Brittle Power.* Brick House Publishing Co., Andover, Mass.
Magnuson, E. 1980. "The Poisoning of America." *Time,* Sept. 22, pp. 58-69.
Margalef, R. 1970. *Perspectives on Ecological Theory.* University of Chicago Press, Chicago, Ill.
Margerum, T. 1979. *Will Local Government Be Liable for Earthquake Losses?* Association of Bay Area Governments, Berkeley, Calif.

Marsh, G. P. 1864. *Man and Nature.* Charles Scribner, New York.
Marsh, W. M. 1978. *Environmental Analysis for Land Use and Site Planning.* McGraw-Hill, New York.
Maugh, T. H. 1979a. "Toxic Waste Disposal a Growing Problem." *Science* 204:4395:819-823.
──── . 1979b. "Hazardous Wastes Technology is Available." *Science* 204:4396:930-933.
──── . 1979c. "Incineration, Deep Wells Gain New Importance." *Science* 204:4398:1188-1190.
──── . 1979d. "Burial is Last Resort for Hazardous Wastes." *Science* 204:4399:1295-1298.
McCloskey, M. 1981. "Environmental Protection Is Good Business." *Sierra* 66:2:31-33.
McCoy, H., and J. Singer. 1979. "How to Audit Community Energy Use." *Practicing Planner,* July.
McHarg, I. 1971. *Design With Nature.* Doubleday/Natural History Press, Garden City, N.Y.
Meadows, D. H., D. W. Meadows, J. A. Randers, and W. W. Behrens. 1972. *The Limits of Growth.* Universe Books, New York.
Melosi, M. V. 1981. "The Cleaning of America." *Environment* 23:8:6-44.
Metcalf and Eddy, Inc. 1971. *Storm Water Management Model.* Vol. 1. Final Report, Environmental Protection Agency, Washington, D.C.
Miller, G. T., Jr. 1971. *Energetics, Kinetics and Life.* Wadsworth Publishing Co., Belmont, Calif.
──── . 1979. *Living in the Environment: Concepts, Consequences and Alternatives.* 2d ed., Wadsworth Publishing Co., Belmont, Calif.
──── . 1982. *Living in the Environment: Concepts, Consequences and Alternatives.* 3d ed., Wadsworth Publishing Co., Belmont, Calif.
Miller, R. D., and E. Dobrovolny. 1959. "Surficial Geology of Anchorage, Alaska, and Vicinity." *U.S. Geological Survey Bulletin,* no. 1093.
Mishan, E. J. 1971. "The Postwar Literature on Externalities: An Interpretative Essay." *Journal of Economic Literature* 1:9:1-28.
Mitchell, B. 1980. "The Politics of Antarctica." *Environment* 22:1:12-41.
Morris, D. 1981. "Self Reliant Cities: The Rise of the New City States." In: *Resettling America,* D. Coates (ed.), Sierra Club Books, San Francisco, Calif., pp. 240-262.
Morrison, P. A., and J. P. Wheeler. 1976. "Rural Renaissance in America?" *Population Bulletin* 31:3:1-26.
Moss, E. (ed.). 1976. *Land Use Controls in the United States.* Dial Press, New York.
Myers, B., and J. Rubin. 1978. "Complying with the Flood Disaster Protection Act." *Real Estate Law Journal* 7:114-131.
National Academy of Sciences (NAS). 1969. *Resources and Man.* NAS, Washington, D.C.
──── . 1974. *Rehabilitation Potential of Western Coal Lands.* Ballinger, Cambridge, Mass.
──── . 1975a. *Air Quality and Stationary Source Emission Control.* NAS, Washington, D.C.
──── . 1975b. *Mineral Resources and the Environment.* NAS, Washington, D.C.

———. 1981. "Atmosphere-Biosphere Interactions: Toward a Better Understanding of the Ecological Consequences of Fossil Fuel Combustion." National Academy Press, Washington, D.C.
National Commission on Water Quality. 1976. Staff Report. Washington, D.C.
National Environmental Policy Act (NEPA). 1969. *Public Law 91-190*, 83 Stat 852.
National Oceanic and Atmospheric Administration (NOAA). 1979. *The First Five Years of Coastal Zone Management.* Office of Coastal Zone Management, U.S. Department of Commerce, Washington, D.C.
Natural Resources Defense Council v. Grant. 1972, 3 ERC 1883, 2 ELR 20185 (E.D., N.C., 1972).
New Republic. 1974. "James Watt's Land Rush." Feature Article, June 29, pp. 22-23.
Nilson, T. H., and B. C. Turner. 1975. "Influence of Rainfall and Ancient Landslide Deposits on Recent Landslides (1950-1971) in Urban Areas of Contra Costa County, California." *U.S. Geological Survey Bulletin,* no. 1388.
Odum, E. 1970. "Optimum Population and Environment: A Georgian Microcosm." *Current History,* vol. 58, pp. 355-359.
Odum, H. T. 1978. "Energy, Ecology, and Economics." In: *Stepping Stones: Appropriate Technology and Beyond,* Schocken Books, New York.
Office of Technology Assessment (OTA). 1978. *Materials and Energy from Waste.* U.S. Government Printing Office, Washington, D.C.
Okagaki, A., and J. Benson. 1979. *County Energy Plan Guidebook.* Institute for Ecological Policies, Fairfax, Va.
Ophuls, W. 1977. *Ecology and the Politics of Scarcity.* W. H. Freeman, San Francisco, Calif.
Oregon Department of Energy (ODOE). 1980. "Weatherization and Alternative Resource Incentives for Oregonians." ODOE, Salem, Ore.
Oregon Department of Environmental Quality (DEQ). 1980. "Uncontrolled (Abandoned) Hazardous Waste Disposal Sites Survey." DEQ, Salem, Ore., Progress Report.
Oregon Statute Annotated. 1979. S459.505.
Page, R., and J. Ferejohn. 1974. "Externalities as Commodities: Comment." *American Economic Review* 64:3:454-459.
Patterson, T. A. 1979. *Land Use Planning: Techniques of Implementation.* Van Nostrand Reinhold, New York.
Peskin, H. M. 1978. "Environmental Policy and the Distribution of Benefits and Costs." In: *Current Issues in U.S. Environmental Policy,* P. R. Portney (ed.), Johns Hopkins University Press, Baltimore, Md., pp. 144-163.
Peskin, H. M., and E. P. Seskin (eds.). 1975. *Cost Benefit Analysis and Water Pollution Policy.* Urban Institute, Washington, D.C.
Peterson, S. 1980. "The Common Heritage of Mankind?" *Environment* 22:1:6-11.
Pierce, C., and J. Heritage. 1980. "The National Environmental Policy Act." *EPA Journal,* Nov./Dec., pp. 29-30.
Pimentel, D., et al. 1976 "Land Degradation: Effects on Food and Energy Resources." *Science* 194:149:155.
Platt, R. 1979. *Options to Improve Federal Non-Structural Response to Floods.* Water Resources Council, Washington, D.C.
Pojasek, R. B. 1978. "Stabilization, Solidification of Hazardous Wastes." *Environmental Science and Technology* 12:4:382-386.

Pope, C. 1984. "Ronald Reagan and the Limits of Responsibility." *Sierra*, May/June, pp. 51-54.

Popper, F. J. 1979. "Ownership: The Hidden Factor in Land Use Planning." In: *Land in America,* R. Anderson (ed.), Lexington Books, Lexington, Mass., pp. 129-135.

Portney, P. R. 1978. "Toxic Substance Policy and the Protection of Human Health." In: *Current Issues in U.S. Environmental Policy,* P. R. Portney (ed.), Johns Hopkins University Press, Baltimore, Md.

Putnam, Hayes, and Bartlett, Inc. 1980. "Comparisons of Estimated and Actual Pollution Control Costs for Selected Industries." Prepared for the Environmental Protection Agency.

RAIN. 1981. *Knowing Home: Studies for a Possible Portland.* RAIN, Portland, Ore.

Randall, J. H. 1940. *The Making of the Modern Mind.* Houghton Mifflin, Cambridge, Mass.

Resource Conservation Committee. 1979. "Choices for Conservation." Final Report to the President and Congress, Washington, D.C.

Resources for the Future. 1980. *Public Opinion on Environmental Issues: Results of a National Public Opinion Survey.* Council on Environmental Quality, Washington, D.C.

Rifkin, J. 1980. *Entropy: A New World View.* Viking Press, New York.

Roberts, P. 1971. "Cross Florida Barge Canal: A Current Appraisal." In: *Business and Economic Dimensions,* College of Business Administration, University of Florida.

Ross, M. H., and R. H. Williams. 1977. "The Potential for Fuel Conservation." *Technology Review* 79:4:49-57.

———. 1982. "The Potential for Fuel Conservation." In: *Perspectives on Energy,* R. Ruedisili and M. W. Firebaugh (eds.), 3d ed., Oxford University Press, New York.

Rowe, P. G., J. Mixon, B. A. Smith, J. B. Blackburn, Jr., G. L. Callaway, and J. L. Gevirtz. 1978. *Principles for Local Environmental Management.* Ballinger, Cambridge, Mass.

Ruckelshaus, W. D. 1972. "Solid Waste Management: An Overview." *Public Management,* Oct.

Samuelson, P. 1954. "The Pure Theory of Public Expenditure." *Review of Economics and Statistics* 49:5:387-389.

Santor, J. D., G. B. Boyd, and F. J. Agardy. 1974. "Water Pollution Aspects of Street Surface Contaminants." *Journal of the Water Pollution Control Federation* 46:3:458-467.

Science. 1981. "EPA and Industry Pursue Regulatory Options." *Science* 211:796-797.

Seldman, N. N. 1976. "High Technology Recycling Mainly Benefits Polluters." *Environmental Action Bulletin,* Feb. 7, pp. 1-3.

Sewell, G. H. 1975. *Environmental Quality Management.* Prentice-Hall, Englewood Cliffs, N.J.

Sheets, K. R. 1981. "Is United States Paving Over Too Much Farmland?" *U.S. News and World Report,* Feb. 2, pp. 47-48.

Shiffman, Y., and A. Page. 1979. "Community Energy Planning: Bridging the Information Gap." *Practicing Planner,* July.

Shreiber, A., P. Gatons, and R. Clemmer. 1976. *The Economics of Urban Problems.* Houghton Mifflin, Boston, Mass.

Sierra Club v. *Froehlke.* 1973. 5 F Supp. 1033, 3 ELR 20248 (S.D. Tex. 1973).
Slosson, J. E. 1969. "The Role of Engineering Geology in Urban Planning." *Colorado Geological Survey Special Publication* (Denver), no. 1.
Soil Conservation Service (SCS). 1981a. *Lane County Soils—Interpretations Defined.* U.S. Department of Agriculture, Eugene, Ore.
———. 1981b. *Soil Survey for Lane County, Oregon.* U.S. Department of Agriculture, Eugene, Ore.
Southern Tier Central Regional Planning and Development Board (STCRPDB). 1978. *Renewable Energy Resource Inventory.* STCRPDB, Corning, N.Y.
Southwick, C. S. 1976. *Ecology and the Quality of Our Environment.* 2d ed. D. Van Nostrand, New York.
Speth, G. 1978. "A Small Price to Pay." *Environment* 20:8:25-28.
Spurr, S. 1970. "Developing a Natural Resource Management Policy." In: *No Deposit—No Return.* Addison-Wesley Publishing Co., Menlo Park, Calif.
Staff of *Environmental Science and Technology.* 1975. "The Hang-ups on Recycling." *Environmental Science and Technology* 9:1015.
Steinhart, P. 1980. "The City and the Inland Sea." *Audubon* 82:5:98-126.
Stobaugh, R. and D. Yergin. 1979. *Energy Future.* Random House, New York.
Stoker, H. S., S. L. Seager, and R. L. Capener. 1975. *Energy.* Scott, Foresman and Co., Glenview, Ill.
Strauss, L. 1953. *National Rights and History.* University of Chicago Press, Chicago, Ill.
Subcommittee on Oversight and Investigations. 1979. *Hazardous Waste Disposal Report.* House Committee on Interstate and Foreign Commerce, U.S. Government Printing Office, Washington, D.C.
Swinton, W. E. 1954. *Fossil Amphibians and Reptiles.* 1st ed. British Museum, London, England.
Technology Review. 1980. "The Chemicals Nobody Wants." *Technology Review,* Jan., pp. 18-19.
Tennessee Valley Authority (TVA). 1978. *Alternatives to Completing the Tellico Dam Project.* TVA, Knoxville, Tenn.
The Real Estate Research Corp. 1974. *The Costs of Sprawl.* Prepared for the Council on Environmental Quality and the Environmental Protection Agency.
Thomas, R. 1978. "Land Treatment." *EPA Journal* 4.7.26.
Thurow, C., W. Toner, and D. Erley. 1975. *Performance Controls for Sensitive Lands: A Practical Guide for Local Administrators.* Office of Research and Development, Environmental Protection Agency, Washington, D.C.
Tobin, R. J. 1984. "Revising the Clean Air Act: Legislative Failure and Administrative Success." In: *Environmental Policy in the 1980's: Reagan's New Agenda,* N. Vig and M. Kraft (eds.), Congressional Quarterly Inc., Washington, D.C.
Toxic Substance Strategy Committee. 1980. *Toxic Chemicals and Public Protection.* U.S. Government Printing Office, Washington, D.C.
Twiss, R. H., and I. M. Heyman. 1976. "Nine Approaches to Environmental Planning." In: *Land Use Planning Politics and Policy,* R. Cowart (ed.), University of California Extension, Berkeley, Calif.
Uhler, R. G., and B. Zycher. 1979. "Energy Forecasting: Coping with Uncertainty." Paper presented at International Conference on Energy Use Management, Los Angeles, Calif.
United Press International (UPI). 1981. "Group of 77 Reject Plan to Mine Seas." *Eugene Register-Guard,* Aug. 8, p. 6A.

U.S. Bureau of Land Management (BLM). 1975. *Range Condition Report.* U.S. Government Printing Office, Washington, D.C.

———. 1978. *Final Environmental Impact Statement—The Proposed Rio Puerco Livestock Grazing Management Program.* U.S. Government Printing Office, Washington, D.C.

U.S. Department of Agriculture (USDA). 1977. *San Joaquin Valley Basin Study.* River Basin Planning Staff, Soil Conservation Service, U.S. Forest Service, and the Economic Research Service, Washington, D.C.

U.S. Department of Agriculture and Council on Environmental Quality. 1981. *The National Agricultural Lands Study.* USDA and CEQ, Washington, D.C.

U.S. Department of Energy (DOE). 1980a. *Monthly Energy Review.* DOE/EIA 0035/80(06), U.S. Government Printing Office, Washington, D.C.

———. 1980b. *The Energy Consumer.* Office of Consumer Affairs, Washington, D.C.

U.S. Department of Health, Education, and Welfare (HEW). 1977. *Statistics Needed For Determining the Effects of the Environment on Health.* National Center for Health Statistics, Washington, D.C.

U.S. Department of Housing and Urban Development (HUD). 1977. *Innovative Zoning: A Digest of the Literature.* Office of Policy Development and Research, U.S. Government Printing Office, Washington, D.C.

U.S. Geological Survey (USGS). 1978. "Field Observations of the December 1977 Windstorm, San Joaquin Valley, California." USGS, Menlo Park, Calif.

U.S. Public Health Service. 1968. *Sanitary Landfill Facts.* Publication no. 1792, U.S. Government Printing Office, Washington, D.C.

U.S. Resources Council. 1978. "Floodplain Management Guidelines for Implementing Executive Order 11988." *Federal Register* 43:6063.

U.S. Water Resources Council. 1978. *Second National Water Assessment.* Vol. 1. U.S. Government Printing Office, Washington, D.C.

———. 1980. *State of the States: Water Resources Planning and Management.* U.S. Government Printing Office, Washington, D.C.

University of Tennessee. 1978. *Study of Alternative Futures for the Little Tennessee River Valley.* University of Tennessee, Knoxville.

Vig, N., and M. Kraft (eds.). 1984. *Environmental Policy in the 1980's: Reagan's New Agenda.* Congressional Quarterly Inc., Washington, D.C.

Vogely, W. A. 1977. "The State of Our Mineral Position: A Provocation." *Technology Review*, Oct./Nov., pp. 65–68.

Walsh, R. G., R. A. Gillman, and J. B. Loomis. 1982. *Wilderness Resource Economics: Recreation Use and Preservation Values.* Dept. of Economics, Colorado State University, and American Wilderness Alliance, Denver, Colo.

Warner, M. L., and E. H. Preston. 1973. *A Review of Environmental Protection Impact Assessment Methodologies.* Report prepared by Battelle-Columbus for Environmental Protection Agency, Washington, D.C.

Washington Post. 1980. "EPA: 1.2 Million May Be Exposed to Toxic Waste." *Washington Post,* June 6.

Washington State University. 1976. *Land Use.* National Task Force on Research Related to Land Use Planning and Policy. College of Agriculture, Pullman, Wash.

Wayne County Planning Commission (WCPC). 1970. *Comprehensive Planning Process for Wayne County.* 3 Vols. WCPC, Detroit, Mich.

Wesner, G. M., et al. 1978. *Energy Conservation in Municipal Wastewater Treatment* EPA-430/9-77-011. U.S. Government Printing Office, Washington, D.C.
Whyte, W. H. 1968. *The Last Landscape.* Doubleday, Garden City, N.Y.
Young, E. 1968. "Urban Planning for Sand and Gravel Needs." *Mineral Information Service* 21:147–150.

Other Titles of Interest from Westview Press

Natural Resource Administration: Introducing a New Methodology for Management Development, edited by C. West Churchman, Spencer H. Smith, and Albert H. Rosenthal

Applied Social Science for Environmental Planning, edited by William Millsap

Alaskan Resources Development: Issues of the 1980s, edited by Thomas A. Morehouse

Conflict and Choice in Resource Management: The Case of Alaska, John S. Dryzek

The Forest Service, Michael Frome

†*The National Park Service,* William C. Everhart

Municipal Water Demand: Statistical and Management Issues, Clive Vaughan Jones, John J. Boland, James E. Crews, C. Frederick DeKay, and John R. Norris

Water and Agriculture in the Western U.S.: Conservation, Reallocation, and Markets, edited by Gary Weatherford, in association with Lee Brown, Helen Ingram, and Dean Mann

Water and Western Energy: Impacts, Issues, and Choices, Steven C. Ballard, Michael D. Devine, and Associates

Economic Benefits of Improved Water Quality: Public Perceptions of Options and Preservations Values, Douglas A. Greenley, Richard G. Walsh, and Robert A. Young

The Natural Geochemistry of Our Environment, David H. Speidel and Allen F. Agnew

†*A Wealth of Wild Species: Storehouse for Human Welfare,* Norman Myers

The Individual vs. the Public Interest: Political Ideology and National Forest Policy, Richard M. Alston

†*Renewable Natural Resources: A Management Handbook for the Eighties,* Dennis L. Little, Robert E. Dils, and John Gray

Managing Air Quality and Scenic Resources at National Parks and Wilderness Areas, edited by Robert D. Rowe and Lauraine G. Chestnut

†Available in hardcover and paperback.

About the Book and Author

Environmental Planning and Management
John H. Baldwin

A comprehensive overview and discussion of all major aspects of environmental planning and management, Professor Baldwin's textbook highlights the causes and interrelationships of environmental problems, emphasizing the important economic and ecological functions of the land as the stage for all human activities and the "source" and "sink" for all physical resources. A detailed analysis of the flow of resources—from acquisition through transformation, distribution, and disposal—is a key feature of the book.

Professor Baldwin proceeds from a review of the overall problems, principles, and practice of environmental planning and management to address the planning and management of water quality and quantity, air quality, hazardous and solid wastes, and energy; the economic costs of environmental controls; and procedures for environmental impact statement writing and review. He concludes by summarizing the needs, alternatives, and practice of community environmental planning and management.

This book is designed to serve as a basic text in courses on policymaking, planning, and management of the environment and on resource management. It also provides an important conceptual bridge for use in urban and regional planning, land use planning, and urban design courses.

John H. Baldwin is an assistant professor in the Department of Planning, Public Policy, and Management and director of environmental studies at the University of Oregon.

Index

Acid rain, 116, 152, 161–162, 291
Acids, 184
Action instruments, 287–289, 292
Activated carbon adsorption, 180
Activated charcoal, 111
Activated sludge system, 177, 178, 179(table), 180, 195
Adjustment assistance, 239–240
Aeration, 178, 180
Africa, 91, 101
Afterburners, 149, 159
Agricultural Stabilization and Conservation Service, 50–53(table)
Agriculture, 25, 26, 27, 54–55(table), 55, 182, 221(table), 278
and erosion, 29, 30, 31, 176–177
and hydrology, 66
production, 29, 182–183
wastes, 141, 199, 201(table)
See also Land use, agricultural
Agriculture, Department of, 29, 40, 177, 267
Air, 90, 141
-borne diseases, 182
quality control and employment, 217–220
quality management, 135, 153–157, 175, 285
See also Air pollution; Environmental impact statement; National ambient air quality standards
Air pollution, 43, 91(table), 127, 141, 206, 209
compared to water pollution, 163
control, 158–162, 291. See also Emissions controls
control costs, 217, 218(table), 219(fig.), 220, 228, 232, 233–236(tables)
control policy, 141, 145–153
and income and race, 232, 236(table)

levels, 138, 146, 147. See also Pollution Standards Index
pollutants, 126, 131, 140, 141, 142–144(tables), 145, 148. See also specific pollutants
reduction, 99, 213. See also Clean Air Act
Roman, 27
See also Environmental impact statement
Alaska, 41–42, 54–55(table), 83–84, 95, 194(table), 233–235(tables)
Alaska Coalition, 41–42
Alaska Lands Bill (1980), 41
Albuquerque-Bernalillo County Planning Department, 280
Alcoa (company), 228
Alcohol, 186
Aldehydes, 141
Algal blooms, 168
Allegheny County (Pa.), 61
Alpine habitat, 10
Alum. See Aluminum, sulfate
Aluminum, 91, 93(table), 97(table), 207, 208, 213
sulfate, 111
American Law Institute, 56, 88
American Planning Association, 59
Ames, S., 1
Ames (Iowa), 210
Aminopterin, 186
Anchorage (Alaska), 84
Andrus, Cecil D., 41
Antarctica, 95
Antiquities Act (1906), 41
Appropriate rights, 105
Appropriate technology, 2
Aquifers, 55, 66
Arab oil embargo (1973, 1974, 1979), 116, 121
Archaeological sites, 108 258(table)
Arctic, 108–109
Areas of critical concern, 75
Argentina, 95(fig.)
Argon, 141

Arizona, 34, 35(table), 54–55(table), 103, 194(table), 203, 233(table), 235(table), 242, 268–274(table)
Arkansas, 54–55(table), 168, 194(table), 234(table)
Arlington (Ore.), 197
Armco Steel Company, 148
Army Corps of Engineers, 32, 35, 50–53(table), 59, 266
Arsenic, 148
Asbestos, 148
Ashby's Law of the Requisite Variety in Cybernetic Systems, 10
Asia, 91, 101
Association of Engineering Geologists, 59
Aswan Dam (Egypt), 31, 108
Atlanta (Ga.), 103
Atomic Energy Commission, 266
Australia, 95(fig.), 101
Automobiles, 99, 219, 220, 221(table), 232
  emissions, 131, 142–143(table), 149–150, 151, 159, 291
  inspection and maintenance program (I/M), 145, 150
AUTO-QUAL model, 139

Bacon, Francis, 15
Bacteria. *See* Fecal coliform bacteria
Baghouse filters, 159, 160(fig.)
Bakersfield (Calif.), 182
Barrier islands, 32, 33, 34
Bases, 184
Basins, 71, 111
BAT. *See* Best available technologies
Beaches, 32, 33
Bedrock, 65, 71
Belgium, 95
Bentonitic clays, 65
Benzene, 148
  chlorinated, 189
Bergen, T. F., 46
Berlin (Germany), 182
Berm sites, 39
Beryllium, 148
Best available technologies (BAT), 38, 146, 169, 171, 174
Best practicable technologies (BPT), 169, 171, 174
Beverage container deposits, 213–214
Biosphere, 9, 162

Biota, 73–74
Birch, D., 241
Birth defects, 185, 186
Blackstone, William, 16
Bogs, 74
Bootlegger Cove (Alaska), 83–84
Boston (Mass.), 103
Bowhead whales, 42
Bowie (Md.), 268–274(table)
BPT. *See* Best practicable technologies
Bridge Canyon Dam, 238
Bromine, 96
Brontosaurus principle, 10–11
Brown, G., 238
Brown, Lester, 227
Bubble policy, 148–149
Building
  design, 219, 285
  materials, 90
  See also Codes
Bureau of Economic Analysis, 228
Bureau of Land Management, 31
Bureau of Reclamation, 113, 238
Burger v. *County of Mendocino* (1975), 267

Cadmium, 148, 165(table), 168
California, 29, 31, 32, 54–55(table), 55, 61–62, 65, 72, 95, 108, 110, 145, 153, 155, 182, 193, 194(table), 230, 231(fig.), 234–235(tables), 268–274(table), 287, 293–295
California, Gulf of, 103
Calumet (Mich.), 182
Calvert Cliff's Coordinating Committee v. *Atomic Energy Commission* (1972), 266
Canada, 94, 162, 291
Cancer, 185, 186, 230. *See also* Carcinogens
Canter, L., 243, 289
Capital goods, 115
Carbon, 285
  adsorption, 180, 195
  dioxide (CO_2), 116, 141, 142–143(table)
  monoxide (CO), 142–144(tables), 145, 149, 150, 152(table), 153, 157, 186
Carcinogens, 142–143(table), 148
Carrying capacity, 11–13, 240, 242
Carter, Jimmy, 38, 41, 112, 247
Catalytic converters, 149
Cattle, 30, 31
Central Park (NYC), 44

Centrifugation, 195
CEQ. See Council on Environmental Quality
Chapin, F. S., Jr., 286
Chemicals, 3, 106(table), 111, 141, 164, 168, 184, 185, 186, 187, 189–190, 192, 193, 206, 219, 220(table), 221(table), 222, 223–224(table)
Chem-Security Systems, Inc. (CSSI) Hazardous Waste Disposable Facility (Arlington, Ore.), 197–198
Cherokee Indians, 108
Chicago (Ill.), 153, 156(table), 233(table), 235(table)
Chile, 95(fig.)
Chlorination. See under Water
Chloromethane, 189
Chromium, 97(table), 98, 106(table)
Cigarette smoking, 186
Claussius, Rudolf, 17
Clays, 63, 64, 65, 68, 83–84, 111
Clean Air Act (1970, 1977), 3, 50–53(table), 141, 145, 146, 147–148, 149, 150, 151–153, 188(table), 228, 232, 233–236(tables), 285
Clean Water Act (1972, 1977), 32, 50–53(table), 169–170, 172, 173, 174, 182, 188(table)
Clean Water Reports (1978), 168
Climate
 change, 109, 116
 conditions, 284
Clivus Maltrum toilet, 183
Coal, 38, 39, 90, 91(table), 114(fig.), 115, 214
Coastal environment, 32–33, 54–55(table), 55, 73, 74, 75, 95
Coastal Zone Management Act (CZMA) (1972), 32, 33(table), 50–53(table)
Cobalt, 96
Codes, 84, 85, 88–89, 119, 287, 292
Colorado, 54–55(table), 57, 194(table), 235(table)
Colorado River, 103, 108
 basin, 102–103
Commentaries on the Laws of England (Blackstone), 16
Commerce, Department of, 228
Commons, 23, 94, 95, 130
Communications, 1, 7, 289, 290
Composting, 183, 195

Comprehensive Plan, Metropolitan Environmental Framework, 280
Comprehensive Planning Process for Wayne County, 279–280
Computer analysis, 78, 79–80(figs.), 139–140, 286
Conditional use permit, 39
Connecticut, 29, 54–55(table), 194(table), 234(table), 268–274(table)
Connection principle, 13–14
Conservation, 5, 6, 40, 41, 82, 108. See also Soils, as renewable resource; under Energy; Water
Conservation of mass, law of, 7, 8, 19, 126, 139
Conservation zones, 75
Consumer price index (CPI), 226–227
Contour and strip cropping, 177
Contra Costa County (Calif.), 61
Control of hazardous substances, 148. See also Hazardous wastes
Coors Brewing Company, 149
Copernicus, 15
Copper, 91, 93(table), 96, 97(table), 99
Corbett, M., 13
Cosmetics, 192
Cost-benefit analysis, 112, 127–129, 131, 151, 171–172, 216–242
Cost subsidies, 239, 240
Council of State Governments, 275
Council on Environmental Quality (CEQ), 2, 29, 50–53(table), 112, 134, 148, 150, 168, 202, 217, 219, 243, 244, 245
 powers, 246–266, 275, 299–301
Coxsackie viruses, 111
CPI. See Consumer price index
Critias (Plato), 27
Critical areas, 75
Crop rotation, 177
CSSI. See Chem-Security Systems, Inc.
Cultural eutrophication, 168
Cultural resources, 108, 113. See also Environmental impact statement
Cyanides, 168
Cyclone precipitators, 159, 160(fig.)
CZMA. See Coastal Zone Management Act

Dams, 31, 34, 35–36, 71, 107–108, 238, 266, 267

Darwin, Charles, 9, 16
Dasmann, R., 28
Davis (Calif.), 287, 293–295
DDT (dichloro-diphenyl-trichloroethane), 163, 171
Decentralist approach, 4, 6
Dee, N., 259
Deep well injection, 195, 196
Deer, 11–12, 242
Defense, Department of, 267
Deforestation, 1, 25, 26, 27, 40
Delaware, 54–55(table), 194(table), 268–274(table)
Delphi technique, 260
Depletion allowances, 214, 292
DES (diethylstilbestrol), 186
Desalinization, 109
Descartes, René, 15
Desertification, 25, 29–32
Deserts, 1, 10, 25
Detoxification, 195
Developing countries, 1, 12, 91, 96, 102
Development capital, 100
Diffusion models, 139
Dikes, 36
Dingell, John, 152
Diocletian, 27
Disaster relief funds, 37, 50–53(table)
Disease agents, 182, 184, 185–186. See also Water, -borne diseases
Distillation, 195, 206
District of Columbia, 192, 193, 194(table)
Diversity and stability, law of, 10
Dow Chemical Company, 228
Drainage, 68–71, 77(fig.), 284, 293
Dredging, 32
Drinking water, 218(table). See also Safe Drinking Water Act
Drugs, 187
Dry scrubbing, 161
Dubos, René, 6, 277
Dunes, 33, 35, 75
 shifting, 60, 74
Dunne, T., 69
DuPont Corporation, 149
Dusts, 159

E. coli, 111
EA. See Environmental assessment
Earthquakes, 35, 60, 84, 231(fig.)
Eastern United States, 103, 105, 222
Ecological cities. See Natural ecosystems, climax state

Ecological principles, 9–14. See also Environmental impact statement
Economic Development Administration, 50–53(table), 240
Economic diversification, 282–283
Economic growth, 92, 115, 216, 227–228
Economics. See Cost-benefit analysis; Socioeconomic systems
Economies of scale, 115
"Edicts on Prices and Occupations" (Diocletian), 27
Effluent charges, 132, 133, 134, 172, 292
Egypt, 26, 31
Einstein, Albert, 7, 17
EIS. See Environmental impact statement
Electricity, 115, 287
 costs, 115–116, 219, 220(table)
 savings, 99, 124
 See also Hydroelectricity; Solar energy
Electrodialysis, 180
Electrostatic precipitators, 159, 160(fig.), 161
Eminent domain, 85, 87, 292
Emissions controls, 137–138, 145, 147, 149, 151, 158–162, 287
 compliance, 149–150, 151(table)
 incentives, 148–149, 162
Endangered species, 3, 42, 258(table)
 federal laws, 50–53(table)
 state laws, 54–55(table)
Endangered Species Act (1973), 50–53(table)
Energy
 conservation, 6, 99, 110, 116, 118, 119(table), 120, 123, 124, 230
 consumption, 6, 44, 90, 91(table), 114, 115, 118, 119, 120(fig.), 183, 214, 278
 control over, 115
 database, 122–123
 demand, 90, 110, 114, 118
 efficiency, 2, 3(table), 115, 118, 119(table), 124, 283
 management, 118–125, 285
 monopoly, 115
 and natural laws, 7–9
 policies, 5, 6, 115, 116
 price, 115, 116, 118
 production, 115, 120–121

recovery, 209-211, 212-213
scarcity, 1, 90, 116
sources. See Coal; Natural gas; Oil; Wood
waste, 114
See also Renewable resources
Energy Digest, 115
Energy Tax Act (1978), 211
Entropy, 8-9, 18, 20, 21, 23, 116, 117(fig.)
Environmental assessment (EA), 248, 249(fig.), 250, 255-262
Environmental change, 9-10. See also Climate, change
Environmental Defense Fund v. Corps of Engineers (1972), 267
Environmental impact statement (EIS), 55, 239, 243, 244, 246-266, 275-276
  format, 251-255
  litigation, 266-267
  and public role, 262-263, 265-266
  review, 263-266
  state, 268-274(table), 275
  types, 244-245
Environmental inventory system, 284-286
Environmentalists, 2, 3, 6, 152, 190, 216, 230, 267
Environmentally unsatisfactory (EU), 264, 265(table)
Environmental performance standards, 87
Environmental planning and management
  additive approach, 279, 280
  comprehensive, 279-289, 293
  cost-benefit impact, 216-242
  costs, 23
  defined, 4
  and employment, 222, 223-224(table), 225(fig.), 241
  engineering approach, 34-36
  goals, 20-24, 83, 131
  implementation, 286-288
  local, 4, 5, 6, 33, 59, 84-85, 136-140, 241, 277-290, 292-296
  models, 139-140, 286
  and politics, 36, 131, 135
  principles of, 7-14
  problems 5, 129-130
  public participation, 289-290, 293
  regional, 291-292

state and federal, 4-5, 32-33, 37, 59, 84-85, 106-107, 112-114, 122, 130-131, 136, 233-235(tables), 267-275, 279, 285, 291-292
See also Agriculture; Air pollution; Energy; Floodplains; Hazardous wastes; Land use; National Environmental Policy Act; Resources; Water; Water pollution
Environmental protection, 2-4, 42, 74, 219(fig.), 222-232. See also Environmental planning and management; Environmental Protection Agency; National Environmental Policy Act
Environmental Protection Agency (EPA)
  administration, 162, 191-192, 199
  budget, 202
  and EIS, 248, 249(fig.), 250, 251, 264, 265(table), 266
  regulations, 50-53(tables), 106, 107, 111, 135, 141, 168, 169, 171-172, 184, 185, 188(table), 189, 190, 195, 196
  studies and information, 99, 105, 137, 138, 139, 161, 170, 182, 183, 184, 187, 195-196, 212, 220, 228, 278-279, 287, 293
Environmental quality (EQ) scale, 259-260
Environmental reservations (ER), 264, 265(table)
EPA. See Environmental Protection Agency
EQ. See Environmental quality scale
ER. See Environmental reservations
Erickson, P. A., 243, 275, 290
Erosion, 26, 27, 32, 66, 231(fig.). See also Agriculture, and erosion; Soils, erosion; Water, erosion; Wind erosion
Ethane, 196
Ethylene dichloride, 148
EU. See Environmentally unsatisfactory
Euphrates River, 26
Evolution, 9-10

Famine, 1
Farmers Home Administration, 50-53(table)
Farmland, 28-29
Faunal habitats, 33, 60, 74. See also Wildlife

Fecal coliform bacteria, 164, 165(table), 166–167(fig.), 168, 171
Federal Energy Administration, 214
Federal Flood Insurance Act (1968), 37, 50–53(table)
Federal Highway Administration, 50–53(table)
Federal Housing Administration, 37
Federal Insecticide, Fungicide, and Rodenticide Act (1947), 188(table)
Federal Land Policy and Management Act (1976), 41
Federal Register, 248, 250, 264
Federal Water Pollution Control Act (1972), 168–169, 170, 285
Ferric chloride, 111
Ferric sulfate, 111
Ferrous sulfate, 111
Fertile Crescent, 26
Fertilizer, 91(table), 164, 177
Fifth Amendment, 45
Finding of no significant impact (FONSI), 248, 250
Fish and wildlife management, 41, 74
Fish and Wildlife Service, 50–53(table), 113–114
Fisheries, 32, 94
Flawn, P. T., 83
Flocculation, 195
Flooding, 26, 27, 31, 34, 35–37, 69, 70(figs.), 108, 231(fig.)
control, 71, 107–108, 283
Floodplains, 33–38, 54–55(table), 55, 85, 107, 113
Floral habitats, 33, 60, 74
Florida, 29, 34, 35(table), 54–55(table), 55, 56, 194(table), 234(table)
Florida Barge Canal, 238
Fluorine, 93(table)
FONSI. *See* Finding of no significant impact
Food
consumption, 91(table)
industry employment, 223–224(table)
pollution control expenditure, 220(table), 221(table)
production, 1, 29
shortages, 1, 27
wastes, 200(fig.)
Forest and Rangeland Renewable Resources Planning Act (RPA) (1974), 40

Forests, 40–41, 74, 278, 281
Forest Service, 40, 41
Fortune list, 241
Fossil fuels, 90, 116, 118. *See also* Coal; Gasoline; Natural gas; Oil
Fourteenth Amendment, 45
France, 95(fig.), 182, 204
Franklin County (Mass.), 120–121
Free markets, 16, 24
Freight rates, 214–215

Galileo, 15
Garrison Diversion project (N.D.), 113
Gaseous pollutant control, 161
Gasoline, 91(table)
Gaussian plume model, 139–140
General Accounting Office, 29, 183
Geological Society of America, 59
Geological Survey, 34, 59, 83, 84, 115, 165
Geology, 60–63, 230, 231(fig.), 284
Georges Bank, 94
Georgia, 54–55(table), 194(table), 268–274(table)
Germany, 172, 182, 204, 207
Gilchrist, J. A., 60
Gillham Dam, 267
Glacier Bay (Alaska), 42
Glass, 200(fig.), 207, 208, 215, 219, 220(table), 221(table), 223–224(table)
Global 2000 Report to the President, The (1980), 1
GNP. *See* Gross national product
Golden Gate Park (San Francisco), 44
Gorsuch (Burford), Anne, 174, 191, 192
Governmental review process, 83
Gracchi brothers, 27
Grading codes, 161–162
Grand Canyon, 42, 238
Great Britain, 95(fig.), 204
Great Falls (Mont.), 34, 35(table)
Great Lakes Region, 222, 291
Greek civilization, 26–27
Greenbelts, 44
Griggs, G. B., 60
Gross national product (GNP), 217, 227–228, 229(fig.)
Groundwater, 29, 38, 66, 71, 73, 101, 105, 107, 109, 182, 284, 295. *See also under* Water pollution
Group of 77, 96

Guam, 193

Hardin, G., 130
Harris, Louis, public opinion polls, 3–4, 152, 173, 186
Haveman, R. H., 216, 222, 240
Hawaii, 54–55(table), 55–56, 194(table), 268–274(table)
Hazardous Materials Transportation Act (1975), 188(table)
Hazardous substances, 148. *See also* Hazardous wastes
Hazardous Waste Management Office (EPA), 191
Hazardous wastes
 characteristics, 184
 cleanup, 191–192, 197, 199
 cleanup costs, 186–187, 190
 control, 193, 195–199
 control policy, 187–193
 costs, 196, 197(table), 218(table), 219(fig.)
 defined, 184
 disposal methods, 195–196, 197(table), 198
 and health, 184, 185–186
 sites, 184, 185, 186, 187, 190, 191, 192, 193, 197
 state policies, 192–193, 194(table), 197, 198–199
 storage methods, 195, 196, 198
 transportation, 198
Heat pollution, 142–143(table), 163, 164(table)
Heavy metals, 163, 164, 168, 182, 184, 195
Helium, 9, 98
Henderson, Hazel, 15, 16, 17, 20, 21, 24
Hippocrates, 27
Historic sites, 108, 113, 258(table)
Honda manufacturers, 149
Hopewell (Va.), 186–187
House Subcommittee on Oversight and Investigations, 184
Housing and Urban Development, Department of (HUD), 37, 50–53(table), 267
Houston (Texas), 153, 156(table)
HUD. *See* Housing and Urban Development, Department of
Hudson, E. A., 118
Huntington (N.Y.), 279
Hurricanes, 32–35
Hydrocarbons, 141, 142–144(tables), 150
 chlorinated, 196

Hydroelectricity, 107, 114(fig.)
Hydrogen, 9
Hydrology, 60, 66, 68–73, 139, 284

I/A. *See* Innovative and alternative system
Idaho, 36, 54–55(table), 194(table)
Illinois, 29, 54–55(table), 153, 193, 194(table), 233(table), 235(table)
I/M. *See* Automobiles, inspection and maintenance program
Impact studies, 13, 22. *See also* Environmental impact statement
Imperial Valley (Calif.), 31, 108
Incineration, 127, 195, 197, 204, 206, 209
Income tax credit, 74
Indiana, 54–55(table), 193, 194(table), 233(table), 235(table), 268–274(table)
Industrial cities. *See* Natural ecosystems, pioneer state
Indus Valley, 31
Infectious hepatitis, 180
Infiltration, 68, 69, 71
Inflation, 222, 226–227
Innovative and alternative (I/A) system, 170, 182, 183(table)
Insecticides, 177
Interest rates, 238–239
Intergovernmental program review (IPR), 175
Interior, Department of the, 112, 267
International Court of Justice, 94
Ionization, 195
Iowa, 29, 54–55(table), 194(table), 210
IPR. *See* Intergovernmental program review
Ireland, 10
Iron ore, 91, 93(table), 96, 97(table), 99, 214, 220(table)
Irrigation, 30, 31, 66, 102
 trickling, 109

Jackson, Henry, 48
Jain, R. K., 243, 257
James River, 186–187
Japan, 95, 196, 207, 228
Johnstown flood, 35–36
Jorgenson, J. A., 118
Justice, Department of, 170

Kaibab Plateau (Ariz.), 11–12, 242
Kaiser, E. J., 286

Kansas City (Mo.), 153, 156(table), 210, 211(table)
Kentucky, 54-55(table), 145, 194(table), 268-274(table)
Kepler, Johannes, 15
Kepone, 186-187
Kormondy, E. J., 11
Kraft, M., 135

Lagoons, 71, 105, 185
Lake George (N.Y.), 182
Lakes, 168, 284, 285
Land and Water Conservation Fund, 50-53(table)
Land development, 28, 29, 32, 33-34, 45, 46, 56, 58, 75, 78, 82-83, 85, 86, 88, 278, 280, 281
  costs, 43-44
  and hydrology, 66, 68, 69, 70(figs.), 73, 77(fig.)
  rights, 87
  and soils, 63-64, 65, 77(fig.), 83-84
  and topography, 60-61, 62-63, 77(fig.), 85
  See also Floodplains; Urbanization
Landfills, 185, 190, 191, 193, 195, 196, 197(table), 203
  sanitary, 204-206
Land ownership, 44-45, 56, 75
LANDSAT satellites, 60
Landscaping, 124, 295
Landslides, 60, 61, 231(fig.)
Land spreading, 195, 196, 197(table)
Land use, 25, 175, 246
  agricultural, 28-29, 30-31, 177, 281
  controls, 84-89, 119, 206, 230, 231(fig.)
  early, 25-28
  federal programs, 47-49, 50-53(table), 55
  and forests, 40-41
  guidance system, 78, 81(fig.), 82-84
  historic, 108
  mining, 39
  nonagricultural, 28
  and ownership, 44-47, 56, 75, 85, 87, 284
  planning, 45-47, 55-84, 278, 281, 282, 284-285, 292, 293
  restrictions, 74-75, 88
  state programs, 48, 54-55(table), 55-56

systems analysis, 57
urban, 43-44
See also Environmental impact statement; Land development; Recreation
Land values, 57, 206, 284
Latin America, 91, 101
Lavelle, Rita, 191, 192
Law of the Sea treaty, 96
Lead (Pb), 93(table), 97(table), 99, 106(table), 144(table), 165(table), 166-167(fig.), 168, 180
Leibniz, Gottfried von, 17
Leopold, Aldo, 47
Leopold, J. B., 69
Levees, 36
Life Science Product Company, 187
Limestone, 111, 161
Limits, 24
Litter, 213
Living organisms, 90, 101
Locke, John, 15-16, 45
London (England), 44
Los Angeles (Calif.), 61-62, 153, 155, 156(table)
  Basin, 108
Louisiana, 54-55(table), 168, 194(table)
Love Canal (N. Y.), 187, 192
Lovins, A., and H., 114
Lubbock (Texas), 182

McCall, Tom, 6
McCloskey, M., 228
Magnesium, 96
Magnuson, E., 186
Malthus, Thomas, 92
Man and Nature (Marsh), 243
Manganese, 93(table), 96, 97(table)
Mapping. See Suitability mapping
Maps, 85, 285-286
Marble Gorge Dam, 238
Margerum, T., 46
Marin County (Calif.), 110
Marsh, George Perkins, 243
Maryland, 54-55(table), 194(table), 268-274(table)
Massachusetts, 54-55(table), 120, 194(table), 210, 268-274(table)
Materials balance model, 19-21, 98-100, 107, 126
Matrix analysis, 260-261
Mechanical world, 15, 16-17, 23, 45
Mediterranean Basin, 26, 31, 101

Mercedes-Benz manufacturers, 149
Mercury, 93(table), 106(table), 148, 165(table), 166-167(fig.), 168, 180
Metals, 90, 91(table), 96, 159, 200(fig.), 207, 208, 209, 219, 220, 221(table), 222, 223-224(table). *See also* Heavy metals
Methane, 180, 183, 184, 196, 204
Methylchloroform, 148
Methyl mercury, 186
Michigan, 29, 54-55(table), 182, 193, 194(table), 268-274(table), 279
Microwave plasma, 196
Mid-Atlantic states, 29
Middle East, 101
Midwest, 73, 105, 222
Miller, G. T., Jr., 17
Minerals, 1, 90, 91, 93(table), 96, 231(fig.), 284
Mining, 27, 38-40, 94, 97-98, 214, 221(table), 278
  waste, 99, 199, 200(fig.), 201(table)
  See also Seabed mining
Minnesota, 54-55(table), 194(table), 268-274(table)
Minnesota Mining and Manufacturing Company (3M), 149, 228
Mississippi, 54-55(table), 194(table), 234(table), 268-274(table)
Mississippi River, 29
Missouri, 54-55(table), 153, 194(table), 210, 211, 234(table)
Modular incinerators, 209
Monoculture, 10
Mono Lake Basin (Calif.), 108
Montana, 29, 34, 35(table), 54-55(table), 194(table), 233(table), 268-274(table)
Motorized craft, 42-43
Mudslides, 37
Multiple-use buildings, 124
Multiple-Use—Sustained-Yield Act (1960), 40, 41
Muskegon (Mich.), 182

NAAQS. *See* National ambient air quality standards
National Academy of Sciences, 162
National ambient air quality standards (NAAQS), 141, 144(table), 145-147, 149, 150, 152, 153, 157
  violations, 152(table), 153
National Cancer Institute, 186
National Commission on Water Quality, 172
National Environmental Policy Act (NEPA) (1969), 243-246, 275-276, 297-301
  court cases, 266-267
  See also Council on Environmental Quality; Environmental impact statement
National Flood Insurance Program, 37
National Forest Management Act (1976), 40
National forests, 40, 41
National Forest System, 40
National grasslands, 40
National Historic Preservation Act, 50-53(table)
National Institute for Environmental Health Sciences, 186
National Institute for Occupational Safety and Health, 186
National monuments, 41
National Park Service, 42-43
National Park Service Management Plan (1980), 42
National Park System, 41, 42, 147, 152
National Pollution Discharge Elimination System (NPDES) permit, 169, 170-171, 172, 174
National welfare measure, 228
National Wilderness Preservation System, 41, 42
National Wildlife Federation, 192, 197
National Wildlife Refuge System, 41, 42
Natural ecosystems, 1-2, 9-14, 57-59, 108, 109, 284
  climax state, 2, 3(table)
  pioneer state, 2, 3(table)
  protection, 21, 22, 74
Natural gas, 90, 91(table), 114(fig.), 115, 116, 149
Natural laws, 6-14, 24
Natural Resources Defense Council v. Grant (1972), 266
Natural rights, 16
Natural selection, 9-10
Nebraska, 54-55(table), 194(table), 233(table), 235(table), 268-274(table)

Neo-Malthusians, 92, 94, 97
NEPA. *See* National Environmental Policy Act
Neutralization, 195
Nevada, 54-55(table), 194(table), 233(table), 235(table), 268-274(table)
New England, 29
New Federalism, 4
New Jersey, 54-55(table), 193, 194(table), 233-235(tables), 268-274(table)
New Mexico, 30, 54-55(table), 194(table), 233(table), 235(table), 280
New Republic, 49
New source performance standards (NSPS), 148
Newton, Isaac, 15, 17
New York City, 103, 153, 155, 156(table), 233-235(tables), 268-274(table)
New York State, 29, 54-55(table), 61, 182, 187, 193, 194(table), 233-235(tables), 268-274(table), 279
New York Times, 115
New Zealand, 95(fig.)
Niagara Falls (N.Y.), 187
Nickel, 93(table), 96, 97(table), 99
Nile River, 26
Nitrates, 164, 171, 180
Nitrogen, 141, 180, 285
 dioxide (NO_2), 144(table), 145, 152(table), 153, 157(fig.)
 oxides, 141, 142-143(table), 149, 150, 161, 162
Nixon, Richard M., 48, 49
Noise pollution, 142-143(table), 218(table)
 Roman, 27
Nonattainment area, 138, 146-147
Nonmonetary economy, 20
North Carolina, 54-55(table), 194(table), 266, 268-274(table)
North Dakota, 54-55(table), 113, 194(table)
Northeastern United States, 232, 291
Norway, 95(fig.)
Notice of intent, 248, 249(fig.), 250
Novum Organum (Bacon), 15
NPDES. *See* National Pollution Discharge Elimination System
NSPS. *See* New source performance standards
Nuclear energy, 114(fig.), 115-116

Nuclear wastes, 190
Nucleic acids, 7

Occupational Safety and Health Act (1970), 188(table)
Oceans, 94, 95, 96
Odum, Eugene, 12
Odum, Harold T., 2
Off-channel facilities, 71
Office of Enforcement. *See* Hazardous Waste Management Office
Office of Management and Budget (OMB), 112, 266
 Circular A-95, 174-175
Office of Surface Mining (OSM), 39, 50-53(table)
Office of Waste Programs Enforcement. *See* Hazardous Waste Management Office
Ohio, 54-55(table), 193, 194(table), 233-235(tables)
Oil, 90, 91(table), 94, 114(fig.), 115, 116, 117(fig.), 118, 219, 221(table)
 high sulfur, 140
 as pollutant, 164, 220(table)
 prices, 116
Oil, Hazardous Substances, and Hazardous Waste Response, Liability, and Compensation Act (1980), 187, 188(table), 191-192
OMB. *See* Office of Management and Budget
100-year flood, 34, 37
On the Origin of Species (Darwin), 9
Open space, 44, 85, 86, 87, 281
 tax incentives, 37
Ordinances, 84, 85, 120, 124
Oregon, 36, 54-55(table), 55, 56, 66, 74, 194(table), 197, 198, 214, 215
 Department of Energy, 122
 Department of Environmental Quality, 198
OSM. *See* Office of Surface Mining
Overgrazing, 25, 27, 30-32
Owens Valley (Calif.), 108
Oxidation, 195
Oxygen, 141, 165(table), 166-167(fig.), 168, 180, 285
Ozone (O_3), 141, 142-144(tables), 145, 149, 150, 153, 157

Pacific Northwest, 147

Paper, 91(table), 200(fig.), 207, 208, 210, 212, 215, 219, 220(table), 221(table), 223–224(table)
Paris (France), 182
Parks, 44. *See also* National Park Service; State parks
Particulates (TPS), 141, 142–144(tables), 145, 148, 149, 150, 152(table), 153, 157
 control, 158–161, 176
Patterson, T. A., 100
PCBs. *See* Polychlorinated biphenols
Pennsylvania, 54–55(table), 61, 193, 194(table)
Perchloroethane, 148
Percolation, 71, 181–182
Performance bond, 40
Permeability, 68, 69, 71
Peskin, H. M., 232
Pesticides, 164, 168, 180, 184, 187, 218(table)
Peugeot manufacturers, 149
Phenols, 168, 184
Phoenix (Ariz.), 34, 35(table), 156(table), 203
Phosphate, 93(table), 164, 171, 180
Phosphorus, 165(table), 166–167(fig.), 168, 180, 285
Photochemical oxidants, 142–143(table), 152(table), 158, 159
Photography, 59–60, 74
Phthalate esters, 189
Physical laws, 7–9
Pits, 105
Planned unit development, 85, 124, 287, 292
Planning commissions, 83, 84, 279–280
Plastic, 91(table), 207, 208, 220(table)
Platinum, 93(table)
Plato, 27
Plutonium, 171
Pneumatic tube collection systems, 204
Poland, 95
Police, 85
Politics of the Social Age, The (Henderson), 15
Pollution, 1, 9, 20, 23, 91, 283
 control policy, 130–132, 136–140, 282
 controls, 126–127, 132–136
 costs, 127–130, 131, 132(table), 216–230, 237–242
 optimum level control model, 127–129
 penalty fee, 135
 Roman, 27
 See also Air pollution; Hazardous wastes; Water pollution
Pollution rights permits, 132, 133–134, 169, 172
Pollution Standards Index (PSI), 153–157
Polychlorinated biphenols (PCBs), 163, 168, 171, 184, 189, 198
Polycyclic organic matter, 148
Ponds, 71, 105, 185
Pools, 105
Population
 distribution, 102, 284, 285
 global, 1, 2, 6, 102
Potassium, 97(table)
Potato blight (1848), 10
POTWs. *See* Publicly owned treatment works
Precipitation, 195
Precipitators, 159–161
Predator control, 12
Preservation, 75, 85
Preston, E. H., 257
Private property, 16, 45–47
Product design, 99–100
Production and consumption model, 18–19, 20
Productivity, 227
Property tax, 29, 74, 86, 87
PSI. *See* Pollution Standards Index
Public good, 45, 47, 130
Public health, safety, and welfare, 21, 22, 85, 123, 131, 136, 145, 146, 203, 227, 230, 237, 240–242
Public investments, 287–289, 292
Publicly owned treatment works (POTWs), 169, 183
Public opinion polls, 2–4, 152, 173, 186
Public services and facilities, 119, 124, 130
Puerto Rico, 193, 267, 268–274(table)
Pyrolysis, 206

Radar imagery, 60
Radiation pollution, 142–143(table)
Radioactive wastes, 126–127, 164(table), 180, 184
Radionuclides, 148
Rainfall, 68, 69, 71, 105, 283
Rangeland, 31, 40

Rationalization, 14, 15–16
RCRA. *See* Resource Conservation and Recovery Act
RDF. *See* Refuse-derived fuel
Reagan, Ronald, 4, 151, 153
Real Estate Research Corporation, 43
Reclamation, 38, 39, 218(table), 219(fig.), 238, 282
Record of decision, 249(fig.), 250–251
Recreation, 41–42, 107, 108, 168, 281
Recycling, 2, 22, 99, 109–110, 124, 126, 127, 195, 196, 198, 207–208, 210, 212, 214, 215, 219, 241, 295
Reefs, 33
Refuse-derived fuel (RDF), 209–211
Renewable resources, 2, 5, 22–23, 40, 90, 100, 114, 116, 278, 282, 283
  and employment, 219
  programs, 122, 123, 124–125
  See also Solar energy
Repairability, 100, 149
Reservoirs, 107, 108, 111
Residuals. *See* Pollution; Wastes
Resin adsorption, 195
Resource Conservation and Recovery Act (RCRA) (1976), 188(table), 190–191, 196, 201–202, 204
Resource Conservation Committee, 213, 214–215
Resource lands, 75, 85, 281
Resource recovery, 208–213
Resources
  access and development, 94–96, 120
  allocation, 16, 23, 47, 96, 295. *See also* Water, resource allocation
  conservation, 230
  consumption, 1, 2, 6, 20, 22, 44, 91, 94, 99, 295
  control, 92
  costs, 92, 94, 96, 98
  global, 1, 6, 92
  management, 92, 94, 98–100, 118, 281, 282, 283, 284, 285
  nonrenewable, 90, 92, 94, 100, 114, 118, 278, 283
  production, 92, 94, 99
  scarcity, 1–2, 9, 21, 23, 92, 100
  stabilization, 100

  substitution, 92, 98
  trade, 1, 23, 96
  See also Energy; Renewable resources; Water
Respiratory disorders, 228
Reverse osmosis, 180, 195
Rhode Island, 54–55(table), 194(table), 268–274(table)
Rifkin, J., 15
Rio Puerco Basin (N.M.), 30
Riparian habitats, 74
Riparian rights, 105
River flows, 108
Rogers, Will, 48
Roman civilization, 27–28
Ross, M. H., 114
RPA. *See* Forest and Rangeland Renewable Resources Planning Act
Rubber, 91(table), 99, 200(fig.), 207, 208, 220(table), 221(table)
Ruckelshaus, William, 162, 174, 191, 192, 199
Ruhr Valley (Germany), 172
Ruhrverband (1904), 172
Runoff, 34, 44, 68, 69, 71, 72(fig.), 139
  as pollutant source, 163–164
Rural-to-urban shift, 43, 45

Safe Drinking Water Act (SDWA) (1974, 1977), 50–53(table), 106–107, 188(table)
St. Lawrence River, 291
Salinization, 30, 31, 73, 108
Salts, 180
Sand County Almanac, A (Leopold), 47
San Diego County (Calif.), 287
San Francisco Bay area, 61, 72, 156(table)
San Joaquin Basin (Calif.), 31, 32
Saugus (Mass.), 210
Scaling, 259
Scenic habitats, 108
Schistosomiasis, 108
Science, 14–15, 26–27
Scoping process, 247, 249
Scottsdale (Ariz.), 203
Scrap iron, 207, 215
Scrubbers, 159, 160(fig.), 161–162
SCS. *See* Soil Conservation Service
SDWA. *See* Safe Drinking Water Act
Seabed mining, 96
Seattle, Chief, 46

Seawater, 96
Second National Water Assessment (1978), 101
Sedimentation, 34, 44, 60, 72, 73(table), 164, 175–176, 195, 283
Sedimentation tank, 177, 178–180
Senate Health and Scientific Research Subcommittee, 185
Septic tank drainfields, 61, 65, 67(table), 88, 180–183
Settling chambers, 159, 160(fig.)
Sewage, 127, 165, 169, 172, 177–183
Sheep, 30, 31
Shore erosion, 37
Siberia, 108
Sierra Club v. Froehlke (1973), 266
Siltation, 26, 27
Silver, 93(table), 98, 106(table)
SIPs. *See* State implementation plans
Site-design review process, 85
Slope, 60–61, 69, 77(fig.), 85, 284
Sludge, 182, 198
Small Business Administration, 37
Smith, Adam, 16, 45
Smith, V. K., 216, 222, 240
Smog, 141, 142–143(table), 158, 159
Smoke, 158
SMSAs. *See* Standard Metropolitan Statistical Areas
Snail darter, 108
Socioeconomic systems, 14–21, 22, 23, 116, 278. *See also* Environmental impact statement
Soddy, Frederick, 17
Sodium aluminate, 111
Sodium bicarbonate, 161
Sodium chloride, 96
Soil Conservation Service (SCS), 50–53(table), 59, 61, 177, 266
 budget, 113
 county soil survey, 65–66
 soil classifications, 63, 64(fig.), 68
Soils, 60, 61, 91(table), 284
 characteristics, 65–66, 67(table), 68, 71, 77(fig.)
 erosion, 29, 30, 31, 69, 72, 74, 164, 176–177
 as renewable resource, 90, 282
 textures, 63–65, 71, 72(fig.)
 See also Landfills
Soil Survey for Land County, Oregon (SCS), 66

Solar energy, 3, 9, 90, 124, 125, 183, 287, 293
Solar evaporation, 198
Solidification and encapsulation, 195, 196, 198
Solid wastes, 1, 20, 99, 126, 141
 collection, 203–204, 214
 costs, 201, 202, 203, 210–211, 212(table), 213, 214, 218(table)
 disposal, 175, 203–215, 287
 management, 201–203, 207, 213–215
 recycling, 127, 207–208, 212, 214
 sites, 199, 203, 204
 sources, 199–201
 transportation, 203, 207, 214–215
 in water, 163, 164, 171, 180
Solvents, 184
Source separation, 208, 212, 295
South Africa, 95
South Dakota, 54–55(table), 145, 194(table), 268–274(table)
Southern United States, 43
Southwestern United States, 65, 73, 105, 232
Soviet Union, 95, 96, 108
Spits, 32
Spruce forests, 10
Standard Metropolitan Statistical Areas (SMSAs), 153, 155, 156(table), 232, 233–235(tables)
State implementation plans (SIPs), 145
State parks, 42
Stationary fuel combustion, 141, 150, 151(table)
Steel, 99, 213, 220(table), 221(table)
Steiger, Sam, 49
STORM model, 139
Stream bank protection, 176
Subdivisions, 84, 85, 124, 287, 293–295
Subsidence, 73, 204, 206
Subsoil, 65
Suburbs, 43, 44
Suffolk County (N.Y.), 29
Suitability mapping, 75–78, 259
Sulfur, 93(table), 97(table), 149
 dioxide (SO_2), 116, 145, 149, 152(table), 157(fig.)
 oxides (SO_x), 141, 142–144(table), 145, 150, 153, 161, 162
 See also Acid rain
Sun Belt, 102

Superfund law. *See* Oil, Hazardous Substances, and Hazardous Waste Response, Liability, and Compensation Act
Surface Mining Control and Reclamation Act (1977), 38–39
Surface water, 30, 100, 105, 106, 107
Survival of the fittest, 9, 17
Swales, 71, 293, 295
Sweden, 204
SWMM model, 139
Synfuels, 5
Synthetic fibers, 91(table)

Tallahassee (Fla.), 34, 35(table)
Tall stacks, 158, 162
Taxes, 29, 37, 74, 85, 86–87, 99, 100, 122, 162, 214, 238, 240, 287, 292. *See also* Effluent charges
Technology, 2, 92, 94, 96, 97–98, 99, 116, 162, 228. *See also* Appropriate technology; Best available technologies; Best practicable technologies
Tellico Dam (Tenn.), 108
Tennessee, 54–55(table), 108, 113, 193, 194(table), 234(table)
Tennessee Valley Authority (TVA), 108
TERA. *See* Transferable emissions reduction assessment
Terracing, 177
Teton Dam (Idaho), 36
Texas, 54–55(table), 153, 168, 182, 193, 194(table), 233–235(tables), 268–274(table)
Thalidomide, 186
Theory of relativity, 7
Thermodynamics, first and second laws of, 7, 8–9, 17–18, 19, 94
Thermonuclear reaction, 7–8
Thin-film surface coating, 109
THM. *See* Trihalomethane
3M. *See* Minnesota Mining and Manufacturing Company
Three Mile Island (TMI), 115
Throughput reduction, 99–100, 109, 118–119, 126, 158
Tiering, 248
Tigris River, 26
Tillage farming, 176–177
Timber, 41, 74
Tin, 93(table), 97(table)
Title II (NEPA), 245–246, 299–301
TMI. *See* Three Mile Island

Tocks Island Dam, 238
Toluene, 148
Tombigbee Waterway (Tenn.), 113
Topography, 60–63
Topsoil, 29, 32, 65, 164
Tornados, 35
Toxic Substances Control Act (TSCA) (1976), 185, 187, 188(table), 189
Toxic Substances Strategy Committee, 192
Toxic wastes, 126, 159, 161, 168, 169, 184, 185, 206
costs, 129, 218(table)
See also Hazardous wastes
TPS. *See* Particulates
Trace elements, 141
Transferable emissions reduction assessment (TERA) program, 146–147
Transportation, Department of, 267
Transportation systems, 119, 141, 150, 158, 219, 220(table), 230, 285
Tri-chloroethylene, 148
Trickling filter, 177–178, 179(table), 180, 195
Trihalomethane (THM), 111–112
TSCA. *See* Toxic Substances Control Act
Tundra, 10
Tungsten, 93(table), 97(table)
TVA. *See* Tennessee Valley Authority
208 plans, 170–171

Udall, Morris, 49
Ul Haque, Inam, 96
Ultrafiltration, 195
United Nations Law of the Sea Conference, 96
Urbanization, 43–44, 45, 58, 60, 70(figs.), 102, 285
Urban Mass Transit Administration, 50–53(table)
Urban planning. *See* Environmental planning and management, local
User fees, 214
U.S. resource claims, 94–95, 96
U.S. Steel Corporation, 149
Utah, 54–55(table), 194(table), 233(table), 235(table), 268–274(table)
Utility financing, 120

Value function graphs, 259–260
Vanport City (Ore.), 36

Vegetative cover, 72, 74, 77(fig.), 176, 177
Vermont, 29, 54-55(table), 55, 56, 86, 194(table)
Veterans Administration, 37
Vig, N., 135
Village Homes subdivision (Davis, Calif.), 287, 293-295
Village of Euclid v. *Amber Realty Company* (1926), 46
Vinyl chloride, 148
Virginia, 54-55(table), 186-187, 194(table), 268-274(table)
Virgin Islands, 193
Volcanos, 35
Volkswagen manufacturers, 149

Wallace, Alfred Russel, 9, 16
Wallisville Dam, 266
Wall Street Journal, 113
Walsh, R. G., 57
Warner, M. L., 257
Washington, 54-55(table), 115, 194(table), 268-274(table)
Washington, D. C., 103, 156(table)
Washington Public Power Supply Systems, 115
Waste Management, Inc., 197
Wastes, 91(table), 94, 99, 105, 126, 281(fig.), 282, 283, 284, 285
 oxygen-demanding, 163, 164-165
 See also Hazardous wastes; Solid wastes; Toxic wastes
Wastewater, 126, 169-170, 177-183
Water
 -borne diseases, 102, 108, 111, 168, 180
 chlorination, 111, 179(table)
 coagulants, 111
 conservation, 109-110, 113
 consumption, 44, 91(table), 102, 103, 104(table), 109, 110(table), 183
 demand, 102, 107, 110
 diversion projects, 30, 34, 36, 107, 108-109, 113
 erosion, 29, 31-32, 60
 evaporation, 108, 109
 filtration, 111
 fishable, swimmable, 169
 management, 101-114, 174-175, 283, 284
 pricing, 109, 112, 287
 quality, 69, 113, 165, 168, 175, 285. *See also* Environmental impact statement
 quality control and employment, 217-220
 recycling, 109, 110
 as renewable resource, 90, 283
 resource allocation, 38, 101, 112, 283
 rights, 105, 109
 shortages, 1, 30, 101-103, 104(fig.), 105, 109
 storage, 108, 111
 supply, 101, 102, 103(fig.), 104(fig.), 107, 108, 109, 112
 table, 73
 treatment, 111-112, 165, 174. *See also* Sewage; Water pollution, control
 waste of, 109-110
 See also Hydrology; Water pollution
Waterless toilets, 183
Water pollution, 30, 32, 71, 88, 91(table), 101, 102, 103, 105-107, 127, 283
 categories, 169
 compared to air pollution, 163
 contaminants, 106(table), 107, 111, 126, 285
 control, 99, 126, 175-183, 214
 control costs, 173, 217, 218(table), 219, 220, 228
 control policy, 165, 168-174
 defined, 162
 degradable and nondegradable, 163
 groundwater, 105-106, 107, 185
 increase rate, 102
 Roman, 27
 sources, point and nonpoint, 163-165, 171, 175-177, 285
 thresholds, 165(table)
 treatment, 163, 169, 177, 183. *See also* Sewage
 violations, 166-167(fig.), 168, 170
 See also Environmental impact statement
Water Resources Council (WRC), 34, 38, 50-53(table), 101, 113
 budget, 113
Water Resources Planning Council, 48, 50-53(table)
Waterwall incinerators, 209
Watt, James, 95
Wayne County (Mich.), 279
Wealth of Nations, The (Smith), 16
Weatherization, 122, 124
Western United States, 30, 43, 105, 222, 232
Wetlands, 27, 31, 60, 74, 75, 281

programs, 32–33, 38, 54–55(table), 55
Wet scrubbers, 159, 160(fig.)
Wilderness areas, 147, 152, 281
Wildlife, 32, 41, 74, 108, 281
 protection, 113
Williams, R. H., 114
Windbreaks, 177
Wind erosion, 29, 31, 32, 72
Wisconsin, 29, 54–55(table), 194(table), 268–274(table)
Wood, 90, 91(table), 114(fig.), 200(fig.)
Worldwatch Institute, 227
WRC. *See* Water Resources Council

Yosemite National Park, 42–43

Zinc, 93(table), 97(table), 99
Zoning, 47, 55, 84, 85–86, 124, 287